C000254883

COPYRIGHT PHILIP'S

POCKET
TRAVEL
ATLAS

IN ASSOCIATION WITH
THE ROYAL GEOGRAPHICAL SOCIETY
WITH THE INSTITUTE OF BRITISH GEOGRAPHERS

CONTENTS

Published in Great Britain in 2014 by Philip's,
a division of Octopus Publishing Group Limited
(www.octopusbooks.co.uk)
Endeavour House, 189 Shaftesbury Avenue,
London WC2H 8JY
An Hachette UK Company (www.hachette.co.uk)

Copyright © 2014 Philip's

Cartography by Philip's

CITY PLANS
Page 46, Dublin: The town plan of Dublin is based on
Ordnance Survey Ireland by permission of the Government
Permit Number 8936. © Ordnance Survey Ireland and
Government of Ireland.

Page 47, Edinburgh, and page 50,
London: This product includes
mapping data licensed from
Ordnance Survey® with the permission of the Controller
of Her Majesty's Stationery Office. © Crown copyright 2014.
All rights reserved. Licence number 100011710.

ISBN 978-1-84907-312-7

A CIP catalogue record for this book is available from the
British Library.

Printed in Hong Kong

Details of other Philip's titles and services can be found
on our website at: www.philips-maps.co.uk

Philip's World Atlases are published in association
with The Royal Geographical Society (with The
Institute of British Geographers).
   The Society was founded in 1830 and given a
Royal Charter in 1859 for 'the advancement of
geographical science'. Today it is a leading world
centre for geographical learning – supporting
education, teaching, research and expeditions, and
promoting public understanding of the subject.
   Further information about the Society and how to
join may be found on its website at: www.rgs.org

WORLD THEMES

4–7	World statistics: countries
8–9	World statistics: cities
10–11	World distance table
12–13	World time zones
14–15	World flight paths
16–17	World air travel
18–19	World tourist destinations
20–21	World climate regions
22–23	World climate graphs
24–25	World temperature
26–27	World pressure and winds
28–29	The land hemisphere 1:133.3M
30–31	The water hemisphere 1:133.3M

CITY PLANS

32	City Plans – general reference
33	Amsterdam
34	Athens
35	Bangkok
36	Barcelona
37	Beijing
38	Berlin
39	Boston
40	Brussels
41	Budapest
42	Cape Town
43	Chicago
44	Copenhagen
45	Delhi
46	Dublin
47	Edinburgh
48	Hong Kong
49	Lisbon
50	London
51	Los Angeles
52	Madrid
53	Mexico City
54	Montreal
55	Moscow
56	Mumbai
57	Munich
58	New Orleans
59	New York
60	Paris
61	Prague
62	Rio de Janeiro

63	Rome
64	San Francisco
65	Singapore
66	Stockholm
67	Sydney
68	Tokyo
69	Toronto
70	Venice
71	Vienna
72	Washington DC

WORLD MAPS

| 73 | World Maps – general reference |

EUROPE

74–75	Europe 1:26.7M
76–77	Scandinavia and the Baltic Lands 1:13.3M
78–79	British Isles 1:6.7M
80–81	Germany and Benelux 1:6.7M
82–83	Central Europe 1:6.7M
84–85	Eastern Europe and the Black Sea 1:13.3M
86–87	Spain and Portugal 1:6.7M
88–89	France 1:6.7M
90–91	Italy and the Adriatic 1:6.7M
92–93	Greece and the Balkans 1:6.7M

ASIA

94–95	Asia 1:67M
96–97	Western Russia and Central Asia 1:26.7M
98–99	Eastern Siberia 1:26.7M
100–101	Japan 1:8.5M
102–103	China and Mongolia 1:26.7M
104–105	North-eastern China and Korea 1:7.8M
106–107	South-eastern China and Taiwan 1:7.8M
108–109	Philippines and Eastern Indonesia 1:16.7M
110–111	South-east Asia 1:16.7M
112–113	Eastern India, Bangladesh and Burma 1:13.3M
114–115	Western India, Pakistan and Sri Lanka 1:13.3M
116–117	Persian Gulf, Iran and Afghanistan 1:13.3M

| 118–119 | The Middle East and Turkey 1:13.3M |
| 120–121 | Arabia and the Horn of Africa 1:20M |

AFRICA

122–123	Africa 1:56M
124–125	North-east Africa 1:20M
126–127	North-west Africa 1:20M
128–129	Central Africa 1:20M
130–131	Southern Africa 1:20M

AUSTRALIA AND OCEANIA

132–133	Australia 1:26.7M
134–135	South-east Australia 1:10.7M
136–137	New Zealand 1:8M
	South-west Pacific 1:72M
	Central Pacific 1:72M

NORTH AMERICA

138–139	North America 1:46.7M
140–141	Western Canada 1:20M
	Alaska 1:38M
142–143	Eastern Canada 1:20M
144–145	North-west USA 1:8M
146–147	North-central USA 1:8M
148–149	North-east USA 1:8M
150–151	South-west USA 1:8M
	Hawai'i 1:13M
152–153	Southern USA 1:8M
154–155	South-east USA 1:8M
156–157	Mexico and Central America 1:20M
158–159	Caribbean Sea 1:20M

SOUTH AMERICA

160–161	South America 1:46.7M
162–163	South America – North-west 1:21.3M
164–165	South America – North-east 1:21.3M
166–167	South America – South 1:21.3M

ANTARCTICA

| 168 | Antarctica 1:46.7M |

INDEX

| 169–232 | Index to World Maps |

Country/Territory	Area (1,000 sq km)	Area (1,000 sq mi)	Population (1,000s)	Density (persons per sq km)	Capital City	Annual Income US$
Afghanistan	652	252	31,108	48	Kabul	1,100
Albania	28.7	11.1	3,011	105	Tirana	8,200
Algeria	2,382	920	38,088	16	Algiers	7,500
American Samoa (US)	0.20	0.08	55	275	Pago Pago	8,000
Andorra	0.47	0.18	85	181	Andorra La Vella	37,200
Angola	1,247	481	18,565	15	Luanda	6,300
Anguilla (UK)	0.10	0.04	16	160	The Valley	12,200
Antigua & Barbuda	0.44	0.17	90	205	St John's	18,400
Argentina	2,780	1,074	42,611	15	Buenos Aires	18,600
Armenia	29.8	11.5	2,974	100	Yerevan	6,300
Aruba (Netherlands)	0.19	0.07	109	574	Oranjestad	25,300
Australia	7,741	2,989	22,263	3	Canberra	43,000
Austria	83.9	32.4	8,222	98	Vienna	42,600
Azerbaijan	86.6	33.4	9,590	111	Baku	10,800
Azores (Portugal)	2.2	0.86	246	112	Ponta Delgada	15,197
Bahamas	13.9	5.4	319	23	Nassau	32,000
Bahrain	0.69	0.27	1,281	1,857	Manama	29,800
Bangladesh	144	55.6	163,655	1,136	Dhaka	2,100
Barbados	0.43	0.17	289	672	Bridgetown	25,100
Belarus	208	80.2	9,626	46	Minsk	16,100
Belgium	30.5	11.8	10,444	342	Brussels	37,800
Belize	23	8.9	334	15	Belmopan	8,800
Benin	113	43.5	9,877	87	Porto-Novo	1,600
Bermuda (UK)	0.05	0.02	69	1,380	Hamilton	86,000
Bhutan	47	18.1	725	15	Thimphu	7,000
Bolivia	1,099	424	10,461	10	La Paz/Sucre	5,500
Bosnia-Herzegovina	51.2	19.8	3,876	76	Sarajevo	8,300
Botswana	582	225	2,128	4	Gaborone	16,400
Brazil	8,514	3,287	201,010	24	Brasília	12,100
Brunei	5.8	2.2	416	72	Bandar Seri Begawan	54,800
Bulgaria	111	42.8	6,982	63	Sofia	14,400
Burkina Faso	274	106	17,813	65	Ouagadougou	1,500
Burma (= Myanmar)	677	261	55,167	81	Rangoon/Naypyidaw	1,700
Burundi	27.8	10.7	10,888	392	Bujumbura	600
Cambodia	181	69.9	15,206	84	Phnom Penh	2,600
Cameroon	475	184	20,549	43	Yaoundé	2,400
Canada	9,971	3,850	34,568	3	Ottawa	43,100
Canary Is. (Spain)	7.2	2.8	1,682	234	Las Palmas/Santa Cruz	19,900
Cape Verde Is.	4.0	1.6	531	133	Praia	4,400
Cayman Is. (UK)	0.26	0.10	54	208	George Town	43,800
Central African Republic	623	241	5,167	8	Bangui	700
Chad	1,284	496	11,193	9	Ndjamena	2,500
Chile	757	292	17,217	23	Santiago	19,100
China	9,597	3,705	1,349,586	141	Beijing	9,800
Colombia	1,139	440	45,746	40	Bogotá	11,100
Comoros	2.2	0.86	752	342	Moroni	1,300
Congo	342	132	4,493	13	Brazzaville	4,800
Congo (Dem. Rep. of the)	2,345	905	75,507	32	Kinshasa	400
Cook Is. (NZ)	0.24	0.09	11	46	Avarua	9,100
Costa Rica	51.1	19.7	4,696	92	San José	12,900
Croatia	56.5	21.8	4,476	79	Zagreb	17,800
Cuba	111	42.8	11,062	100	Havana	10,200
Curaçao (Netherlands)	0.44	0.17	147	334	Willemstad	15,000
Cyprus	9.3	3.6	1,155	124	Nicosia	24,500
Czech Republic	78.9	30.5	10,163	129	Prague	27,200

Listed above are the principal countries and territories of the world. If a territory is not completely independent, then the country it is associated with is named. The area figures give the total area of land, inland water and ice.

Country/Territory	Area (1,000 sq km)	Area (1,000 sq mi)	Population (1,000s)	Density (persons per sq km)	Capital City	Annual Income US$
Denmark	43.1	16.6	5,556	129	Copenhagen	37,800
Djibouti	23.2	9.0	792	34	Djibouti	2,700
Dominica	0.75	0.29	73	97	Roseau	14,300
Dominican Republic	48.5	18.7	10,220	211	Santo Domingo	9,700
East Timor	14.9	5.7	1,172	79	Dili	8,800
Ecuador	284	109	15,439	54	Quito	10,600
Egypt	1,001	387	85,294	85	Cairo	6,600
El Salvador	21.0	8.1	6,109	291	San Salvador	7,500
Equatorial Guinea	28.1	10.8	704	25	Malabo	25,700
Eritrea	118	45.4	6,234	53	Asmara	1,200
Estonia	45.1	17.4	1,266	28	Tallinn	22,400
Ethiopia	1,104	426	93,877	85	Addis Ababa	1,300
Falkland Is. (UK)	12.2	4.7	3	0	Stanley	55,400
Faroe Is. (Denmark)	1.4	0.54	50	36	Tórshavn	30,500
Fiji	18.3	7.1	897	49	Suva	4,900
Finland	338	131	5,266	16	Helsinki	35,900
France	552	213	65,952	119	Paris	35,700
French Guiana (France)	90.0	34.7	250	3	Cayenne	8,300
French Polynesia (France)	4.0	1.5	277	69	Papeete	22,000
Gabon	268	103	1,640	6	Libreville	19,200
Gambia, The	11.3	4.4	1,883	167	Banjul	2,000
Georgia	69.7	26.9	4,556	65	Tbilisi	6,100
Germany	357	138	81,147	227	Berlin	39,500
Ghana	239	92.1	25,200	105	Accra	3,500
Gibraltar (UK)	0.006	0.002	29	4,833	Gibraltar Town	43,000
Greece	132	50.9	10,773	82	Athens	23,600
Greenland (Denmark)	2,176	840	58	0.03	Nuuk	38,400
Grenada	0.34	0.13	110	324	St George's	13,800
Guadeloupe (France)	1.7	0.66	406	239	Basse-Terre	7,900
Guam (US)	0.55	0.21	160	291	Agana	28,700
Guatemala	109	42.0	14,373	132	Guatemala City	5,300
Guinea	246	94.9	11,176	45	Conakry	1,100
Guinea-Bissau	36.1	13.9	1,661	46	Bissau	1,200
Guyana	215	83.0	740	3	Georgetown	8,500
Haiti	27.8	10.7	9,894	356	Port-au-Prince	1,300
Honduras	112	43.3	8,448	75	Tegucigalpa	4,800
Hungary	93.0	35.9	9,939	107	Budapest	19,800
Iceland	103	39.8	315	3	Reykjavik	40,700
India	3,287	1,269	1,220,800	371	New Delhi	4,000
Indonesia	1,905	735	251,160	132	Jakarta	5,200
Iran	1,648	636	79,854	48	Tehran	12,800
Iraq	438	169	31,858	73	Baghdad	7,100
Ireland	70.3	27.1	4,776	68	Dublin	41,300
Israel	20.6	8.0	7,707	374	Jerusalem	34,900
Italy	301	116	61,482	204	Rome	29,600
Ivory Coast (= Côte d'Ivoire)	322	125	22,401	70	Yamoussoukro	1,800
Jamaica	11.0	4.2	2,910	265	Kingston	9,000
Japan	378	146	127,253	337	Tokyo	37,100
Jordan	89.3	34.5	6,482	73	Amman	6,100
Kazakhstan	2,725	1,052	17,737	7	Astana	14,100
Kenya	580	224	44,038	76	Nairobi	1,800
Kiribati	0.73	0.28	103	141	Tarawa	6,400
Korea, North	121	46.5	24,720	204	Py ngyang	1,800
Korea, South	99.3	38.3	48,955	493	Seoul	33,200
Kosovo	10.9	4.2	1,848	170	Pristina	7,600

The population figures are 2013 estimates. The annual income is the Gross Domestic Product per capita in US dollars. The figures are the latest available, usually 2013 estimates.

Country/Territory	Area (1,000 sq km)	Area (1,000 sq m)	Population (1,000s)	Density (persons per sq km)	Capital City	Annual Income US$
Kuwait	17.8	6.9	2,695	151	Kuwait City	42,100
Kyrgyzstan	200	77.2	5,548	28	Bishkek	2,500
Laos	237	91.4	6,695	28	Vientiane	3,100
Latvia	64.6	24.9	2,178	34	Riga	19,100
Lebanon	10.4	4.0	4,132	397	Beirut	15,800
Lesotho	30.4	11.7	1,936	64	Maseru	2,200
Liberia	111	43.0	3,990	36	Monrovia	700
Libya	1,760	679	6,002	3	Tripoli	11,300
Liechtenstein	0.16	0.06	37	231	Vaduz	89,400
Lithuania	65.2	25.2	3,516	54	Vilnius	22,600
Luxembourg	2.6	1.0	515	198	Luxembourg	77,900
Macedonia (= FYROM)	25.7	9.9	2,087	81	Skopje	10,800
Madagascar	587	227	22,599	38	Antananarivo	1,000
Madeira (Portugal)	0.78	0.30	268	344	Funchal	25,800
Malawi	118	45.7	16,778	142	Lilongwe	900
Malaysia	330	127	29,628	90	Kuala Lumpur/Putrajaya	17,500
Maldives	0.30	0.12	394	1,313	Malé	9,100
Mali	1,240	479	15,969	13	Bamako	1,100
Malta	0.32	0.12	411	1,284	Valletta	27,500
Marshall Is.	0.18	0.07	70	389	Majuro	8,700
Martinique (France)	1.1	0.43	412	375	Fort-de-France	14,400
Mauritania	1,026	396	3,438	3	Nouakchott	2,200
Mauritius	2.0	0.79	1,322	661	Port Louis	16,100
Mayotte (France)	0.37	0.14	213	576	Mamoundzou	4,900
Mexico	1,958	756	116,221	59	Mexico City	15,600
Micronesia, Fed. States of	0.70	0.27	106	151	Palikir	7,300
Moldova	33.9	13.1	3,620	107	Kishinev	3,600
Monaco	0.001	0.0004	31	31,000	Monaco	65,500
Mongolia	1,567	605	3,227	2	Ulan Bator	5,900
Montenegro	14.0	5.4	653	47	Podgorica	11,900
Montserrat (UK)	0.10	0.39	5	50	Brades	8,500
Morocco	447	172	32,649	73	Rabat	5,500
Mozambique	802	309	24,097	30	Maputo	1,200
Namibia	824	318	2,183	3	Windhoek	8,200
Nauru	0.02	0.008	9	450	Yaren	5,000
Nepal	147	56.8	30,430	207	Katmandu	1,500
Netherlands	41.5	16.0	16,805	405	Amsterdam/The Hague	41,400
New Caledonia (France)	18.6	7.2	264	14	Nouméa	37,700
New Zealand	271	104	4,365	16	Wellington	30,400
Nicaragua	130	50.2	5,789	45	Managua	4,500
Niger	1,267	489	16,899	13	Niamey	800
Nigeria	924	357	174,508	189	Abuja	2,800
Northern Mariana Is. (US)	0.46	0.18	51	111	Saipan	13,600
Norway	324	125	4,723	15	Oslo	55,400
Oman	310	119	3,154	10	Muscat	29,800
Pakistan	796	307	193,239	243	Islamabad	3,100
Palau	0.46	0.18	21	46	Melekeok	10,500
Panama	75.5	29.2	3,559	47	Panamá	16,500
Papua New Guinea	463	179	6,432	14	Port Moresby	2,900
Paraguay	407	157	6,623	16	Asunción	6,800
Peru	1,285	496	29,849	23	Lima	11,100
Philippines	300	116	105,721	352	Manila	4,700
Poland	323	125	38,384	119	Warsaw	21,100
Portugal	88.8	34.3	10,799	122	Lisbon	22,900
Puerto Rico (US)	8.9	3.4	3,674	413	San Juan	16,300
Qatar	11.0	4.2	2,042	186	Doha	102,100
Réunion (France)	2.5	0.97	841	336	St-Denis	6,200

Country/Territory	Area (1,000 sq km)	Area (1,000 sq mi)	Population (1,000s)	Density (persons per sq km)	Capital City	Annual Income US$
Romania	238	92.0	21,790	92	Bucharest	13,200
Russia	17,075	6,593	142,500	8	Moscow	18,100
Rwanda	26.3	10.2	12,013	457	Kigali	1,500
St Kitts & Nevis	0.26	0.10	51	196	Basseterre	16,300
St Lucia	0.54	0.21	163	302	Castries	13,100
St Vincent & the Grenadines	0.39	0.15	103	264	Kingstown	12,100
Samoa	2.8	1.1	195	70	Apia	6,200
San Marino	0.06	0.02	32	533	San Marino	55,000
São Tomé & Príncipe	0.96	0.37	187	195	São Tomé	2,200
Saudi Arabia	2,150	830	26,940	13	Riyadh	31,300
Senegal	197	76.0	13,300	68	Dakar	2,100
Serbia	78	29.9	7,243	93	Belgrade	11,100
Seychelles	0.46	0.18	91	198	Victoria	25,900
Sierra Leone	71.7	27.7	5,613	78	Freetown	1,400
Singapore	0.68	0.26	5,460	8,029	Singapore City	62,400
Slovak Republic	49.0	18.9	5,488	112	Bratislava	24,700
Slovenia	20.3	7.8	1,993	98	Ljubljana	27,400
Solomon Is.	28.9	11.2	597	21	Honiara	3,400
Somalia	638	246	10,252	16	Mogadishu	600
South Africa	1,221	471	48,601	40	Cape Town/Pretoria	11,500
Spain	498	192	47,371	95	Madrid	30,100
Sri Lanka	65.6	25.3	21,676	330	Colombo	6,500
Sudan	1,886	728	34,848	18	Khartoum	2,600
Sudan, South	620	239	11,090	18	Juba	1,400
Surinam	163	63.0	567	3	Paramaribo	12,900
Swaziland	17.4	6.7	1,403	81	Mbabane	5,700
Sweden	450	174	9,119	20	Stockholm	40,900
Switzerland	41.3	15.9	7,996	194	Berne	46,000
Syria	185	71.5	22,457	121	Damascus	5,100
Taiwan	36.0	13.9	23,300	647	Taipei	39,600
Tajikistan	143	55.3	7,910	55	Dushanbe	2,300
Tanzania	945	365	48,262	51	Dodoma	1,700
Thailand	513	198	67,448	131	Bangkok	9,900
Togo	56.8	21.9	7,154	126	Lomé	1,100
Tonga	0.65	0.25	106	163	Nuku'alofa	8,200
Trinidad & Tobago	5.1	2.0	1,225	240	Port of Spain	20,300
Tunisia	164	63.2	10,836	66	Tunis	9,900
Turkey	775	299	80,694	104	Ankara	15,300
Turkmenistan	488	188	5,113	10	Ashkhabad	9,700
Turks & Caicos Is. (UK)	0.43	0.17	48	112	Cockburn Town	29,100
Tuvalu	0.03	0.01	11	367	Fongafale	3,500
Uganda	241	93.1	34,759	144	Kampala	1,500
Ukraine	604	233	44,573	74	Kiev	7,400
United Arab Emirates	83.6	32.3	5,474	65	Abu Dhabi	29,900
United Kingdom	242	93.4	63,396	262	London	37,300
United States of America	9,629	3,718	316,669	33	Washington, DC	52,800
Uruguay	175	67.6	3,324	19	Montevideo	16,600
Uzbekistan	447	173	28,662	64	Tashkent	3,800
Vanuatu	12.2	4.7	262	21	Port-Vila	4,800
Vatican City	0.0004	0.0002	839	2,097,500	Vatican City	-
Venezuela	912	352	28,459	31	Caracas	13,600
Vietnam	332	128	92,478	279	Hanoi	4,000
Virgin Is. (UK)	0.15	0.06	28	187	Road Town	42,300
Virgin Is. (US)	0.35	0.13	105	300	Charlotte Amalie	14,500
Yemen	528	204	25,408	48	Sana'	2,500
Zambia	753	291	14,222	19	Lusaka	1,800
Zimbabwe	391	151	13,183	34	Harare	600

8 WORLD STATISTICS: CITIES

	Population (1,000s)		Population (1,000s)		Population (1,000s)		Population (1,000s)
Afghanistan		**China**		Yiyang	1,318	**Finland**	
Kabul	3,097	Shanghai	20,208	Huai'an	1,316	Helsinki	1,134
Algeria		Beijing	15,594	Handan	1,306	**France**	
Algiers	2,916	Guangzhou	10,849	Tai'an	1,276	Paris	10,620
Angola		Shenzhen	10,630	Suqian	1,258	Marseilles	1,489
Luanda	5,068	Chongqing	9,977	Jining	1,246	Lyon	1,488
Humabo	1,098	Wuhan	9,158	Chifeng	1,238	Lille	1,042
Argentina		Tianjin	8,744	Jingmen	1,228	**Georgia**	
Buenos Aires	13,528	Dongguan	7,280	Nanyang	1,227	Tbilisi	1,121
Córdoba	1,556	Hong Kong	7,122	Yuzhou	1,226	**Germany**	
Rosario	1,283	Chengdu	6,670	Xining	1,225	Berlin	3,462
Armenia		Foshan	6,486	Zaozhuang	1,211	Hamburg	1,796
Yerevan	1,116	Nanjing	5,866	Zaoyang	1,210	Munich	1,364
Australia		Harbin	5,687	Tianshui	1,199	Cologne	1,006
Sydney	4,543	Shenyang	5,568	Yueyang	1,184	**Ghana**	
Melbourne	3,961	Hangzhou	5,448	Yongzhou	1,182	Accra	2,573
Brisbane	2,039	Xi'an	4,975	Baoding	1,177	Kumasi	2,019
Perth	1,649	Shantou	4,175	Mudanjiang	1,171	**Greece**	
Adelaide	1,198	Zhengzhou	3,964	Liupanshui	1,149	Athens	3,414
Austria		Qingdao	3,797	Anyang	1,144	**Guatemala**	
Vienna	1,720	Jinan	3,697	Leshan	1,143	Guatemala City	1,168
Azerbaijan		Changchun	3,694	Hengyang	1,135	**Guinea**	
Baku	2,123	Taiyuan	3,495	Xiaomen	1,130	Conakry	1,786
Bangladesh		Kunming	3,472	Xiaoshan	1,130	**Haiti**	
Dhaka	15,391	Suzhou	3,463	Yixing	1,129	Port-au-Prince	2,207
Chittagong	5,239	Wuxi	3,366	Yinchuan	1,119	**Honduras**	
Khulna	1,781	Dalian	3,359	Quanzhou	1,097	Tegucigalpa	1,088
Belarus		Changsha	3,335	Zigong	1,087	**Hungary**	
Minsk	1,861	Ürümqi	3,123	Putian	1,084	Budapest	1,737
Belgium		Hefei	3,012	Zhangjiakou	1,072	**India**	
Brussels	1,949	Fuzhou	2,897	Jingzhou	1,070	Delhi	22,654
Bolivia		Xiamen	2,880	Fuyu	1,068	Mumbai	19,744
Santa Cruz	1,719	Zhongshan	2,862	Jixi	1,067	Kolkata	14,402
La Paz	1,715	Shijiazhuang	2,841	Yulin	1,060	Chennai	8,784
Brazil		Zibo	2,797	Mianyang	1,052	Bangalore	8,614
São Paulo	19,924	Ningbo	2,755	Zhuzhou	1,047	Hyderabad	7,837
Rio de Janeiro	11,960	Wenzhou	2,733	Xinyang	1,045	Ahmedabad	6,425
Belo Horizonte	5,487	Lanzhou	2,555	Pingdingshan	1,041	Pune	5,100
Pôrto Alegre	3,933	Guiyang	2,525	Zhanjiang	1,041	Surat	4,661
Salvador	4,061	Nanchang	2,411	Lianyungang	1,017	Jaipur	3,102
Recife	3,733	Changzhou	2,405	Linqing	1,009	Kanpur	2,928
Fortaleza	3,591	Jinxi	2,268	Jiamusi	1,006	Lucknow	2,926
Curitiba	3,188	Xuzhou	2,242	Xiangfan	1,006	Nagpur	2,511
Campinas	2,846	Nanning	2,136	Huaibei	1,005	Indore	2,188
Brasília	3,813	Nanchong	2,046	**Colombia**		Coimbatore	2,180
Belém	2,069	Wanxian	1,963	Bogotá	8,743	Patna	2,059
Goiânia	2,095	Baotou	1,953	Medellín	3,694	Bhopal	1,900
Vitória	1,695	Jilin	1,942	Cali	2,453	Vadodara	1,829
Santos	1,820	Tangshan	1,927	Barranquilla	1,900	Agra	1,763
Manaus	1,848	Huizhou	1,856	Bucaramanga	1,120	Visakhapatnam	1,746
Natal	1,293	Weifang	1,752	**Congo**		Ludhiana	1,622
São Luís	1,275	Anshan	1,694	Brazzaville	1,611	Kochi	1,620
Guarulhos	1,222	Tianmen	1,676	**Congo (Dem. Rep.)**		Nashik	1,579
Maceió	1,177	Shangqiu	1,650	Kinshasa	8,798	Vijayawada	1,511
Joinville	1,065	Lu'an	1,647	Lubumbashi	1,556	Madurai	1,472
Florianópolis	1,043	Haikou	1,624	Mbuji-Mayi	1,504	Varanasi	1,443
João Pessoa	1,094	Qiqihar	1,616	**Costa Rica**		Meerut	1,434
Bulgaria		Daqing	1,603	San José	1,515	Rajkot	1,406
Sofia	1,174	Yangzhou	1,603	**Croatia**		Jamshedpur	1,346
Burma		Xinghua	1,587	Zagreb	1,067	Faridabad	1,330
(Myanmar)		Luoyang	1,575	**Cuba**		Srinagar	1,285
Rangoon	4,457	Pingxiang	1,562	Havana	2,116	Ghaziabad	1,277
Mandalay	1,063	Yantai	1,557	**Czech Republic**		Jabalpur	1,273
Naypyidaw	1,060	Xiantao	1,528	Prague	1,276	Asansol	1,248
Cambodia		Hohhot	1,499	**Denmark**		Allahabad	1,223
Phnom Penh	1,550	Linyi	1,454	Copenhagen	1,206	Aurangabad	1,201
Cameroon		Xianyang	1,450	**Dominican Republic**		Dhanbad	1,190
Douala	2,449	Luzhou	1,447	Santo Domingo	2,191	Amritsar	1,190
Yaoundé	2,432	Neijiang	1,441	**Ecuador**		Solapur	1,155
Canada		Huainan	1,436	Guayaquil	2,287	Jodhpur	1,149
Toronto	5,573	Changde	1,429	Quito	1,622	Raipur	1,140
Montréal	3,856	Suining	1,401	**Egypt**		Ranchi	1,137
Vancouver	2,267	Datong	1,390	Cairo	11,169	Gwalior	1,111
Calgary	1,216	Liuzhou	1,390	Alexandria	4,494	Guwahati	1,075
Ottawa	1,208	Fushun	1,379	**El Salvador**		Bhilainagar-Durg	1,069
Edmonton	1,142	Xintai	1,334	San Salvador	1,605	Chandigarh	1,034
Chile		Yancheng	1,330	**Ethiopia**		Thiruvananthapuram	1,034
Santiago	20,208	Heze	1,318	Addis Ababa	2,979	Tiruchchirapalli	1,028

	Population (1,000s)		Population (1,000s)		Population (1,000s)		Population (1,000s)
...ota	1,013	**Mali**		Omsk	1,156	**United States**	
...rivandrum	1,010	Bamako	2,037	Kazan	1,147	**of America**	
...alicut	1,007	**Mexico**		Chelyabinsk	1,135	New York	19,832
...ndonesia		Mexico City	20,446	Rostov	1,092	Los Angeles	13,053
...akarta	9,769	Guadalajara	4,525	Ufa	1,064	Chicago	9,522
...urabaya	2,787	Monterrey	4,213	Volgograd	1,022	Dallas-Fort Worth	6,701
...andung	2,429	Puebla	2,335	**Rwanda**		Houston	6,177
Medan	2,118	Tijuana	1,820	Kigali	1,004	Philadelphia	6,019
...emarang	1,573	Toluca	1,748	**Saudi Arabia**		Washington, DC	5,860
...alembang	1,455	León	1,653	Riyadh	5,451	Miami	5,763
Makassar	1,387	Ciudad Juárez	1,338	Jedda	3,578	Atlanta	5,458
...atam	1,034	Torreón	1,242	Mecca	1,591	Boston	4,641
...an		Querétaro	1,143	Medina	1,142	San Francisco	4,456
...ehran	7,304	San Luis Potosí	1,061	**Senegal**		Riverside-	
...ashhad	2,713	Mérida	1,040	Dakar	3,035	San Bernardino	4,350
...araj	1,635	**Mongolia**		**Serbia**		Phoenix-Mesa	4,330
...sfahan	1,781	Ulan Bator	1,184	Belgrade	1,135	Detroit	4,292
...abriz	1,509	**Morocco**		**Singapore**		Seattle	3,552
...hiraz	1,321	Casablanca	3,046	Singapore City	5,188	Minneapolis-St Paul	3,422
...hvaz	1,082	Rabat	1,843	**Somalia**		San Diego	3,177
...om	1,065	Fès	1,088	Mogadishu	1,554	Tampa-St Petersburg	2,843
...aq		**Mozambique**		**South Africa**		St Louis	2,796
...aghdad	6,036	Maputo	1,150	Johannesburg	3,844	Baltimore	2,753
Mosul	1,494	**Nepal**		Cape Town	3,562	Denver	2,645
...rbil	1,039	Katmandu	1,015	Durban	3,012	Pittsburgh	2,361
...reland		**Netherlands**		Pretoria	1,501	Charlotte	2,297
Dublin	1,121	Amsterdam	1,056	Vereeniging	1,200	Portland	2,290
...srael		Rotterdam	1,014	Port Elizabeth	1,119	San Antonio	2,234
...el Aviv-Yafo	3,381	**New Zealand**		**Spain**		Orlando	2,224
...aifa	1,054	Auckland	1,452	Madrid	6,574	Sacramento	2,196
...aly		**Niger**		Barcelona	5,570	Cincinnati	2,129
...ome	3,298	Niamey	1,297	**Sudan**		Cleveland	2,064
Milan	2,909	**Nigeria**		Khartoum	4,632	Kansas City	2,039
...aples	2,373	Lagos	11,223	**Sweden**		Las Vegas	2,001
...urin	1,613	Kano	3,375	Stockholm	1,385	Columbus	1,944
...ory Coast (Côte d'Ivoire)		Ibadan	2,949	**Syria**		Indianapolis	1,929
...bidjan	4,288	Abuja	2,153	Aleppo	3,164	San Jose	1,894
...apan		Port Harcourt	1,894	Damascus	2,650	Austin	1,834
...okyo	37,217	Kaduna	1,524	Homs	1,369	Nashville	1,727
Osaka-Kobe	11,494	Benin City	1,359	**Taiwan**		Virginia Beach-Norfolk	1,700
...agoya	3,328	Ogbomosho	1,075	Taipei	2,730	Providence	1,601
...apporo	2,742	**Pakistan**		T'aichung	1,244	Milwaukee	1,567
...yoto	1,804	Karachi	13,876	Kaohsiung	1,560	Jacksonville	1,378
...ukuoka-Kitakyushu	2,868	Lahore	7,566	Tainan	1,205	Memphis	1,342
Hiroshima	2,119	Faisalabad	3,038	**Tanzania**		Oklahoma	1,297
...endai	2,428	Rawalpindi	2,164	Dar es Salaam	3,588	Louisville	1,251
...ordan		Multan	1,775	**Thailand**		Richmond	1,232
...mman	1,179	Gujranwala	1,767	Bangkok	8,426	New Orleans	1,227
...azakhstan		Hyderabad	1,701	Samut Prakan	1,212	Hartford	1,214
...lmaty	1,426	Peshawar	1,523	**Togo**		Raleigh	1,189
...enya		**Panama**		Lomé	1,524	Birmingham	1,137
Nairobi	3,363	Panamá	1,426	**Tunisia**		Buffalo	1,134
...orea, North		**Paraguay**		Tunis	2,385	Salt Lake City	1,124
...yo'ngyang	2,843	Asunción	2,139	**Turkey**		Rochester	1,082
...orea, South		**Peru**		Istanbul	11,253	Grand Rapids	1,006
Seoul	9,736	Lima	9,130	Ankara	4,194	**Uruguay**	
...usan	3,372	**Philippines**		Izmir	2,927	Montevideo	1,672
...ncheon	2,622	Manila	11,862	Bursa	1,713	**Uzbekistan**	
...aegu	2,447	Davao	1,565	Adana	1,468	Tashkent	2,227
...aejeon	1,538	**Poland**		Gaziantep	1,198	**Venezuela**	
...wangju	1,503	Warsaw	1,723	Konya	1,057	Caracas	3,242
...won	1,159	**Portugal**		**Uganda**		Maracaibo	2,310
...lsan	1,100	Lisbon	2,843	Kampala	1,659	Valencia	1,866
...uwait		Porto	1,367	**Ukraine**		Barquisimeto	1,245
...uwait City	2,406	**Puerto Rico**		Kiev	2,829	Maracay	1,115
...ebanon		San Juan	2,475	Kharkov	1,451	**Vietnam**	
...eirut	2,022	**Romania**		Odessa	1,010	Ho Chi Minh City	6,405
...ibya		Bucharest	1,937	**United Arab Emirates**		Hanoi	2,955
...ripoli	1,127	**Russia**		Dubai	1,978	Can Tho	1,004
Madagascar		Moscow	11,621	**United Kingdom**		**Yemen**	
...ntananarivo	1,987	Saint Petersburg	4,866	London	9,005	Sana'	2,419
Malaysia		Novosibirsk	1,478	Birmingham	2,272	**Zambia**	
...uala Lumpur	1,556	Yekaterinburg	1,355	Manchester	2,213	Lusaka	1,802
...ang	1,190	Nizhni Novgorod	1,245	Liverpool	1,519	**Zimbabwe**	
...hore Bharu	1,045	Samara	1,166	Glasgow	1,137	Harare	1,542

...ted above are the principal cities with more than 1,000,000 inhabitants. The figures are taken from the most recent
...nsus or estimate available (usually 2011), and as far as possible are for the metropolitan area or urban agglomeration.

Kms

	Beijing	Buenos Aires	Cairo	Caracas	Chicago	Hong Kong	Honolulu	Johannesburg	Kolkata	Lagos	London	Los Angeles
Beijing		11972	4688	8947	6588	1220	5070	7276	2031	7119	5057	625
Buenos Aires	19268		7341	3167	5599	11481	7558	5025	10268	4919	6917	612
Cairo	7544	11814		6340	6127	5064	8838	3894	3541	2432	2180	758
Caracas	14399	5096	10203		2502	10166	6009	6847	9609	4810	4664	361
Chicago	10603	9011	3206	4027		7783	4247	8689	7978	5973	3949	174
Hong Kong	1963	18478	8150	16360	12526		5543	6669	1653	7360	5980	723
Honolulu	8160	12164	14223	9670	6836	8921		11934	7048	10133	7228	255
Johannesburg	11710	8088	6267	11019	13984	10732	19206		5256	2799	5637	1036
Kolkata	3269	16524	5699	15464	12839	2659	11343	8459		5727	4946	815
Lagos	11457	7916	3915	7741	9612	11845	16308	4505	9216		3118	771
London	8138	11131	3508	7507	6356	9623	11632	9071	7961	5017		544
Los Angeles	10060	9852	12200	5812	2804	11639	4117	16676	13120	12414	8758	
Mexico City	12460	7389	12372	3586	2726	14122	6085	14585	15280	11071	8936	249
Moscow	5794	13477	2902	9938	8000	7144	11323	9161	5534	6254	2498	976
Mumbai	4757	14925	4355	14522	12953	4317	12914	6974	1664	7612	7190	1400
Nairobi	9216	10402	3536	11544	12883	8776	17282	2927	6179	3807	6819	1554
New York	10988	8526	9020	3430	1145	12950	7980	12841	12747	8477	5572	393
Paris	8217	11051	3210	7625	6650	9630	11968	8732	7858	4714	342	908
Rio de Janeiro	17338	1953	9896	4546	8547	17704	13342	7113	15073	6035	9299	1015
Rome	8126	11151	2133	8363	7739	9284	12916	7743	7219	4039	1431	1018
Singapore	4478	15879	8267	18359	15078	2599	10816	8660	2897	11145	10852	1412
Sydney	8949	11800	14418	15343	14875	7374	8168	11040	9138	15519	16992	1207
Tokyo	2099	18362	9571	14164	10137	2874	6202	13547	5141	13480	9562	881
Wellington	10782	9981	16524	13122	13451	9427	7513	11761	11354	16050	18814	1081

The table above shows air distances in kilometres and miles between 30 major citie

Mexico City	Moscow	Mumbai	Nairobi	New York	Paris	Rio de Janeiro	Rome	Singapore	Sydney	Tokyo	Wellington	
7742	3600	2956	5727	6828	5106	10773	5049	2783	5561	1304	6700	**Beijing**
4591	8374	9275	6463	5298	6867	1214	6929	9867	7332	11410	6202	**Buenos Aires**
7687	1803	2706	2197	5605	1994	6149	1325	5137	8959	5947	10268	**Cairo**
2228	6175	9024	7173	2131	4738	2825	5196	11407	9534	8801	8154	**Caracas**
1694	4971	8048	8005	711	4132	5311	4809	9369	9243	6299	8358	**Chicago**
8775	4439	2683	5453	8047	5984	11001	5769	1615	4582	1786	5857	**Hong Kong**
3781	7036	8024	10739	4958	7437	8290	8026	6721	5075	3854	4669	**Honolulu**
9063	5692	4334	1818	7979	5426	4420	4811	5381	6860	8418	7308	**Johannesburg**
9494	3438	1034	3839	7921	4883	9366	4486	1800	5678	3195	7055	**Kolkata**
6879	3886	4730	2366	5268	2929	3750	2510	6925	9643	8376	9973	**Lagos**
5552	1552	4467	4237	3463	212	5778	889	6743	10558	5942	11691	**London**
1549	6070	8700	9659	2446	5645	6310	6331	8776	7502	5475	6719	**Los Angeles**
Mexico City	6664	9728	9207	2090	5717	4780	6365	10321	8058	7024	6897	**Mexico City**
724	*Moscow*	3126	3942	4666	1545	7184	1477	5237	9008	4651	10283	**Moscow**
656	5031	*Mumbai*	2816	7793	4356	8332	3837	2432	6313	4189	7686	**Mumbai**
4818	6344	4532	*Nairobi*	7358	4029	5548	3350	4635	7552	6996	8490	**Nairobi**
8264	7510	12541	11842	*New York*	3626	4832	4280	9531	9935	6741	8951	**New York**
9200	2486	7010	6485	5836	*Paris*	5708	687	6671	10539	6038	11798	**Paris**
7693	11562	13409	8928	7777	9187	*Rio de Janeiro*	5725	9763	8389	11551	7367	**Rio de Janeiro**
8243	2376	6175	5391	6888	1105	9214	*Rome*	6229	10143	6127	11523	**Rome**
8610	8428	3914	7460	15339	10737	15712	10025	*Singapore*	3915	3306	5298	**Singapore**
969	14497	10160	12153	15989	16962	13501	16324	6300	*Sydney*	4861	1383	**Sydney**
304	7485	6742	11260	10849	9718	18589	9861	5321	7823	*Tokyo*	5762	**Tokyo**
100	16549	12370	13664	14405	18987	11855	18545	8526	2226	9273	*Wellington*	**Wellington**

Miles

nown as 'great-circle' distances, these measure the shortest routes between the cities.

The world is divided into 24 time zones, each centred on meridians at 15° intervals, which is the longitudinal distance the Sun travels every hour. The Prime Meridian running through Greenwich in London, England, passes through the middle of the first time zone. Zones to the east of Greenwich are ahead of Universal Time (UT) by one hour for every 15° of longitude, while zones to the west are behind UT by one hour.

When it is 12 noon at the Greenwich meridian, 180° east it is midnight of the same day, while at 180° west the day is only just beginning. To overcome this, the International Date Line was established in 1883 – an imaginary line which approximately follows the 180th meridian. Therefore, if one travelled eastwards from Japan (140° East) towards Samoa (170° West), one would pass from Sunday night straight into Sunday morning.

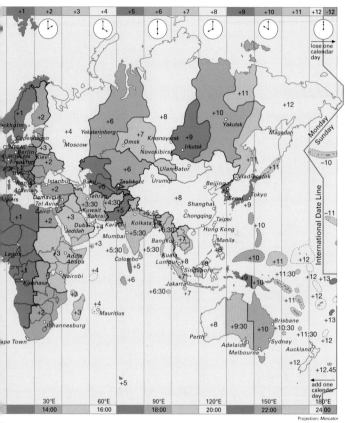

Projection: Mercator

TIME DIFFERENCES FROM GMT (LONDON)

BEIJING	+8	BANGKOK	+7
CHICAGO	−6	DELHI	+5.30
JO'BURG	+2	LAGOS	+1
LOS ANGELES	−8	MEXICO CITY	−6
MOSCOW	+4	NEW YORK	−5
PARIS	+1	ROME	+1
SYDNEY	+10	TEHRAN	+3.30
TOKYO	+9	TORONTO	−5

KEY TO TIME ZONES MAP

10   Hours behind or ahead of UT or Coordinated Universal Time

Zones using UT (GMT)

Zones behind UT (GMT)

International boundaries

Actual solar time, when time at Greenwich is 12:00 (noon)

Zones ahead of UT (GMT)

Half-hour zones

Time-zone boundaries

International Date Line

Note: Certain time zones are affected by the incidence of Daylight Saving Time in countries where it is adopted.

COPYRIGHT PHILIP'S

WORLD'S BUSIEST AIRPORTS

Total passengers in millions (2012)

1. ATLANTA HARTSFIELD INTL. (ATL) 95.5
2. BEIJING CAPITAL INTL. (PEK) 81.9
3. LONDON HEATHROW (LHR) 70.0
4. TOKYO HANEDA (HND) 66.8
5. CHICAGO O'HARE INTL. (ORD) 66.6
6. LOS ANGELES INTL. (LAX) 63.7
7. PARIS CHARLES DE GAULLE (CDG) 61.6
8. DALLAS/FORT WORTH INTL. (DFW) 58.6
9. JAKARTA INTL. (CGK) 57.8
10. DUBAI INTL. (DXB) 57.7

The flight paths shown on the map above usually follow the shortest, most direct route from A to B, known as the *great-circle route*. A great circle is any circle that divides the globe into equal halves. Aircraft do not always fly along great-circle routes, however. Lack of search and rescue and emergency landing provisions, together with limits on fuel consumption and minimum flying altitudes, mean that commercial aircraft do not usually fly across Antarctica.

Projection: *Oblique Azimuthal Equidistant*

FLIGHT TIMES FROM LONDON		**FLIGHT TIMES FROM NEW YORK**	
ATHENS	4hrs 05mins	FRANKFURT	8hrs 35mins
AUCKLAND	24hrs 20mins	JOHANNESBURG	17hrs 45mins
BANGKOK	14hrs 30mins	MEXICO CITY	5hrs 45mins
BUENOS AIRES	14hrs 20mins	PARIS	8hrs 15mins
HONG KONG	14hrs 10mins	ROME	9hrs 35mins
LOS ANGELES	12hrs 00mins	SANTIAGO	12hrs 55mins
MOSCOW	3hrs 50mins	SINGAPORE	23hrs 10mins
MUMBAI (BOMBAY)	11hrs 15mins	TOKYO	14hrs 35mins
NEW YORK	6hrs 50mins	VANCOUVER	7hrs 25mins

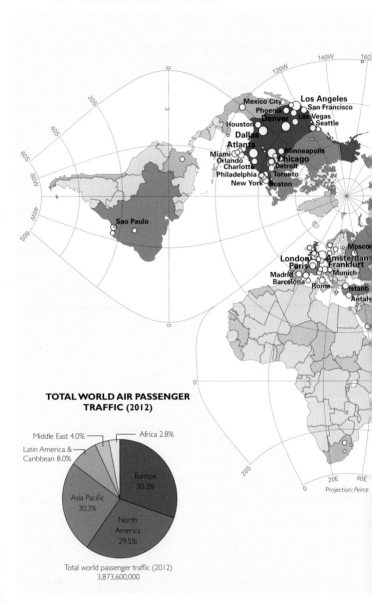

TOTAL WORLD AIR PASSENGER TRAFFIC (2012)

Africa 2.8%
Middle East 4.0%
Latin America & Caribbean 8.0%
Europe 30.3%
Asia Pacific 30.3%
North America 29.5%

Total world passenger traffic (2012)
3,873,600,000

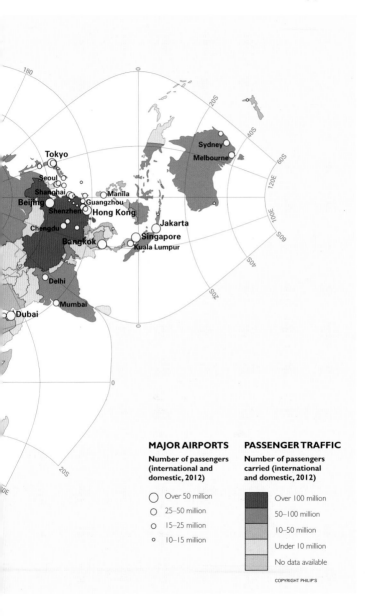

MAJOR AIRPORTS

Number of passengers
(international and
domestic, 2012)

○ Over 50 million

○ 25–50 million

○ 15–25 million

○ 10–15 million

PASSENGER TRAFFIC

Number of passengers
carried (international
and domestic, 2012)

Over 100 million

50–100 million

10–50 million

Under 10 million

No data available

COPYRIGHT PHILIP'S

UNESCO WORLD HERITAGE SITES 2014

Total sites = 981 (759 cultural, 193 natural, 29 mixed)

Region	Cultural sites	Natural sites	Mixed sites
Africa	48	36	4
Arab States	68	4	2
Asia & Pacific	154	57	10
Europe & North America	399	60	10
Latin America & Caribbean	90	36	3

NB Some sites are trans-boundary, therefore total figures may not add up.

Europe at larger scale

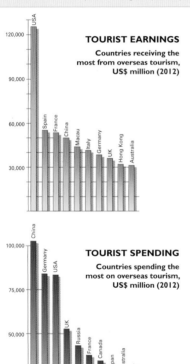

TOURIST EARNINGS

Countries receiving the most from overseas tourism, US$ million (2012)

TOURIST SPENDING

Countries spending the most on overseas tourism, US$ million (2012)

Movement of tourists

More than 10 million

5 – 10 million

3 – 5 million

Less than 3 million

TOURIST DESTINATIONS

Projection: *Peirce*

Destinations

- ■ Cultural & historical centres
- ☐ Coastal resorts
- ☐ Ski resorts
- ■ Centres of entertainment
- ■ Places of pilgrimage
- ■ Places of great natural beauty

☐ Other tourist destinations

COPYRIGHT PHILIP'S

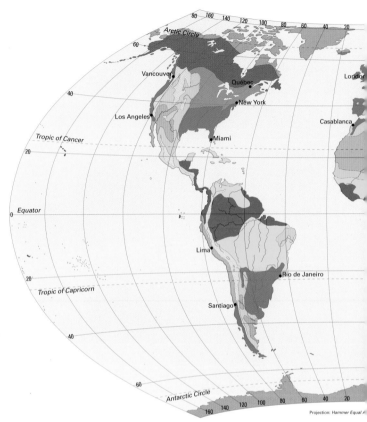

Projection: Hammer Equal A

Climate is weather in the long term: the seasonal pattern of temperature and precipitation averaged over a period of time. Temperature roughly follows latitude, and is warmest near the equator and coldest near the poles. The interplay of various factors, however, namely the differential heating of land and sea, the influence of land masses and mountain ranges on winds and ocean currents, and the effect of vegetation, all combine to add complexity. Thus New York and Naple share almost the same latitude, but the resulting climates are quite differen Most scientists are now in agreeme that the world's climate is changing, du partly to atmospheric pollution. By th year 2050, average world temperature are predicted to rise by between 1.5° and 2.8°C to make the climate hott than it has been at any time during th last 120,000 years. Climate graphs fo 24 cities are given on pages 22 and 2

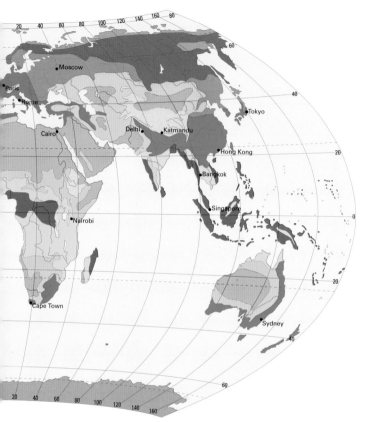

SEASONAL WEATHER EXTREMES

- **Caribbean**
  Hurricanes – August to October

- **Northern Latitudes**
  Blizzards – November to March

- **Southern Asia**
  Cyclones and typhoons – June to November

- **Southern Asia**
  Monsoon rains – July to October

CLIMATIC REGIONS

- Tropical climate (hot and wet)
- Desert climate (hot and very dry)
- Savanna climate (hot with dry season)
- Steppe climate (warm and dry)
- Mild climate (warm and wet)
- Continental climate (cold with wet winter)
- Subarctic climate (very cold winter)
- Polar climate (very cold and dry)
- Mountainous climate (altitude affects climate)
- Lima ● Climate graphs on pages 22 and 23

Note: Climate comprises a description of the condition of the atmosphere over a considerable area for a long time (at least 30 years).

22 WORLD CLIMATE GRAPHS

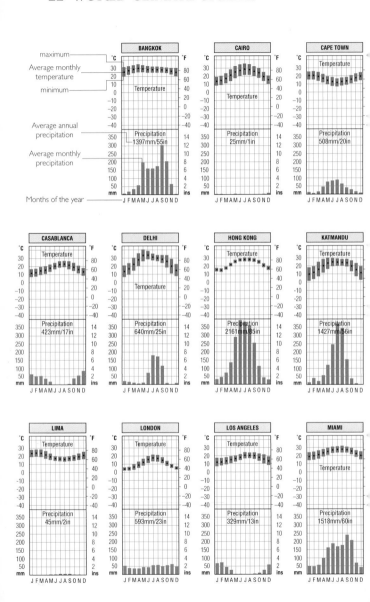

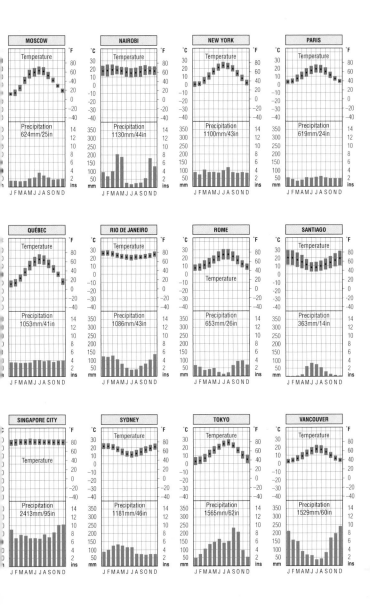

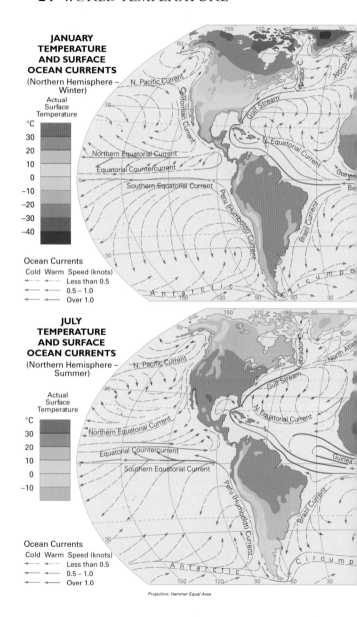

JANUARY TEMPERATURE AND SURFACE OCEAN CURRENTS
(Northern Hemisphere – Winter)

Actual Surface Temperature
°C
30
20
10
0
-10
-20
-30
-40

Ocean Currents
Cold Warm Speed (knots)
Less than 0.5
0.5 – 1.0
Over 1.0

JULY TEMPERATURE AND SURFACE OCEAN CURRENTS
(Northern Hemisphere – Summer)

Actual Surface Temperature
°C
30
20
10
0
-10

Ocean Currents
Cold Warm Speed (knots)
Less than 0.5
0.5 – 1.0
Over 1.0

Projection: *Hammer Equal Area*

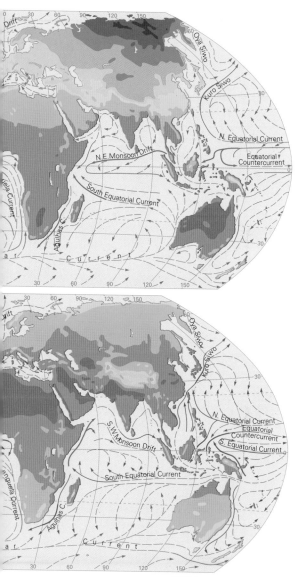

Projection: *Hammer Equal Area*

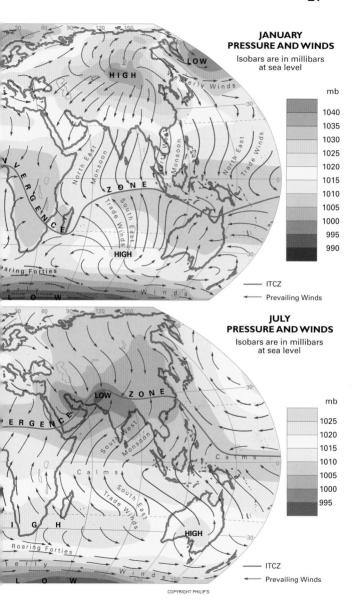

JANUARY PRESSURE AND WINDS
Isobars are in millibars at sea level

mb
1040
1035
1030
1025
1020
1015
1010
1005
1000
995
990

ITCZ
Prevailing Winds

JULY PRESSURE AND WINDS
Isobars are in millibars at sea level

mb
1025
1020
1015
1010
1005
1000
995

ITCZ
Prevailing Winds

COPYRIGHT PHILIP'S

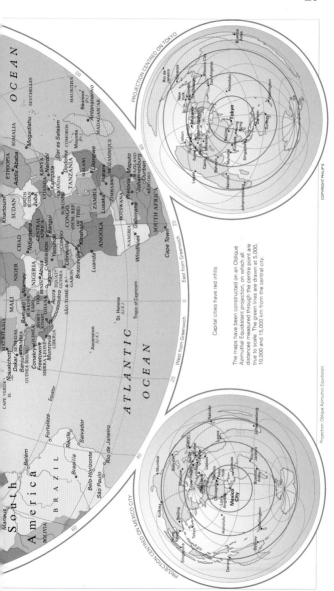

29

Capital cities have red infills

The maps have been constructed on an Oblique Azimuthal Equidistant projection, on which all distances measured through the centre point are true to scale. The green lines are drawn at 5,000, 10,000 and 15,000 km from the central city.

PROJECTION CENTRED ON TOKYO

PROJECTION CENTRED ON MEXICO CITY

Projection: Oblique Azimuthal Equidistant

COPYRIGHT PHILIP'S

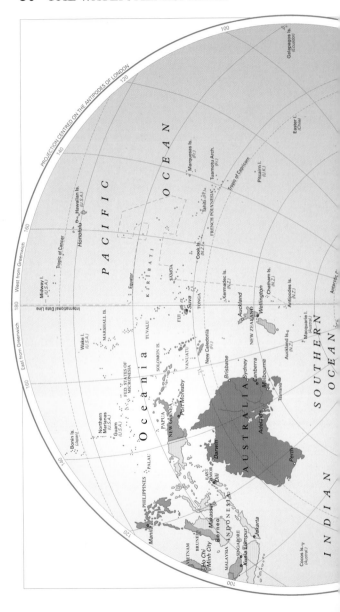

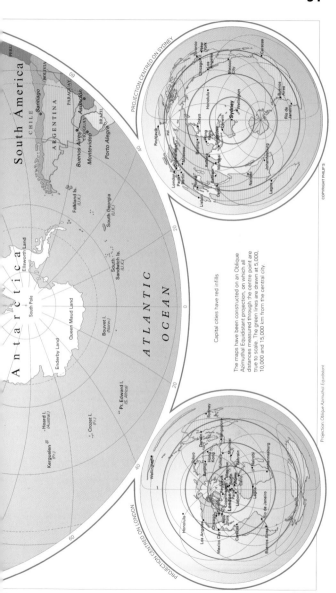

South America

CHILE

Santiago

BOLIVIA

PARAGUAY

ARGENTINA

PERU

BRAZIL

Asunción

Buenos Aires

URUGUAY

Montevideo

Porto Alegre

Falkland Is.
(U.K.)

South Georgia
(U.K.)

South
Sandwich Is.
(U.K.)

Antarctica

Ellsworth Land

South Pole

Queen Maud Land

Enderby Land

Bouvet I.
(Norw.)

Pr. Edward I.
(S. African)

Crozet I.
(Fr.)

Heard I.
(Austral.)

Kerguelen
(Fr.)

ATLANTIC

OCEAN

PROJECTION CENTRED ON SYDNEY

Sydney

PROJECTION CENTRED ON LONDON

London

Capital cities have red infills

The maps have been constructed on an Oblique
Azimuthal Equidistant projection, on which all
distances measured through the centre point are
true to scale. The green lines are drawn at 5,000,
10,000 and 15,000 km from the central city.

Projection: Oblique Azimuthal Equidistant

COPYRIGHT PHILIP'S

CITY PLANS

33	Amsterdam	**53**	Mexico City
34	Athens	**54**	Montréal
35	Bangkok	**55**	Moscow
36	Barcelona	**56**	Mumbai
37	Beijing	**57**	Munich
38	Berlin	**58**	New Orleans
39	Boston	**59**	New York
40	Brussels	**60**	Paris
41	Budapest	**61**	Prague
42	Cape Town	**62**	Rio de Janeiro
43	Chicago	**63**	Rome
44	Copenhagen	**64**	San Francisco
45	Delhi	**65**	Singapore
46	Dublin	**66**	Stockholm
47	Edinburgh	**67**	Sydney
48	Hong Kong	**68**	Tokyo
49	Lisbon	**69**	Toronto
50	London	**70**	Venice
51	Los Angeles	**71**	Vienna
52	Madrid	**72**	Washington DC

GENERAL REFERENCE

	Limited-access highway	✝	Abbey/cathedral
	Through route	†	Church of interest
	Secondary road	⊞	Hospital
	Other road	☾	Mosque
	Limited access/ pedestrian road	▲	Shrine
	Railroad	✡	Synagogue
	Tramway/cable car	⛩	Temple
	Elevated railroad	𝒊	Tourist information
	Railroad station	☐	Public building
⊖⊖ⓊⓂⓈ	Subway station	Museum	Place of interest

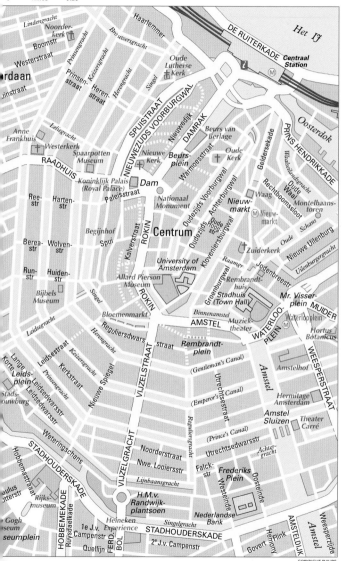

0   km   0.5

0   miles   0.25

Lindengracht
Noorder-
kerk
Boomstr
Westerstraat
Haarlemmer
DE RUITERKADE
Het IJ
Centraal
Station
Oosterdok
PRINS HENDRIKKADE

Brouwersgracht
Prinsengracht
Keizersgracht
Herengracht
Singel
Oude
Lutherse
Kerk

rdaan
jinstraat
Prinsen-
straat
Heren-
straat

SPUISTRAAT
NIEUWEZIJDS VOORBURGWAL
Nieuwendijk
DAMRAK
Beurs van
Berlage
Geldersekade

Anne
Frankhuis
Leliegracht
Westerkerk
Spaarpotten
Museum
Nieuwe
Kerk
Beurs-
plein
Oude
Kerk
Warmoesstraat
Oude
Waag
Rechtboomssloot
Montelbaans-
toren
Waterlandsgracht

RAADHUIS
Koninklijk Palais
(Royal Palace)
Dam
Paleisstraat
Nationaal
Monument
Ouderzijds Voorburgwal
Oudezijds Achterburgwal
Waag
Nieuw-
markt
Nieuw-
markt
Oude Schans

Ree-
str
Harten-
str
Kalverstraat
ROKIN
Begijnhof
Spui
Centrum
Oude
Hoog-
str
Kloveniersburgwal
Zuiderkerk
Nieuwe Uilenburg
Uilenburgergracht

Berea-
str
Wolven-
str
University of
Amsterdam
Raamgr
Jodenbreestr

Run-
str
Huiden-
str
Allard Pierson
Museum
ROKIN
Groenburgwal
Rembrandt-
huis
Stadhuis
Town Hall
Mr. Visser-
plein
MUIDER

Bijbels
Museum
Singel
Bloemenmarkt
Binnenamstel
AMSTEL
Muziek-
theater
WATERLOO-
PLEIN
Waterlooplein
Hortus
Botanicus

Leidsegracht
Reguliersdwars
straat
Rembrandt-
plein
Amstel
Amstelhof
WEESPERSTRAAT

Lange
Korte
Leids-
plein
stads-
ouwburg
Leidsestraat
Kerkstraat
Leidsedwarsstr
Leidsedwarsstr
Prinsengracht
Keizersgracht
Herengracht
Nieuwe Spiegel
VIJZELSTRAAT
(Gentleman's Canal)
Utrechtsestraat
(Emperor's Canal)
Reguliersgracht
(Prince's Canal)
Hermitage
Amsterdam
Amstel
Sluizen
Theater
Carré

Weteringschans
Noorderstraat
Nwe. Looiersstr
Lijnbaansgracht
Utrechtsedwarsstr
Falck-
str
Frederiks
Plein
Achter-
gracht

Hobbemastraat
STADHOUDERSKADE
VIJZELGRACHT
H.M.v.
Randwijk-
plantsoen
Oostende
AMSTELDIJK
Amstel
Weesperzijde

aulus
tterstr
Rijks-
museum
HOBBEMAKADE
Ruysdaelkade
Heineken
Experience
1e J.v.
Campenstr
FERD.
BOL
Singelgracht
Nederlandse
Bank
Weesperzijde
Amstel

Gogh
seum
seumplein
Quellijn
2e J.v. Campenstr
STADHOUDERSKADE
Govert Flinck
Govert
Henny

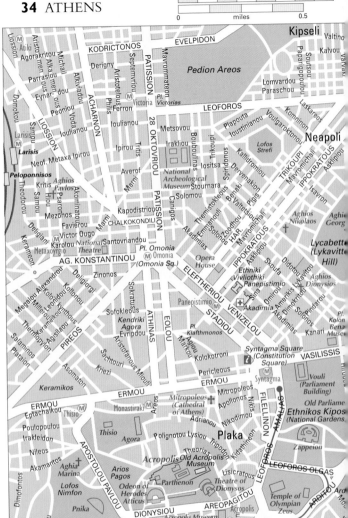

COPYRIGHT PHILIP'S

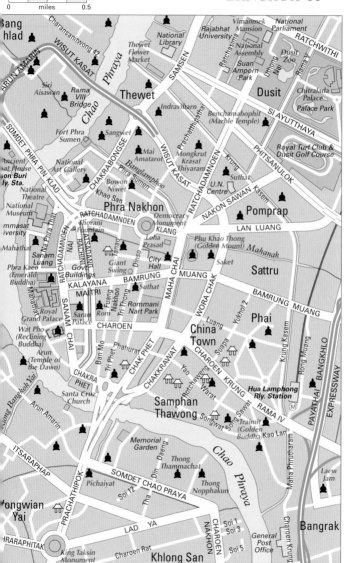

Map labels:

0 km 1
0 miles 0.5

Bang Phlad
Charansanitwong 42
WISUT KASAT
ARUN AMARIN
Thewet Flower Market
National Library
Rajabhat University
Vimanmek Mansion
National Parliament
RATCHWITHI
Chao Phraya
SAMSEN
Ratchasima
National Assembly
Suan Amporn Park
Uthong Nai
Dusit Zoo
Rama V
Siri Aisawan
Rama VIII Bridge
Thewet
Dusit
Chitralada Palace
Palace Park
Fort Phra Sumen
Sangwet
Indraviharn
Benchamabophit (Marble Temple)
SI AYUTTHAYA
SOMDET PHRA PIN KLAO
Mai Amatarot
Prachathipathai
Mongkrut Krasat Thiyaram
PHITSANULOK
Royal Turf Club & Dusit Golf Course
Ancient Seat House on Buri Fly. Sta.
National Art Gallery
CHAKRABONGSE
Banglamphoo
Phra Sumen
WISUT KASAT
RATCHADAMNOEN
Krung
Suthat
National Theatre
Bowon Niwet
Khao San
U.N. Centre
National Museum
Phra Athit Thai
Phra Nakhon
RATCHADAMNOEN
Democracy Monument
NAKON SAWAN Kasan
Pomprap
Thammasat University
Niorani Fountain
RACHINI
KLANG
LAN LUANG
Mahathat
NAI
Loha Prasad
Phu Khao Thong (Golden Mount)
Mahanak
Phra Kaeo (Emerald Buddha)
Sanam Luang
RATCHADAMNOEN
Giant Swing
Tanao
Dinso
City Hall
MAHA CHAI
Saket
Sattru
Mahathat
Govt Buildings
KALAYANA
BAMRUNG
MUANG
WORA CHAK
BAMRUNG MUANG
Royal Grand Palace
SANAM CHAI
MAITRI
Fuang Nakhon
Tri Thong
Suthat
Rommani Nart Park
Luang
Yukhol 2
Phai
Wat Pho (Reclining Buddha)
Saran Palace
Rom
CHAROEN
China Town
Supha
Krung Kasem
Arun (Temple of the Dawn)
Ban Mo
Tri Phet
Phahurat
CHAK PHET
CHAKKRAWAT
Yao
Rotchawet
Warat
CHAROEN KRUNG
Song Sawat
Traimit (Golden Buddha)
Rong Muang
BANGKHLO
Wongs Bangkok Yai
CHAKRA PHET
Santa Cruz Church
Arun Amarin
Samphan Thawong
Songwat
Hua Lamphong Rly. Station
RAMA IV
Kao Lan
PAYATHAI
EXPRESSWAY
ITSARAPHAP
Memorial Garden
Daeng
Thong Thammachat
Chao Phraya
Maha Phrutharam
Wongwian Yai
Pichaiyat
Dim
Tha
Thong Nopphakun
SOMDET CHAO PRAYA
Soi 12
Soi 1
Soi 3
CHAROEN NAKHON
Laew Jam
Bangrak
HRARAPHITAK
PRACHATHIPOK
LAD YA
Charoen Rat
Khlong San
Soi 5
General Post Office
Charoen Krung
King Taksin Monument

COPYRIGHT PHILIP'S

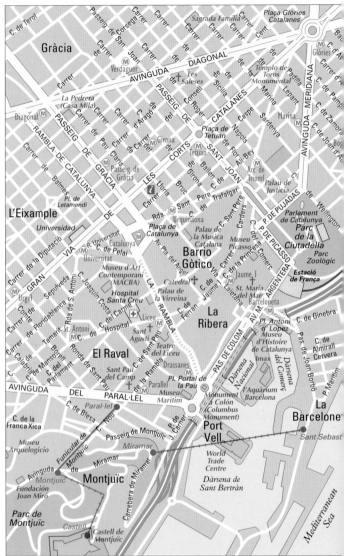

0 km 2

0 miles 1

atihutong

Wenhuiyuan Lu

XINJIEKOUWAI DAJIE

XINJIE-MENWAI D.

Rendinghu Park

Andeli

Andelizhong Lu

Qinghianhu Park

Qingnian Lake

INGMENWAI DAJIE

Temple of Earth

Altar of the Earth

huiyuan Lu

Jishuitan (M)

Ande Lu

Gouloudajie (M)

Andingmen (M)

Ditan Park

Yonghegong

DESHENGMENXI D.

DESHENGMENDONG D.

ANDINGMENXI D.

Museum

Lama Temple

DESHENGMENNEI DAJIE

Huifeng Xihai

Dashiqiao

Jingutou D.

Baochao

Beiluoguxi

Andingmennei Dajie

Capital Library and Mus.

YONGHEGONG

Xu Beihong Mem. Hall

Former Res. of Song Qingling

Houhaibeiyan

Guloux Dajie

ZHIMENXI DAJIE

Xinjiekou

Houhai

Bell Tower

Guloudong Dajie

Beixinqiao

XINJIEKOUBEI D.

Deshengmen

XINJIEKOUNAN

Guanghua

Drum Tower

Jiaodaokounan Dajie

DONGSIBEI

Xizhimen

Macaochang Jie

Hugousi

Panthéon of Mei Lanfang

Houhananyan

Di'anmenwai Dajie

Nanluoguxi

Nanluoguxi

DONGSIBEI

XINJIEKOUNAN

Daijio Baochan

Dingfu

Music Conservatory of China

Qianhai

Zhangzizhong Lu

Zhaodengyu

Huguosi People's Theatre

Qianfu

DI'ANMENXI D.

DI'ANMENDONG D.

ING'ANLIXI-JIE

Ping'anli (M)

XISIBEI DAJIE

Aimin Jie

Bei Hai Park

Di'anmennei Dajie

Dongcheng

Xun seum

Xisibei 3 T

Dahongluochang

Xishiku Jie

Bei Hai

Beiheyan Dajie

National Art Gallery

Xicheng

XISIBEI DAJIE

Xihuangchenggen

Baita

Children's Palace

Meishuguandongjie (M)

CHENGMENNEI Xisi DAJIE

XISINAN DAJIE

Dajie

Beijing Library (N. Cathedral)

Jade Island

Jingshan Park

WUSI D.

DONGSIXI D.

Geological Museum

XI'ANMEM DAJIE

WENJIN JIE

JINGSHANQIAN

Dongsi Mosque

ding ong

Fengsheng H.

Taipingqiao Dajie

XIDANBEI DAJIE

Jie

Fuyou Jie

Zhonghai

Beichang

Imperial Palace Mus.

Beichizi Dajie

Beiheyan Dajie

Capital Theatre

Wangfujing Dajie

DONGSINAN

Picai Hutong

XIDAN DAJIE

Lingjing Hutong

Lingjing Hutong

Forbidden City

Beijing Children's Art Theatre

uan nan

Cultural Palace for Nationalities

Heng 2

Taipusi

Nanchang

Working People's Cult. Pal.

Nanchizi Dajie

Nanheyan Dajie

Pudusi

Dongdan

Nanhai

Zhongshan Park

Wangfujing (M)

KINGMENNEI DAJIE

XICHANG'AN JIE

Great Hall of the People

DONGCHANG'AN JIE

Tian'anmendong (M)

Xinwenhua Jie

Xidan (M)

Xirongxian Hutong

Tian'anmenxi (M)

Tian'anmen Square

Zhengyi Lu

Municipal Offices

Dongdan Park

gchunjie

Nantang (South Cathedral)

National Grand Theatre

Mao Mausoleum

Mus. of Chinese Revolution and Chinese History

Chongwenmen (M)

Xuanwumen (M)

Hepingmen (M)

QIANMEN

QIANMEN-

XUANWUMENXI DAJIE

XUANWUMEN-DONG DAJIE

QIANMEN-XI DAJIE

Qianmen (M)

Xidamochang Jie

DONG D.

Shangxie Jie

Haibai H.

Nanxinhua Jie

QIANMEN DAJIE

Xianyukou

Xinlong Jie

Changchun Jie

Liulichang Jie

Dazhalan Jie

Meishi Jie

ZHUSHIKOUDONG DAJIE

Xicaochang Hutong

Qianmen

Chongwen

Baoguo

Caishikou (M)

Tiantan Lu

NG'ANMENNEI DAJIE

LUOMASHI DAJIE

ZHUSHIKOUXI DAJIE

Tiantan Park

Huguang Opera Museum

Liyuan Theatre

COPYRIGHT PHILIP'S

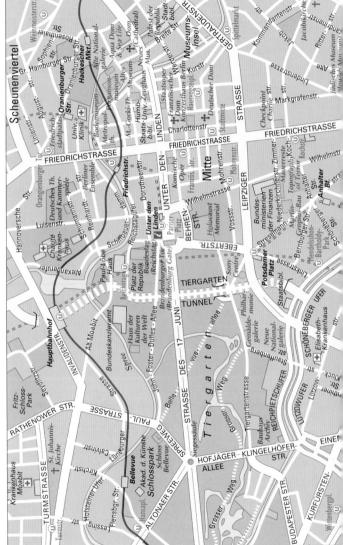

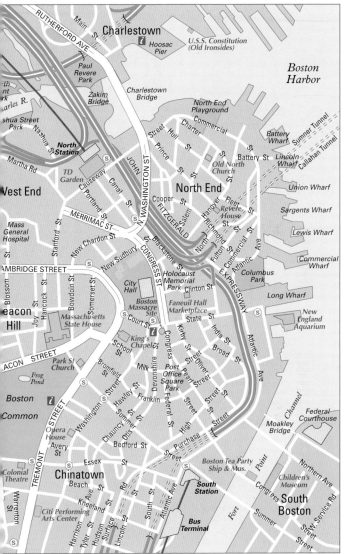

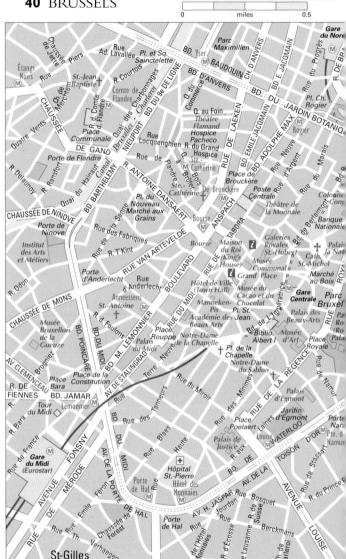

St-Gilles

COPYRIGHT PHILIP'S

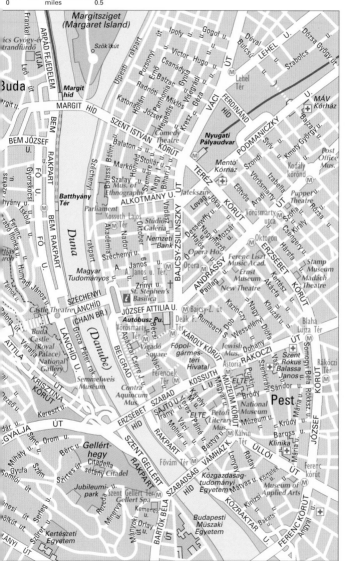

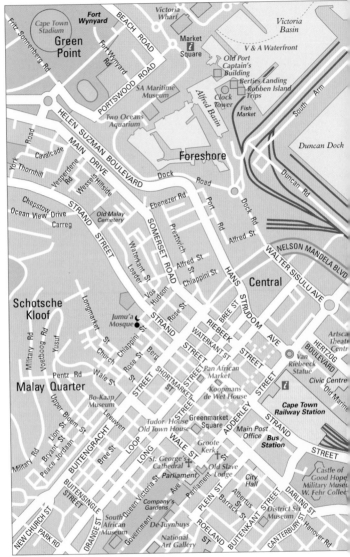

Cape Town Stadium

Fort Wynyard

Green Point

BEACH ROAD

Victoria Wharf

Victoria Basin

Fritz Sonnenberg Rd

Fort Wynyard Rd

PORTSWOOD ROAD

Market Square

V & A Waterfront

Old Port Captain's Building

SA Maritime Museum

Bertie's Landing

Robben Island Trips

HELEN SUZMAN BOULEVARD

Two Oceans Aquarium

Clock Tower

Alfred Basin

Fish Market

MAIN DRIVE

Foreshore

South Arm

Duncan Dock

Cavalcade

Road

York

Thornhill

Vesperdene Rd

Wessel's

Hillside

STRAND STREET

Dock

Road

Chepstow Drive

Ocean View

Carreg

Old Malay Cemetery

Ebenezer Rd

Duncan Rd

SOMERSET ROAD

Prestwich

Port Rd

Dock Rd

Alfred St

NELSON MANDELA BLVD

Waterkant St

Loader

Alfred St

Chiappini St

HANS STRIJDOM AVE

WALTER SISULU AVE

Vos

Hudson

Central

Schotsche Kloof

Longmarket

Jumu'a Mosque

STRAND

Rose St

BREE STREET

Artsca Theatre Centr

Van Riebeeck Statue

Military Rd

Voetboog Rd

Yusuf

Church

Chiappini

Berg

STREET

RIEBEEK

STREET

HERTZOG BOULEVARD

Civic Centre

Rose St

WATERKANT

Old Marine

Pentz Rd

Wale St

SHORTMARKET

STREET

Pan African Market

Cape Town Railway Station

Malay Quarter

Bo-Kaap Museum

Leeuwen

ST

STREET

Koopmans de Wet House

Upper Bloem St

Lion St

Bryant St

Peace Jordaan

BUITENGRACHT

Bree St

LOOP

Tudor House Old Town House

Greenmarket Square

ADDERLEY

STRAND

Military Rd

STREET

WALE ST

Main Post Office

Bus Station

STREET

Groote Kerk

LONG

St. George's Cathedral

Old Slave Lodge

City Hall

Castle of Good Hope Military Museu W. Fehr Collec

BUITENSINGLE

Parliament

St.

Parliament Ave

PLEIN ST

Albertus

DARLING

Queen Victoria St

Company's Gardens

De Tuynhuys

BARRACK St

BUITENKANT

District Six Museum

NEW CHURCH ST

PARK RD

ORANGE ST

South African Museum

Government

ROELAND ST

Hanover Rd

Canterbury St

National Art Gallery

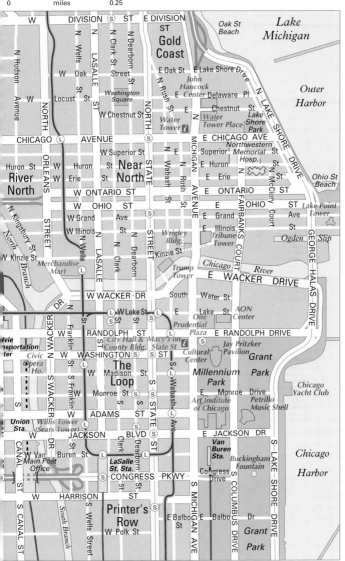

0 km 0.5
0 miles 0.25

Lake Michigan

Oak St Beach

Gold Coast

Outer Harbor

DIVISION ST
E DIVISION ST

N Hudson Avenue

N Wells St

N LASALLE Street

N Clark St

N Dearborn Street

W Oak St

Locust St

Washington Square

W Chestnut St

E Oak St
E Lake Shore Drive

John Hancock Center
Delaware Pl

Chestnut

Water Tower Place

Lake Shore Park

N LAKE SHORE DRIVE

CHICAGO AVENUE
E CHICAGO AVE

Water Tower

River North

Huron St

W Huron St

W Erie St

Near North

W Superior St

W Ontario St

W Ohio St

N ORLEANS STREET

N State St

N Wabash St

N Rush St

N MICHIGAN AVENUE

Northwestern Memorial Hosp.

E Superior St

E Huron St

E Erie St

E ONTARIO ST

E Ohio St

Ohio St Beach

N McCLURG COURT

N FAIRBANKS COURT

Lake Point Tower

Kingsbury St

W Grand Ave

W Illinois St

E Grand Ave

E Illinois St

Tribune Tower

Ogden Slip

GEORGE HALAS DRIVE

North Branch

W Kinzie St

Merchandise Mart

Wrigley Bldg.

Kinzie St

Chicago River

WACKER DR

Trump Tower

W WACKER DR

South Water St

E WACKER DRIVE

Franklin St

S Wells St

N LaSalle St

Clark St

Dearborn St

W Lake St
E Lake St

One Prudential Plaza

AON Center

RANDOLPH ST
E RANDOLPH DRIVE

Civic Opera Ho.

City Hall & County Bldg.
Macy's on State St

Jay Pritzker Pavilion

Cultural Center

Grant Park

W WASHINGTON ST

The Loop

W Madison St

Monroe St

W ADAMS ST

Millennium Park

E Monroe Drive

Art Institute of Chicago

Petrillo Music Shell

Chicago Yacht Club

S WACKER DR

Willis Tower (Sears Tower)

JACKSON BLVD
E JACKSON DR

Union Sta.

W Van Buren St

Main Post Office

LaSalle St. Sta.

CONGRESS PKWY

Van Buren Sta.

Congress Drive

Buckingham Fountain

Chicago Harbor

S CANAL ST

S COLUMBUS DRIVE

S LAKE SHORE DRIVE

W HARRISON ST

Printer's Row

W Polk St

South Branch

E Balbo Ave

Grant Park

COPYRIGHT PHILIP'S

━━━Ⓛ━━━ Elevated rail lines

Østerbro

BLEGDAMSVEJ

Ryesgade

Sortedam Dossering

Sortedam Sø

DAG HAMMARSKJÖLDS ALLÉ

Garnisons
Kirkegård

Kristianiagade

Hovedvej

ØSTBANEGADE

F. Bernstorffs Allé

Den I
Havf
(Litt
Mern

ØSTER SØGADE

Farimagsgade

Holmens
Kirkegård

Østerport
Sta.

Kastellet
(Citadel)

Forbindelsesvej

Fredens
Bro

Stockholmsgade

GRØNNINGEN

Sortedam Sø

ØSTER SØGADE

Statens museet
for Kunst (Fine
Art Museum)

Østre Anlæg

Frihedsmuseet
(Museum of Danis
Resistance Movem

Farimagsgade

Kommune
Hospital

Geologisk
Museet

VOLDGADE

Gernersgade

Nyboder

Fredericiagade

Klerkegade

STORE KONGENSGADE

BREDGADE

Kunstindustrimuseo
(Decorative Art Muse

gade

GOTHERS GADE

Botanisk
Have

Botanisk
Museum

ØSTER

Rosenborg Have
(King's Garden)

Rosenborg
Slot (Castle)
Crown Jewels

Klerkegade

Borgergade

Adelgade

Amalienborg
Slot (Palace)

Inderha

Frederiksborggade

Arbejdermus.
(Workers Museum)

Vendersgade

Israels
Plads

Nørreport
Sta.

Kongens
Have

Krompmansgade

GOTHERS GADE

Skt. Annæ Plads

Amalie

NØRRE VOLDGADE

Ørsteds
Parken

Frolstræde

Nørre

Rundetaarn
(Round Tower)

Købmager

gade

Pilestræde

Kongens
Nytorv

Charlottenborg

Operahu
(Opera Hou

Skt. Peters Str.

Post & Tele
Museum

Universitet

Domkirken

Helligånds
Kirke

Øster gade

Bremerholm

Nyhavn

Nyhavn

JUELSGADE

Det Kongelige Teater
(Royal Theatre)

Studie Str.

Vestergade

Fredriksberg
gade

Rådhusstræde

Nyg.

Vimmelsk

Læderstræde

Nybrogade

Hans Christian
Andersen's Ho.

Thorvaldsen's
Museum

Borsgade

Holbers
Gade

Havnegade

Christians

Haevns Kanal

H.C.

Rådhus-
pladsen

Farvergade

Ripley's

Storm

Frederiksholms Kanal

Christiansborg
Slotsholmsgade

Slotsholmen

Ministerialbyg.

Christiansborg
Slot (Palace)

KNIPPELSBRO TORVE

Dansk
Arkitektur
Centre

Strandgade

Bådsmandsstræde

Christian

ANDERSENS

Rådhus-
museet

National-
museet

(City
Hall)

Vestervold

BOULEVARD

Gade

CHRISTIANS

BRYGGE

Det Kongelige Bibliotek
(Royal Library)

Bådsmandsstræde

Prinse

Tivoli

Koncertsal
(Concert Hall)

Ny
Carlsberg
Glyptotek

Politigård

Hambrosgade

Inderhavnen

Christians
Kirke

Overgaden
Overgaden

Dronningens

Prinsesse

GADE

Amagergade

Stadsgrave

Hovedbane-
gården

BERNSTORFFSGADE

Tietgensgade

Mitchellsgade

KALVEBOD
BRYGGE

Langebro

Ved Kanalen

Langebrogade

Christianshavn

Central
Postbygning

AMAGER BOULEVARD

Amagerbro

COPYRIGHT PHILIPS

0   km   0.5
0   miles   0.25

0 km 2

0 miles 1

BOULEVARD ROAD

Tilak Park

Interstate Bus Terminal

Nicholson Rd

St. Stephen's

St. James

ZORAWAR SINGH MARG

Yamuna

Old City

GRAND TRUNK RD

adar Bazar

NAYA BAZAR

SHRADHANAN

Old Delhi Station

SHYAMA PRASAD

MUKHERJI MARG

Mahatma Gandhi Park

Town Hall

Library Jain Mandir

CHANDNI

CHAUK

NETAJI SUBHASH

River

Lal Qila (Red Fort)

Vijay Ghat

QUTAB ROAD

Lalkuan Bazar Road

Fathepur

Sunehri

Nai Sarak

Sisganj

Guari Shankar

Jama Masjid

Kasturba Hospital Marg

Bazar

Chitli Qabar Marg

MAHATMA GANDHI MARG

Darya Ganj

Ajmeri Gate Road

Ghaziuddin

Kalan

SH BANDHU GUPTA RD

ahar anj

in Bazar Road

CHELMSFORD ROAD

Ramlila Grounds

Holy Trinity

Eye

ASAF ALI ROAD

JAWAHARLAL

NEHRU MARG

New Delhi Station

Delhi Gate

Raj Ghat

Gandhi Museum

Northern Railway

NCHKUIAN MARG

VIVEKANAND RD

Jahangir Road

DEEN DAYAL UPADHYAYA MARG

LNJP Narain

Mirdard Marg

Feroz Shah Kotla Cricket Stadium

Kotla

BAHADUR SHAH ZAFAR MG

Feroz Shah Kotla Fort

Velodrome

RING ROAD

Doll Museum

Indira Gandhi Indoor Stadium

CONNAUGHT

Connaught Place

CIRCUS

Ranjit Singh Marg

Babar Rd

Marg

VIKAS MARG

BA KHARAK SINGH MARG

BARAKHAMBA ROAD

Tolstoy

KASTURBA GANDHI MARG

Halley Rd

Natural History Museum

Bhagwan Das

SIKANDRA ROAD

MATHURA ROAD

MAHATMA GANDHI MARG

SANSAD MARG

Mantar Rd

FIROZ SHAH ROAD

Copernicus Marg

SHOKA

Jantar

Canning

Supreme Court

ST AMENT

RAISINA RD

Dr. Rajender Prasad Road

JANPATH

Jaswant Singh Road

Road

TILAK MARG

Crafts Museum

New Delhi

Indira Gandhi Centre of Arts

Rajpath

India Gate

National Stadium

Rafi

National Museum

Maulana Azad Rd

AKBAR ROAD

SHAHJAHAN RD

SHERSHAH RD

National Gallery of Modern Art

Purana Qila (Old Fort)

OTILAL NEHRU MG

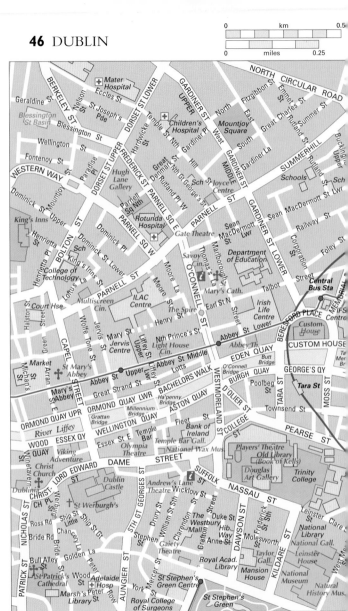

Light Rail (LUAS)

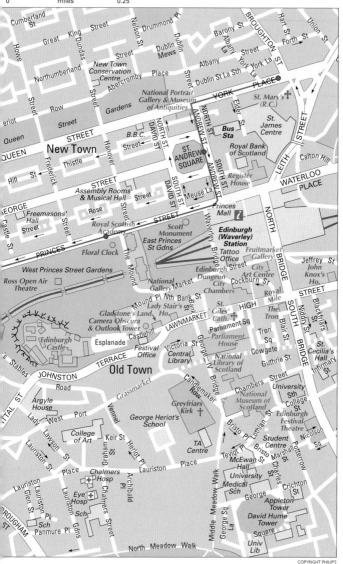

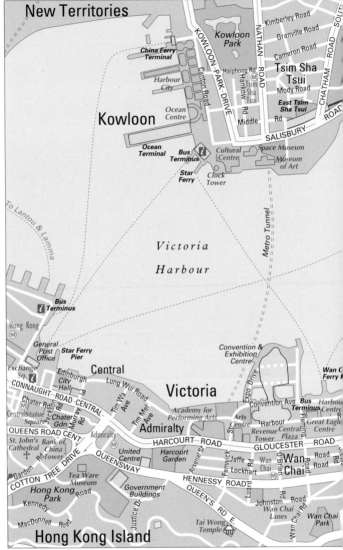

New Territories

Kowloon

China Ferry Terminal

Kowloon Park

Kimberley Road

Granville Road

Cameron Road

Harbour City

Haiphong Rd

Tsim Sha Tsui

Hankow Rd

Mody Road

East Tsim Sha Tsui

Ocean Centre

Middle Rd

SALISBURY

Ocean Terminal

Bus Terminus

Cultural Centre

Space Museum

Museum of Art

Star Ferry

Clock Tower

To Lantou & Lamma

Victoria Harbour

Metro Tunnel

Bus Terminus

Hong Kong

General Post Office

Star Ferry Pier

Central

Lung Wui Road

Victoria

Convention & Exhibition Centre

Wan Ch Ferry

Exchange Sq.

Edinburgh City Hall

Tim Wa Ave

Tim Mei Ave

Academy for Performing Arts

Arts Centre

Convention Ave

Bus Terminus

Harbour Centre

Great Eagle Centre

Chater Rds

Chater Gdn

Murray Rd

Admiralty

Harbour

Revenue Tower

Central Plaza

Central Statue Square

QUEENS ROAD CENT

CONNAUGHT ROAD CENTRAL

St. John's Cathedral

Bank of China Tower

HARCOURT ROAD

GLOUCESTER

Arsenal St.

O'Brien

Jaffe

Fenwick

Wan Chai

Road

Road

ROAD

Garden

COTTON TREE DRIVE

QUEENSWAY

United Centre

Harcourt Garden

Lockhart

Wan Chai

Tea Ware Museum

Road

HENNESSY ROAD

Johnston

Road

Hong Kong Park

Kennedy

Government Buildings

QUEEN'S RD.

Justice D.

Wan Chai Lanes

Wan Chai Rd

Wan Chai Park

MacDonnell Road

Hong Kong Island

Tai Wong Temple

COPYRIGHT PHILIPS

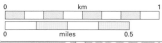

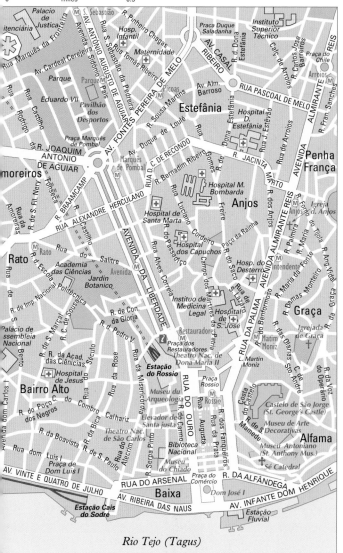

Rio Tejo (Tagus)

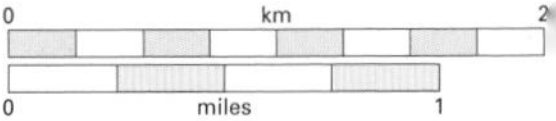

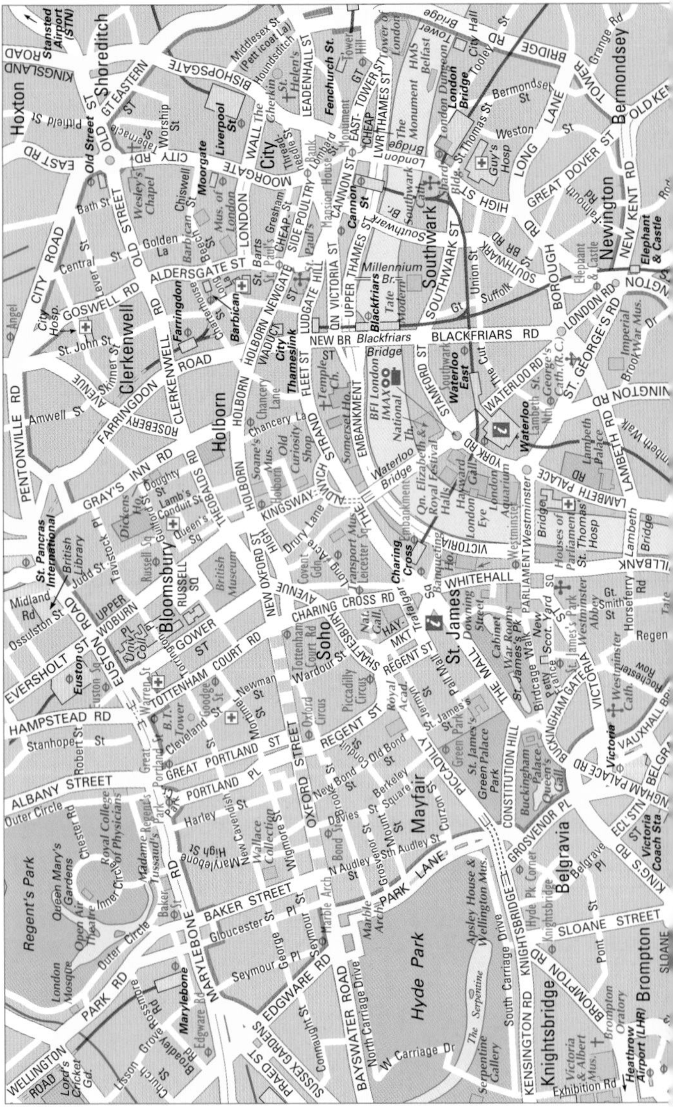

km
0 ... 2

miles
0 ... 1

Congestion Charging Zone

COPYRIGHT PHILIP'S

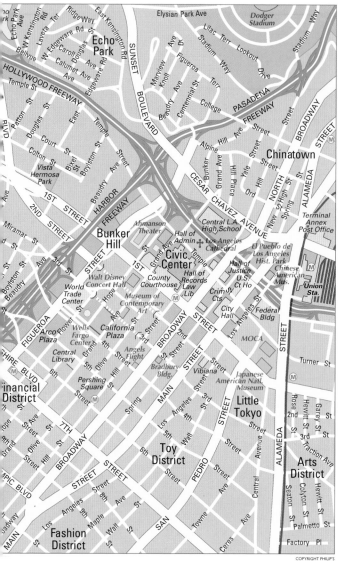

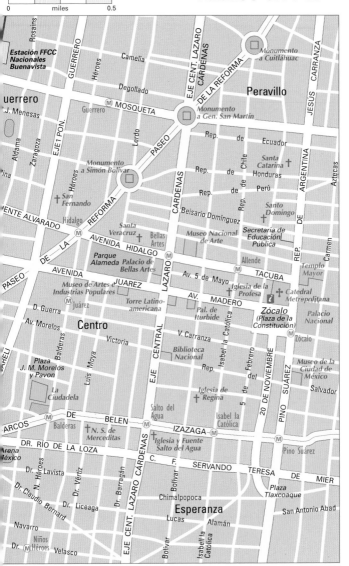

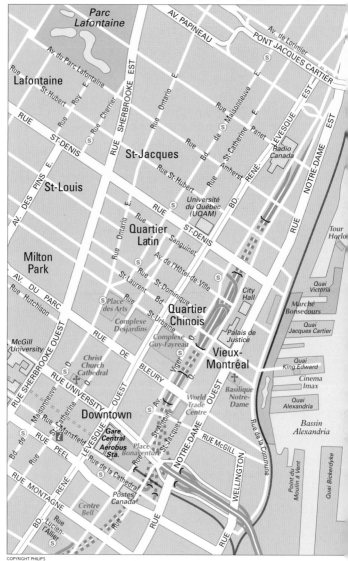

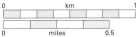

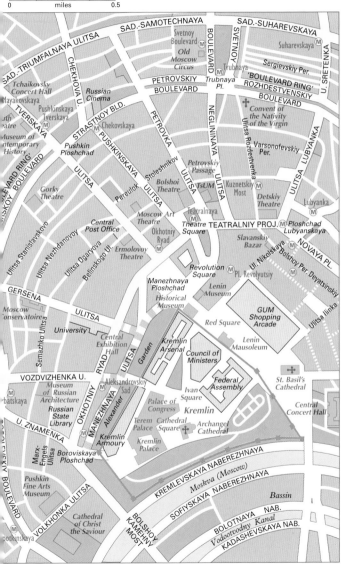

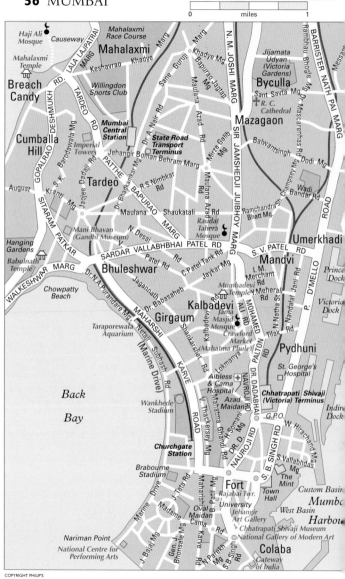

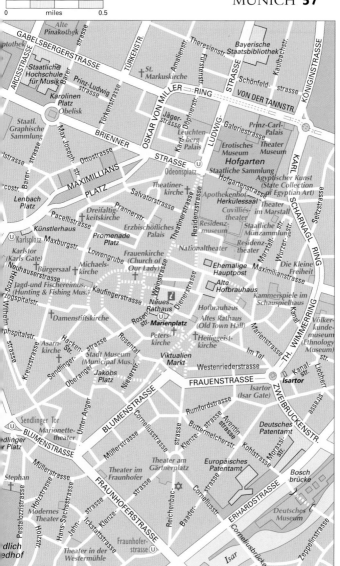

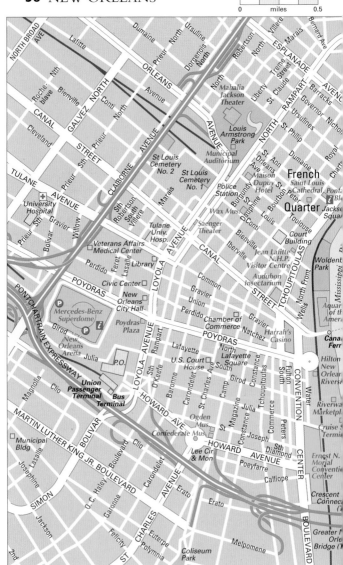

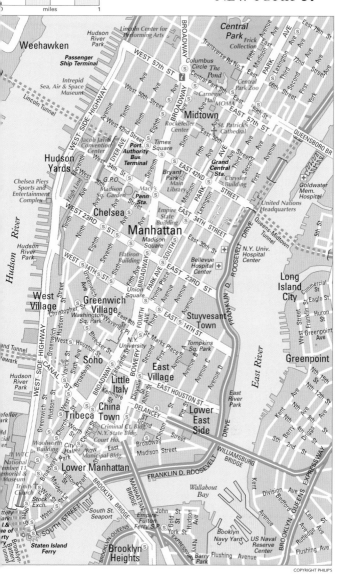

km 2

miles 1

Weehawken

Hudson River Park

Lincoln Center for Performing Arts

Central Park

Frick Collection

Transverse Rd No. 1

Passenger Ship Terminal

Intrepid Sea, Air & Space Museum

Lincoln Tunnel

WEST 57th ST

Columbus Circle

The Pond

Central Park S.th

Central Park Zoo

BROADWAY

West 50th Street

Carnegie Hall

MOMA

Midtown

EAST 57th ST

Rockefeller Center

St. Patrick's Cathedral

East 50th

Jacob Javits Convention Center

West 42nd Street

Times Square

EAST 42ND

Grand Central Sta.

Port Authority Bus Terminal

Bryant Park

Chrysler Building

QUEENSBORO BR

Hudson Yards

WEST 34th

G.P.O.

Madison Sq. Garden

Penn Sta.

Macy's

Main Library

EAST 34TH STREET

United Nations Headquarters

Goldwater Mem. Hospital

Chelsea Piers Sports and Entertainment Complex

WEST 23RD

Empire State Building

East 30th St

Queens-Midtown Tunnel

Hudson River

Chelsea

Manhattan

Madison Square

EAST 23RD ST

N.Y. Univ. Hospital Center

Hudson River Park

WEST 14TH ST

Flatiron Building

Bellevue Hospital Center

Long Island City

West Village

Greenwich Village

Union Square

East 8th

EAST 14TH ST

Stuyvesant Town

Commercial St

Eagle St

Huron St

Greenpoint Ave

WEST SIDE HIGHWAY

Christopher St

Washington Sq. Park

Waverly Pl

N.Y. University

St Marks Place

Tompkins Sq. Park

Greenpoint

Nth 15th

Nth 12th St

Bleecker St

Houston St

East Village

East River

and Tunnel ewark

Soho

BROADWAY

BOWERY

EAST HOUSTON ST

East River Park

Kent

Berry

Hudson River Park

Little Italy

Kenmare

DELANCEY

Lower East Side

efeller ark

Tribeca

China Town

Criminal Ct. Bldg.

N.Y. State Bldg.

Court Ho.

Clinton

WILLIAMSBURG BRIDGE

WEST SIDE HIGHWAY

CANAL

Woolworth Building

City Hall

Municipal Bldg.

Broadway

Madison Street

FRANKLIN D. ROOSEVELT

Division Ave

Bedford

Lower Manhattan

Wallabout Bay

WtC

National ember 11, Museum

Trinity Church

Wall St

Stock Exch.

South St Seaport

Empire-Fulton Ferry S.P.

John St

Gold St

Brooklyn Navy Yard

US Naval Reserve Center

Lee Ave

Rutledge St

ttery ark L.& se of rty

SOUTH STREET

Staten Island Ferry

BROOKLYN QUEENS

MANHATTAN BRIDGE

Brooklyn Heights

Barry Flushing Avenue

Brooklyn Bridge Park

York St

Flushing Ave

COPYRIGHT PHILIP'S

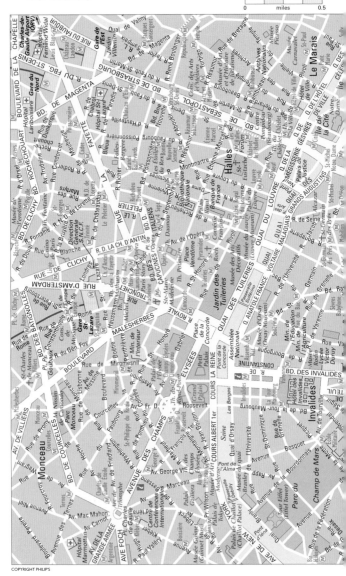

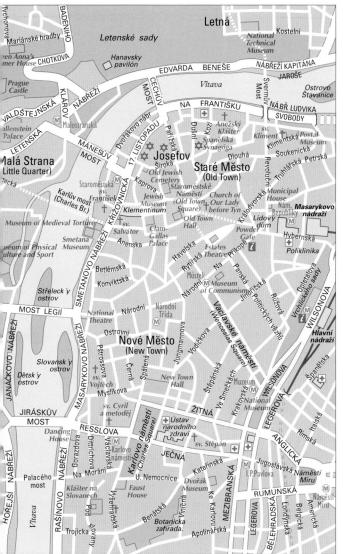

Letná

National Technical Museum

Kostelní

Mariánské hradby

Letenské sady

BADENÍHO

CHOTKOVA

Hanavsky pavilón

NÁBŘEŽÍ KAPITÁNA

JAROŠE

EDVARDA BENEŠE

Prague Castle

KLÁROV

NÁBŘEŽÍ

Vltava

Svermův Most

Ostrovo Šťavanice

CECHŮV MOST

NA FRANTIŠKU

NÁBŘ. LUDVIKA

SVOBODY

WALDŠTEJNSKÁ

Malostranská

Dvořákovo nábř

Anežský Klášter

Dušní

Kozí

sv. Kliment

Postal Museum

Pařížská

Španělská Synagóga

Klimentská

Wallenstein Palace

LETENSKÁ

MÁNESŮV MOST

17. LISTOPADU

Josefov

Soukenická

Dlouhá

Staré Město

Revoluční

Truhlářská

Petrská

Malá Strana (Little Quarter)

Široká

(Old Town)

Staroměstská

Karlův most (Charles Br.)

sv. Františe

KŘIŽOVNICKÁ

Old Jewish Cemetery

Kaprova

Staroměstskě Náměstí (Old Town Square)

Church of Our Lady before Tyn

Municipal House

tecká

Klementinum

Jewish Museum

Nám. Republiky

Masarykovo nádraží

Museum of Medieval Torture

SMETANOVO NÁBŘEŽÍ

Smetana Museum

sv. Salvátor

Clam-Gallas Palace

Old Town Hall

Lidový dům

Hybernská

Powder Gate

useum of Physical ulture and Sport

Anenska

Havelská

Estates Theatre

Na Příkopě

Poliklinika

Betlémská

Rytířská

Panská

Opletalova

Konviktská

Můstek

Národní

Jindřišská

Politických věžňů

Ružová

Vrchlického sady

Střelecký ostrov

Museum of Communism

WILSONOVA

MOST LEGIÍ

National Theatre

Národní

Národní Třída

Václavské náměstí (Wenceslas Square)

Hlavní nádraží

JANÁČKOVO NÁBŘEŽÍ

MASARYKOVO NÁBŘEŽÍ

Ostrovní

Nové Město

Pštrossova

Vodičkova

Jungmannova

Španělska

Slovanský ostrov

Dětský ostrov

(New Town)

Černá

Spálená

New Town Hall

Štěpánská

Ve Smečkách

Krakovská

National Museum

sv. Vojtěch

Myslíkova

ŽITNÁ

Muzeum

JIRÁSKŮV MOST

sv. Cyril a metoděj

Ústav národní zdraví

LEGEROVA

WILSONOVA

Italská

Římská

Dancing House

RESSLOVA

Karlovo náměstí (Charles Square)

Dittrichova

Václavská

JEČNÁ

sv. Štěpán

ANGLICKA

NÁBŘEŽÍ

Na Moráni

U. Nemocnice

Kateřinská

I.P.Pavlova

Jugoslávská

Náměstí Miru

Palackého most

HOŘEJŠÍ

RAŠÍNOVO

Klášter na Slovanech

Faust House

Dvořák Museum

Ke Karlovu

MEZIBRANSKÁ

RUMUNSKÁ

Náměstí Miru

Americká

Vltava

Pod

Vyšehradská

Benátská

Viničná

LEGEROVA

BĚLEHRADSKÁ

Belgická

Londýnská

Trojicka

slavany

Botanická zahrada.

Apolinářská

0 ──── km ──── 1

0 ──── miles ──── 0.5

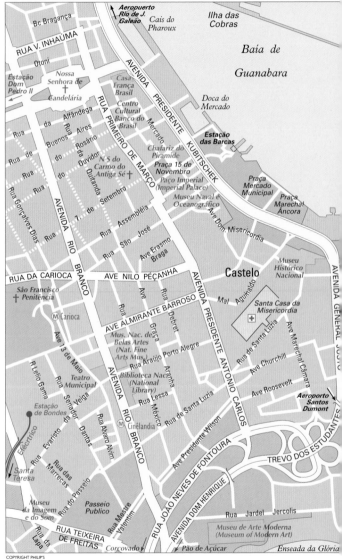

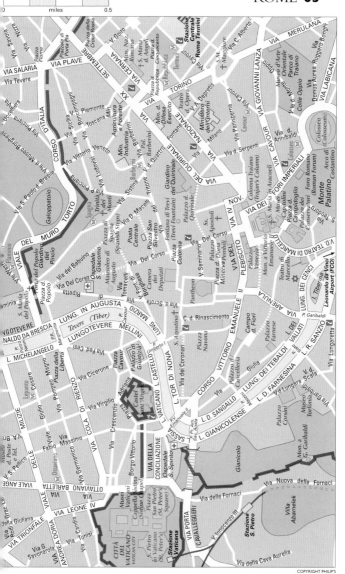

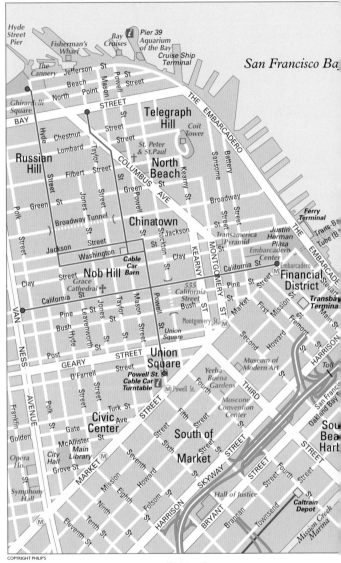

Cable Car route

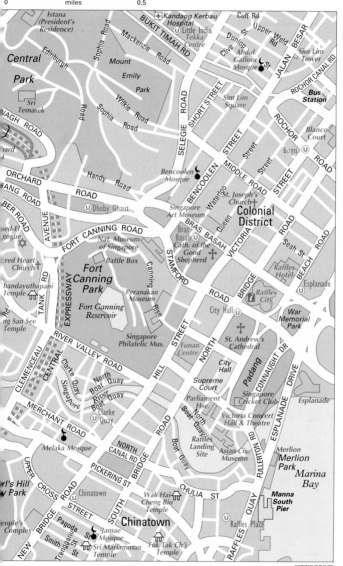

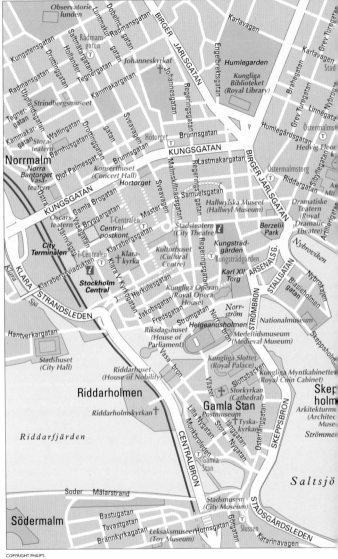

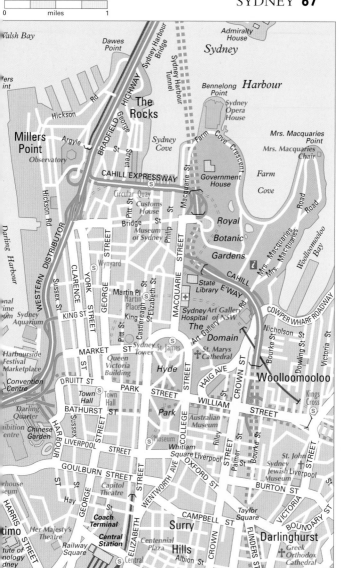

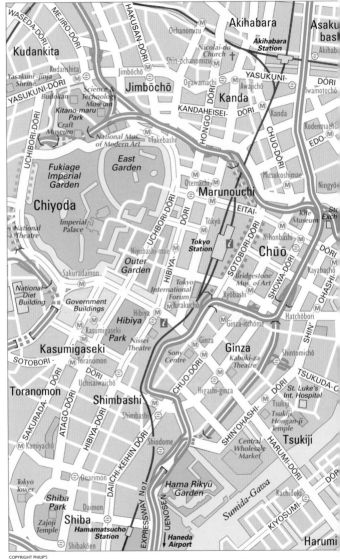

⊖ Toei Subway ⓜ Tokyo Metro

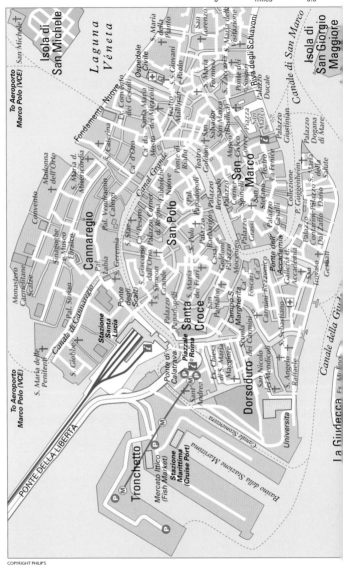

Ⓟ Car parks   --- Vaporetti   ⓜ— Monorail
          (water buses)   (Venice People Mover)

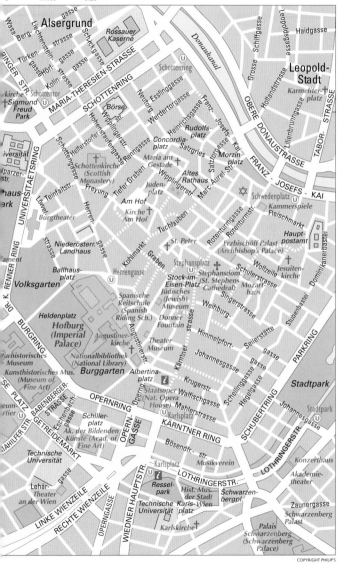

km
0   0.5
miles
0   0.25

Alsergrund

gasse
Rossauer
Kaserne

Wasa-
Berg-

Liechtenstein-
strasse
Schrekgasse

Türken-
gasse
Höri-
strasse
gasse

RINGER STR.
kirche
Schottentor
Sigmund
Freud
Park
Kolin-
strasse

MARIA-THERESIEN-STRASSE

SCHOTTENRING
Schottenring
Neutor
Esslinggasse
Werdertorgasse

Börse
str.
Wipplingerstr.
Hohenstaufengasse

Donaukanal

Schiffgasse
Grosse
Hollandstrasse

OBERE DONAUSTRASSE
FRANZ-JOSEFS-KAI

Haidgasse
Leopoldsgasse

Leopold-
Stadt

Karmeliter-
platz

Lilienbrunngasse
TABOR-

Franz-
Josefs-Kai

STRASSE

universität
Stadtparzer-
str.

Schottengasse
Helfersdorferstr
Renngasse

Concordia-
platz
Maria am
Gestade
Salzgries

Rudolfs-
platz
Heinrichsgasse

Morzin-
platz

JOSEFS-KAI

haus-
park

Schottenkirche
(Scottish
Monastery)

Teinfaltstr.
Löwel

Freyung
Tiefer Graben

Wipplingerstr.
Judenplatz

Altes
Rathaus

Marc-Aurel-St.

Schwedenplatz

Kammerspiele
Fleischmarkt

UNIVERSITAETSRING

Am Hof
Kirche
Am Hof

Herren-

Tuchlauben

Rotenturmgasse

Haupt-
postamt

Burgtheater
Niederöster.
Landhaus

gasse
strasse

Kohlmarkt

Graben
St. Peter

Rotenturmstr.

Erzbischöff Palast
(Archbishop's Palace)

Jesuiten-
kirche

Dominikanerbastei

DR. K. RENNER RING

Ballhaus-
platz

Herrengasse

Stephansplatz

Stock-im-
Eisen-Platz

Wollzeile
Schulerstrasse

Mozart-
haus

Parlament

Volksgarten

Spanische
Reitschule
(Spanish
Riding Sch.)

Stephansdom
(St. Stephens
Cathedral)
Jüdisches
(Jewish)
Museum

Singerstrasse

Stubenbastei

PARKRING

Heldenplatz
Hofburg
(Imperial
Palace)

Augustinerkirche

Donner
Fountain

Weihburg

Himmelpfort-

Sellerstätte

Stadtpark

BURGRING

Naturhistorisches
Museum

Nationalbibliothek
(National Library)

Theater
Museum

Kärntner

Johannesgasse

Schellinggasse

Hegelgasse

SCHUBERTRING

strasse
gasse

Kunsthistorisches Mus.
(Museum of
Fine Art)

Burggarten

Albertina-
platz

Krugerstr.

Johannesgasse
Stadtpark

museum
Quartier

BABENBERGER-
STRASSE

OPERNRING

Staatsoper
(Nat. Opera
House)

Walfischgasse
Mahlerstrasse

LOTHRINGERSTR.

Konzerthaus

MARIAHILFER STR. GETREIDEMARKT

Eschenbach-
gasse

OPERN-
GASSE

Schiller-
platz
Ak. der Bildenden
Künste (Acad. of
Fine Art)

Karlsplatz

KÄRNTNER RING

Akademie-
theater

Technische
Universität

Bösendfr-
str.
Musikverein

Karlsplatz

Lehár-
Theater
an der Wien

LINKE WIENZEILE

RECHTE WIENZEILE

OPERNGASSE

WIEDNER HAUPTSTR.

Ressel-
park

Technische
Universität

Hist. Mus.
der Stadt
Karls-
platz

Hist. Mus. der Stadt
Karls-Wien

Schwarzen-
bergpl.

Zaunergasse

Schwarzenberg
Palast

Karlskirche

Palais
Schwarzenberg
(Schwarzenberg
Palace)

COPYRIGHT PHILIP'S

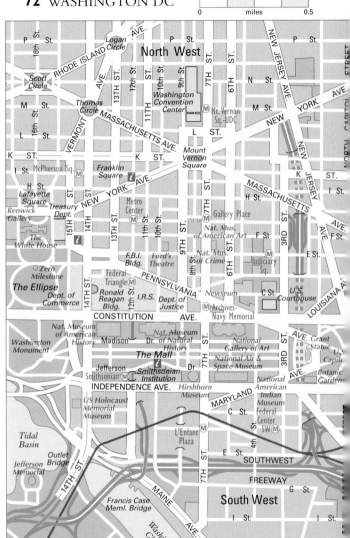

WORLD MAPS – GENERAL REFERENCE

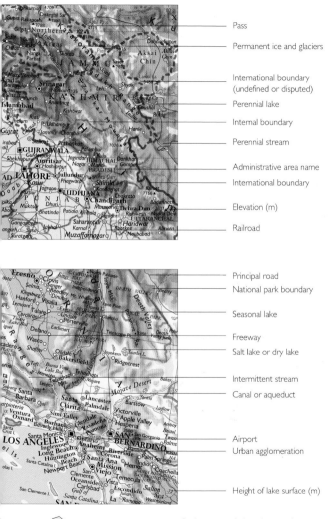

Pass

Permanent ice and glaciers

International boundary
(undefined or disputed)

Perennial lake

Internal boundary

Perennial stream

Administrative area name

International boundary

Elevation (m)

Railroad

Principal road

National park boundary

Seasonal lake

Freeway

Salt lake or dry lake

Intermittent stream

Canal or aqueduct

Airport

Urban agglomeration

Height of lake surface (m)

Settlements

Capital cities have red infills

Settlement symbols and type styles vary
according to the scale of each map and
indicate the importance of towns rather
than specific population figures.

Projection: Bonne   West from Greenwich   0   East from Greenwich   5

m ft

0
200   600
1000   3000
2000   6000
4000   12 000

■ LONDON Capital Cities

ICELAND
on same scale

West from Greenwich

NORWEGIAN SEA

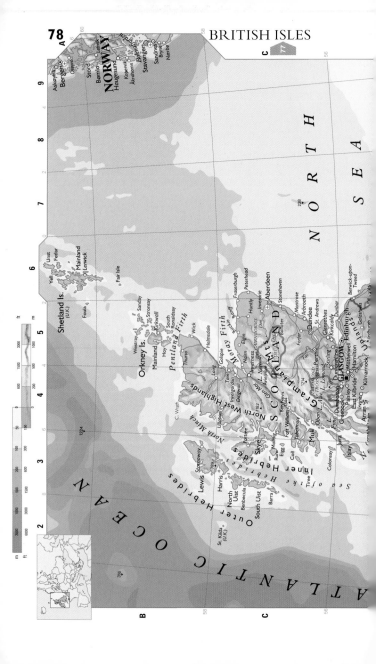

NORWAY

Askvoll
Bergen
Osøyro
Stord
Bømlo
Haugesund
Kopervik
Åkrehamn
Stavanger
Sandnes
Bryne
Nærbø

Shetland Is.
(U.K.)
Unst
Yell
Fetlar
Mainland
Lerwick

Fair Isle

Foula

Orkney Is.
Westray
Sanday
Stronsay
Mainland
Kirkwall
Rousay
Hoy
South
Ronaldsay
Pentland Firth
Wick
Helmsdale

C. Wrath
Thurso

Lewis
Stornoway

Harris

North
Uist
Benbecula
South Uist
Barra

St. Kilda
(U.K.)

Outer Hebrides

North Minch

Ullapool
Loch
Maree
Dingwall
Inverness
Loch Ness

Skye
Rum
Eigg
Coll
Tiree
Muck
Mull
Colonsay

Inner Hebrides

Sea of the Hebrides

Jura
Islay

SCOTLAND

North West Highlands
Ben Nevis
1344

Fort William

Oban

Golspie
Loch
Shin
Tain
Nairn
Elgin
GRAMPIAN MTS.
1311
Huntly
Moray Firth
Ballater

Fraserburgh
Peterhead

Aberdeen
Stonehaven

Grampian Mts.
Inverary
Forfar
Montrose
Arbroath
Dundee
St. Andrews
L. Lomond
Perth
Stirling
Dunfermline
Kirkcaldy
Dumbarton
GLASGOW
Greenock
Paisley
East Kilbride
Hamilton
Motherwell
Kilmarnock

Southern Uplands
Berwick-upon-Tweed

Edinburgh
Dunbar
Glenrothes

1224

238

NORTH SEA

ATLANTIC OCEAN

N

B

C

m | ft
6000 |
3000 | 2000
1500 | 1000
600 | 500
300 | 200
180 | 100
50 | 0

ft | m
6000 | 2000
3000 | 1500
1500 | 500
600 | 200
300 | 100
180 | 50
0 | 0

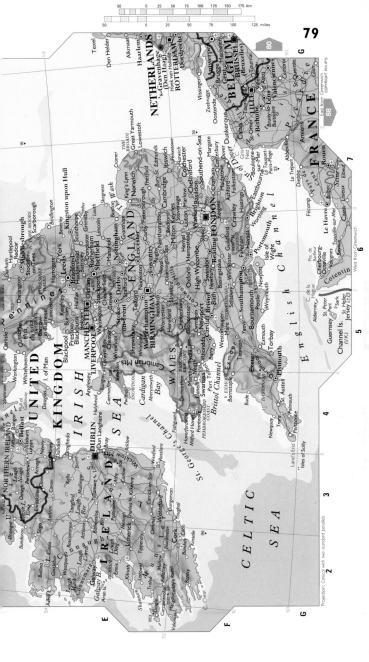

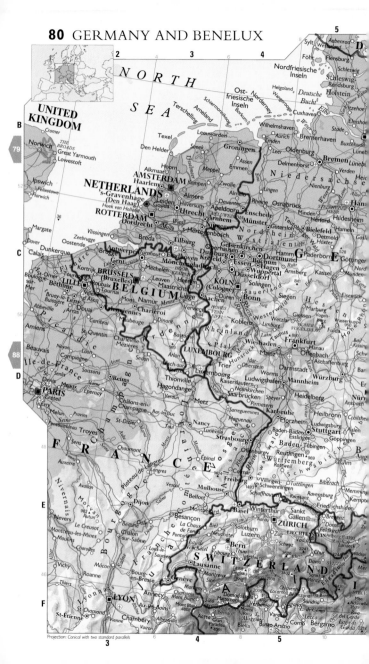

Projection: Conical with two standard parallels

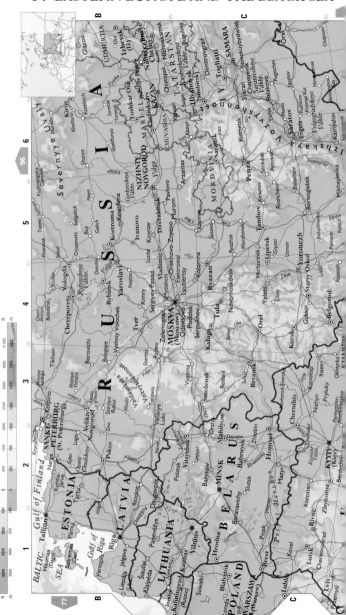

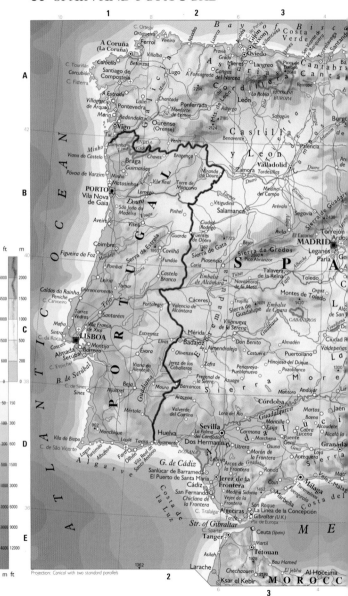

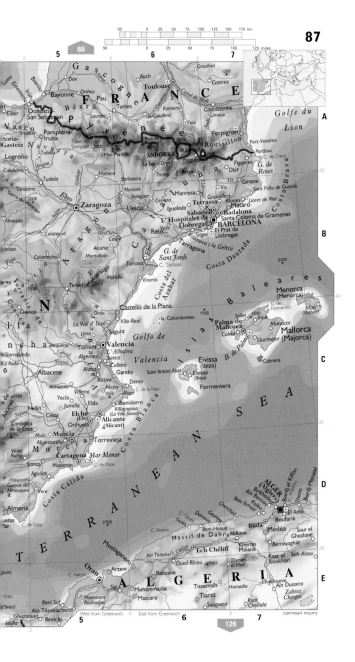

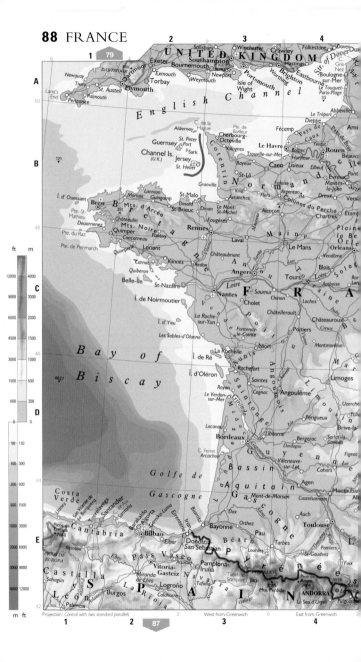

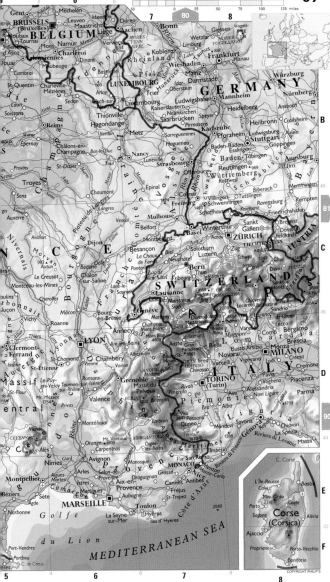

50 0 25 50 75 100 125 150 175 km
50 0 25 50 75 100 125 miles

East from Greenwich

COPYRIGHT PHILIP'S

Projection: Conical with two standard parallels

m ft
4000 12000
3000 9000
2000 6000
1000 3000
500 1500
200 600
0 0

m ft
4300 12000
3000 9000
2000 6000
1000 3000
500 1500
200 600

126

IONIAN SEA

Brindisi
Lecce
Otranto
Nardò Galatina
Francavilla Fontana
Gallipoli
Martina Franca
Taranto
Golfo di Taranto

Rossano
Crotone
Catanzaro
ASPROMONTE
Reggdi Calabria
Nicastro
Cosenza
Lamezia
Vibo Valentia
Palmi
Gioia Tauro
Str. di Messina
Messina
Giarre
Acireale
CATÁNIA
Augusta
Siracusa
Avola
Noto
Módica
Ragusa
C. Passero
Pozzallo
Vittória

IONIAN SEA

Stromboli
Salina
Isole Eólie
Lipari
Vulcano
Milazzo
Barcellona Pozzo di Gotto
Monti Nébrodi
Etna
Adrano
Enna
Paternò
Caltagirone
Gela
Comiso

Ústica (Italy)

Palermo
Termini Imerese
Cefalù
S i c i l i a
Caltanissetta
Canicattì
Licata
Porto Empédocle
Sciacca
Gozo
Valletta
MALTA

Érice
Trápani
Isole Égadi
Favignana
Marsala
Mazara del Vallo
Castelvetrano

Pantelleria (Italy)

Linosa
Isole Pelagie (Italy)
Lampione
Lampedusa

MEDITERRANEAN SEA

TYRRHENIAN SEA

Sardegna (Sardinia)

Alghero
Bosa
Macomer
Oristano
G. di Oristano
Iglésias
Carbonia
Sant'Antíoco
San Pietro
G. di Palmas
C. Spartivento
Quartu Sant'Elena
Cágliari
G. di Cágliari
C. Carbonara

ALGERIA

TUNISIA

Bizerte
TUNIS
Golfe de Tunis
Menzel-Bourguiba
Nabeul
Hammamet
Golfe de Hammamet
Sousse
Monastir
Mahdia
Kairouan
Sfax

Béja
El Kef
Kasserine
Tébessa
Souk-Ahras
Guelma
Aïn Beïda

Is. de la Galite (Tunisia)

C. Blanc

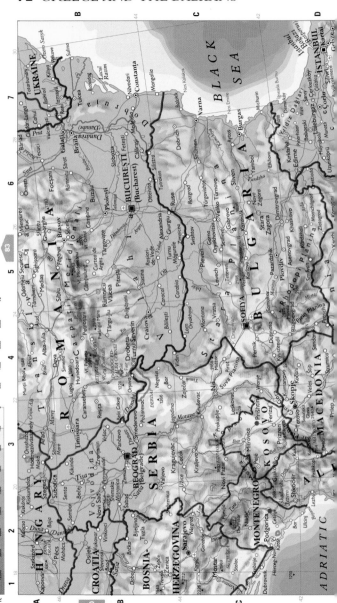

100 0 200 400 600 800 1000 1200 1400 km
100 0 200 400 600 800 1000 miles

Barents Sea

Novaya Zemlya

Kara Sea

North Sea

NORWAY

SWEDEN

FINLAND

Murmansk

Onega

Anderma

Vorkuta

Novyy Port

Novyy Ure

KOMI

Salekhard

GERMANY

Berlin

Warsaw

ESTONIA

LATVIA

LITH.

St Petersburg

KARELIA

Arkhangelsk

Ukhta

Syktyvkar

R U

Serov

Surgut

Nizhnevart

BELARUS

MOSCOW

Rybinsk

Yaroslavl

Kotlas

Vologda

Kirov

Glazov

Perm

Nizhny Tagil

Tobolsk

Tyumen

POLAND

UKRAINE

Kiev

Smolensk

Nizhny Novgorod

Kazan

Izhevsk

Ufa

Yekaterinburg

Serov

ROMANIA

Tula

Ryazan

Penza

BASHKORTOSTAN

Chelyabinsk

Omsk

Novosibirsk

Belgrade

Danube

Odesa

Rostov

Voronezh

Samara

Orenburg

Kustanay

Pavlodar

Novokuznetsk

BULGARIA

CRIMEA

Don

Volgograd

Uralsk

Orsk

Astana

Semey

Karaganda

Oskemen

ALTAY

GREECE

Black Sea

ISTANBUL

Samsun

GEORGIA

Stavropol

Astrakhan

Atyrau

K A Z A K H S T A N

L. Balkhash

TURKEY

Ankara

Erzurum

ARMENIA

AZER.

Baku

Aral

Aral Sea

Taraz

Bishkek

Ala

Tirümq

SINK

CYPRUS

Nicosia

Adana

Yerevan

Tabriz

UZBEKISTAN

Urganch

Syrdarya

Tashkent

KYRGYZSTAN

Tarim

Kashi

Mediterranean Sea

SYRIA

Aleppo

Mosul

KARAKUM

TURKMENISTAN

Samarkand

TAJIKISTAN

Dyushabe

Hotan

Alexandria

ISRAEL

Beirut

Damascus

Kirkuk

Caspian Sea

Ashkhabad

Mashhad

CAIRO

Suez

JORDAN

Amman

BAGHDAD

TEHRAN

Kabul

Peshawar

Srinagar

JAMMU & KASHMIR

EGYPT

Nile

Medina

Basra

Abadan

Kermanshah

Esfahan

I R A N

Qom

Yazd

Herat

AFGHANISTAN

Qandahar

Islamabad

Rawalpindi

Faisalabad

LAHORE

Red Sea

SAUDI

RIYADH

KUWAIT

BAHRAIN

Al Manamah

QATAR

Shiraz

Kerman

Zahedan

Quetta

Multan

DELHI

Bareilly

Jeddah

Mecca

Medina

Dubai

Abu Dhabi

UNITED ARAB EMIRATES

Bandar Abbas

G. of Oman

Jodhpur

New Delhi

Agra

Jaipur

Kanpur

Lucknow

Kathmandu

NEPAL

Patna

ARABIA

Abha

Doha

Muscat

KARACHI

Hyderabad

AHMADABAD

 Vadodara

Bhopal

Allahabad

Varanasi

Janshedpur

Sana

OMAN

Surat

Indore

Jabalpur

I N D I A

KOLKA

Calcutt

YEMEN

Aden

G. of Aden

Socotra

MUMBAI (Bombay)

PUNE

HYDERABAD

Vishakha

Kakinada

B e

ETHIOPIA

DJIBOUTI

Addis Ababa

Hargesia

SOMALIA

Panaji

Vijayawada

Nellore

Arabian Sea

Mangalore

BANGALORE (Bengaluru)

CHENNAI (Madras)

Pondicherry

A f r i c a

KENYA

Mogadishu

Lakshadweep Is. (India)

Coimbatore

Cochin

Madurai

Trivandrum

Jaffna

SRI LANKA

Colombo

Mombasa

Equator

MALDIVES

Malé

I N D I A N

O C E

TANZANIA

Dar es Salaam

Aldabra Is. (Seych.)

SEYCHELLES

Victoria

COMOROS

Chagos Arch.

East from Greenwich

Projection: Bonne

m ft

0

200 600

1000 3000

2000 6000

4000 12000

6000 18000

8000 24000

Katmandu ● Capital Cities

RUSSIA
1 Adygea
2 Karachey-Cherkessia
3 Kabardino-Balkaria
4 North Ossetia-Alaniya
5 Ingushetia
6 Chechenia
7 Dagestan
8 Mordvinia
9 Chuvashia
10 Mari El
11 Tatarstan
12 Udmurtia

AZERBAIJAN
13 Naxçivan

GEORGIA
14 Ajaria
15 Abkhazia

COPYRIGHT PHILIP'S

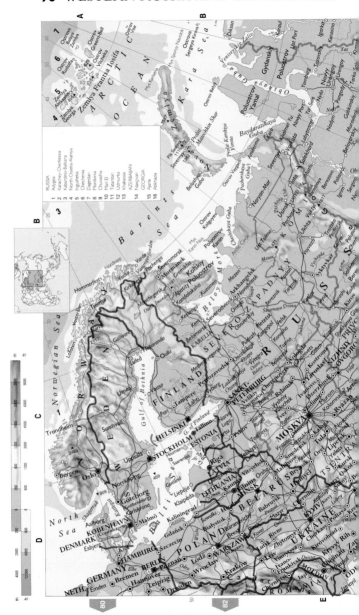

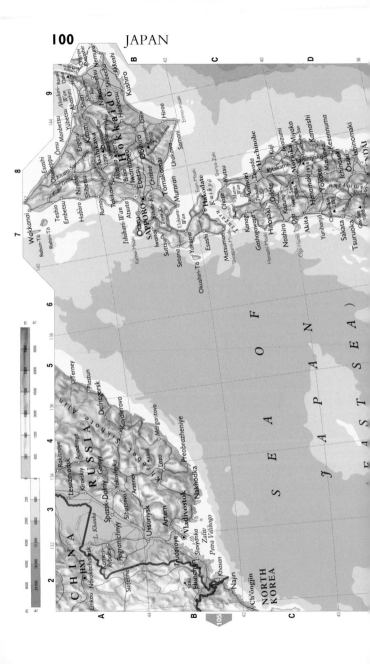

CHINA

RUSSIA

Erkou
Novokachalinsk
L'sozavodsk
Rukinoye
Kirovskiy
Ananьevo
Spassk-Dalniy
Gornyy
Yakovlevka
Dalnegorsk
Plastun
Terney
Sihote-Alin
Sitaevo
Shkotovo
Arsenev
Luzo
Yasse
Margaritovo
Olga
Pogranichnyy
Spassk-Dalniy
Ussuriysk
Artem
Kavderovo
Preobrazheniye
Kamen-Rybolov
L. Khanka
Suifenhe
Vladivostok
Nakhodka
Slavyanka
Zaliv
Petra Velikogo
Hunchun
Trudovoye
Khasan
Najin
Ch'ŏngjin
NORTH KOREA

S E A   **O F**   **J A P A N**   **(**   **E A S T**   **S E A** **)**

H O K K A I D Ō

Wakkanai
Rebun-Tō
Rishiri-Tō
Esashi
Otoineppu
Ōmu
Monbetsu
Kitami-Sammyaku
Engaru
Abashiri
Wan
Shari
Rausu
Oshiri
Shibetsu
Kushiro
Akkeshi
Nemuro
Shiretoko Hantō
Teshio
Asahikawa
Daisetsu-Zan
Asahi-dake 2290
Kunashiri
Haboro
Nayoro
Kitami
Bibai
Furano
Kushiro
Hiroo
Erimo-misaki
Rumoi
Iwamizawa
Obihiro
Ashibetsu-Kō
Otaru
SAPPORO
Chitose
Tomakomai
Urakawa
Samani
Ishikari-Wan
Iwanai
Ebetsu
Yūbari
Kamui-misaki
Suttsu
Noboribetsu
Muroran
Uchiura-Wan
Setana
Shiraoi
Toyako-Ko
Uchiura
Wan
Esan-misaki
Okushiri-Tō
Yakumo
Hakodate
Kaikyō
Matsumae-Misaki
Shiriya-Zaki
Shirakami-Misaki
Henashi-Misaki
Mutsu
Ōma
Tappi-Zaki
Ōata
Mutsu-Wan
Shimokita Hantō

Aomori
Kanagi
Goshogawara
Hirosaki
Towada
Odate
Kazuno
Kuji
Iwaizumi
Hachinohe
Towada-Ko
Morioka
Ōu-Sammyaku
Sammyaku
Miyako
Nakinobe-San
Noshiro
Oga-Hantō
Akita
Kakunodate
Kamaishi
Yokote
Hanamaki
Ichinoseki
Kesennuma
Yurihonjō
Honjō
Ōfunato
Kitakami
Sakata
Shinjō
Kitakami-Sammyaku
Shishinomaki
Tsuruoka

SENDAI

m ft

8000   24,000
6000   18,000
4000   13,000
2000   6600
200   660
0

m ft
7000   23,000
5000   16,000
3000   9000
1500   4500
600   1200
250   600
0

105

A   B   C   D

44   42   40   38

132   134   136   138   140   142   144

1   2   3   4   5   6   7   8   9

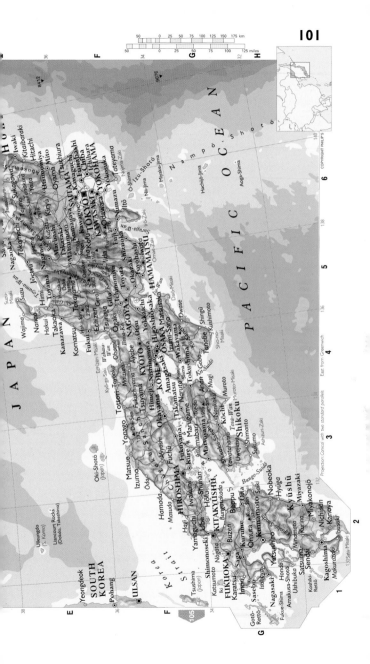

50 0 25 50 75 100 125 150 175 km
50 0 25 50 75 100 125 miles

J A P A N

P A C I F I C   O C E A N

SOUTH
KOREA

Yeongdeok
Pohang

ULSAN

Ulleungdo
(S. Korea)

Liancourt Rocks
(Dokdo, Takeshima)

Oki-Shoto
(Japan)

Matsue
Izumo
Yonago
Tottori

Hamada
Masuda
Hagi

HIROSHIMA
Iwakuni
Kure
Fuchū
Tsuyama
Okayama

Shimonoseki
Yamaguchi
Ube

KITAKYUSHU
Buzen
Shunan
Hōfu

FUKUOKA
Karatsu
Kurume
Ōmuta

Tosu
Saga
Ōita
Beppu

Nagasaki
Isahaya
Amakusa-Shoto
Ushibuka

Nobeoka
Hyūga

KYŪSHŪ
Miyazaki
Miyakonojō

Kagoshima
Kanoya
Ibusuki
Makurazaki
Sendai

Tsushima
(Japan)

Gotō
Retto
Fukue-Shima

Kōshiki-
Retto

Koror
Strait

Tsushima
Strait

Matsuyama
Imabari
Marugame
Takamatsu
Shikoku
Kōchi
Sukumo
Uwajima

Tokushima
Muroto

Muroto-Misaki

Tosa-Wan
Ashizuri-Zaki

KYOTO
KOBE
OSAKA
Wakayama
Kii-Suidō

NAGOYA
Yokkaichi
Tsu
Matsusaka

TOKYO
YOKOHAMA
KAWASAKI
CHIBA
SAITAMA

Hamamatsu
Shizuoka
Numazu
Itō

Suruga-Wan

Izu-Shoto
O-Shima

Miyake-Jima
Niijima

Hachijō-Jima
Aogo-Shima

Izu-Shoto

PACIFIC OCEAN

East from Greenwich

Projection: Conical with two standard parallels

COPYRIGHT PHILIP'S

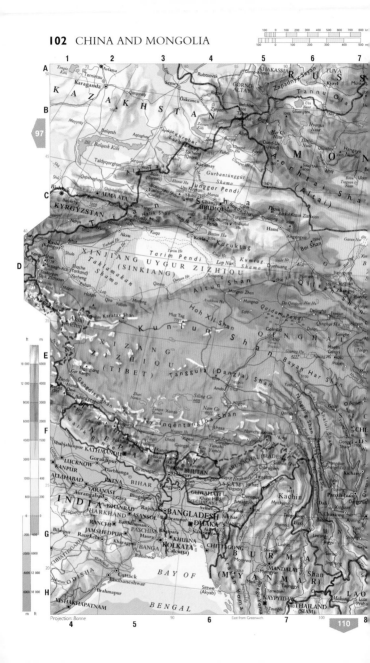

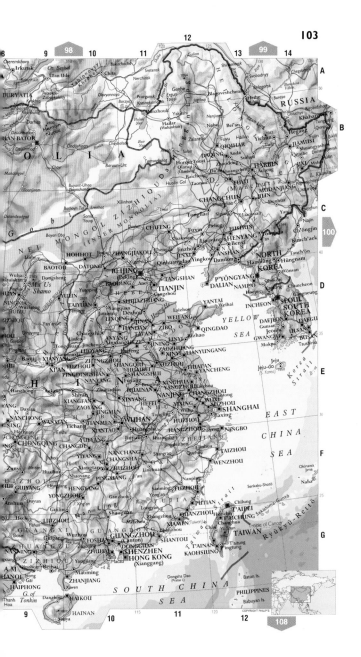

Projection: Conical Orthomorphic with two standard parallels

50 0 50 100 150 200 km
50 0 50 100 150 miles

RUSSIA
Vladivostok

JILIN

Gongzhuling Yantongshan Mingyuegue Shixian Tumen
Yinmacheng Siping Liaoyuan Panshi Songhua Kanji Namyang Hunchun Kraskino
Changtu Xifeng Dongfeng Meihekou Huinan Baishan Antu Helong Longjing Hoeryong Aoji Khasan
Kaiyuan Shanchengzhen Jingyu Quanyang Baihe 1677 Musan Unggi Sosura
Tieling Qingyuan Jiaohe Jiangyuan Songjianghe Changbai Shan Puryŏng Pugodong Najin
Liao He Hunjiang Shiren Linjiang Changbai 2744 Hapsan Nanam Ch'ŏngjin Odaejin
NYANG FUSHUN Tonghua Huch'ŏn Hyesan Kyŏngsŏng
Benxi Xinbin Qinghecheng Huanren 1846 Kasan-dong Pyŏngsan Kapsan Kilchu
SHAN Tianshifu Lianshanguan Manp'o Puksubŏng 2522 Iwŏn Tanch'ŏn Muduan
cheng Kuandian Shuiku Pyŏktong Koin Changjin Kwangdong Kimch'aek (Sŏngjin)
Fengcheng Chu Uiju Taegwan Kanggye Ch'osan Chunghung Changjin Sinhung Pukch'ŏng
Xiuyan Dandong Sinŭiju Pukch'ŏng Huich'ŏn Oro Hongwŏn Sinch'ang
Langtou Yongamp'o Kusŏng Kusŏng **NORTH** Tŏkch'ŏn Hamhŭng
Gushan Sŏnch'ŏn Anju Sunch'ŏn Yŏnghung Chŏngp'yŏng Hŭngnam
Donggang Sinanju Sukch'ŏn **KOREA** Kowŏn Tongjosŏn-man
Yalu Jiang Sinmi-do Sukch'ŏn Munch'ŏn Anbyŏn Wŏnsan **SEA OF**
Korea **P'YŎNGYANG** Chinnamp'o Kangdong Tongdang Kosan Kojŏ **JAPAN**
Bay **NAMP'O** Songnim Suan Sepo-ri Hoeyang 1638 Kosŏng Gangseong (EAST SEA)
Cho-do Sariwŏn Simmok P'yŏnggang Chŏngo-ri 1708 Sokcho Yang-yang
Changyŏn Chaeryŏng Sinch'ŏn Nam-ch'ŏn Cheorwon Cheorwon Jumunjin Ullŭngdo 984
Baengnyeongdo Haeju Kŭmch'ŏn Kimhwa Hwacheon Chuncheon Gangneung (S. Korea)
(S. Korea) Ongjin Yonan Kaesŏng Munsan Uijeongbu Hongcheon Donghae Samcheok
Bucheon **SEOUL** **SEONGNAM** Yeongwol Uljin
INCHEON **GOYANG** Anyang Yong-in Wonju
Ansan **SUWON** Ichon Yecheon Yeongju
Pyeongtaek Chungju Jecheon Yeongdeok
Cheonan **SOUTH** Cheongju Yecheon Andong Yeongdeok
Seosan Hongseong **KOREA** Sangju Uiseong Heunghae
Anmyeondo Gongju Nonsan Gimcheon Yeongcheon Pohang
Boryeong Gangyeong Seonsan Gumi Gyeongju
Gunsan Iksan Waegwan **DAEGU** Cheongdo **ULSAN**
Gimje Jeonju Geochang Goryeong Miryang
Jeong-eup Namwon Jinsan Hamyang Hapcheon Changnyeong Gimhae
GWANGJU Damyang 1915 Jinju Masan **BUSAN**
Naju Hwasun Hadong Sacheon **Chang-won** Geoje
Mokpo Suncheon Boseong Beolgyo Yeosu Tong-yeong Korea Strait Tsushima
Heuksando Yesan Gwangyang (Japan)
(S. Korea) Jindo Haenam 649 Izuhara
Soheuksando Iki
(S. Korea) **JAPAN**
Jeju Haehyop Karatsu
Jeju Jeju-do (S. Korea) Sasebo Imari
Hallim Hallasan Kashima
Daejeong Namjeju Nakadori-Shima Omura Isahaya
Seogwipo Nagasaki
Fukue-Shima Kuchinotsu

YELLOW SEA
(HUANG HAI)

Gyeonggi-man

Korea
Bay

Liaodong

42
40
38
36
34

A B C D E F

101

103 126 East from Greenwich 128 7 8

COPYRIGHT PHILIP'S

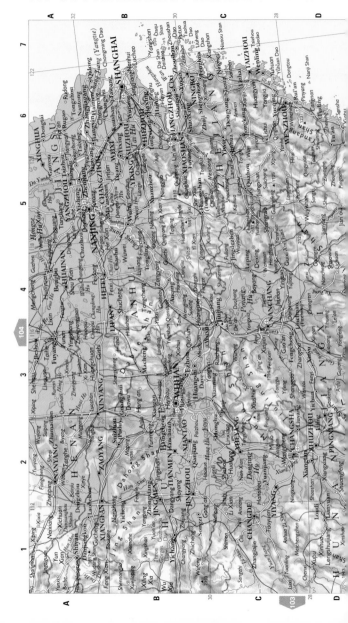

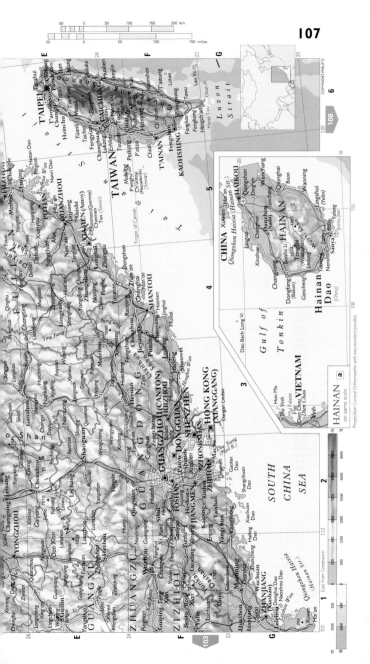

50   0   50   100   150   200 km
50   0   50   100   150 miles

East from Greenwich

E   24   **F**   22   **G**

E   26   **F**   22   **G**

COPYRIGHT PHILIP'S

Projection: Conical Orthomorphic with two standard parallels

HAINAN
on same scale
a

TAIPEI
Taoyuan
Hsinchu
TAICHUNG
Yuanlin
Fengyuan
Changhua
T A I W A N
Chiai
TAINAN
Fengshan
KAOHSIUNG
Hualien
Taitung
Hsiaoliuchiu

P'enghu
Ch'üntao
(Pescadores)

L u z o n   S t r a i t

Lan Yü

120   108

Hengch'un

Tropic of Cancer

CHINA   Xuwen   Hai'an (Str.)   **HAIKOU**   Wenchang
Qiongzhou Haixia (Hainan)   Qinglan
Qiongshan   Ding'an   Qionghai
Lingao   Chengmai   Jiaji
Danzhou (Nada)   Tunchang   Wanning
Xinzhou
Changjiang   Baisha L.   Qiongzhong   Lingshui
Baishaling   (Yelin)
HAINAN
Dongfang (Basuo)   1654   Wuzhishan   Yaxian   Jinmu Jiao
Gancheng   Ledong   Tongshi   Sanya

**Hainan
Dao**   (Qiong)

110

*G u l f   o f
T o n k i n*

Dao Bach Long Vi

VIETNAM
Hon Me
Tho Vinh   Chau Chau
Vinh   Dien Bien   Chau Chau
Phu   Mui Falaise

106   108

FUJIAN
Fuzhou   **FUZHOU**
Minhou
Yongtai
Putian
Yunxiao   **QUANZHOU**
Jinjiang   Shishi
XIAMEN (Amoy)
Nan'an
Longhai   Jinmen (Quemoy)
Tao (Tawar)
Zhangpu
Dongshan

SHANTOU
Chaozhou   Chenghai
Chaoyang
Puning   Jieyang   Raoping
Haimen
Huilai
Lufeng

G U A N G D O N G
Heyuan   Zijin
Huizhou   Huidong
DONGGUAN
SHENZHEN
**HONG KONG
(XIANGGANG)**
Dangan Liedao

**S O U T H
C H I N A
S E A**

**GUANGZHOU
(CANTON)**
Sanshui   Panyu
FOSHAN   Humen
Heshan   Shunde   Nansha
JIANGMEN   Zhongshan
Xinhui   **ZHUHAI**
Taishan   Doumen
Yangjiang   Shangchuan
Dao
Xiachuan
Dao
Hailing
Dao

**G U A N G X I
Z H U A N G Z U**
YONGZHOU
Cangwu
Wuzhou
Guiping
Pingnan   Xinyi
ZHANJIANG
Leizhou
Haikang
Xuwen
Qiongzhou Haixia
(Hainan Str.)

110   112   114   116   118   120

22   24   26

m   ft
9000
6000
4500
3000
1500
600
300
0   0
600
2000   m

103   108

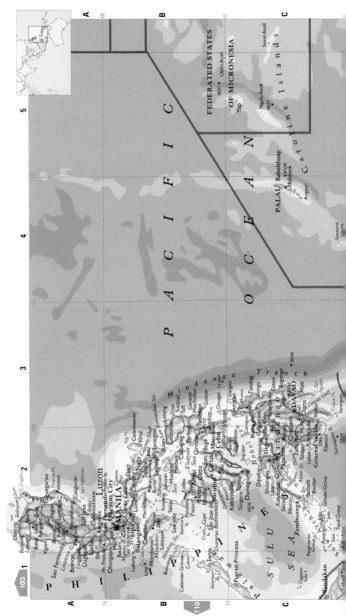

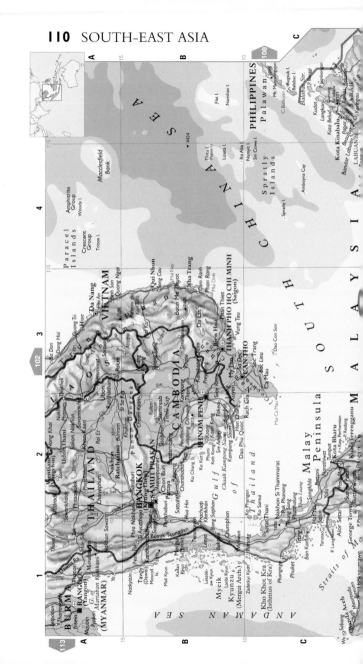

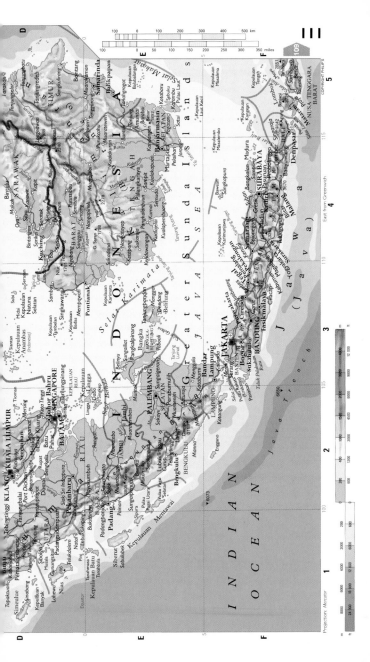

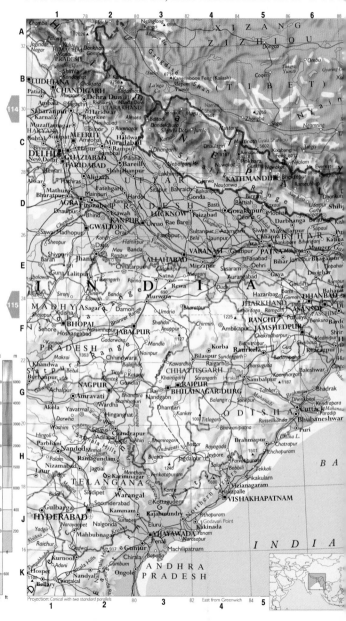

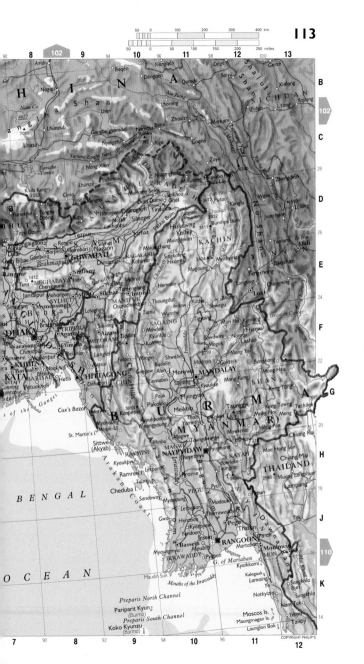

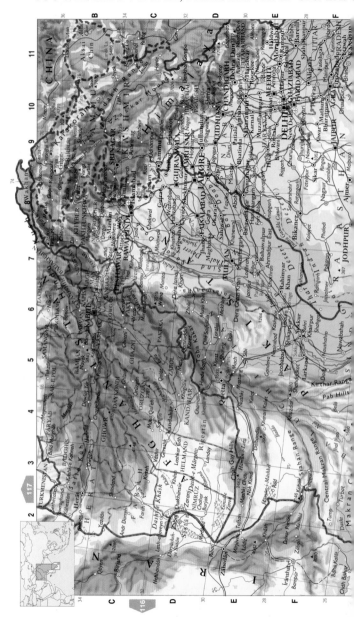

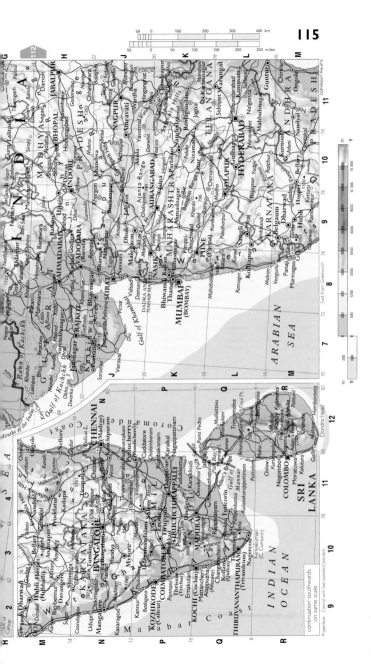

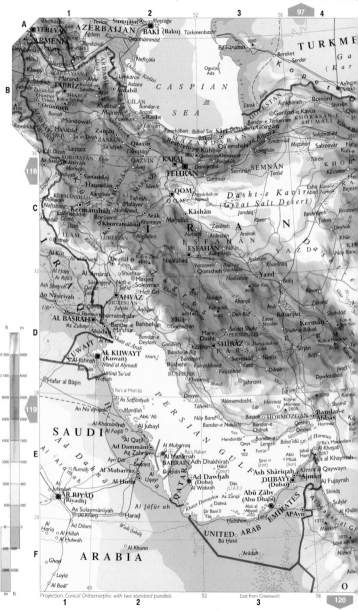

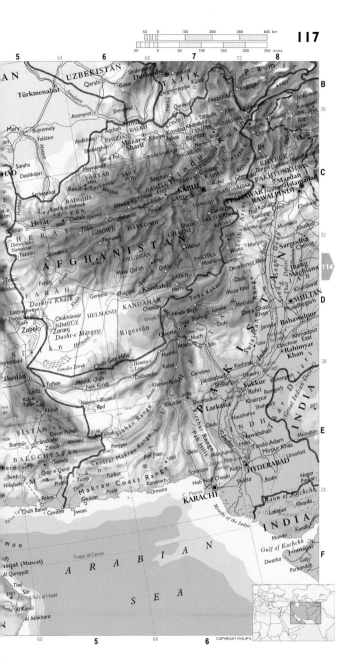

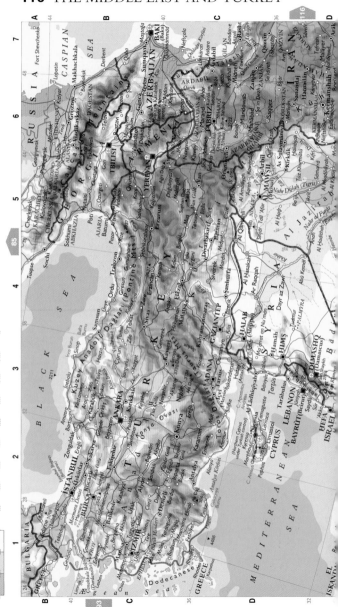

50 0 100 200 300 400 km
50 0 50 100 150 200 250 miles

116
120
125
124

PERSIAN GULF

KUWAIT
AL KUWAYT (Kuwait)
Al Aḥmadī
Mīnā' al Aḥmadī
Mīnā' Su'ūd
Wafrah
Ḥafar al Bāṭin

AL BAŞRAH
Az Zubayr
Ar Rifā'ī
Ash Shaţrah
As Samāwah
An Nāşirīyah
UR
As Salmān
Al 'Amārah

Abū 'Alī
Al 'Ubayl
Al Qaţīf
Az Zahrān
Ad Dammām
Al Muḥarraq
BAHRAIN
Al Hufūf
Harad
Al Jāfūrah
Al Khunn
Al Jafūrah

An Nu'ayrīyah
As Saffānīyah
Al Manīfah
Al Fudūl

AD DAHNĀ'

Al Qaşab
Ad Dilam
Al Ḥarīq
Al Ḥulwah
Layla
Al Badī'

AR RIYĀD (Riyadh)
Al 'Arama
Marāt
Thādiq
Rumāh
As Sulaymānīyah
Al Kharj

Buraydah
'Unayzah
Ar Rass
Mabā'ij
Al Ghāt
Riḍā
Shaqrā'
Al Qaşim
Ad Dawādimī
Al 'Uwayqīlah
Ghazala
Al Hamār
Al Ḥaddār
Al Quway'īyah
'Afīf
Al Dawādimī

AN NAFŪD
Al Jawf
Sakākah
Al 'Ulayyānīyah
Al 'Ubaylah
Tūmān
Ḥā'il
Jabal Shammar
Ḥarrat al 'Uwayriḍ
Madā'in Şāliḥ
Al 'Ulā
Şafājah
Taymā'
Al Akhḍar
Ḥarrat Khaybar

SAUDI ARABIA

AL MADĪNAH (Medina)
Al Ḥanākīyah
Al Mudhnab
Mahd adh Dhahab
Uruq Şubay'
Al Mudawwarah
Ḥarrat al Kishb
Ḥarrat Nawāşif
Al Ḥawīyah
AL MAKKAH (Mecca)
At Tā'if
Zaymah
'Usfān
Rābigh
Maştūrah

JIDDAH (Jedda)
Al Qunfudhah
Dhahabān
Ra's Bān
Ra's al Baḥr

RED SEA

Yanbu' al Baḥr
Umm Lajj
Wajh
Shaybārah
Ḥasāniyah
Ḥanak
Ḍubā'
Al Muwayliḥ
Maqnā

EGYPT

EL QÂHIRA (Cairo)
Es Suweis (Suez)
Khalig el Suweis
Gebel Shā'ib al Banāt
Es Sinā'
Bûr Safâga
Hurghada
Qena
THEBES
El Uqşur (Luxor)
El Ballâs
El Khârga
Edfu
Aswân
El Sâddât

Es Sahrâ' esh Sharqiya

Tropic of Cancer

PYRAMIDS
EL GÎZA
Helwân
El Faiyûm
Beni Suef
El Minya
Mallawi
Asyûṭ
Girga
Nag Hammâdi
Nag' Ḥammâdi
Kôm Ombo
Idfu

Gebel
HALA'IB TRIANGLE
Muḥammad Qol

SUDAN
Es Sahrâ' en Nûbiya

Wâdi Halfa
Dunqula
Buḥairat en Nâşir (Lake Nasser)

PERSIA (IRAN)
Behbehān
Bandar-e Deylam
Bandar-e Māhshahr
Khorramshahr
AHVĀZ

Projection: Conical Orthomorphic with two standard parallels

East from Greenwich

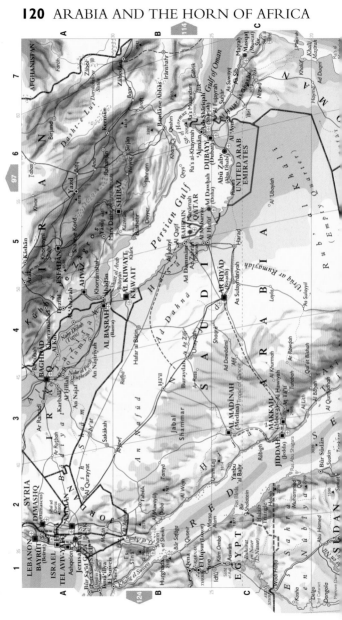

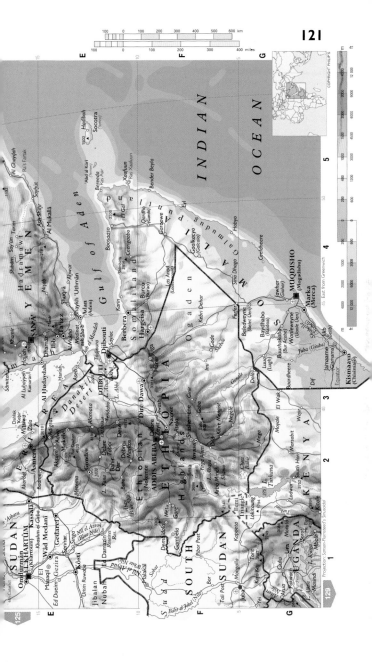

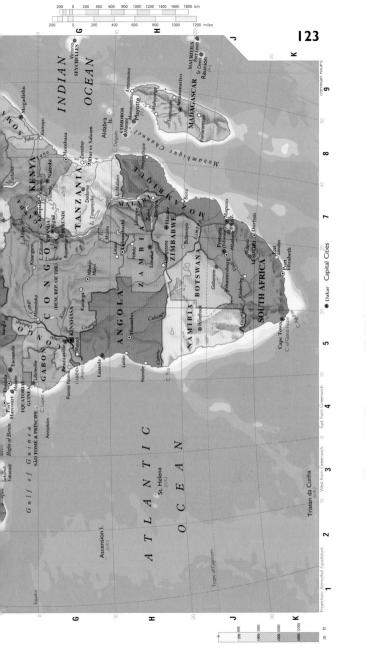

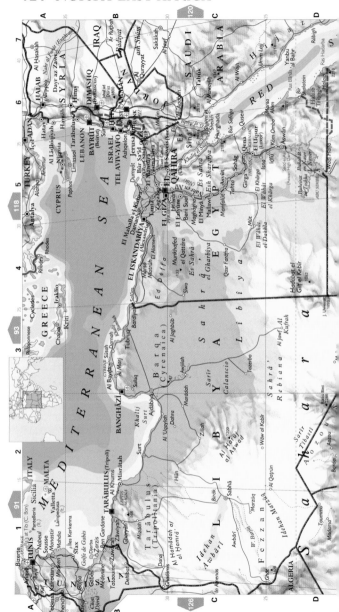

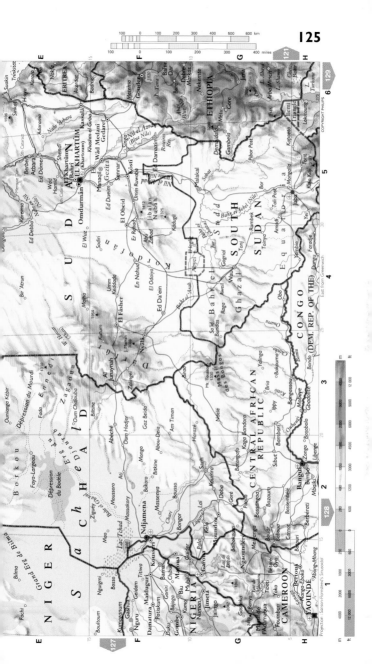

100 0 100 200 300 400 500 600 km
100 0 100 200 300 400 miles

ERITREA
Suakin
Trinkitat
Tokar
Nakfa
Karora
Haiya
Karora
Bodhei
Metema
Gonder
L. Tana
Bahir Dar
Dese
Nekemte
ETHIOPIA
Metu
Abay (Blue Nile)
Debre Markos
Gore
Arba Minch
L. Abaya
L. Turkana
Jima

Berber
Atbara
Nahr Atbara
Kassala
Khashm el Girba
Gedaref
Nil el Azraq (Blue Nile)
Roseires Res.
Ed Damazin
Dembidolo
Gambela

Shendi
AL KHARTUM
Khartum Bahri
EL KHARTUM
Wad Medani
Sennar
Singa
Metu

Omdurman
Ed Dueim
Kosti
Managil
Gezira
Sennar
Malakal
Sobat
Pibor Post

SUDAN
El Wiz
Sodiri
Umm Ruwaba
En Nahud
El Obeid
Abu Zabad
Kadugli
Jibal Nuba
Nubah
1412
1325
Nil el Abyad
Nuer
Bor
Bahr el Jebel (Nile)
SOUTH
SUDAN
Juba
Kapoeta
Torit
Kao Gai
Boma

Bir Atrun
Kutum
Mellit
Umm Keddada
El Odaiya
Kaga
Abyei
Ngok
Tur
Raqaba
Bahr el Arab
Aweil
Wau
Gogrial
Tonj
Rumbek
Amadi
Yambio
Maridi
Yei
Mongalla

El Fasher
Nyala
Ed Da'ein
Nuba
Buram
Raga
Sopo
Oba
EQUATORIA
Ondur
Zémio

DARFUR
Al Junaynah
Zalingei
Birao
Mt. Toussoro
Massifs des Bongos
Bria
Kotto
Bangassou
CONGO (DEM. REP. OF THE)
Dungu
Faradje

Ennedi
Fada
Oum Chalouba
Bitrine
Goz Beida
Am Timan
Haraze
Ndélé
Kaga Bandoro
Ippy
Mobaye
Gbadolite

Borkou
Ounianga Kebir
Fada
Depression du Mourdi
Zaghawa
Abéché
Oum Hadjer
Mongo
Ati
Bokoro
Sarh
Kyabé
Sibut
CENTRAL AFRICAN REPUBLIC
Bambari
Bangui
Zongo

Dépression du Bodélé
Zouar
Faya-Largeau
Koro Toro
Bahr el Ghazal
Massakory
Moussoro
Massenya
Bousso
Bongor
Laï
Doba
Goré
Paoua
Bossangoa
Bozoum
Bossembélé
Boali
Mbaïki

Tibesti
Zouar
Bilma
Grand Erg de Bilma
Nguigmi
Bol
Lac Tchad
Ndjamena
Kousséri
Bongor
Kélo
Pala
Bébédjia
Moundou
Baïbokoum
Ngaoundéré
Berbérati
Carnot
Nola

NIGER
Fachi
Boultoum
Nguru
Damatura
Maiduguri
Geidam
Kukawa
Titwa
Maroua
Garoua
Ngaoundéré
CAMEROON
Bertoua
Abong-Mbang

NIGERIA
Potiskum
Gombe
Biu
Mubi
Numan
Yola
Jimeta
Mandara Mts.
Chubi
Banyo
Foumban
YAOUNDÉ
Eséka
Mbalmayo

Projection: Sanson-Flamsteed's Sinusoidal
COPYRIGHT PHILIP'S
East from Greenwich

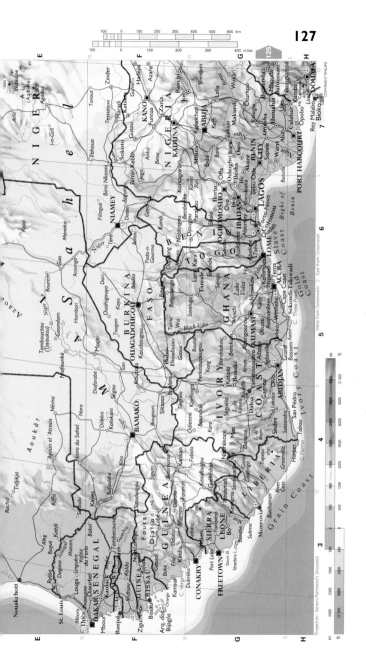

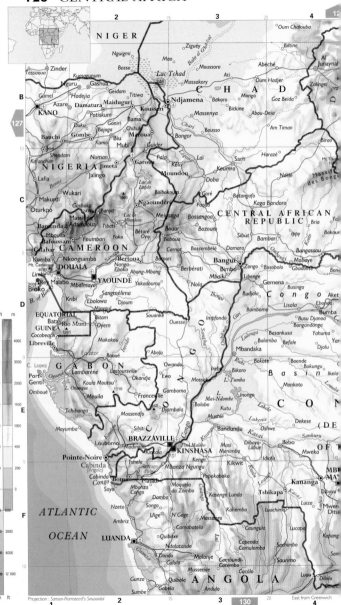

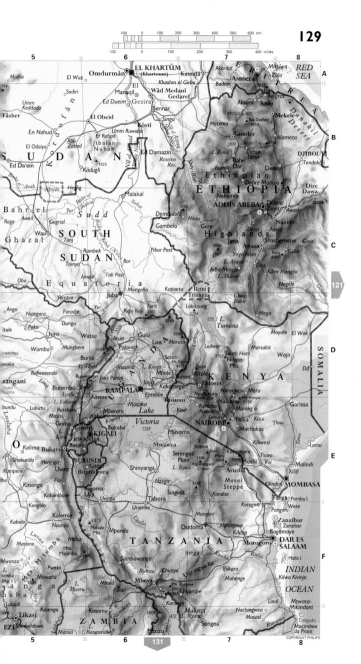

100 0 100 200 300 400 500 600 km
100 0 100 200 300 400 miles

5 **6** **7** **8**

Malha
El Wuz
Omdurmân **EL KHARTÛM**
(Khartoum) Kassalâ
Akordat
Mitsiwa
Zula
**RED
SEA**
A

Umm
Keddada
Sodiri
El
Managil
Khashm el Girba
Badme
Asmera
E R I T R E A

Fâsher
En Nahud
Ed Dueim
Gezira
Wâd Medani
Gedaref
Aksum
Adigrat
Adwa
Mekele
Danakil

K o r d o f â n
El Obeid
Er Rahad
Jibalan
Nubah
Sennar
Singa
Nile
Metema
Gonder
Ras Dashen
4533
Alameta
Desert
B

S U D A N
Ed Da'ein
Abu
Zabad
Kâdugli
1325
Ed Damazin
Roseires
Res.
L. Tana
Bahir
Dar
Debre
Tabor
Dese
DJIBOUTI
Tendaho

B a h r e l
Arab
Heglig
Abyei
Malakal
Ethiopia
Buro
Blue Nile
Debre Markos
Dire
Dawa

Raga
Aweil
Jur
Bahr el
Ghazal
Sobat
Sudd
Dembidolo
Metu
ADDIS ABEBA
Zeyit
Debre
Awash
Gorgol
C

Gogrial
Wau
Tonj
**SOUTH
SUDAN**
Gambela
Gore
H i g h l a n d s
Jima
Awasa
Nazret
Shashemene
Gimir

Obo
Amadi
Rumbek
Bor
Pibor Post
Yirga Alem
L. Abaya
Dila
Kibre Mengist
Goba
Batu

E q u a t o r i a
Tali Post
Toinya
Mongalla
Kapoeta
Ilemi
Triangle
Arba Minch
L. Shamo
Negele

Ango
Niangara
Yambio
Yei
Juba
Torit
Lokitaung
Chew
Bahir
Mega

Faradje
Dungu
Kajo Kaji
L.
Turkana
Moyale
El Wak

Isiro
Watsa
Gulu
Lira
Moroto
Lodwar
South Horn
Ndoto
Mts.
Marsabit
Wajir
SOMALIA
D

Mungbere
Bunia
Pakwach
Soroti
Mt. Elgon
Kitale
Dif

Bafwasende
L. Albert
Fort Portal
Masindi
Mbale
Tororo
Eldoret
KENYA
Meru

Butembo
Beni
Ruwenzori
L. Kyoga
Jinja
Kakamega
Nyahururu
Mt. Kenya
5199
Nanyuki
Garissa

Lubutu
Goma
Rutshuru
Masisi
Kasese
KAMPALA
Entebbe
Kisumu
Kericho
Nakuru
Murang'a
Thika
Kitui

KIGALI
Gisenyi
Butare
Masaka
Kabale
Bukoba
Lake
Victoria
Kisii
Limuru
NAIROBI
Machakos
E

Bukavu
RWANDA
Gitega
Musoma
Mwanza
L. Natron
Kilimanjaro
5895
Kibwezi
Lamu

Uvira
BURUNDI
Bujumbura
Shinyanga
Serengeti
Plain
Ngorongoro
Crater
Moshi
Arusha
Voi
Malindi
Kilifi

Fizi
Kigoma-
Ujiji
Nzega
Singida
Kondoa
Masai
Steppe
MOMBASA

Kasongo
Kabambare
Uvinza
Tabora
Dodoma
Korogwe
Tanga
Pemba I.
Wete
Pangani

Kalemie
Nyunzu
Mahale
Mts.
Mpanda
Uramba
Manyoni
Mpwapwa
Kilosa
Morogoro
Zanzibar
Bagamoyo
**DAR ES
SALAAM**
Mafia I.

Kongolo
Kabalo
Mariano
TANZANIA
Iringa
Rufiji
INDIAN
F

Kasongo
Pweto
L. Rukwa
Sumbawanga
Chunya
Mbeya
Mt. Rungwe
2067
Njombe
Ifakara
Mahenge
Kilwa Kivinje
OCEAN

Likasi
Shinkolobwe
Kasenga
Kasama
ZAMBIA
L. Malawi
(L. Nyasa)
Songea
Lindi
Nachingwea
Mtwara-
Mikindani

Mansa
Mbala
L.
Mweru
Karonga
Mzuzu
Masasi
Mocimboa
da Praia

5 **6** **7** **8**

121

COPYRIGHT PHILIP'S

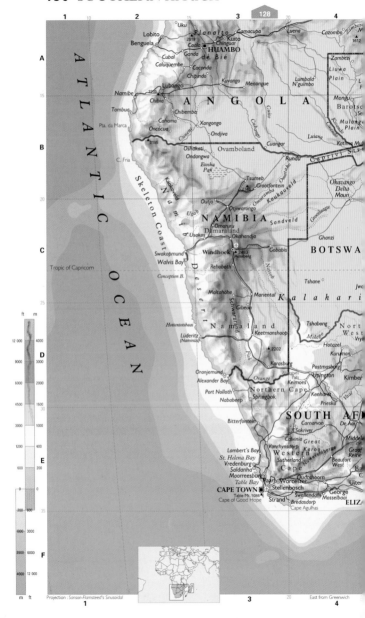

ft   m

12 000   4000

9000   3000

6000   2000

4500   1500

3000   1000

1200   400

600   200

0   0

200   600

1000   3000

2000   6000

4000   12 000

m   ft

Projection : Sanson-Flamsteed's Sinusoidal

East from Greenwich

ATLANTIC OCEAN

ANGOLA

Lobito
Benguela
Uku
Planalto
Camacupa
Luena
Cazombo
Caala
Kuito
Chinguar
HUAMBO
de Bié
Ganda
Cubal
Caluquembe
Caconda
Chipindo
Kuvango
Menongue
Lumbala
N'guimbo
Lubango
Namibe
Chibia
Chibemba
Xangongo
Ondjiva
Cahama
Oncócua
Cunene
Cuito
Cuando
Cuangar
Rundu

Zombezi
Liuwa
Plain
Zambezi
Mongu
Barotse
Mulonga
Plain
Katima Mul
Kalongola

Caprivi Strip

Okavango
Delta
Maun

NAMIBIA

C. Fria
Skeleton Coast
Namib
Desert
Oshakati
Ondangwa
Etosha
Pan
Ovamboland
Tsumeb
Grootfontein
Otavi
Omaruru
Outjo
Otjiwarongo
Sandveld
Kaokoveld
Ghanzi
Ugab
Usakos
Damaraland
Okahandja
Windhoek
Auasberg
Gobabis
Rehoboth
Swakopmund
Walvis Bay
Conception B.
Tropic of Capricorn
Maltahöhe
Mariental
Gibeon
Hottentotsbaai
Namaland
Schwarzrand
Keetmanshoop
Tshabong
Lüderitz
(Naminüs)
Fish
Karasburg
Postmasburg
Hotazel
Kuruman
Oranjemund
Alexander Bay
Orange
Keimoes
Upington
Port Nolloth
Nababeep
Springbok
Kenhardt
Prieska

BOTSWA

Kalahari

Tshane

Nort
West
Vry

Kimber

NORTHERN CAPE

SOUTH AF

Carnarvon
De Aar
Middel
Bitterfontein
Calvinia
Sakriver
Vanrhynsdorp
Great Karoo
Sutherland
Nuweveldberge
Beaufort
West
Graaf
Reine
Lambert's Bay
St. Helena Bay
Vredenburg
Saldanha
Moorreesburg
Table Bay
Paarl
Stellenbosch
Worcester
Swartberge
Oudtshoorn
George
Mosselbaai
Uiter
CAPE TOWN
Table Mt. 1086
Cape of Good Hope
Strand
Swellendam
Bredasdorp
Cape Agulhas
Western Cape
ELIZA

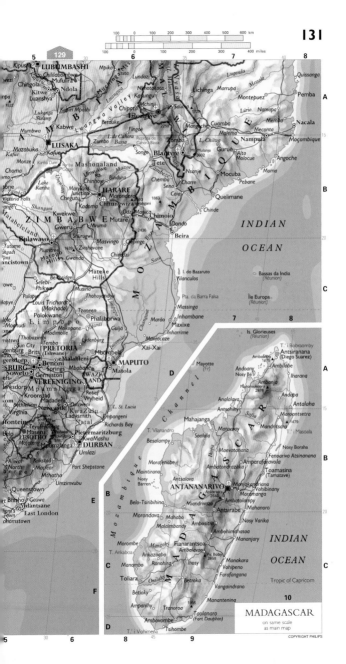

MADAGASCAR
on same scale
as main map

COPYRIGHT PHILIPS

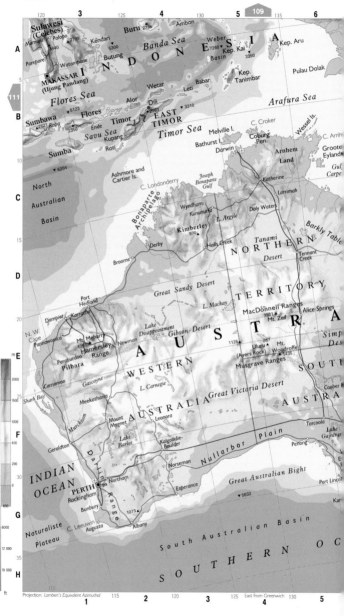

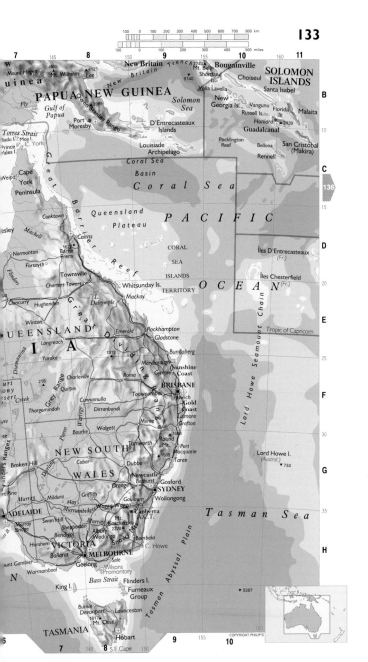

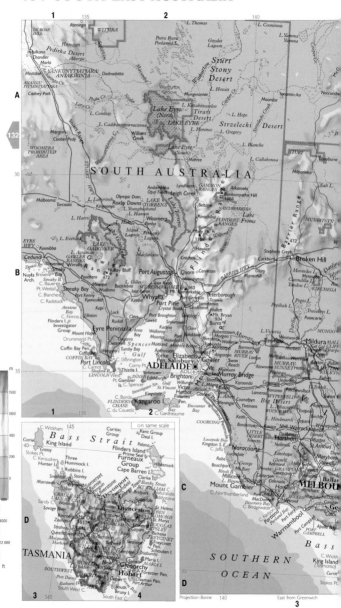

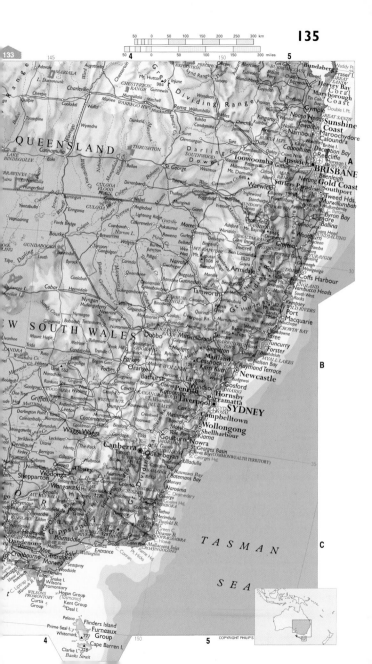

50 0 50 100 150 200 250 300 km
50 0 50 100 150 200 miles

4 **5**

QUEENSLAND

Great Dividing Range

Mt Hutton
984

Adavale
Cheepie
Quilpie
Toompine
Charleville
Augathella
Mitchell
Injune
Chesterton Range
Mungallala
Mitchell
Roma
Wallumbilla
Miles
Chinchilla
Dalby
Kingaroy
Nambour
Oakey
Toowoomba
Caboolture
Deception Bay
Redcliffe

MARIALA
Augathella
WARREGO R.
Surat
Condamine
Tara
Dalby
BUNYA MTS.
Kumbia

Cunnamulla
Bollon
St George
Dirranbandi
Thallon
Mungindi
Goondiwindi
Inglewood
Stanthorpe
Warwick
Clifton
Millmerran
Pittsworth
Gatton
Ipswich
BRISBANE
Beenleigh

GREAT SANDY
Bundaberg
Waddy Pt
Childers
Hervey Bay
Maryborough
Gympie
Noosa Heads
Sunshine Coast
Maroochydore
Caloundra
Bribie I.
Moreton I.

Double I. Pt

THRUSTON
SOUTHWOOD
Darling Downs

NEW SOUTH WALES

Hungerford
Bourke
Brewarrina
Walgett
Lightning Ridge
Collarenebri
Moree
Ashford
Inverell
Glen Innes
Grafton
Woodburn
Ballina
Byron Bay
Lismore

Coffs Harbour
Nambucca Heads

Cobar
Nyngan
Coonamble
Gilgandra
Narrabri
Gunnedah
Tamworth
Armidale
NEW ENGLAND
Walcha
Kempsey
Port Macquarie

Mt Kaputar
1508

GREAT DIVIDING RANGE

Broken Hill
Wilcannia
Menindee
Ivanhoe
Mount Hope
Condobolin
Parkes
Forbes
Dubbo
Wellington
Mudgee
Singleton
Maitland
Cessnock
Newcastle
Raymond Terrace
Nelson Bay
Forster
Tuncurry
Taree
CROWDY BAY
WALLIS LAKES

Griffith
Hillston
Hay
Narrandera
Leeton
Cootamundra
Young
Cowra
Bathurst
Orange
Lithgow
Katoomba
Penrith
Windsor
Gosford
Hornsby
Parramatta
Liverpool
SYDNEY

BLUE MTS.

Wagga Wagga
Junee
Temora
Wyalong
Grenfell
Boorowa
Yass
Goulburn
Mittagong
Bowral
Camden
Campbelltown
Liverpool
Wollongong
Kiama
Shellharbour

Albury
Wodonga
Holbrook
Tumut
Tumbarumba
Gundagai
Canberra
Queanbeyan
Nowra
Jervis Bay (COMMONWEALTH TERRITORY)
Georges Basin
St Georges Hd

Shepparton
Wangaratta
Benalla
Mansfield
Cooma
Bombala
Bega
Merimbula
Eden
Batemans Bay
Bateman Bay
Moruya
Narooma
C. Dromedary

VICTORIA

Dandenong
Cranbourne
Moe
Morwell
Traralgon
Sale
Bairnsdale
Lakes Entrance
Orbost

GIPPSLAND

WILSONS PROMONTORY
Hogan Group (Tasmania)
Kent Group
Deal I.

TASMAN SEA

Flinders Island
Furneaux Group
Cape Barren I.
Clarke I.
718
Banks Strait
Prime Seal I.
Whitemark

A

B

30

C

35

COPYRIGHT PHILIP'S

4 150 **5**

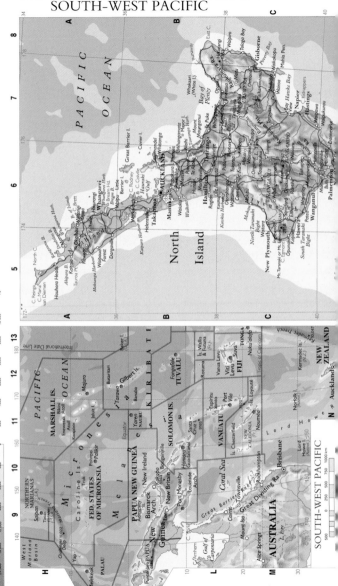

SOUTH-WEST PACIFIC

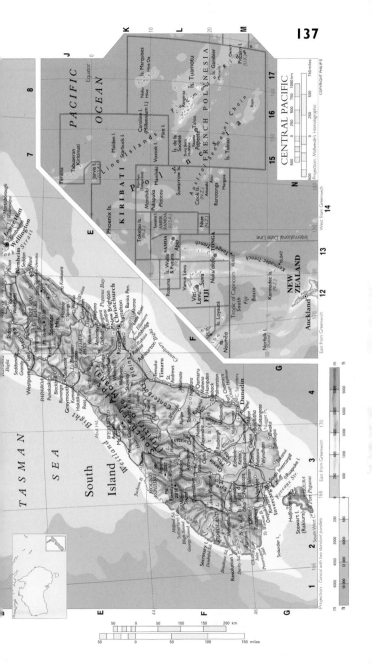

CENTRAL PACIFIC

PACIFIC OCEAN

Equator

Is. Marquises

Caroline I.
(Millennium I.)

FRENCH POLYNESIA

Is. Tuamotu

Is. Gambier
Pitcairn I.
(U.K.)

Line Islands

Tabuaeran
Kiritimati

Teraina

Maiden I.

Jarvis I.

Starbuck I.

Vostok I.

Flint I.

Is. de la
Société

Tahiti
Papeete

Is. Tubuai

KIRIBATI

Phoenix Is.

Penrhyn
(Tongareva)

Pukapuka

Manihiki
Rakahanga

Suwarrow Is.

Cook Is.
(N.Z.)

Rarotonga

Aitutaki

Mangaia

Tokelau Is.
(N.Z.)

Swains I.
(U.S.A.)

AMER.
SAMOA

Niue
(N.Z.)

International Date Line

Rotuma

Is. Wallis
& Futuna

SAMOA
Apia

Tonga Trench

TONGA

Nuku'alofa

10,882

West from Greenwich

Vanua Levu

FIJI

Viti
Levu

Suva

Tropic of Capricorn

Fiji
Basin

South

Kermadec Trench

10,047

Kermadec Is.

Is. Loyauté

Nouméa

Norfolk I.
(Austr.)

NEW
ZEALAND

Auckland

East from Greenwich

TASMAN

SEA

South
Island

Murrahborough
Waikawaru

Picton

Blenheim

Seddon

Ward

Cook Strait

Wellington

Upper Hutt
Lower Hutt

Spenser
Mts.

Westport

Greymouth

Hokitika

Ross

WESTLAND

Christchurch

Canterbury
Plains

Dunedin

Invercargill

Stewart I.
(Rakiura)

Foveaux Str.

Ruapuke I.

MOUNT
ASPIRING

Queenstown

Milford Sd.

Secretary I.

Resolution I.

Solander I.

Projection: Conical with two standard parallels

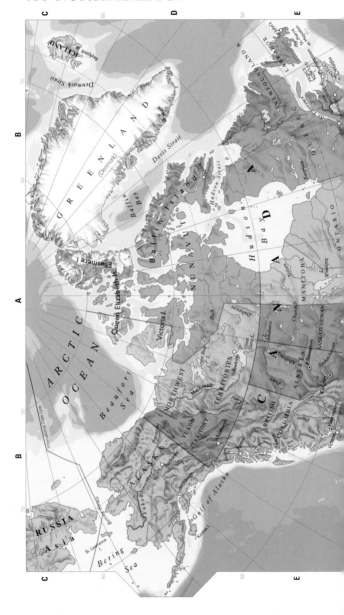

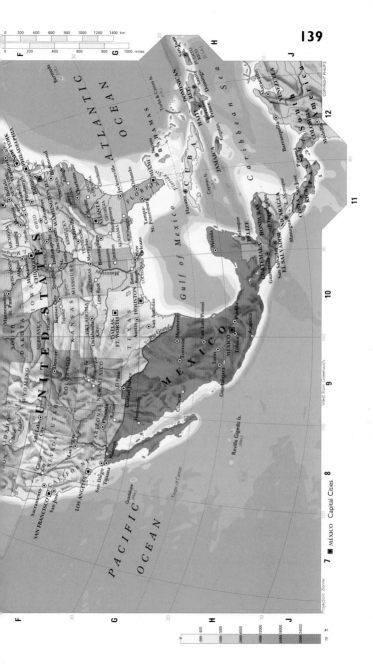

139

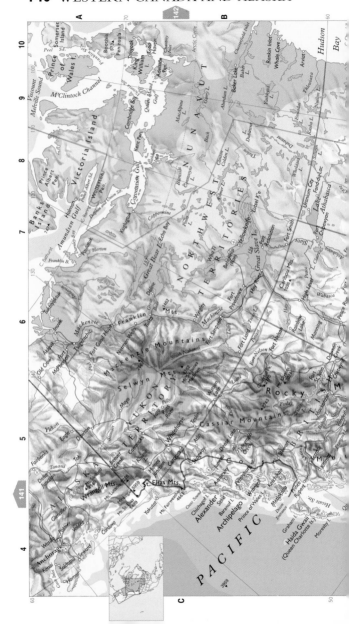

100 0 100 200 300 400 500 600 km

100 0 100 200 300 400 miles

COPYRIGHT PHILIPS

Map labels

ONTARIO

MANITOBA

SASKATCHEWAN

ALBERTA

UNITED STATES

NORTH DAKOTA

SOUTH DAKOTA

MONTANA

NEBRASKA

MINNESOTA

WISCONSIN

IOWA

WASHINGTON

ALASKA

U.S.S.R.

PACIFIC OCEAN

BERING SEA

CHUKCHI SEA

GULF OF ALASKA

Aleutian Islands

Lake Winnipeg

Lake of the Woods

Brooks Range

Winnipeg

Selkirk

St. Paul

Minneapolis

Duluth

Superior

Omaha

Edmonton

Calgary

Vancouver

Seattle

Fairbanks

Anchorage

Nome

Inset

ALASKA

100 0 100 200 300 400 500 600 km

100 0 100 200 300 400 miles

Projection : Bonne

Karaginskoye

Karaginsk

Ozero

Near Is.

Rat Is.

Andreanof Is.

Adak I.

Amchitka I.

Attu I.

Elevation scale

m   ft

4000 13000

2000 6000

1000 3000

400 1200

200 600

0 0

m   ft

6000 18000

4000 12000

2000 6000

1500 4500

900 3000

600 1800

300 600

0 0

99

146

143

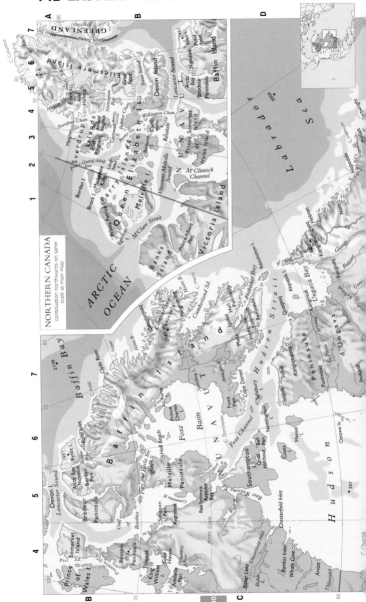

NORTHERN CANADA
continuation northwards on same
scale as main map

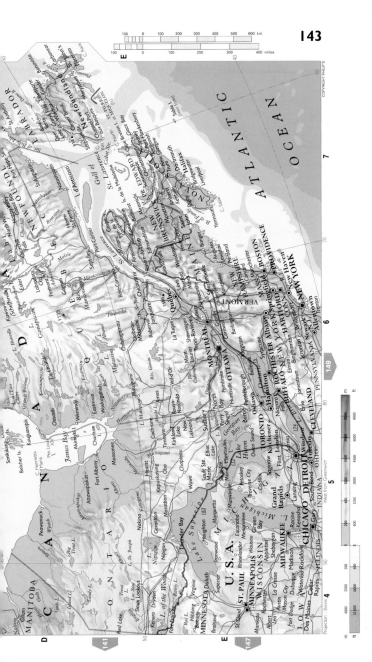

100 0 100 200 300 400 500 600 km
100 0 100 200 300 400 miles

E

COPYRIGHT PHILIP'S

A T L A N T I C

O C E A N

LABRADOR

NEWFOUNDLAND

St-Pierre & Miquelon (Fr.)

Gulf of St. Lawrence

PRINCE EDWARD I.

NOVA SCOTIA

NEW BRUNSWICK

MAINE

QUÉBEC

NEW HAMPSHIRE

VERMONT

MASS.

BOSTON

PROVIDENCE

CONN.

R.I.

HARTFORD

NEW HAVEN

NEW YORK

MONTRÉAL

OTTAWA

ALBANY

ROCHESTER

BUFFALO

NEW YORK

PENNSYLVANIA

TORONTO

DETROIT

CLEVELAND

Ohio

CANADA

ONTARIO

MANITOBA

James Bay

Lake Superior

Lake Huron

Lake Michigan

MICHIGAN

WISCONSIN

U.S.A.

MINNESOTA

ST. PAUL

MINNEAPOLIS

CHICAGO

MILWAUKEE

ILLINOIS

INDIANA

IOWA

Des Moines

Cedar Rapids

Duluth

West from Greenwich

Projection: Bonne

m   ft

149

147

141

147

1   VANCOUVER   2   3   120   4   118   5

Nanaimo   Surrey   Coquitlam
  Island Coast   New Westminster   Chilliwack
PACIFIC   Vancouver Island   Ferndale   Lynden
  Str. of Juan de Fuca   BRITISH

B

Victoria   Bellingham   NORTH CASCADES NAT. PARK
  Esquimalt   Mt. Baker   Omak   Oroville   Grand Forks
Port Angeles   Anacortes   Oak Hbr.   Sedro Woolley   Winthrop   Okanogan   Tonasket   Republic   Kettle Falls
La Push   Port Townsend   Mount Vernon   Glacier Peak 3213   Chelan   Brewster   Colville
OLYMPIC   Mt. Olympus 2428   Everett   Darrington   Franklin D. Roosevelt L.   Newport
NAT. PARK   Snohomish   Coulee Dam   Deer Park   Post Falls

C

Ocean Park   SEATTLE   Leavenworth   Grand Coulee   Davenport   Spokane   Opportunity   Coeur d'Alene
Hoquiam   Bellevue   Chelan   Coulee City   Cheney   Rosalia
Aberdeen   Tacoma   Renton   Kent   Wenatchee   Columbia Basin
Grays Harbor   Olympia   Lacey   Ephrata   Moses Lake   Garfield   Oakesdale
Westport   Tumwater   Enumclaw   WASHINGTON   Quincy   Othello Land   Colfax   Pullman   Moscow

46

Long Beach   Raymond   Centralia   Chehalis   Ellensburg   HANFORD REACH   Connell
Ocean City   Toledo   Yakima   Selah   Clarkston   Lewiston
Astoria   Kelso   Mt. St.   Union Gap   Wapato   Richland   Waitsburg   Winchester
Seaside   St. Helens   Helens   Toppenish   Kennewick   Pasco   Walla Walla

D

PORTLAND   Battle Ground   Grandview   Prosser   Milton-Freewater   HELLS CANYON NAT. REC. AREA
Tillamook   Hillsboro   Vancouver   Hood River   The Dalles   Hermiston   Weston   Enterprise
  Beaverton   Gresham   Cascade Locks   Wasco   Arlington   Pendleton   Elgin
  McMinnville   Newberg   Oregon City   Mt. Hood 3427   Pilot Rock
Newport   Dallas   Salem   Keizer   Woodburn   Maupin   Condon   Heppner   La Grande   Wallowa
  Philomath   Albany   Stayton   Mt. Jefferson 3199   Madras   Grass Valley   North Powder   Wallowa Mts.
  Corvallis   Lebanon   Candon   Fossil   Baker City

E

Florence   Junction City   Sweet Home   JOHN DAY FOSSIL BEDS   John Day   Haines
  Eugene   McKenzie   Sisters   NAT. MON.   Mitchell   Dayville   Prairie City   Huntington
North Bend   Springfield   Sister 3159   Redmond   Prineville   Spray   Brogan   Council
Coos Bay   Cottage Grove   Bend   O R E G O N   Seneca   Ontario   Payette
Coquille   Drain   Oakridge   NEWBERRY   Brothers   Juntura   Nyssa   Eagle
Myrtle Point   Sutherlin   La Pine   NAT. VOLCANIC MON.   Harney Basin   Crane   Caldwell   Nampa   Meridian
Cape Blanco   Roseburg   Chemult   Silver Lake   Riley   Malheur L.   Murphy   Boise
Port Orford   Myrtle Creek   SILVER LAKE   Harney L.   Burns   Mountain
Gold Beach   Canyonville   Crater Lake   Summer L.   Steens Mountain 2962   Jordan Valley   Bruneau

F

Brookings   Grants Pass   White City   CRATER LAKE NAT. PARK   Paisley   Alvord Desert
SMITH RIVER NAT. REC. AREA   Central Point   Mt. McLoughlin 2894   Fort Klamath   Summer Lake
Crescent City   Medford   Talent   Klamath Falls   Valley Falls   Lakeview   McDermitt   Owyhee
REDWOOD NAT. PARK   Ashland   Altamont   Merrill   Winnemucca   Santa Rosa Range   Elko
  Hornbrook   Dorris   Clear Lake   Warner Mts.   Paradise Valley   Spring Creek
Klamath   Yreka   Tulelake   LAVA BEDS NAT. MON.   Adel   Golconda   Dunphy   Carlin

CALIFORNIA   Weed   McCloud   Canby   Alturas   Middle Alkali L.   Battle Mountain   Ruby Mts.
McKinleyville   Mt. Shasta   Bieber   Lower Alkali L.   Winnemucca   Diamond Mts.
Eureka   Thompson   Burney   Eagle L.   Black Rock Desert   Gerlach   Lovelock
Fortuna   Redding   Shasta L.   LASSEN VOLCANIC NAT. PARK   Honey L.   Trinity Range   Austin
Scotia   Anderson   Lassen Peak   Susanville   Gabbs

G

Garberville   Red Bluff   Westwood   Greenville   Carson Sink   Stillwater Ra.   Toiyabe Ra.
Daytonville   Corning   Paradise   Quincy   Wadsworth   Fernley   Fallon   Mt. Jefferson 3642
Ft. Bragg   Willits   Orland   Chico   Portola   Truckee   Reno   Sparks   N E V A D A   Shoshone Mountains   Hot Creek Ra.
Mendocino   Ukiah   Oroville   Yuba City   Nevada City   Virginia City   Carson City   Yerington   Currant
Pt. Arena   Lakeport   Marysville   Grass Valley   Carson   South Lake Tahoe   Schurz   Walker L.   Luning
Cloverdale   Clearlake   Olivehurst   Auburn   Mt. Grant 3428   Hawthorne
Healdsburg   Calistoga   Woodland   Roseville   El Dorado Camino   Jackson   San Andreas
Windsor   St. Helena   Davis   SACRAMENTO   Lodi
Santa Rosa   Napa   Vacaville   Arden-Arcade   Elk Grove
Petaluma   Vallejo   Concord   Galt
San Rafael   Berkeley   Richmond
POINT REYES NAT. SEASHORE   San Francisco   Golden Gate

⊞ ⊛ State Capitals

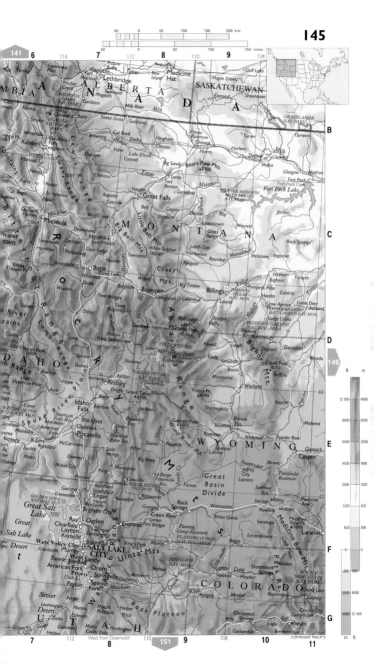

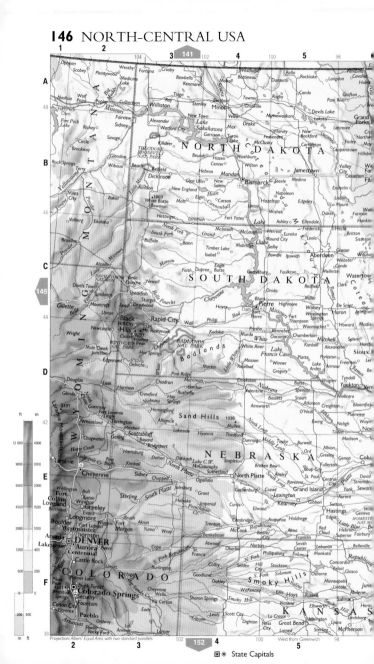

Projection: Albers' Equal Area with two standard parallels

West from Greenwich

⊠ ⊛ State Capitals

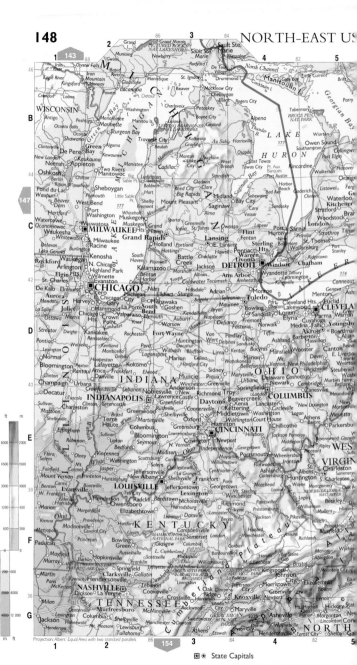

Thurso Lachute
Fort Pembroke Buckingham St-Hyacinthe Sherbrooke
Coulonge Gatineau Rockland MONTREAL Longueuil Granby Magog Coaticook
Renfrew Hull Salaberry-de-Valleyfield St-Jean- Newport Island Pond B
OTTAWA CORNWALL Richelieu St. Albans Groveton
Carleton Smiths Falls Prescott Massena Malone Plattsburgh Lancaster Berlin
Place Ogdensburg Dannemora Champlain Whitefield
Brockville Potsdam Burlington Montpelier Lebanon Laconia Rochester C
Kingston Napanee Clayton Long Gouverneur Saranac Lake Barre Hanover Concord Dover
Belleville Lake Tupper Lake Randolph Manchester
Picton Watertown Lake Ticonderoga George Rutland Claremont Nashua Haverhill
Cobourg ADIRONDACK Lake Glens Keene Lawrence
Port Hope LAKE ONTARIO Pulaski PARK Falls Bennington Fitchburg Lowell C. Ann
TORONTO Oswego Rome Saratoga Sp. Greenfield Leominster Lynn Cambridge
Niagara Falls ROCHESTER Fulton Utica Amsterdam Northampton Worcester Newton BOSTON
Lockport Oneida Schenectady Pittsfield MASS Quincy Brockton
BUFFALO Seneca Geneseo Syracuse Johnstown ALBANY Chicopee Holyoke Woonsocket Taunton CAPE COD
Hamburg NEW YORK Auburn Cortland Oneonta Catskill Springfield HARTFORD PROVIDENCE Fall River New Bedford
Gowanda Ithaca Cooperstown Kingston New Britain CONN R.I. Newport Nantucket
Salamanca Olean Wellsville Corning Elmira Binghamton Sidney Middletown Danbury Waterbury New London Martha's Vineyard
Jamestown Bradford Williamsport Scranton Wilkes-Barre Stroudsburg Hazleton Newton New Haven Long Island Montauk
Oil City Coudersport Milton Bloomsburg Easton Patterson E. Orange Bridgeport Norwalk Southampton
PENNSYLVANIA Bethlehem Allentown NEWARK NEW YORK Riverhead D
Indiana State College Harrisburg Reading Pottstown Princeton Perth Amboy Freeport Levittown
PITTSBURGH Johnstown Holidaysburg Lancaster PHILADELPHIA Trenton NEW JERSEY ATLANTIC
Chambersburg Gettysburg York Norristown Willingboro OCEAN
Uniontown Hagerstown Frederick Westminster Upper Darby Camden E
Cumberland Hanover Wilmington Vineland Pleasantville
Martinsburg Rockville Aberdeen DELAWARE Atlantic City
BALTIMORE Dundalk Dover Ocean City
Winchester MARYLAND Annapolis Easton Milford North Wildwood
Front Royal Arlington Cambridge Cape May
WASHINGTON Alexandria Salisbury Berlin
Harrisonburg Culpeper D.C. Dale City Charles Lewes Delaware Bay
Staunton Fredericksburg Orange Colonial Salisbury Chincoteague
Waynesboro Charlottesville Ashland Beach Pocomoke City ASSATEAGUE ISLAND NAT. SEASHORE
VIRGINIA West Onancock Accomac
Lynchburg Buena Point F
Lexington Vista Heights RICHMOND Williamsburg Gloucester Cape Charles
Roanoke Altavista Hopewell Newport News Hampton Cape Charles
Blackstone Petersburg Portsmouth Virginia
South Boston Danville Emporia Franklin NORFOLK Beach Chesapeake
Eden Roxboro Murfreesboro Suffolk
Greensboro Oxford Henderson Roanoke Rapids Elizabeth City Albemarle Sd.
Burlington Wake Edenton
Durham Forest Rocky Mount Williamston CAPE HATTERAS G
Thomasville Chapel Hill Wilson NAT. SEASHORE
Asheboro RALEIGH Bethel
CAROLINA Sanford Goldsboro Greenville Pamlico Sound
Smithfield Kinston New Bern CAPE HATTERAS

50 0 50 100 150 200 km
50 0 50 100 150 miles

155 6 West from Greenwich 7

Edmundston
CANADA
St-Leonard
Fort Grand A
Kent Falls
Eagle Van
Lake Buren
Fort Andover
Fort Fairfield Island
Eagle L. Presque Isle Ashland Mars Hill Woodstock
Chesuncook Houlton B
BAXTER
STATE PARK
Chamberlain Patten
L. Mt. Katahdin Chesuncook L. Millinocket
Moosehead Sherman
L. Mills Lincoln
Flagstaff Greenville Dover- West C
L. Foxcroft Lincoln Grand
MAINE Milo Lake
Bingham Dover Old Town
Rangeley Skowhegan Orono Calais
Moosehead Farmington Pittsfield Bangor Brewer
NEW Mexico Waterville Woodland D
HAMPSHIRE Rumford Belfast Ellsworth
Mt. Washington Norway Augusta Mt. Desert I.
Groveton Berlin Auburn Gardiner Camden ACADIA NAT. PARK
Lisbon Falls Bath Rockland Machias
LEWISTON Bad
Laconia Brunswick
Sanford Saco Portland Casco B. 44
Rochester Biddeford
Dover Kittery Gulf of
Portsmouth Maine
Newburyport 68 12

continuation
eastwards
on same scale

COPYRIGHT PHILIP'S

☒ ☀ State Capitals

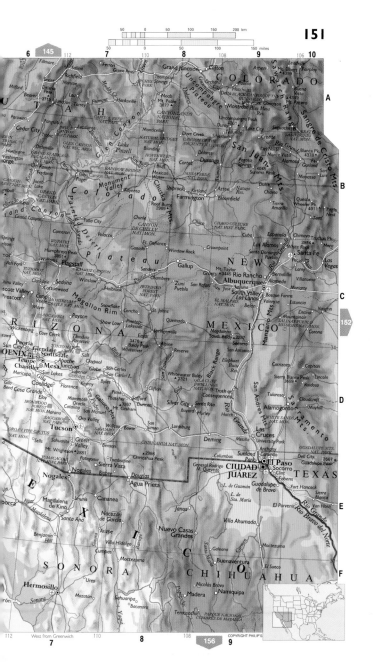

State Capitals

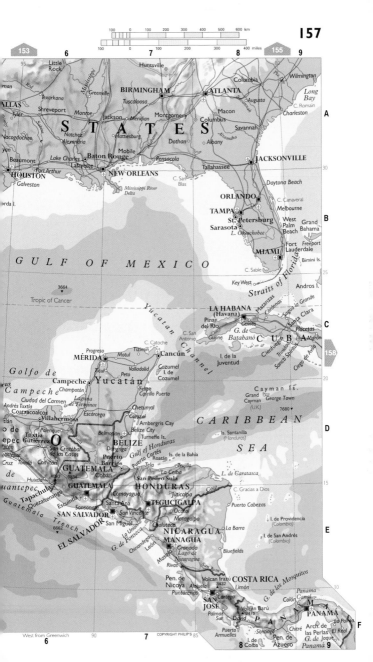

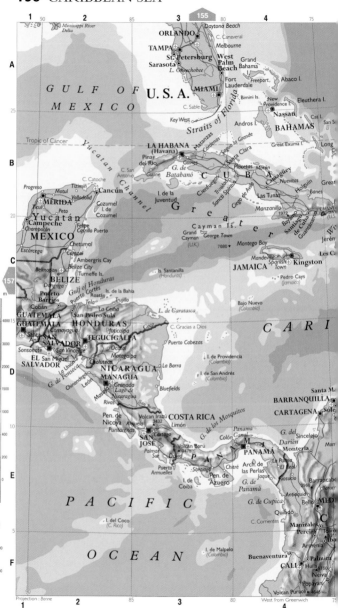

157

1 90 **2** 85 **3** 80 **4** 75

GULF OF U.S.A.

MEXICO

Mississippi River Delta

ORLANDO
TAMPA
St. Petersburg
Sarasota
L. Okeechobee
C. Canaveral
Melbourne
West
Palm
Beach
Fort
Lauderdale
Daytona Beach
Grand
Bahama
Freeport·
Abaco I.

MIAMI
C. Sable
Key West
Bimini Is.
New
Providence I.
Eleuthera I.
Nassau
BAHAMAS
Andros I.
Cat I.
San S

Straits of Florida

Tropic of Cancer

Yucatan Channel

Progreso
Motul
Tizimín
Valladolid
MÉRIDA
Ticul
Peto
Yucatán
Champotón
Campeche
MEXICO
Escárcega
Chetumal
C. Catoche
C. San
Antonio
Cancún
Cozumel
I. de
Cozumel

LA HABANA
(Havana)
Pinar
del Río
Güines
Matanzas
Cárdenas
Sagua la Grande
Santa Clara
Placetas
Morón
CUBA
Camagüey
Nuevitas
G. de
Batabanó
Cienfuegos
Trinidad
Sancti Spíritus
Ciego de Ávila
Las Tunas
Holguín
Bones
Manzanillo
1972
Bayam
Santiago
de Cuba
Guantán
Great Exuma I.
Long

Greater

I. de la
Juventud

Felipe
Carrillo Puerto
Ambergris Cay
Belmopán
Corozal
Belize City
BELIZE
Dangriga
Puerto
Barrios
Cobán

Cayman Is.
Grand
Cayman
George Town
(U.K.)
7680
Montego Bay
Mandeville
Spanish
Town
JAMAICA
Kingston
Pedro Cays
(Jamaica)

Is. Santanilla
(Honduras)

GUATEMALA
GUATEMALA
Comayagua
San
Vincente
SAN
SALVADOR
EL
SALVADOR
Sonsonate
San Miguel
La Unión
Gulf of Honduras
Puerto Cortés
Roatán
Is. de la Bahía
La Ceiba
San Pedro Sula
HONDURAS
TEGUCIGALPA
Juticalpa
Ocotal
Choluteca
G. de Fonseca
Tela
Trujillo
L. de Caratasca
C. Gracias a Dios
Puerto Cabezas

CARI

15

Santa M

BARRANQUILLA
CARTAGENA
Sole

NICARAGUA
MANAGUA
Granada
Lago de
Nicaragua
Rivas
León
Masaya
Bluefields
La Barra
I. de Providencia
(Colombia)
I. de San Andrés
(Colombia)

Bajo Nuevo
(Colombia)

10

Pen. de
Nicoya
Puntarenas
Volcán Irazú
3432
COSTA RICA
Limón
Cartago
SAN
JOSÉ
Palmar
Sur
Volcán Barú
3477
David
Puerto
Armuelles
I. de
Coiba
Santiago
Chitré
Pen. de
Azuero
G. de
Panamá
PANAMÁ
Colón
Panamá
Canal
Arch. de
las Perlas
Jaqué
La Palma
El Real
Riosucio
G. del
Darién
Sincelejo
Montería
G. de los Mosquitos
Bello
MED
Manizales
Pereira
Armenia
Quibdó
C. Corrientes
Antioquia
Yarumal
Barrancabe
G. de Cupica

PACIFIC

I. del Coco
(C. Rica)
I. de Malpelo
(Colombia)

Buenaventura
CALI
Palmira
Huila
Neiva
Popayán
Volcán Puracé 4646

OCEAN

1 90 **2** 85 **3** 80 **4** West from Greenwich 75

ft   m
12 000 4000
9000   3000
6000   2000
4500   1500
3000   1000
1200   400
600   200
0   0
200   600
2000   6000
4000 12 000
4000 18 000
m   ft

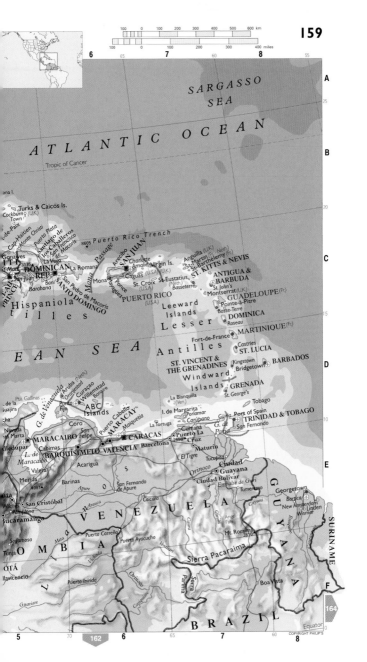

100 0 100 200 300 400 500 600 km
100 0 100 200 300 400 miles

6 7 8

A

SARGASSO SEA

ATLANTIC OCEAN

B

Tropic of Cancer

ana I.

Turks & Caicos Is.
Cockburn (U.K.)
Town

-de-Paix
Cap-Haitien
Monte Christi
Puerto Plata
Santiago de
los Caballeros
San Francisco
de Macorís
La Vega
Gonaïves
La Romana
Mars
DOMINICAN
REP.
San Juan
Bani
San Pedro de Macorís
Barahona
SANTO DOMINGO

8605 Puerto Rico Trench

SAN JUAN
Arecibo
Charlotte
Amalie
Caguas
Ponce
St. Croix
(U.S.A.)
Virgin Is.
(U.S.A.)(U.K.)

Anguilla (U.K.)
St. Martin (Neth.)
St. Barthélemy (Fr.)
ST. KITTS & NEVIS
St-Eustatius,
(Neth.)
Basseterre
ANTIGUA &
BARBUDA
St. John's
Montserrat(U.K.)
GUADELOUPE(Fr.)
Pointe-à-Pitre
Basse-Terre
DOMINICA
Roseau

C

Mona
Mayagüez
PUERTO RICO
(U.S.A.)

Hispaniola
t i l l e s

Leeward
Islands
Lesser

Mona
Passage

MARTINIQUE(Fr.)
Fort-de-France

EAN SEA

Antilles
Castries
ST. LUCIA

D

ST. VINCENT &
THE GRENADINES
Windward
Islands
Kingstown
Bridgetown
BARBADOS

GRENADA
St. George's
Tobago

Pta. Gallinas
de la
Guajira
cha

Aruba (Neth.)
Oranjestad
Curaçao
Willemstad
Bonaire
ABC
Islands

Punto
Fijo

La Blanquilla
(Ven.)
I. de Margarita
Porlamar
La Tortuga
Caripano
Güiria
Port of Spain
San Fernando
TRINIDAD & TOBAGO
G. de
Paria

E

Nevada
nt Marta
Bleduper

San
Coro
Felipe
Puerto Cabello
Maiquetía
MARACAY
VENEZUELA(Neth.)
G. de

MARACAIBO
Cabimas
BARQUISIMETO VALENCIA
L. de
Maracaibo
Valera
Mérida
4981
Barinas

CARACAS
Barcelona
Maturín
El Tigre
Tucupita
Ciudad
Guayana
Ciudad Bolívar
Embalse de Guri
Cumaná
Puerto La
Cruz
2594

Cumaná

Georgetown

SURINAME

ata
San Cristóbal
Wilches
Pamplona
Bucaramanga

Apure
San Fernando
de Apure
Caicara

Orinoco
Tumeremo

G U Y A N A

Bartica
New Amsterdam
Linden
Wismar

Sogamoso
Tunja
O M B I A
OTÁ
llavicencio

Meta
Puerto Carreño
Arauca

Puerto Ayacucho

Caura
Mt. Roraima
2810
Sierra Pacaraima

Cuyuni

Essequibo

Guainía
Puerto Inírida

Orinoco
Vichada

Guaviare

Ventuari

Parima
Sierra
Parima

Boa Vista

B R A Z I L

Equator

164

F

COPYRIGHT PHILIP'S

5 162 6 7 60 8

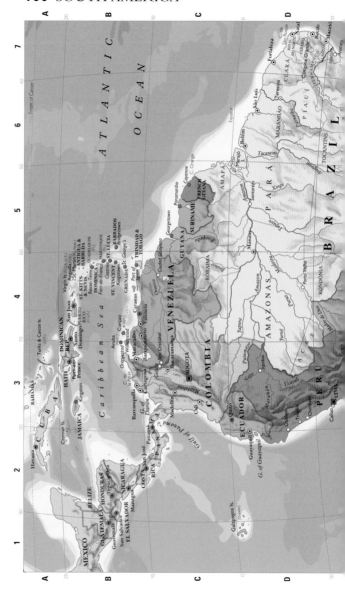

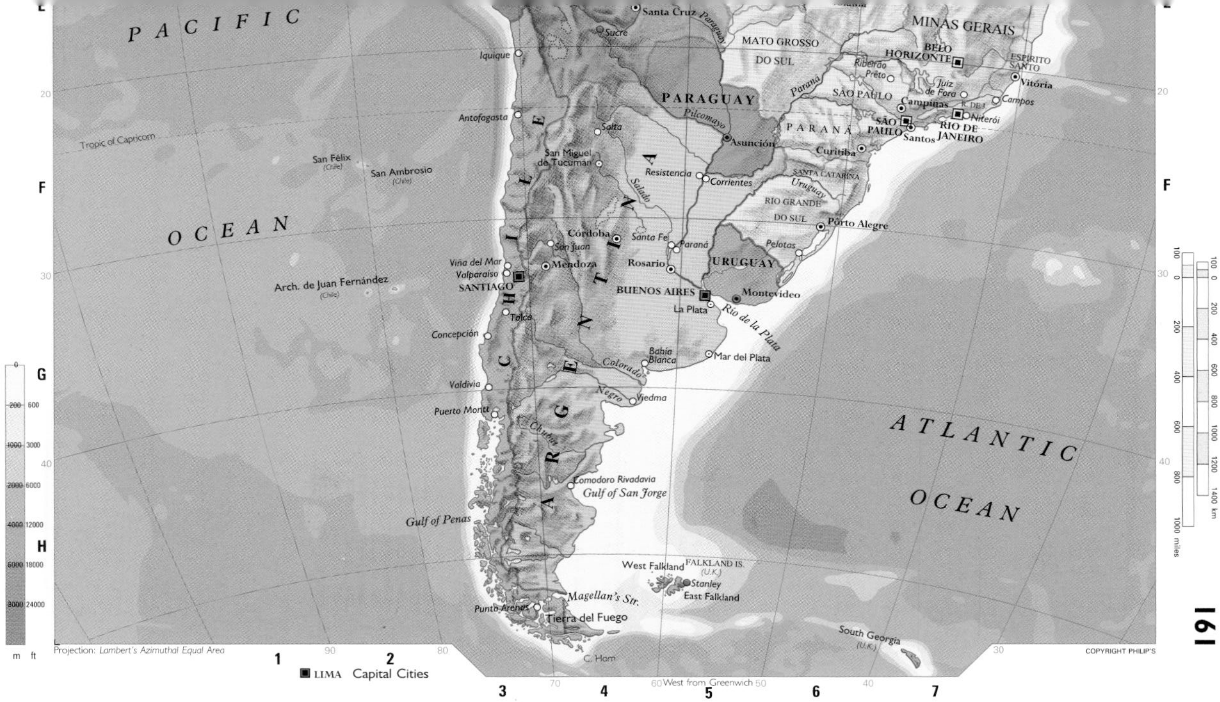

100 0 200 400 600 800 1000 1200 1400 km

100 0 200 400 600 800 1000 miles

COPYRIGHT PHILIP'S

F

20

30

40

PACIFIC OCEAN

ATLANTIC OCEAN

Tropic of Capricorn

MINAS GERAIS

ESPÍRITO SANTO

Vitória

Campos

BELO HORIZONTE

Rio Doce

Niterói

RIO DE JANEIRO

SÃO PAULO

Santos

Juiz de Fora

Paraíba

MATO GROSSO DO SUL

PARANÁ

SANTA CATARINA

Paranaguá

Curitiba

Ponta Grossa

Paraná

RIO GRANDE DO SUL

Pôrto Alegre

Santa Cruz (Paraguay)

Sucre

PARAGUAY

ASUNCIÓN

Pilcomayo

URUGUAY

Uruguay

Corrientes

Resistencia

Salta

Santa Fé

Paraná

Montevideo

Río de la Plata

BUENOS AIRES

La Plata

Mar del Plata

San Miguel de Tucumán

Salado

Córdoba

San Juan

Rosario

Pelotas

Iquique

Antofagasta

San Félix (Chile)

San Ambrosio (Chile)

Arch. de Juan Fernández (Chile)

Mendoza

Viña del Mar

Valparaíso

SANTIAGO

Concepción

Valdivia

Puerto Montt

Gulf of Penas

Bahía Blanca

Colorado

Negro

Viedma

Comodoro Rivadavia

Gulf of San Jorge

Trelew

Chubut

Tierra del Fuego

Punta Arenas

Magellan's Str.

C. Horn

West Falkland

FALKLAND IS. (U.K.)

Stanley

East Falkland

South Georgia (U.K.)

ARGENTINA

CHILE

60 West from Greenwich 50

40

30

20

LIMA Capital Cities

Projection: Lambert's Azimuthal Equal Area

m ft

6000 24000

4000 12000

3000 9000

2000 6000

1000 3000

600 1800

300 600

0

G **H**

1 **2** **3** **4** **5** **6** **7**

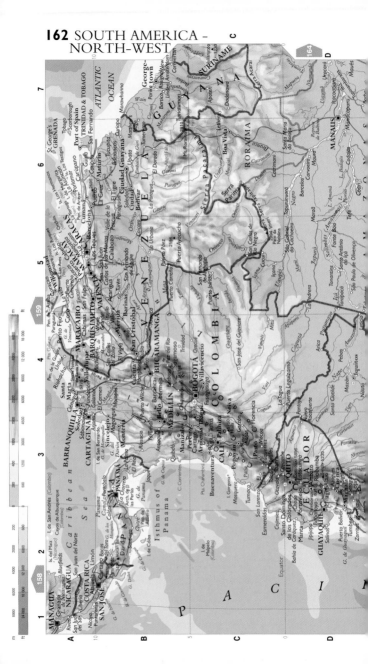

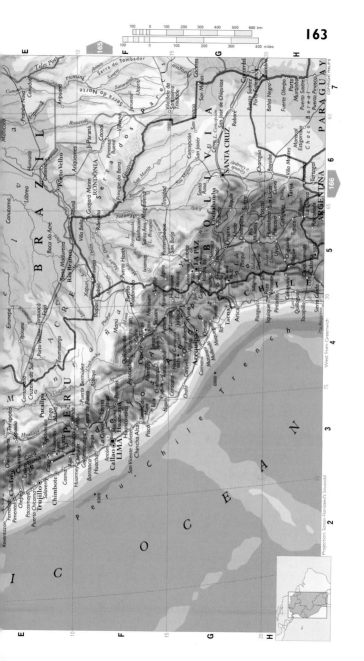

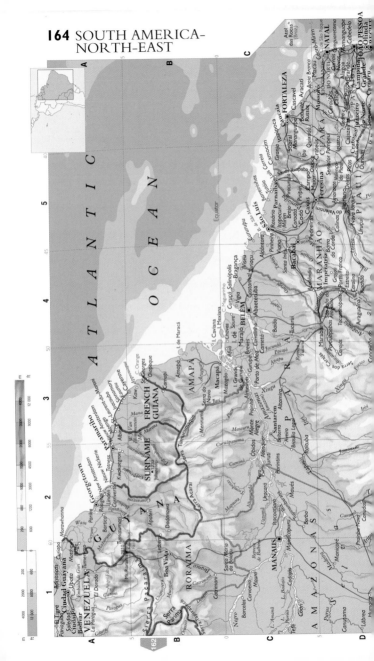

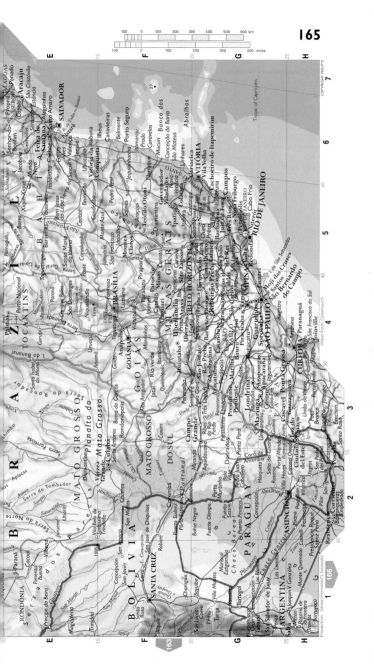

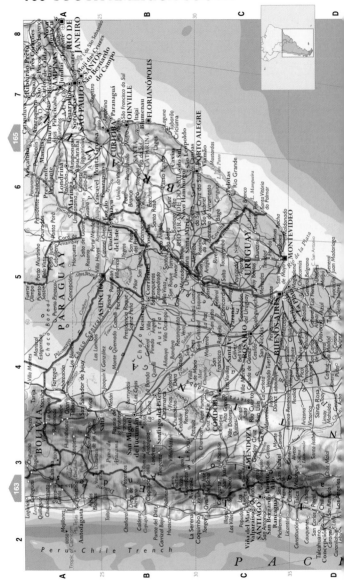

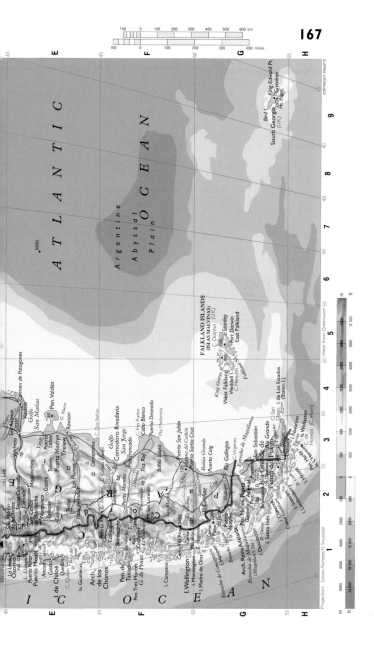

167

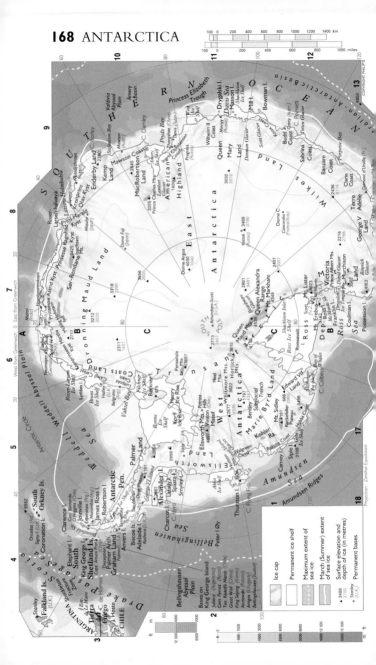

100 0   200   400   600   800   1000 1200 1400 km
100 0   200   400   600   800   1000 miles

COPYRIGHT PHILIP'S

Ice cap

Permanent ice shelf

Maximum extent of
sea ice

March (Summer) extent
of sea ice

▲ 3488 Surface elevation and
  3700   depth of ice (in metres)

★ Stanley Permanent bases
  (U.K.)

Projection: Zenithal Equidistant

Index to Map Pages

The index contains the names of all principal places and features shown on the world maps. Physical features composed of a proper name (Erie) and a description (Lake) are positioned alphabetically by the proper name. The description is positioned after the proper name and is usually abbreviated:

Erie, L. **148 C5**

Where a description forms part of a settlement or administrative name, however, it is always written in full and put in its true alphabetical position:

Lake Charles **153 D7**

Names beginning St. are alphabetized under Saint, but Sankt, Sant, Santa and San are all spelt in full and are alphabetized accordingly.

The number in bold type which follows each name in the index refers to the number of the map page where that feature or place will be found. This is usually the largest scale at which the place or feature appears.

The letter and figure which are in bold type immediately after the page number give the grid square on the map page, within which the feature is situated.

Rivers are indexed to their mouths or confluences, and carry the symbol ➔ after their names. The following symbols are also used in the index: ■ country, ☑ overseas territory or dependency, ☐ first order administrative area, △ national park, ◠ regional park.

A

A Coruña **86 A1**
A Estrada **86 A1**
A Fonsagrada **86 A2**
Aachen **80 C4**
Aalborg **77 D7**
Aalen **80 D6**
Aarhus **77 D8**
Aba **127 G7**
Abaco I. **158 A4**
Ābādān **119 E7**
Ābādeh **116 D3**
Abadla **126 B5**
Abaetetuba **164 C4**
Abancay **163 F4**
Abarqū **116 D3**
Abashiri **100 A9**
Abashiri-Wan **100 B9**
Abay **97 E8**
Abaya, L. **129 C7**
Abbeville **88 A4**
Abbot Ice Shelf **168 B2**
ABC Islands **159 D6**
Abd al Kūrī **121 E5**
Abéché **125 F3**
Abel Tasman △ **136 D5**
Abeokuta **127 G6**
Abercorn **135 A5**
Aberdeen *Australia*
  135 B5
Aberdeen *U.K.* **78 C5**
Aberdeen *S. Dak., U.S.A.*
  146 C5
Aberdeen *Wash., U.S.A.*
  144 C2
Aberystwyth **79 E4**
Abidjan **127 G5**
Abilene **152 C4**
Abitibi, L. **143 E6**
Abkhazia ☐ **85 E5**
Abminga **134 A1**
Abohar **114 D9**
Abomey **127 G6**
Abong-Mbang **128 D2**
Abou-Deïa **125 F2**
Absaroka Range **145 D9**
Abū 'Alī **119 F7**
Abu Dhabi = Abū Ẓaby
  116 E3
Abu Hamed **125 E5**
Abū Kamāl **118 D5**
Abū Madd, Ra's **119 F4**
Abu Zabad **125 F4**
Abū Ẓāby **116 E3**
Abuja **127 G7**
Abunã **163 E5**
Abunã ➔ **163 E5**
Abut Hd. **137 E4**
Acaponeta **156 C3**
Acapulco **156 D5**
Acarigua **162 B5**

Aberdeen *U.K.* **78 C5**
Aceh ☐ **110 D1**
Achalpur **115 J10**
Acharnes **93 E4**
Acheloos ➔ **93 E3**
Achill I. **79 E1**
Achinsk **98 D7**
Acireale **91 F5**
Acklins I. **158 B5**
Aconcagua, Cerro
  166 C3
Aconquija, Mt. **166 B3**
Açores, Is. dos **122 C1**
Acraman, L. **134 B2**
Acre ☐ **163 E4**
Acre ➔ **163 E5**
Ad Dahnā **119 F7**
Ad Dammām **119 F7**
Ad Dawādimī **119 F6**
Ad Dawḥah **116 E2**
Ad Dilam **119 G6**
Ad Dīwānīyah **119 E6**
Ada **153 B5**
Adair, C. **142 B6**
Adaja ➔ **86 B3**
Adam **116 F4**
Adamaoua, Massif de l'
  125 G1
Adamawa Highlands =
  Adamaoua, Massif de l'
  125 G1

Accra **127 G5**
Adamello, Mte. **90 A3**
Adaminaby **135 C4**
Adams, Mt. **144 C3**
Adam's Bridge **115 Q11**
'Adan **121 E4**
Adana **118 C3**
Adarama **125 E5**
Adare, C. **168 B15**
Adaut **109 F4**
Adavale **135 A3**
Adda ➔ **90 B2**
Addis Abeba **121 F2**
Adelaide **134 B2**
Adelaide I. **168 A3**
Adelaide Pen. **140 B10**
Adélie, Terre **168 A14**
Aden = 'Adan **121 E4**
Aden, G. of **121 E4**
Adi **109 E4**
Adige ➔ **90 B4**
Adilabad **115 K11**
Adirondack Mts. **149 C8**
Admiralty I. **140 C6**
Admiralty Is. **136 K9**
Adonara **109 F2**
Adoni **115 M10**
Adour ➔ **88 E3**
Adra **86 D4**
Adrano **91 F5**
Adrar **126 D6**
Adrar des Iforas **126 E6**

Adriatic Sea 90 C5
Adua 109 E3
Ægean Sea 93 E5
Aerhtai Shan 102 B6
Afghanistan ■ 117 C6
'Afīf 119 G5
Afuá 164 C3
Afyon 118 C2
Agadez 127 E7
Agadir 126 B4
Agartala 113 F8
Agats 109 F5
Agboville 127 G5
Agde 89 E5
Agen 88 D4
Aghios Efstratios 93 E5
Aghiou Orous, Kolpos
  93 D5
Agra 114 F10
Ağri 85 F5
Agri → 91 D6
Ağri Daği 118 C6
Agrigento 91 F4
Agrinio 93 E3
Água Clara 165 G3
Agua Prieta 156 A3
Aguarico → 162 D3
Aguas Blancas 166 A3
Águilas 87 D5
Agulhas, C. 130 E4
Agung, Gunung 111 F5
Agusan → 108 C3
Ahaggar 126 D7
Ahar 118 C6
Ahipara B. 136 A5
Ahiri 115 K12
Ahmadabad 115 H8
Ahmadnagar 115 K9
Ahmadpur East 114 E7
Ahvāz 119 E7
Ahvenanmaa = Åland
  77 C10
Aḥwar 121 E4
Aigues-Mortes 89 E6
Aija 163 E3
Aikawa 101 D6
Aiken 155 C7
Aïn Ben Tili 126 C4
Aïn Sefra 126 B5
Aïr 127 E7
Air Force I. 142 C6
Aisne → 89 B5
Aitutaki 137 L14
Aix-en-Provence 89 E6
Aix-la-Chapelle = Aachen
  80 C4
Aix-les-Bains 89 D6
Aizawl 113 F9
Aizuwakamatsu 101 E6
Ajaccio 89 F8
Ajanta Ra. 115 J9

Ajaria □ 85 E5
Ajdābiyā 124 B3
Ajka 82 E3
'Ajmān 116 E3
Ajmer 114 F9
Ajo, C. de 86 A4
Akaroa 137 E5
Akelamo 109 D3
Aketi 128 D4
Akhisar 93 E6
Akimiski I. 143 D5
Akita 100 D7
Akjoujt 127 E3
Akkeshi 100 B9
'Akko 118 D3
Aklavik 140 B6
Akola 115 J10
Akordat 129 A7
Akpatok I. 142 C7
Akranes 76 C1
Akron 148 D5
Aksai Chin 114 B11
Aksaray 118 C3
Akşehir 118 C2
Aksu 102 C4
Aktsyabrski 83 B9
Akure 127 G5
Akureyri 76 B2
Al Amādīyah 118 C5
Al 'Amārah 119 E6
Al 'Aqabah 119 E3
Al 'Aramah 119 F6
Al Ashkhara 117 F4
Al Badī' 119 G6
Al Başrah 119 E6
Al Baydā 124 B3
Al Fadīlī 119 E7
Al Fallūjah 118 D5
Al Fāw 119 E7
Al Fujayrah 116 E4
Al Ḥaddār 119 G6
Al Hāmad 119 E4
Al Ḥamar 119 G6
Al Ḥamrā' 119 F4
Al Ḥarīq 119 G6
Al Ḥasakah 118 C5
Al Ḥayy 119 D6
Al Ḥillah Iraq 119 D6
Al Ḥillah Si. Arabia
  119 G6
Al Hoceïma 126 A5
Al Ḥudaydah 121 E3
Al Hufūf 119 F7
Al Ḥulwah 119 G6
Al Jāfūrah 119 F7
Al Jaghbūb 124 C3
Al Jahrah 119 E6
Al Jalāmīd 119 E4
Al Jawf Libya 124 D3
Al Jawf Si. Arabia 119 E4
Al Jazirah 118 D5
Al Jubayl 119 F7

Al Jubaylah 119 F6
Al Junaynah 125 F3
Al Khābūrah 116 F4
Al Khalīl 119 E3
Al Kharsānīyah 119 F7
Al Khaṣab 116 E4
Al Kufrah 124 D3
Al Kūt 119 D6
Al Kuwayt 119 E7
Al Lādhiqīyah 118 D3
Al Luḥayyah 121 D3
Al Madīnah 119 F4
Al Majma'ah 119 F6
Al Manāmah 116 E2
Al Marj 124 B3
Al Mawṣil 118 C5
Al Midhnab 119 F6
Al Mubarraz 119 F7
Al Muḥarraq 116 E2
Al Mukallā 121 E4
Al Mukhā 121 E3
Al Musayyib 119 D6
Al Muwaylih 119 F3
Al Qadimah 119 G4
Al Qā'iyah 119 F5
Al Qāmishlī 118 C5
Al Qaṣim 119 F5
Al Qaṭīf 119 F7
Al Qaṭrūn 124 D2
Al Qurayyāt 117 F4
Al Qurnah 119 E6
Al 'Ulā 119 F4
Al 'Uqayr 119 F7
Al 'Uwaynid 119 F6
Al 'Uwayqīlah 119 E5
Al 'Uyūn 119 F5
Al Wakrah 116 E2
Alabama □ 154 C4
Alabama → 154 D4
Alaçam Dağları 93 E7
Alagoa Grande 164 D6
Alagoas □ 165 D6
Alagoinhas 165 E6
Alajuela 158 D3
Alamosa 151 B10
Åland 77 C10
Alanya 118 C2
Alapayevsk 97 D7
Alappuzha 115 Q10
Alaşehir 93 E7
Alaska □ 141 B4
Alaska, G. of 141 C5
Alaska Peninsula 141 C4
Alaska Range 141 B4
Alatyr 84 C6
Alausi 162 D3
Alawoona 134 B3
Alba 90 B2
Albacete 87 C5
Albacutya, L. 134 C3
Albanel, L. 143 D6
Albania ■ 93 D3

Albany Australia 132 H2
Albany Ga., U.S.A.
  155 D5
Albany N.Y., U.S.A.
  149 C9
Albany Oreg., U.S.A.
  144 D2
Albany → 143 D5
Albardón 166 C3
Albemarle 155 B7
Alberche → 86 C4
Alberga → 134 A2
Albert, L. Africa 129 D6
Albert, L. Australia
  134 C2
Albert Nile → 129 D6
Albertville 89 D7
Albi 88 E5
Albina 164 A3
Alborán 86 E4
Ålborg = Aalborg 77 D7
Alborz, Reshteh-ye
  Kūhhā-ye 116 B3
Albuquerque 151 C9
Albury 135 C4
Alcalá de Henares 86 B4
Alcalá la Real 86 D4
Álcamo 91 F4
Alcañiz 87 B5
Alcántara 164 C5
Alcántara, Embalse de
  86 C2
Alcantarilla 87 D5
Alcaraz, Sierra de 87 C4
Alcaudete 86 D3
Alcázar de San Juan
  86 C4
Alchevsk 85 D4
Alcoy 87 C5
Aldabra Is. 123 G8
Aldan → 99 C10
Alderney 79 G5
Aleg 127 E3
Alegrete 166 C1
Alençon 88 B4
Aleppo = Ḥalab 118 C4
Alert 142 A7
Alès 89 D6
Alessándria 90 B2
Ålesund 76 C7
Aleutian Is. 141 C2
Alexander Arch. 141 C6
Alexander I. 168 A3
Alexandra Australia
  135 C4
Alexandra N.Z. 137 F3
Alexandria = El
  Iskandarîya 124 B4
Alexandria Romania
  92 C5
Alexandria La., U.S.A.
  153 D7

Alexandria *Va., U.S.A.* 149 E7
Alexandrina, L. 134 C2
Alexandroupoli 92 D5
Aleysk 97 D9
Algarve 86 D1
Algeciras 86 D3
Algemesí 87 C5
Alger 126 A6
Algeria ■ 126 C6
Algha 97 E6
Alghero 91 D2
Algiers = Alger 126 A6
Algorta 87 A4
'Alī al Gharbī 119 D6
'Alī Khēl 114 C6
Aliağa 93 E6
Alicante 87 C5
Alice Springs 132 E5
Aligarh 114 F11
Alīgūdarz 118 D7
Alipur 114 E7
Alipur Duar 113 D7
Aliwal North 131 E5
Aljustrel 86 D1
Alkmaar 80 B3
All American Canal 150 D5
Allahabad 112 E3
Allegheny → 149 D5
Allegheny Mts. 149 F5
Allentown 149 D8
Aller → 80 B5
Allier → 89 C5
Allora 135 A5
Alma Ata = Almaty 97 E8
Almada 86 C1
Almadén 86 C3
Almansa 87 C5
Almanzor, Pico 86 B3
Almanzora → 87 D5
Almaty 97 E8
Almazán 87 B4
Almeirim 164 C3
Almelo 80 B4
Almendralejo 86 C2
Almería 87 D4
Almora 114 E11
Alnwick 78 D6
Alon 113 F10
Alor 109 F2
Alor Setar 110 C2
Alps 80 E5
Alsace □ 89 B7
Alsasua 87 A4
Alta Gracia 166 C4
Altai = Aerhtai Shan 102 B2
Altamira 164 C3
Altamura 91 D6
Altanbulag 103 A9
Altay 102 B5

Altea 87 C5
Altiplano 163 G5
Alto Araguaia 165 F3
Alto Molocue 131 B7
Alton 147 F9
Altoona 149 D6
Altun Shan 102 D5
Alusi 109 F4
Alvear 166 B5
Alwar 114 F10
Alxa Zuoqi 103 D9
Alzira 87 C5
Am Timan 125 F3
Amadi 125 G5
Amadjuak L. 142 C4
Amagasaki 101 F4
Amahai 109 E3
Amakusa-Shotō 101 G2
Amaliada 93 F3
Amalner 115 J9
Amambay, Cordillera de 166 A5
Amankeldi 97 D7
Amapá 164 B3
Amarante 164 D5
Amarillo 152 B3
Amaro, Mte. 90 C5
Amarpur 113 D7
Amasra 118 B3
Amazonas □ 162 D6
Amazonas → 164 C3
Ambala 114 D10
Ambalavao 131 C9
Ambanja 131 A9
Ambato 162 D3
Ambatolampy 131 B9
Ambatondrazaka 131 B9
Amberg 81 D6
Ambergris Cay 157 D7
Amberley 137 E5
Ambikapur 112 F4
Ambilobé 131 A9
Ambo 163 F3
Amboise 88 C4
Ambon 109 E3
Ambositra 131 C9
Ambovombe 131 D9
Amboyna Cay 110 C4
Ambriz 128 F2
Amchitka I. 141 C1
Amderma 96 C7
Ameca 156 C4
Ameland 80 B3
American Highland 168 B10
American Samoa ☑ 137 L13
Americus 155 C5
Amersfoort 80 B4
Amery Ice Shelf 168 A10
Ames 147 D8
Amherst 143 E7
Amiata, Mte. 90 C3
Amiens 88 B5

'Ammān 119 E3
Amorgos 93 F5
Amos 143 E6
Ampanihy 131 C8
Ampenan 111 F5
Amper → 81 D6
Amravati 115 J10
Amreli 115 J7
Amritsar 114 D9
Amroha 114 E11
Amsterdam 80 B3
Amstetten 81 D8
Amudarya → 97 E6
Amund Ringnes I. 142 B4
Amundsen Gulf 140 A7
Amundsen Sea 168 B1
Amuntai 111 E5
Amur → 99 D12
Amurang 109 D2
An Nafūd 119 E5
An Najaf 119 D6
An Nu'ayrīyah 119 F7
Anabar → 98 B9
Anaconda 145 C7
Anadolu 118 C2
'Ānah 118 D5
Anaheim 150 D4
Anakapalle 112 J4
Anambas, Kepulauan 111 D3
Anamur 118 C3
Anan 101 G4
Anantnag 114 C9
Ananyiv 87 D16
Anápolis 165 F4
Anār 116 D3
Anārak 116 C3
Añatuya 166 B4
Anchorage 141 B5
Anci 104 C2
Ancohuma, Nevado 163 G5
Ancón 163 F3
Ancona 90 C4
Ancud 167 E2
Ancud, G. de 167 E2
Andalgalá 166 B3
Andalucía □ 86 D3
Andalusia 154 D4
Andaman Is. 95 G11
Andaman Sea 110 B1
Andapa 131 A9
Anderson 148 D3
Anderson → 140 B7
Andes, Cord. de los 163 G4
Andhra Pradesh □ 115 M11
Andijon 97 E8
Andikhvoy 117 B6

Andoany 131 A9
Andorra ■ 87 A6
Andorra La Vella 87 A6
Andreanof Is. 141 C2
Ándria 90 D6
Andros 93 F5
Andros I. 158 B4
Andújar 86 C3
Andulo 128 G3
Aneto, Pico de 87 A6
Angara → 98 D7
Angarsk 98 D8
Angaston 134 B2
Ånge 76 C9
Angeles 108 A2
Ångermanälven → 76 C9
Angers 88 C3
Angledool 135 A4
Anglesey 79 E4
Ango 129 D5
Angoche 131 B7
Angola ■ 130 A3
Angoulême 88 D4
Angoumois 88 D4
Angren 97 E8
Anguilla ☑ 159 C7
Anhui □ 106 B4
Anjou 88 C3
Ankaboa, Tanjona 131 C8
Ankang 103 E9
Ankara 118 C3
Ankaratra 131 B9
Ann Arbor 148 D3
Annan 79 D5
Annapolis 149 E7
Annecy 89 D7
Anning 102 G8
Anniston 154 C5
Annobón 123 G4
Anqing 106 B4
Anshan 105 B5
Anshun 103 F9
Ansongo 127 E6
Ansudu 109 E5
Antabamba 163 F4
Antakya = Hatay 118 C4
Antalaha 131 A10
Antalya 118 C2
Antalya Körfezi 118 C2
Antananarivo 131 B9
Antarctic Pen. 168 A4
Antarctica 168 C
Antequera 86 D3
Anti Atlas 126 C4
Antibes 89 E7
Anticosti, Î. d' 143 E7
Antigonish 143 E7
Antigua & Barbuda ■ 159 C7
Antikythira 93 G4

Antioquia 162 B3
Antofagasta 166 A2
Antonina 166 B7
Antrim 79 D3
Antsirabe 131 B9
Antsiranana 131 A9
Antsohihy 131 A9
Antwerpen 80 C3
Anupgarh 114 E8
Anvers = Antwerpen 80 C3
Anvers I. 168 A3
Anxi 102 C7
Anxious B. 134 B1
Anyang 104 D1
Anzhero-Sudzhensk 97 D9
Ânzio 90 D4
Aoga-Shima 101 G6
Aomori 100 C7
Aoraki Mount Cook 137 E4
Aosta 90 B1
Apalachicola → 154 E5
Apaporis → 162 D5
Aparri 108 A2
Apeldoorn 80 B3
Apia 137 L13
Apiacás, Serra dos 163 E7
Aplao 163 G4
Apo, Mt. 108 C3
Apolo 163 F5
Apoteri 162 C7
Appalachian Mts. 149 F5
Appennini 90 B3
Appleton 148 B1
Aprilia 90 D4
Apucarana 166 A6
Apure → 162 B5
Apurímac → 163 F4
Aqaba = Al 'Aqabah 119 E3
Aqaba, G. of 119 E3
Āqchah 117 B6
'Aqrah 118 C5
Aqtöbe 97 D6
Aqtoghay 97 E8
Aquidauana 165 G2
Aquitain, Bassin 88 D3
Ar Ramādī 118 D5
Ar Raqqah 118 D4
Ar Rass 119 F5
Ar Rifā'ī 119 E6
Ar Riyāḍ 119 F6
Ar Ruṭbah 118 D5
Ar Ruwayḍah 119 G6
Ara 112 E5
'Arab, Bahr el → 125 D4
Arab, Shatt al → 119 E7
Arabian Desert = Es Sahrâ' Esh Sharqîya 124 C5

Arabian Gulf = Persian Gulf 116 E2
Arabian Sea 94 G8
Araç 118 B3
Aracaju 165 E6
Aracati 164 C6
Araçatuba 165 G3
Aracena 86 D2
Araçuaí 165 F5
Arad 82 E5
Arafura Sea 109 F4
Aragón □ 87 B5
Aragón → 87 A5
Araguacema 164 D4
Araguaia → 164 D4
Araguari 165 F4
Araguari → 164 B4
Arak 126 C6
Arakan Coast 113 H9
Arakan Yoma 113 H10
Aral 97 E7
Aral Sea 97 E6
Aran I. = Arranmore 78 D2
Aran Is. 79 E2
Aranda de Duero 86 B4
Aranjuez 86 B4
Arapgir 118 C4
Arapiraca 165 D6
Arapongas 166 A6
Araraquara 165 G4
Ararat 134 C3
Ararat, Mt. = Ağrı Dağı 118 C6
Araripe, Chapada do 164 D6
Aras, Rûd-e → 118 B7
Arauca 162 B4
Arauca → 162 B5
Araxá 165 F4
Araya, Pen. de 162 A6
Árbatax 91 E2
Arbîl 118 C6
Arbroath 78 C5
Arcachon 88 D3
Arckaringa Cr. → 134 A2
Arcos de la Frontera 86 D3
Arcot 115 N11
Arctic Bay 142 B5
Arda → 92 D6
Ardabīl 118 C7
Ardahan 118 B5
Ardenne 80 D3
Ardestān 116 C3
Ardlethan 135 B4
Ardmore 152 B5
Ardrossan 134 B2
Arecibo 159 C6
Areia Branca 164 C6
Arendal 77 D7
Arequipa 163 G4

Arévalo 86 B3
Arezzo 90 C3
Arganda del Rey 86 B4
Argentan 88 B3
Argentário, Mte. 90 C3
Argentina ■ 166 D3
Argentino, L. 167 G2
Argeş → 92 B6
Arghandab → 114 D4
Argolikos Kolpos 93 F4
Argos 93 F4
Argostoli 93 E3
Århus = Aarhus 77 D8
Ariadnoye 100 A4
Arica Chile 163 G4
Arica Colombia 162 D4
Ariquemes 163 E6
Arinos → 163 F7
Aripuanã 163 E6
Aripuanã → 162 E6
Ariquemes 163 E6
Arizona 166 D3
Arizona □ 151 C7
Arjona 162 A3
Arkansas □ 153 B7
Arkansas → 153 C8
Arkansas City 152 A5
Arkhangelsk 96 C5
Arklow 79 E3
Arkt023 135 B4
Arkticheskiy, Mys 98 A7
Arlanzón → 86 A3
Arlberg pass 80 E6
Arlbergtunnel 80 E6
Arles 89 E6
Arlington Va., U.S.A. 149 E7
Arlington Wash., U.S.A. 144 B2
Arlon 80 D3
Armagh 79 D3
Armavir 85 D5
Armenia 162 C3
Armenia ■ 85 E5
Armidale 135 B5
Arnaud → 142 C6
Arnauti, C. 118 D3
Arnhem 80 C3
Arnhem, C. 132 C6
Arnhem Land 132 C5
Arno → 90 C3
Arno Bay 134 B2
Arnsberg 80 C5
Arqalyk 97 D7
Arran 78 D4
Arranmore 78 D2
Arras 89 A5
Arrecife 126 C3
Arrée, Mts. d' 88 B2
Arrow L. 137 F3
Arthur → 134 D3

Arthur's Pass 137 E4
Artigas 166 C5
Artois 88 A5
Artsyz 83 E9
Artvin 118 B5
Aru, Kepulauan 109 F4
Arua 129 D6
Aruanã 165 E3
Aruba ⬚ 159 D6
Arunachal Pradesh □ 113 C10
Arusha 129 E7
Aruwimi → 128 D4
Arviat 140 B10
Arxan 103 B11
Arys 97 E7
Arzamas 84 B5
As Saffānīyah 119 E7
As Samāwah 119 E6
As Sulaymānīyah Iraq 118 D6
As Sulaymānīyah Si. Arabia 119 F6
As Summān 119 F6
As Suwaydā' 118 D4
Aş Şuwayrah 119 E6
Asahikawa 100 B8
Asansol 112 B6
Ascension I. 123 G2
Aschaffenburg 80 D5
Aschersleben 81 C6
Áscoli Piceno 90 C4
Ascope 163 E3
Aseb 121 E3
Asenovgrad 92 C5
Ash Shāmīyah 119 E6
Ash Shāriqah 116 E3
Ash Shaṭrah 119 E6
Ash Shu'bah 119 E6
Ashburton 137 E4
Asheville 155 B6
Ashford Australia 135 A5
Ashford U.K. 79 F7
Ashgabat 97 F6
Ashizuri-Zaki 101 C4
Ashmyany 83 A7
Ashqelon 119 E3
Ashtabula 148 D5
Ashuanipi, L. 143 D7
Asia, Kepulauan 109 D4
Asifabad 115 K11
Asinara 90 D2
Asinara, G. dell' 90 D2
Asino 97 D9
Asipovichy 83 B9
'Asīr 120 D3
Asir, Ras 121 E5
Asmara = Asmera 129 A7
Asmera 129 A7
Aspiring, Mt. 137 F3
Assam □ 113 D9
Assen 80 B4

Assiniboia 141 D9
Assiniboine → 141 D10
Assis 166 A6
Assisi 90 C4
Astana 97 D8
Asti 90 B2
Astipalea 93 F6
Astorga 86 A2
Astoria 144 C2
Astrakhan 85 D6
Asturias □ 86 A3
Asunción 166 B5
Aswân 124 D5
Asyût 124 E5
At Ṭafilah 119 E3
Aṭ Ṭā'if 120 C3
Atacama, Desierto de 166 A3
Atacama, Salar de 166 A3
Atalaya 163 F4
Atamyrat 97 F7
Atapupu 109 F2
Atâr 126 D3
Atasū 97 E8
Atauro 109 F3
Atbara 125 E5
'Atbara, Nahr → 125 E5
Atbasar 97 D7
Athabasca 141 C8
Athabasca → 140 C8
Athabasca, L. 140 C8
Athens = Athína 93 F4
Athens Ala., U.S.A. 154 B4
Athens Ga., U.S.A. 155 C6
Athína 93 F4
Athlone 79 E3
Athos 93 D5
Athy 79 E3
Ati 125 F2
Atlanta 155 C5
Atlantic City 149 E8
Atlas Mts. = Haut Atlas 126 B4
Atrek → 116 B3
Atsuta 100 B7
Attapeu 110 E5
Attawapiskat 143 D5
Attawapiskat → 143 D5
Attock 114 C8
Attur 115 P11
Atuel → 166 D3
Atyraū 97 E6
Aubagne 89 E6
Aube → 89 B5
Aubenas 89 D6
Auburn 154 C5
Auburn Ra. 135 A5
Aubusson 88 D5
Auch 88 E4
Auckland 136 B6

Aude → 89 E5
Augathella 135 A4
Augsburg 80 D6
Augusta Italy 91 F5
Augusta Ga., U.S.A. 155 C7
Augusta Maine, U.S.A. 149 B11
Aunis 88 C3
Auponhia 109 E3
Aurangabad Bihar, India 112 E5
Aurangabad Maharashtra, India 115 K9
Aurich 80 B4
Aurillac 88 D5
Aurora Colo., U.S.A. 146 F2
Aurora Ill., U.S.A. 148 D1
Austin Minn., U.S.A. 147 D8
Austin Tex., U.S.A. 152 D5
Austral Seamount Chain 137 M16
Australia ■ 132 E6
Australian Capital Territory □ 135 C4
Austria ■ 81 E8
Autun 89 C6
Auvergne □ 89 D5
Auvergne, Mts. d' 89 D5
Auxerre 89 C5
Avallon 89 C5
Aveiro Brazil 164 C2
Aveiro Portugal 86 B1
Āvej 118 D7
Avellaneda 166 C5
Avellino 91 D5
Aversa 91 D5
Avesta 77 C9
Avezzano 90 C4
Aviemore 78 C5
Avignon 89 E6
Ávila 86 B3
Avilés 86 A3
Avoca → 134 C3
Avola 91 F5
Avon → 140 B9
Awaji-Shima 101 F4
Awash 121 F3
Awatere → 137 D6
Awbārī 124 C1
Awbārī, Idehan 124 C1
Awjilah 124 C3
Axel Heiberg I. 142 B5
Axim 127 H5
Axios → 93 D4
Ayabaca 162 D3
Ayabe 101 F4
Ayacucho Argentina 166 D5

Ayacucho Peru 163 F4
Ayaköz 97 E9
Ayamonte 86 D2
Ayaviri 163 F4
Aybak 117 B7
Aydın 93 F6
Ayers Rock = Uluru 132 F5
Ayeyarwady = Irrawaddy → 113 K10
Aylmer, L. 140 B8
Ayn Dār 119 F7
Ayr 78 D4
Aytos 93 C6
Ayu, Kepulauan 109 D4
Ayvacık 93 E6
Ayvalık 93 E6
Az Zahrān 119 F7
Az Zarqā 118 D4
Az Zilfī 119 F6
Az Zubayr 119 E6
Azamgarh 112 D4
Āzarbāyjān-e Gharbī □ 118 C6
Āzarbāyjān-e Sharqī □ 118 C6
Azare 127 F8
Azerbaijan ■ 85 E6
Azogues 162 D3
Azov 85 D4
Azov, Sea of 85 D4
Azuaga 86 C3
Azuero, Pen. de 158 E3
Azul 166 D5
Azur, Côte d' 89 E7

B

Ba Don 110 A3
Baardheere 121 G3
Bab el Mandeb 121 E3
Bābā, Koh-i- 114 B5
Baba Burnu 93 E6
Babadag 83 B7
Babaeski 92 D6
Babahoyo 162 D3
Babar 109 E4
Babo 109 E4
Bābol 116 B3
Bābol Sar 116 B3
Babruysk 83 B9
Babuyan Chan. 108 A2
Babylon 119 D6
Bacabal 164 C5
Bacan, Kepulauan 109 E3
Bacarra 108 A2
Bacău 83 E8
Back → 140 B9
Bacolod 108 B2
Bad Ischl 81 E7
Bad Kissingen 80 C6
Badajoz 86 C2

Badalona 87 B7
Badampahar 112 F6
Badanah 119 E5
Badarinath 114 D11
Badas, Kepulauan 111 D3
Baddo → 114 E4
Bade 109 F5
Baden 81 D9
Baden-Baden 80 D5
Baden-Württemberg □ 80 D5
Badgastein 81 E7
Bādghīs □ 114 B3
Badin 115 G6
Badlands 146 D3
Baena 86 D3
Baeza 86 D4
Baffin B. 142 B7
Baffin I. 142 C6
Bafing → 127 F3
Bafoulabé 127 F3
Bāfq 116 D3
Bāft 116 D4
Bafwasende 129 D5
Bagamoyo 129 F7
Baganga 108 C3
Bagansiapiapi 111 D2
Bagdarin 98 D9
Bagé 166 C5
Baghdād 118 D6
Bagheria 91 E4
Baghlān 114 A6
Baguio 108 A2
Bahamas ■ 158 A4
Baharampur 112 E7
Bahawalpur 115 E4
Bahía □ 165 E5
Bahía, Is. de la 157 D7
Bahía Blanca 166 D4
Bahía de Caráquez 162 D2
Bahía Laura 167 F3
Bahía Negra 163 H7
Bahraich 112 D3
Bahrain ■ 116 E2
Baia Mare 83 E6
Baïbokoum 125 G2
Baie-Comeau 143 E7
Baie Verte 143 E8
Ba'ījī 118 D5
Baikal, L. = Baykal, Oz. 98 D8
Băilești 92 B4
Bā'ir 119 E4
Bairnsdale 135 C4
Baitadi 112 C3
Baiyin 103 D8
Baja 82 E4
Baja, Pta. 156 B1
Baja California 156 A1
Bajimba, Mt. 135 A5

Bakel 127 F4
Baker, L. 140 B10
Baker, Mt. 144 B3
Baker I. 136 J13
Baker Lake 140 B10
Bakersfield 150 C3
Bākhtarān = Kermānshāh 118 D6
Bakı 85 E6
Bakony 82 E3
Bakouma 128 C4
Baku = Bakı 85 E6
Bakutis Coast 168 B1
Balabac I. 110 C5
Balabac Str. 110 C5
Balabalangan, Kepulauan 111 E5
Balaghat Ra. 115 K10
Balaguer 87 B6
Balaklava 85 E3
Balakovo 84 C6
Balashov 84 C5
Balaton 82 E3
Balbina, Represa de 162 D7
Balchik 92 C7
Balclutha 137 G3
Baleares, Is. 87 C7
Baleine → 142 D7
Baler 108 A2
Baleshwar 112 G6
Bali 111 F5
Balıkeşir 93 E6
Balikpapan 111 E5
Balimbing 108 C1
Balkan Mts. = Stara Planina 92 C4
Balkanabat 97 F6
Balkh 117 B6
Ballarat 134 C3
Ballater 78 C5
Ballina Australia 135 A5
Ballina Ireland 79 D2
Ballinasloe 79 E2
Ballymena 79 D3
Balmaceda 167 F2
Balmoral 134 C3
Balonne → 135 A4
Balqash 97 E8
Balqash Köli 97 E8
Balrampur 112 D4
Balranald 134 B3
Balsas → 156 D4
Balta 83 D9
Bălți 83 E8
Baltic Sea 77 D9
Baltimore 149 E7
Baluchistan □ 114 F4
Balya 93 E6
Bam 116 D4
Bama 125 F1

Bamako 127 F4
Bambari 128 C4
Bamberg 80 D6
Bamenda 127 G8
Bāmīān □ 114 B5
Bampūr 117 E5
Ban Kantang 110 C1
Banaba 136 K11
Banalia 129 D5
Bananal, I. do 165 E3
Bânâs, Ras 124 D6
Band-e Torkestan 117 C6
Banda, Kepulauan 109 E3
Banda Aceh 110 C1
Banda Banda, Mt. 135 B5
Banda Elat 109 F4
Banda Sea 109 F3
Bandanaira 109 E3
Bandar-e Abbās 116 E4
Bandar-e Anzalī 118 C7
Bandar-e Chārak 116 E3
Bandar-e Deylam 119 E7
Bandar-e Emām Khomeynī 118 D6
Bandar-e Lengeh 116 E3
Bandar-e Rīg 116 D2
Bandar-e Torkeman 116 B3
Bandar Labuan 110 C5
Bandar Lampung 111 F3
Bandar Seri Begawan 110 D5
Bandar Sri Aman 111 D4
Bandera 166 B4
Bandırma 93 D7
Bandon 79 F2
Bandundu 128 E3
Bandung 111 F3
Banff Canada 141 C8
Banff U.K. 78 C5
Bang Saphan 110 B1
Bangalore 115 N10
Bangassou 128 D4
Banggai, Kepulauan 109 E2
Banggi, Pulau 110 C5
Banghāzī 124 B3
Bangka Sulawesi, Indonesia 109 D3
Bangka Sumatera, Indonesia 111 E3
Bangka, Selat 111 E3
Bangkinang 111 D2
Bangko 111 E2
Bangkok 110 B2
Bangladesh ■ 113 E7
Bangong Co 114 B11
Bangor Down, U.K. 79 D4

Bangor Gwynedd, U.K. 79 E4
Bangor U.S.A. 149 B11
Bangued 108 A2
Bangui 128 D3
Bangweulu, L. 129 G6
Baní 159 C5
Banī Walīd 124 B1
Bāniyās 118 D3
Banja Luka 90 B6
Banjarmasin 111 E4
Banjul 127 F2
Bankipore 112 E5
Banks I. 140 A7
Banks Pen. 137 E5
Banks Str. 134 D4
Bankura 112 F6
Bantry 79 F2
Banswara 115 H9
Banyak, Kepulauan 111 D1
Banzare Coast 168 A13
Baoding 104 C1
Baoji 103 E9
Baoshan 102 F7
Baotou 103 C10
Bapatla 112 K3
Ba'qūbah 118 D6
Bar Montenegro 92 C2
Bar Ukraine 83 D8
Bar-le-Duc 89 B6
Barabai 111 E5
Baracoa 158 B5
Barahona 159 C5
Barail Range 113 E9
Barakaldo 87 A4
Barakpur 113 F7
Baramula 114 B9
Baran 115 G10
Baranavichy 83 B8
Baranof I. 141 C6
Barapasi 109 E5
Barat Daya, Kepulauan 109 F3
Barbacena 165 G5
Barbados ■ 159 D8
Barbastro 87 A6
Barberton 112 F6
Barbosa 162 B4
Barcellona Pozzo di Gotto 91 E5
Barcelona Spain 87 B7
Barcelona Venezuela 162 A6
Barcelos 162 D6
Bardaï 124 D2
Barddhaman 112 F6
Bardīyah 124 B4
Bareilly 114 E11
Barfleur, Pte. de 88 B3
Barhi 112 E5
Bari 90 D6
Bari Doab 114 D8

Barīdī, Ra's 119 F4
Barinas 162 B4
Baring, C. 140 B8
Barisal 113 F8
Barisan, Pegunungan 111 E2
Barito → 111 E4
Barkly Tableland 132 D6
Bârlad → 83 F8
Barlee, L. 132 F2
Barletta 90 D6
Barmedman 135 B4
Barmer 114 G7
Barmera 134 B3
Barnaul 97 D9
Barnsley 79 E6
Barnstaple 79 F4
Baro 127 G7
Baroda = Vadodara 115 H8
Barotseland 130 B4
Barpeta 113 D8
Barqa 124 C3
Barquísimeto 162 A5
Barra Brazil 165 E5
Barra U.K. 78 C3
Barra do Corda 164 D4
Barra Falsa, Pta. da 131 C7
Barraba 135 B5
Barranca Lima, Peru 163 F3
Barranca Loreto, Peru 162 D3
Barrancabermeja 162 B4
Barrancas 162 B6
Barrancos 86 C2
Barranqueras 166 B4
Barranquilla 162 A4
Barreiras 165 E5
Barreirinhas 164 C5
Barreiro 86 C1
Barren, Nosy 131 B8
Barretos 165 G4
Barrie 143 E6
Barrier Ra. 134 B3
Barrington Tops 135 B5
Barringun 135 A4
Barrow 141 A4
Barrow-in-Furness 79 D5
Barry 79 F5
Barsi 115 K9
Barsoi 112 E6
Barstow 150 C4
Bartica 162 B7
Bartin 118 B3
Bartlesville 153 A6
Barysaw 83 A9
Bāsa'idū 116 E3
Basankusa 128 D3
Basarabeasca 83 E9
Basel 80 E4

Bashākerd, Kūhhā-ye 117 E4
Bashkortostan □ 97 D6
Basilan I. 108 C2
Basilan Str. 108 C2
Basildon 79 F7
Basingstoke 79 F6
Basle = Basel 80 E4
Basque Provinces = País Vasco □ 87 A4
Basra = Al Başrah 119 E6
Bass Str. 133 H8
Bassano del Grappa 90 B3
Bassas da India 131 C7
Basse-Terre 159 C7
Bassein 113 J10
Basseterre 159 C7
Bastak 116 E3
Bastar 112 H3
Basti 112 D4
Bastia 89 E8
Bastogne 80 C3
Bata 128 D1
Bataan 108 B2
Batabanó, G. de 158 B3
Batac 108 A2
Batagai 99 C11
Batamay 99 C10
Batang 102 A7
Batangafo 125 G2
Batangas 108 B2
Batanta 108 E4
Batdambang 110 B2
Batemans Bay 135 C5
Bath 79 F5
Bathurst Australia 135 B4
Bathurst Canada 143 E7
Bathurst, C. 140 A7
Bathurst Harb. 134 D4
Bathurst I. 142 B3
Bathurst Inlet 140 B9
Batlow 135 C4
Batman 118 C5
Batna 126 A7
Baton Rouge 153 D8
Batouri 128 D2
Battipáglia 91 D5
Battle Creek 148 C3
Batu 121 F2
Batu, Kepulauan 111 E1
Batu Pahat 111 D2
Batuata 109 F2
Baturaja 111 E2
Baturité 164 C6
Bau 111 D4
Baubau 109 F2
Baucau 109 F3
Bauchi 127 F7
Bauer, C. 134 B1
Bauld, C. 143 D8
Bauru 165 G4

Bautzen 81 C8
Bavaria = Bayern □ 81 D6
Bawdwin 113 F11
Bawean 111 F4
Bawku 127 F5
Bay City 148 C4
Bay View 136 C7
Bayamo 158 B4
Bayan Har Shan 102 E7
Bayanaūyl 97 D8
Bayanhongor 103 B8
Baybay 108 B2
Baydhabo 121 G3
Bayern □ 81 D6
Bayeux 88 B3
Bayındır 93 E6
Baykal, Oz. 98 D8
Bayombong 108 A2
Bayonne 88 E3
Bayovar 163 E2
Bayqongyr 97 E7
Baýramaly 97 F7
Bayramiç 93 E6
Bayreuth 81 D6
Bayrūt 118 D3
Baytown 153 E6
Baza 87 D4
Bazaruto, I. do 131 C7
Bé, Nosy 131 A9
Beachport 134 C2
Beagle, Canal 167 G3
Beardmore Glacier 168 C14
Béarn 88 E3
Beauce, Plaine de la 88 B4
Beaudesert 135 A5
Beaufort 110 C5
Beaufort Sea 138 B6
Beaufort West 130 E4
Beaumont 153 D6
Beaune 89 C6
Beauvais 88 B5
Beaver → 141 C9
Beawar 114 F9
Bečej 92 B3
Béchar 126 B5
Bedford 79 E6
Beenleigh 135 A5
Be'er Sheva 119 E3
Beersheba = Be'er Sheva 119 E3
Befale 128 D4
Bega 135 C4
Behbehān 119 E7
Behshahr 116 B3
Bei Jiang → 107 F2
Bei'an 103 B13
Beihai 103 G9
Beijing 104 C2

Beilpajah 135 B3
Beira 131 B6
Beirut = Bayrūt 118 D3
Beitbridge 131 C6
Beja Portugal 86 C2
Béja Tunisia 124 A1
Bejaïa 126 A7
Béjar 86 B3
Bejestān 116 C4
Békéscsaba 82 E5
Bela India 112 E4
Bela Pakistan 114 F5
Bela Crkva 92 B3
Bela Vista Brazil 166 A5
Bela Vista Mozam. 131 D6
Belarus ■ 84 C2
Belau = Palau ■ 108 C4
Belawan 111 D1
Belcher Chan. 142 B4
Belcher Is. 143 D6
Beledweyne 121 G4
Belém 164 C4
Belev 84 C4
Belfast 79 D4
Belfort 89 C7
Belgaum 115 M9
Belgium ■ 80 C3
Belgorod 84 C4
Belgrade = Beograd 92 B3
Beli Drim → 92 C3
Belinyu 111 E3
Belitung 111 E3
Belize ■ 157 D7
Belize City 157 D7
Belkovskiy, Ostrov 98 B11
Bell Peninsula 142 C5
Bell Ville 166 C4
Bella Unión 166 C5
Bella Vista 166 B5
Bellary 115 M10
Bellata 135 A4
Belle-Île 88 C2
Belle Isle 143 D8
Belle Isle, Str. of 143 D8
Belleville Canada 143 E6
Belleville U.S.A. 147 F10
Bellingen 135 B5
Bellingham 144 B2
Bellingshausen Sea 168 A2
Bellinzona 89 C8
Belluno 90 A4
Belmonte 165 F6
Belmopan 157 D7
Belo Horizonte 165 F5
Belo-Tsiribihina 131 B8
Beloit 147 D10
Belokorovichi 83 C9
Belomorsk 96 C4

Belonia 113 F8
Belorussia = Belarus ■ 84 C2
Belovo 97 D9
Beloye, Ozero 84 A4
Beloye More 76 B13
Belozersk 84 A4
Beltana 134 B2
Belterra 164 C3
Belukha 97 E9
Beluran 110 C5
Belyy, Ostrov 96 B8
Belyy Yar 97 D9
Bembéréke 127 F6
Bemidji 147 B7
Ben Lomond N.S.W., Australia 135 B5
Ben Lomond Tas., Australia 134 D4
Ben Nevis 78 C4
Bena 127 F7
Benalla 135 C4
Benares = Varanasi 112 E4
Benavente 86 A3
Benbecula 78 C3
Benbonyathe Hill 134 B2
Bend 144 D3
Bender Beyla 121 F5
Bendigo 135 C3
Benevento 90 D5
Bengal, Bay of 113 J7
Bengaluru = Bangalore 115 N10
Bengbu 104 F2
Benghazi = Banghāzī 124 B3
Bengkalis 111 D2
Bengkulu 111 E2
Benguela 130 A2
Beni 129 D5
Beni → 163 F5
Beni Mellal 126 B4
Beni Suef 124 C5
Benidorm 87 C5
Benin ■ 127 G6
Benin, Bight of 127 H6
Benin City 127 G7
Benito Juárez 166 D5
Benjamin Constant 162 D4
Benoni 131 D5
Bent 116 E4
Benteng 109 F2
Benton Harbor 148 C2
Benue → 127 G7
Benxi 105 B5
Beo 108 D3
Beograd 92 B3
Beppu 101 G2
Berat 93 D2
Berau, Teluk 109 E4

Berber 125 E5
Berbera 121 E4
Berbérati 128 D3
Berbice → 162 B7
Berdsk 97 D9
Berdyansk 85 D4
Berdychiv 83 D9
Berebere 109 D3
Bereeda 121 E5
Berehove 83 D6
Berekum 127 G5
Berestechko 83 C7
Berezhany 83 D7
Berezniki 96 D6
Berezovo 96 C7
Berga 87 A6
Bergama 93 E6
Bérgamo 90 B2
Bergen 76 C7
Bergerac 88 D4
Berhala, Selat 111 E2
Bering Sea 141 C1
Bering Strait 141 B3
Berja 87 D4
Berkeley 154 H2
Berkner I. 168 B4
Berlin 81 B7
Bernburg 81 C6
Bernina, Piz 89 C8
Beroun 82 D2
Berri 134 B3
Berry Australia 135 B5
Berry France 88 C5
Bershad 83 D9
Bertoua 128 D2
Berwick-upon-Tweed
78 D6
Besalampy 131 B8
Besançon 89 C7
Besar 111 E5
Bessarabiya 83 E9
Bessemer 154 C4
Betanzos 86 A1
Bétaré Oya 128 C2
Bethel 141 B3
Bethlehem S. Africa
131 D5
Bethlehem U.S.A. 149 D8
Béthune 89 A5
Betong 111 D4
Betroka 131 C9
Bettiah 112 D5
Betul 115 J10
Beverley 79 E6
Beverly Hills 150 C3
Beyneu 97 E6

Beypazarı 118 B2
Beyşehir Gölü 118 C2
Béziers 89 E5
Bhachau 115 H7
Bhadrak 112 G6
Bhadravati 115 N9
Bhagalpur 112 E6
Bhakra Dam 114 D10
Bhamo 113 E11
Bhandara 115 J11
Bhanrer Ra. 115 H11
Bharatpur 114 F10
Bhatpara 113 F7
Bhavnagar 115 J8
Bhawanipatna 112 H4
Bhilainagar-Durg 112 G3
Bhilwara 115 G9
Bhima → 115 L10
Bhind 114 F11
Bhiwandi 115 K8
Bhiwani 114 E10
Bhola 113 F8
Bhopal 115 H10
Bhubaneshwar 112 G5
Bhuj 115 H6
Bhusawal 115 J9
Bhutan ■ 113 D8
Biak 109 E5
Biała Podlaska 83 B6
Białogard 82 A2
Białystok 83 B6
Biaro 109 D3
Biarritz 88 E3
Bibai 100 B7
Biberach 80 D5
Bida 127 G7
Bidar 115 L10
Biddeford 149 C10
Bié, Planalto de 130 A3
Bielefeld 80 B5
Biella 90 B2
Bielsk Podlaski 83 B6
Bielsko-Biała 82 D4
Bien Hoa 110 B3
Bienville, L. 143 D6
Big Spring 152 C3
Big Trout L. 143 D5
Biğa 93 D6
Bigadiç 93 E7
Biggar 141 C9
Biggenden 135 A5
Bighorn → 145 C10
Bighorn Mts. 145 D10
Bihać 90 B5
Bihar 112 E5
Bihor, Munţii 83 E6
Bijagós, Arquipélago dos
127 F2
Bijapur Chhattisgarh,
India 112 H3

Bijapur Karnataka, India
115 L9
Bījār 118 D6
Bijnor 114 E11
Bikaner 114 E8
Bikini Atoll 136 H11
Bila Tserkva 83 D10
Bilara 114 F8
Bilaspur 112 F4
Bilauk Taungdan 110 B1
Bilbao 87 A4
Bilecik 85 E3
Bilhorod-Dnistrovskyy
85 D3
Billings 145 D9
Bilma 125 E1
Biloxi 153 D9
Biltine 125 F3
Bima 109 F1
Bina-Etawah 115 G11
Binalbagan 108 B2
Binalong 135 B4
Bīnālūd, Kūh-e 116 B4
Bindura 131 B5
Bingara 135 A5
Binghamton 149 C8
Bingöl 118 C5
Binh Dinh 110 B3
Binh Son 110 A3
Binjai 111 D1
Binnaway 135 B4
Binongko 109 F2
Bintan 111 D2
Bintangau 111 D4
Bintulu 111 D4
Bintuni 109 E4
Bioko 128 D1
Bir 115 K9
Bîr Atrun 125 E4
Bîr Mogreïn 126 C3
Birāk 124 C1
Birchip 134 C3
Birecik 118 C4
Bireuen 110 C1
Birmingham U.K. 79 E6
Birmingham U.S.A.
154 C4
Birmitrapur 112 F5
Birni Nkonni 127 F7
Birnin Kebbi 127 F6
Birr 79 E3
Birrie → 135 A4
Birsk 97 D6
Biru 115 N9
Bisa 109 E3
Biscay, B. of 88 D2
Biscoe Is. 168 A3
Bishkek 97 E8
Biskra 126 B7
Bismarck 146 B4
Bismarck Arch. 136 K9

Bissau 127 F2
Bistriţa 83 E7
Bistriţa → 83 E8
Bitlis 118 C5
Bitola 92 D3
Bitterfontein 130 E3
Bitterroot Range 145 D6
Biu 125 F1
Biwa-Ko 101 F5
Biysk 97 D9
Bizerte 124 A1
Bjelovar 90 B6
Black Forest =
  Schwarzwald 80 D5
Black Hills 146 D3
Black Sea 85 E3
Black Volta → 127 G5
Blackball 137 E4
Blackburn 79 E5
Blackpool 79 E5
Blackwater → 79 E2
Blagodarnyy 85 D5
Blagoevgrad 92 C4
Blagoveshchensk 99 D10
Blanc, Mont 89 D7
Blanca, B. 167 D4
Blanca, Costa 87 C5
Blanca Peak 151 B10
Blanche, C. 134 B1
Blanche, L. 134 A2
Blanes 87 B7
Blantyre 131 B6
Blayney 135 B4
Blenheim 137 D5
Blida 126 A6
Bligh Sound 137 F2
Bloemfontein 131 D5
Bloemhof 131 D5
Blois 88 C4
Bloomington Ill., U.S.A.
147 E10
Bloomington Ind., U.S.A.
148 E2
Blue Mts. 144 D4
Blue Nile = Nîl el Azraq →
125 E5
Blue Ridge 155 A7
Bluefields 158 D3
Bluff 137 G3
Blumenau 166 B7
Bo 127 G3
Bo Hai 104 C3
Bo Hai Haixia 104 C4
Boa Vista 162 C6
Bobadah 135 B4
Bobbili 112 H4
Bobo-Dioulasso 127 F5
Bóbr → 82 B2
Bobraomby, Tanjon' i
131 A9
Boby, Pic 131 C9
Boca do Acre 163 E5

Boca Raton **155 F7**
Bochum **80 C4**
Bodaybo **98 D9**
Boden **76 B10**
Bodensee **89 C8**
Bodhan **115 K10**
Bodø **76 B8**
Bodrog **82 D5**
Bodrum **93 F6**
Boende **128 E4**
Bogalusa **153 D9**
Bogan Gate **135 B4**
Boggabilla **135 A5**
Boggabri **135 B5**
Bogo **108 B2**
Bogong, Mt. **135 C4**
Bogor **111 F3**
Bogotá **162 C4**
Bogotol **97 D9**
Bogra **113 E7**
Bohemian Forest =
  Böhmerwald **81 D7**
Böhmerwald **81 D7**
Bohol □ **108 C2**
Bohol Sea **108 C2**
Boise **144 E5**
Boise City **152 A2**
Bojador, C. **126 C3**
Bojana → **92 D2**
Bojnūrd **116 B4**
Bokhara → **135 A4**
Bokoro **125 F2**
Bolan Pass **114 E5**
Bolbec **88 B4**
Bole **102 C4**
Bolekhiv **83 D6**
Bolesławiec **81 C8**
Bolhrad **83 F9**
Bolivia ■ **163 G6**
Bollon **135 A4**
Bolobo **128 E3**
Bologna **90 B3**
Bologoye **84 B3**
Bolsena, L. di **90 C3**
Bolshevik, Ostrov **98 B8**
Bolshoy Begichev, Ostrov
  98 B9
Bolshoy Lyakhovskiy,
  Ostrov **99 B12**
Bolton **79 E5**
Bolu **85 E3**
Bolvadin **118 C2**
Bolzano **90 A3**
Bom Jesus da Lapa
  165 E5
Boma **128 F2**
Bombala **135 C4**
Bombay = Mumbai
  115 K8
Bomboma **128 D3**
Bomu → **128 D4**
Bonaire **159 D6**

Bonang **135 C4**
Bonavista **143 E8**
Bondo **128 D4**
Bondoukou **127 G5**
Bone, Teluk **109 E2**
Bonerate **109 F2**
Bonerate, Kepulauan
  109 F2
Bongor **125 F2**
Bonifacio **89 F8**
Bonn **80 C4**
Bonney, L. **134 C3**
Bonoi **109 E5**
Bontang **111 D5**
Bonthe **127 G3**
Bontoc **108 A2**
Booligal **135 B3**
Boonah **135 A5**
Boorindal **135 B4**
Boorowa **135 B4**
Boosaaso **121 E4**
Booué **128 E2**
Bor Serbia **92 B4**
Bor South Sudan **125 G5**
Boraha, Nosy **131 B9**
Borås **77 D8**
Borāzjān **116 D2**
Borba **162 D7**
Borda, C. **134 C2**
Bordeaux **88 D3**
Borden I. **142 B2**
Borden Pen. **142 B5**
Bordertown **134 C3**
Bordj Flye Ste-Marie
  126 C5
Bordj in Eker **126 D7**
Bordj Omar Driss **126 C7**
Borger **152 B3**
Borhoyn Tal **103 C10**
Borisoglebsk **84 C5**
Borja **162 D3**
Borkou **125 E2**
Borkum **80 B4**
Borley, C. **168 A9**
Borneo **111 D4**
Bornholm **77 D8**
Borongan **108 B3**
Borovichi **84 B3**
Borşa **83 E7**
Borūjerd **118 D7**
Boryslav **83 D6**
Bosa **91 D2**
Bosanska Gradiška
  90 B6
Boshrūyeh **116 C4**
Bosna → **90 B7**
Bosnia-Herzegovina ■
  90 B6
Bosnik **109 E5**

Bosobolo **128 D3**
Bosporus = İstanbul
  Boğazı **92 D7**
Bossangoa **128 C3**
Bosso **125 F1**
Bosten Hu **102 C5**
Boston U.K. **79 E6**
Boston U.S.A. **149 C10**
Bothnia, G. of **76 C10**
Bothwell **134 D4**
Botletle → **130 C4**
Botoşani **83 E8**
Botswana ■ **130 C4**
Botucatu **165 G4**
Bouaké **127 G4**
Bouar **128 C3**
Bouârfa **126 B5**
Bougainville I. **136 K10**
Bougouni **127 F4**
Boulder **146 E2**
Boulogne-sur-Mer **88 A4**
Bouna **127 G5**
Boundiali **127 G4**
Bourbonnais **89 C5**
Bourem **127 E5**
Bourg-en-Bresse **89 C6**
Bourg-St-Maurice **89 D7**
Bourges **88 C5**
Bourgogne □ **89 C6**
Bourke **135 B4**
Bournemouth **79 F6**
Bowen Mts. **135 C4**
Bowman I. **168 A12**
Bowral **135 B5**
Bowraville **135 B5**
Boyne → **79 E3**
Boyoma, Chutes **129 D5**
Boz Dağları **93 E7**
Bozburun **93 F7**
Bozcaada **93 E6**
Bozdoğan **93 F7**
Bozeman **145 D8**
Bozen = Bolzano **90 A3**
Bozoum **128 C3**
Bra **90 B1**
Brač **90 C6**
Bracciano, L. di **90 C4**
Bräcke **76 C9**
Bradenton **155 F6**
Bradford **79 E6**
Braga **86 B1**
Bragança Brazil **164 C4**
Bragança Portugal **86 B2**
Brahmanbaria **113 F8**
Brahmani → **112 G6**
Brahmapur **112 H5**
Brahmaputra → **113 F7**
Braidwood **135 C4**
Bräila **83 F8**
Branco → **162 D6**
Brandenburg **81 B7**
Brandon **141 D10**
Braniewo **82 A4**

Bransfield Str. **168 A4**
Brantford **148 C5**
Brasiléia **163 F5**
Brasília **165 F4**
Braşov **83 F7**
Brassey, Banjaran
  110 D5
Bratislava **82 D3**
Bratsk **98 D8**
Braunau **81 D7**
Braunschweig **80 B6**
Brava, Costa **87 B7**
Bravo del Norte, Rio =
  Grande, Rio → **156 B5**
Brawley **150 D5**
Bray **79 E3**
Bray, Pays de **88 B4**
Brazil ■ **165 E4**
Brazos → **153 E6**
Brazzaville **128 E3**
Brčko **90 B7**
Breaksea Sd. **137 F2**
Bream B. **136 A6**
Bream Hd. **136 A6**
Brecon **79 F5**
Breda **80 C3**
Bredasdorp **130 E4**
Bregenz **80 E5**
Breiðafjörður **76 B1**
Brejo **164 C5**
Bremen **80 B5**
Bremerhaven **80 B5**
Bremerton **144 C2**
Brennerpass **81 E6**
Bréscia **90 B3**
Breslau = Wrocław **82 C3**
Bressanone **90 A3**
Brest Belarus **83 B7**
Brest France **88 B1**
Bretagne □ **88 B2**
Brett, C. **136 A6**
Brewarrina **135 A4**
Bria **125 G3**
Briançon **89 D7**
Bribie I. **135 A5**
Bridgeport **149 D9**
Bridgetown **159 D8**
Bridgewater **143 E7**
Bridgewater, C. **134 C3**
Bridlington **79 D6**
Bridport **134 D4**
Brigham City **145 F7**
Bright **135 C4**
Brighton Australia **134 C2**
Brighton U.K. **79 F6**
Bríndisi **91 D6**
Brisbane **135 A5**
Brisbane → **135 A5**
Bristol U.K. **79 F5**
Bristol U.S.A. **155 A6**
Bristol B. **141 C3**
Bristol Channel **79 F4**
British Isles **79 D4**

British Virgin Is. ☑ **159 C7**
Brittany = Bretagne □ **88 B2**
Brive-la-Gaillarde **88 D4**
Brno **82 D3**
Brock I. **142 B2**
Brocken **80 C6**
Brodeur Pen. **142 B5**
Brodnica **82 B4**
Brody **83 C7**
Broken Hill **134 B3**
Brooks Range **141 B5**
Broome **132 D3**
Brown, Pt. **134 B1**
Brownsville **153 G5**
Brownwood **152 D4**
Bruay-la-Buissière **89 A5**
Bruce, Mt. **132 E2**
Bruck an der Mur **81 E8**
Brugge **80 C2**
Brumado **165 E5**
Brunei = Bandar Seri Begawan **110 D5**
Brunei ■ **110 D4**
Brunner, L. **137 E4**
Brunswick = Braunschweig **80 B6**
Brunswick **155 D7**
Brunswick, Pen. de **167 G2**
Brussel **80 C3**
Brussels = Brussel **80 C3**
Bruthen **135 C4**
Bruxelles = Brussel **80 C3**
Bryan **153 D5**
Bryan, Mt. **134 B2**
Bryansk **84 D5**
Bu Craa **126 C3**
Buapinang **109 E2**
Bucak **118 C2**
Bucaramanga **162 B4**
Buchach **83 D7**
Buchanan **127 G3**
Bucharest = Bucureşti **92 B6**
Buckie **78 C5**
Buckleboo **134 B2**
Bucureşti **92 B6**
Budalin **113 F10**
Budapest **82 E4**
Budd Coast **168 A12**
Bude **79 F4**
Budennovsk **85 E5**
Budgewoi **135 B5**
Budjala **128 D3**
Buenaventura **162 C3**
Buenos Aires **166 C5**
Buffalo **149 C6**
Bug → **82 B5**
Buga **162 C3**
Bugel, Tanjung **111 F4**

Bugsuk I. **110 C5**
Bugun Shara **103 B8**
Buguruslan **97 D6**
Buh → **85 D3**
Buir Nur **103 B11**
Bujumbura **129 E5**
Bukavu **129 E5**
Bukhara = Buxoro **97 F7**
Bukittinggi **111 E2**
Bukoba **129 E6**
Bula **109 E4**
Bulahdelah **135 B5**
Bulan **108 B2**
Bulawayo **131 C5**
Buldan **93 E7**
Bulgan **103 B8**
Bulgaria ■ **92 C5**
Buli, Teluk **109 D3**
Buliluyan, C. **110 C5**
Bulloo → **135 A3**
Bulloo L. **134 A3**
Bulls **136 D6**
Bulukumba **109 F2**
Bulun **98 B10**
Bumba **128 D4**
Bumhpa Bum **113 D11**
Bunbury **132 G2**
Bundaberg **135 A5**
Bundi **115 G9**
Bundoran **79 D2**
Bungo-Suidö **101 G3**
Bunia **129 D6**
Bunji **114 B9**
Buntok **111 E4**
Bunyu **111 D5**
Buol **109 D2**
Buon Ma Thuot **110 B3**
Buorkhaya, Mys **99 B11**
Buqayq **119 F7**
Bûr Safâga **124 C5**
Bûr Sa'îd **124 B5**
Bûr Sûdân **125 E6**
Buraydah **119 F5**
Burco **121 F4**
Burdur **118 C2**
Burgas **92 C6**
Burgos **86 A4**
Burgundy = Bourgogne □ **89 C6**
Burhaniye **93 E6**
Burhanpur **115 J10**
Burias I. **108 B2**
Buriram **110 A2**
Burkina Faso ■ **127 F5**
Burlington Iowa, U.S.A. **147 E9**
Burlington N.C., U.S.A. **155 A8**
Burlington Vt., U.S.A. **149 B9**
Burma ■ **113 G11**
Burnie **134 D4**

Burnley **79 E5**
Burnside → **140 B9**
Burqān **119 E6**
Burqin **102 B5**
Burra **134 B2**
Burren Junction **135 B4**
Burrinjuck, L. **135 C4**
Burruyacú **166 B3**
Burton **127 G7**
Buru **109 E3**
Burundi ■ **129 E6**
Burutu **127 G7**
Bury St. Edmunds **79 E7**
Busan **105 E8**
Büshehr **116 D2**
Businga **128 D4**
Busto Arsízio **90 B2**
Busu Djanoa **128 D4**
Busuanga I. **108 B1**
Buta **129 D4**
Butare **129 E5**
Butaritari **136 J12**
Butembo **129 D5**
Butha Qi **103 B12**
Buton **109 E2**
Butte **145 C7**
Butterworth **110 C2**
Butuan **108 C3**
Buturlinovka **84 C5**
Buurhakaba **121 G3**
Buxoro **97 F7**
Buxtehude **80 B5**
Buy **84 B5**
Buyant-Uhaa **103 C10**
Büyük Menderes → **93 F6**
Büyükçekmece **92 D7**
Buzău **93 D6**
Buzău → **83 F8**
Buzen **101 G2**
Buzi → **131 B6**
Buzuluk **97 D6**
Byarezina → **83 B10**
Byaroza **83 B7**
Bydgoszcz **82 B3**
Byelorussia = Belarus ■ **84 C2**
Bykhaw **83 B10**
Bylot I. **142 B6**
Byrd, C. **168 A3**
Byrock **135 B4**
Byron Bay **135 A5**
Byrranga, Gory **98 B8**
Bytom **82 C4**
Bytów **82 B2**

C

Ca Mau **110 C3**
Caála **130 A3**
Cabanatuan **108 A2**
Cabedelo **164 D7**
Cabimas **162 A4**
Cabinda **128 F2**

Cabinet Mts. **145 C6**
Cabo Blanco **167 F3**
Cabo Frio **165 G5**
Cabo Pantoja **162 D3**
Cabonga, Réservoir **143 E6**
Caboolture **135 A5**
Cabora Bassa Dam = Cahora Bassa, Lago de **131 B6**
Cabot Str. **143 E8**
Cabra **86 D3**
Cabrera **87 C7**
Cabriel → **87 C5**
Čačak **92 C3**
Cáceres Brazil **163 G7**
Cáceres Spain **86 C2**
Cachimbo, Serra do **165 D2**
Cachoeira **165 E6**
Cachoeira do Sul **166 C6**
Cachoeiro de Itapemirim **165 G5**
Cacólo **128 G3**
Caconda **130 A3**
Cadibarrawirracanna, L. **134 A2**
Cadiz Phil. **108 B2**
Cádiz Spain **86 D2**
Cádiz, G. de **86 D2**
Cadney Park **134 A1**
Caen **88 B3**
Caetité **165 E5**
Cagayan de Oro **108 C2**
Cágliari **91 E2**
Cágliari, G. di **91 E2**
Caguas **159 C6**
Cahora Bassa, Lago de **131 B6**
Cahors **88 D4**
Cahul **83 F9**
Caicara **162 B5**
Caicó **164 D6**
Caird Coast **168 B5**
Cairns **133 D8**
Cairo = El Qâhira **124 B5**
Cairo **153 A9**
Cajamarca **163 E3**
Cajazeiras **164 D6**
Calabar **127 H7**
Calábria □ **91 E6**
Calais **88 A4**
Calama Brazil **163 E6**
Calama Chile **166 A3**
Calamar **162 A4**
Calamian Group **108 B1**
Calamocha **87 B5**
Calang **110 D1**
Calapan **108 B2**
Cälăraşi **92 B6**
Calatayud **87 B5**

Calauag **108 B2**
Calavite, C. **108 B2**
Calbayog **108 B2**
Calca **163 F4**
Calcutta = Kolkata
 113 F7
Caldas da Rainha **86 C1**
Caldera **166 B2**
Caldwell **144 E5**
Caledon → **131 E5**
Calgary **141 C8**
Cali **162 C3**
Calicut = Kozhikode
 115 P9
California □ **150 B3**
California, G. de **156 B2**
Calingasta **166 C3**
Callabonna, L. **134 A3**
Callao **163 F3**
Caloundra **135 A5**
Caltagirone **91 F5**
Caltanissetta **91 F5**
Calulo **128 G2**
Calvi **89 E8**
Calvià **87 C7**
Calvinia **130 E3**
Camabatela **128 F3**
Camacupa **130 A3**
Camagüey **158 B4**
Camaná **163 G4**
Camargue **89 E6**
Camarones **167 E3**
Cambodia ■ **110 B3**
Cambrai **89 A5**
Cambrian Mts. **79 E5**
Cambridge *N.Z.* **136 B6**
Cambridge *U.K.* **79 E7**
Cambridge *U.S.A.*
 149 C10
Cambridge Bay **140 B9**
Cambundi-Catembo
 128 G3
Camden *Ark., U.S.A.*
 153 C7
Camden *N.J., U.S.A.*
 149 E8
Cameroon ■ **128 C2**
Cameroun, Mt. **128 D1**
Cametá **164 C4**
Caminha **86 B1**
Camira Creek **135 A5**
Camocim **164 C5**
Campana, I. **167 F1**
Campánia □ **91 D5**
Campbell Town **134 D4**
Campbellton **143 E7**
Campbelltown **135 B5**
Campbeltown **78 D4**
Campeche **157 D6**
Campeche, Golfo de
 157 D6
Camperdown **134 C3**

Câmpina **83 F7**
Campina Grande **164 D6**
Campinas **166 A7**
Campo Grande **165 G3**
Campo Maior **164 C5**
Campobasso **90 D5**
Campos **165 G5**
Campos Belos **165 F6**
Câmpulung **83 F7**
Camrose **141 C8**
Çan **93 D6**
Can Tho **110 B3**
Canada ■ **140 C8**
Cañada de Gómez
 166 C4
Çanakkale **93 D6**
Çanakkale Boğazı **93 D6**
Cananea **156 A5**
Cananeia **165 G6**
Canarias, Is. **126 C2**
Canary Is. = Canarias, Is.
 126 C2
Canavieiras **165 F6**
Canberra **135 C4**
Candelo **135 C4**
Canelones **166 C5**
Cañete **166 D2**
Cangas del Narcea **86 A2**
Canguaretama **164 D6**
Canguçu **166 C6**
Cangzhou **104 C2**
Caniapiscau → **142 D7**
Caniapiscau, L. **143 D7**
Canicattì **91 F4**
Çankırı **118 B3**
Cann River **135 C4**
Cannes **89 E7**
Canoas **166 B6**
Canora **141 C9**
Canowindra **135 B4**
Cantabria □ **86 A4**
Cantábrica, Cordillera
 86 A3
Cantal, Plomb du **89 D5**
Canterbury **79 F7**
Canterbury Bight **137 F4**
Canterbury Plains **137 E4**
Canton **148 D5**
Canudos **163 E7**
Canutama **163 E6**
Cap-Haïtien **159 C5**
Capanaparo → **162 B5**
Cape Barren I. **134 D4**
Cape Breton I. **143 E7**
Cape Coast **127 G5**
Cape Girardeau **153 A9**
Cape Town **130 E3**
Cape Verde Is. ■ **122 E1**
Cape York Peninsula
 133 C7
Capela **165 E6**
Capim → **164 C4**
Capraia **90 C2**

Capri **91 D5**
Caprivi Strip **130 B4**
Captains Flat **135 C4**
Caquetá → **162 D5**
Caracal **92 B5**
Caracas **162 A5**
Caracol **165 D5**
Carajás, Serra dos
 164 D3
Caransebeş **83 F6**
Caratasca, L. de **158 C3**
Caratinga **165 F5**
Caraúbas **164 D6**
Caravaca de la Cruz
 87 C5
Caravelas **165 F6**
Caraveli **163 G4**
Carballo **86 A1**
Carbonara, C. **91 E2**
Carbondale **153 A9**
Carbonear **143 E8**
Carbónia **91 E2**
Carcassonne **88 E5**
Carcross **140 B6**
Cardamon Hills **115 Q10**
Cárdenas **158 B3**
Cardiff **79 F5**
Cardigan B. **79 E4**
Cardston **141 D8**
Carei **83 E6**
Carhué **166 D4**
Caria **93 F7**
Cariacica **165 G5**
Caribbean Sea **158 D5**
Cariboo Mts. **141 C7**
Carinda **135 B4**
Carinhanha **165 E5**
Caripito **162 A6**
Carlisle **79 D5**
Carlow **79 E3**
Carlsbad **152 C1**
Carmacks **140 B6**
Carmarthen **79 F4**
Carmaux **88 D5**
Carmen de Patagones
 167 E4
Carmona **86 D3**
Carnac **88 C2**
Carnarvon *Australia*
 132 E1
Carnarvon *S. Africa*
 130 E4
Carnegie, L. **132 F3**
Carnot **128 D3**
Carnot, C. **134 B2**
Carolina **164 D4**
Caroline I. **137 K15**
Caroline Is. **136 J10**
Caroní → **162 B6**
Caroona **135 B5**
Carpathians **82 D5**
Carpaţii Meridionali **83 F7**

Carpentaria, G. of **132 C6**
Carpentras **89 D6**
Carpi **90 B3**
Carrara **90 B3**
Carrauntoohill **79 E2**
Carrick-on-Suir **79 E3**
Carrieton **134 B2**
Carrizal Bajo **166 B2**
Carson City **144 G4**
Cartagena *Colombia*
 162 A3
Cartagena *Spain* **87 D5**
Cartago *Colombia*
 162 C3
Cartago *Costa Rica*
 158 E3
Carterton **137 D6**
Carthage **153 A6**
Cartwright **142 D8**
Caruaru **164 D6**
Carúpano **162 A6**
Carvoeiro **162 D6**
Carvoeiro, C. **86 C1**
Casa Nova **165 D5**
Casablanca **126 B4**
Cascade Ra. **144 F2**
Cascais **86 C1**
Cascavel **166 A6**
Cáscina **90 C3**
Caserta **90 D5**
Casiguran **108 A2**
Casilda **166 C4**
Casino **135 A5**
Casiquiare → **162 C5**
Casma **163 E3**
Casper **145 E10**
Caspian Sea **97 C5**
Castellammare di Stábia
 91 D5
Castelló de la Plana
 87 C5
Castelo Branco **86 C2**
Castelsarrasin **88 D4**
Castelvetrano **91 F4**
Casterton **134 C3**
Castilla-La Mancha □
 86 C4
Castilla y Leon □ **86 A3**
Castlebar **79 E2**
Castleblayney **79 D3**
Castlemaine **135 C3**
Castlereagh → **135 B4**
Castres **88 E5**
Castries **159 D7**
Castro **167 E2**
Castro Alves **165 E6**
Castuera **86 C3**
Cat I. **158 B4**
Catalão **165 F4**
Çatalca **92 D7**
Catalonia = Cataluña □
 87 B6

Cataluña □ 87 B6
Catamarca 166 B3
Catanduanes □ 108 B2
Catanduva 165 G4
Catánia 91 F5
Catanzaro 91 E6
Catarman 108 B2
Cateel 108 C3
Catoche, C. 157 C7
Catrimani 162 C6
Catskill Mts. 149 C8
Cauca → 162 B4
Caucaia 164 C6
Caucasus Mountains 85 E5
Caungula 128 F3
Cauquenes 166 D2
Caura → 162 B6
Cauvery → 115 P11
Caux, Pays de 88 B4
Cavan 79 D3
Cavendish 134 C3
Caviana, I. 164 B3
Cavite 108 B2
Cawndilla L. 134 B3
Caxias 164 C5
Caxias do Sul 166 B6
Cayambe 162 C3
Cayenne 164 A3
Cayman Is. ☑ 158 C3
Cazombo 130 A4
Ceará □ 164 D6
Ceará-Mirim 164 D6
Cebollar 166 B3
Cebu 108 B2
Cecil Plains 135 A5
Cedar L. 141 C10
Cedar Rapids 147 E9
Cedro 164 D6
Ceduna 134 B1
Ceel Gaal 121 E5
Ceel Waaq 129 D8
Ceeldheere 121 E4
Ceerigaabo 121 E4
Cefalù 91 E5
Cegléd 82 E4
Celaya 156 C4
Celebes = Sulawesi 109 E2
Celebes Sea 109 D2
Celje 90 A5
Celle 80 B6
Celtic Sea 79 F2
Central, Cordillera 162 C3
Central African Rep. ■ 128 C4
Central Makran Range 114 F4
Cephalonia = Kefalonia 93 E3
Ceram = Seram 109 E3

Ceres 166 B4
Cerignola 90 D5
Çerkeş 118 B3
Çerkezköy 92 D6
Cerro de Pasco 163 F3
Cervera 87 B6
Cesena 90 B4
České Budějovice 82 D2
Českomoravská Vrchovina 82 D2
Çeşme 93 E6
Cessnock 135 B5
Cetinje 92 C2
Cetraro 91 E5
Ceuta 86 E3
Cévennes 89 D5
Ceylon = Sri Lanka ■ 115 R12
Chachapoyas 163 E3
Chachran 114 E7
Chad ■ 125 E2
Chad, L. = Tchad, L. 125 F1
Chadileuvú → 166 D3
Chagos Arch. ☑ 94 J9
Chāh Bahar 117 E5
Chāh Gay Hills 114 E3
Chahār Borjak 114 D3
Chaibasa 112 F5
Chakhānsūr 114 D3
Chakradharpur 112 F5
Chakwal 114 C8
Chala 163 G4
Chalhuanca 163 F4
Chalisgaon 115 J9
Chalkida 93 E4
Chalky Inlet 137 G2
Challapata 163 G5
Chalon-sur-Saône 89 C6
Châlons-en-Champagne 89 B6
Chaman 114 D5
Chamba 114 C10
Chambal → 114 F11
Chambéry 89 D6
Chamical 166 C3
Chamonix-Mont Blanc 89 D7
Champagne 89 B6
Champaign 148 D1
Champlain, L. 149 B9
Chañaral 166 B2
Chandigarh 114 D10
Chandler 134 A1
Chandpur 113 F8
Chandrapur 115 K11
Chang Jiang → 106 B6
Changanacheri 115 Q10
Changane → 131 C6
Changbai Shan 105 A8
Changchun 103 C13
Changde 106 C1

Changhua 107 E6
Changsha 106 C2
Changzhi 103 D10
Changzhou 106 B5
Chania 93 G5
Chanion, Kolpos 93 G4
Channapatna 115 N10
Channel Is. 79 G5
Channel-Port aux Basques 143 E8
Chantada 86 A2
Chanthaburi 110 B2
Chantrey Inlet 140 B10
Chanute 153 A6
Chao Phraya → 110 B2
Chaoyang 104 B4
Chaozhou 107 F4
Chapala, L. de 156 C4
Chapayevsk 84 C6
Chapleau 143 E5
Chara 99 D9
Charagua 163 G6
Charaña 163 G5
Chari → 125 F1
Chārīkār 114 B6
Charleroi 80 C3
Charles, C. 149 F8
Charleston S.C., U.S.A. 155 C8
Charleston W. Va., U.S.A. 148 E5
Charleville 135 A4
Charleville-Mézières 89 B6
Charlotte 155 B7
Charlotte Amalie 159 C6
Charlottesville 149 E6
Charlottetown 143 E7
Charlton 134 C3
Charlton I. 143 D6
Charolles 89 C6
Charters Towers 133 E8
Chartres 88 B4
Chascomús 166 D5
Châteaubriant 88 C3
Châteaulin 88 B1
Châteauroux 88 C4
Châtellerault 88 C4
Chatham 79 F7
Chatrapur 112 H5
Chattahoochee → 154 D5
Chattanooga 154 B5
Chaukan Pass 113 D11
Chaumont 89 B6
Chaves Brazil 164 C4
Chaves Portugal 86 B2
Cheb 82 C1
Cheboksary 84 B6
Chech, Erg 126 D5
Chechenia □ 85 E6

Chechnya = Chechenia □ 85 E6
Cheduba I. 113 H9
Cheepie 135 A4
Chegga 126 C4
Chegutu 131 B6
Chehalis 144 C2
Cheju = Jeju 105 F7
Chelforó 167 D3
Chełm 83 C6
Chełmno 82 B4
Chelmsford 79 F7
Cheltenham 79 F5
Chelyabinsk 97 D7
Chelyuskin, Mys 98 B8
Chemba 131 B6
Chemnitz 81 C7
Chenab → 114 C7
Chengde 104 B2
Chengdu 103 E8
Chengjiang 102 G8
Chennai 115 N12
Chenzhou 103 F10
Cheom Ksan 105 D7
Cheongju 105 D7
Chepén 163 E3
Chepes 166 C3
Cher → 88 C4
Cherbourg-Octeville 88 B3
Cherdyn 96 C6
Cherepanovo 97 D9
Cherepovets 84 B4
Chergui, Chott ech 126 B6
Cherkasy 84 D3
Cherlak 97 D8
Chernaya 98 B6
Chernihiv 84 C3
Chernivtsi 83 D7
Chernobyl = Chornobyl 83 C10
Cherrapunji 113 E8
Cherven 83 B9
Chervonohrad 83 C7
Cherykaw 83 B10
Chesapeake 149 G7
Chesapeake B. 149 E7
Cheshskaya Guba 96 C5
Chester U.K. 79 E5
Chester U.S.A. 149 E8
Chesterfield 79 E6
Chesterfield, Îs. 136 L10
Chesterfield Inlet 140 B10
Chesterton Ra. 135 A4
Chetumal 157 D7
Cheviot Hills 78 D5
Chew Bahir 125 H6
Cheyenne 146 E2
Cheyenne → 146 C4
Chhapra 112 E5

Chhatarpur 115 G11
Chhindwara 115 H11
Chi → 110 A2
Chiai 107 F6
Chiávari 90 B2
Chiavenna 90 A2
Chiba 101 F7
Chibemba 130 B2
Chibia 130 B2
Chibougamau 143 E6
Chicago 148 D2
Chichagof I. 141 C6
Chichester 79 F6
Chickasha 152 B5
Chiclana de la Frontera
86 D2
Chiclayo 163 E3
Chico 144 G3
Chico → Chubut,
Argentina 167 E3
Chico → Santa Cruz,
Argentina 167 F3
Chicoutimi 143 E6
Chidambaram 115 P11
Chidley, C. 142 C7
Chiemsee 81 E7
Chiese → 90 B3
Chieti 90 C5
Chifeng 104 A3
Chiguana 163 H5
Chihuahua 156 B3
Chik Bollapur 115 N10
Chikmagalur 115 N9
Chilapa 156 D5
Chilas 114 B9
Chilaw 115 R11
Childers 135 A5
Chile ■ 166 D2
Chilete 163 E3
Chililabombwe 131 A5
Chilka L. 112 H5
Chillán 166 D2
Chiloé, I. de 167 E2
Chilpancingo 156 D5
Chilung 107 E6
Chilwa, L. 131 B7
Chimborazo 162 D3
Chimbote 163 E3
Chimboy 97 E6
Chimkent = Shymkent
97 E7
Chimoio 131 B6
Chin □ 113 F9
China ■ 103 E8
Chinandega 157 E7
Chincha Alta 163 F3
Chinchilla 135 A5
Chinde 131 B7
Chindwin → 113 G10
Chingola 131 A5
Chinguetti 126 D3
Chinhoyi 131 B6

Chiniot 114 D8
Chinon 88 C4
Chióggia 90 B4
Chios 93 E6
Chipata 131 A6
Chiquián 163 F3
Chiquinquira 162 B4
Chirchiq 97 E7
Chiredzi 131 C6
Chirmiri 112 F4
Chisasibi 143 D6
Chişinău 83 E9
Chistopol 84 B7
Chita 98 D9
Chitral 114 B7
Chitré 158 E3
Chittagong 113 F8
Chittaurgarh 115 G9
Chittoor 115 N11
Chiusi 90 C3
Chivasso 90 B1
Chivilcoy 166 B4
Choele Choel 167 D3
Chojnice 82 B3
Cholet 88 C3
Choluteca 157 E7
Choma 131 B5
Chomolungma = Everest,
Mt. 112 C6
Chomutov 82 C1
Chon Buri 110 B2
Chone 162 D3
Ch'ŏngjin 105 B8
Chongqing 103 F9
Chonos, Arch. de los
167 F2
Chop 83 D6
Chora Sfakion 93 G5
Chornobyl 83 C10
Chortkiv 83 D7
Chorzów 82 C4
Chos-Malal 166 D2
Choszczno 82 B2
Chotila 115 H7
Choybalsan 103 B10
Christchurch 137 E5
Christmas I. = Kiritimati
137 J15
Chubut → 167 E3
Chudskoye, Ozero 84 B2
Chūgoku-Sanchi 101 F3
Chula Vista 144 D5
Chulucanas 162 E2
Chulym → 97 D9
Chumbicha 166 B3
Chumphon 110 B1
Chuna → 98 D7
Chuncheon 105 D7
Chungking = Chongqing
103 F9
Chunya 129 F6

Chuquibamba 163 G4
Chuquicamata 166 A3
Chur 89 C8
Churachandpur 113 E9
Churchill 140 C10
Churchill → Man.,
Canada 140 C10
Churchill → Nfld. & L.,
Canada 143 D7
Churchill, C. 140 C10
Churchill Falls 143 D7
Churchill L. 141 C9
Churu 114 E9
Chushal 114 C11
Chusovoy 96 D6
Chuvashia □ 84 B6
Ciadâr-Lunga 83 E9
Cicero 148 D2
Ciechanów 82 B5
Ciego de Ávila 158 B4
Ciénaga 162 A4
Cienfuegos 158 B3
Cieza 87 C5
Cijara, Embalse de 86 C3
Cimişlia 83 E9
Cimone, Mte. 90 B3
Cinca → 87 B6
Cincar 90 C6
Cincinnati 148 E3
Çine 93 F7
Cinto, Mte. 89 E8
Circle 141 B5
Cirebon 111 F3
Citlaltépetl = Orizaba,
Pico de 156 D5
Città di Castello 90 C4
Ciudad Bolívar 162 B6
Ciudad de México
156 D5
Ciudad del Carmen
157 D6
Ciudad Guayana 162 B6
Ciudad Juárez 156 A3
Ciudad Madero 156 C5
Ciudad Mante 156 C5
Ciudad Obregón 156 B3
Ciudad Real 86 C4
Ciudad Rodrigo 86 B2
Ciudad Victoria 156 C5
Civitanova Marche 90 C4
Civitavécchia 90 C3
Cixi 106 B6
Cizre 118 C5
Clare 134 B2
Clarence → Australia
135 A5
Clarence → N.Z. 137 E5
Clarence, I. 167 G2
Clarence I. 168 A4
Clarie Coast 168 A13
Clarke I. 134 D4
Clarksdale 153 B8

Clarksville 154 A4
Claveria 108 A2
Clear, C. 79 F2
Clearwater 155 F6
Clearwater Mts. 145 C6
Clermont-Ferrand 89 D5
Cleveland 148 D5
Clifden 137 G2
Clifton 135 A5
Clinton N.Z. 137 G3
Clinton U.S.A. 147 E9
Clinton Colden L. 140 B9
Clones 79 D3
Clonmel 79 E3
Clovis 152 B2
Cluj-Napoca 83 E6
Clunes 134 C3
Clutha → 137 G3
Clyde 137 F3
Clyde → 78 C4
Clyde, Firth of 78 D4
Clyde River 142 B7
Coari 162 D6
Coast Mts. 140 C7
Coast Ranges 144 F2
Coats I. 142 C5
Coats Land 168 B5
Coatzacoalcos 157 D6
Cobar 135 B4
Cobh 79 F2
Cobija 163 F5
Cobram 135 C4
Coburg 81 C6
Cocanada = Kakinada
112 J4
Cochabamba 163 G5
Cochin = Kochi 115 Q10
Cochin China =
Nam-Phan 110 B3
Cochrane 143 E5
Cochrane, L. 167 F2
Cockburn 134 B3
Cockburn, Canal 167 G2
Coco → 158 D3
Cocobeach 128 D1
Cod, C. 149 C10
Codajás 162 D6
Codó 164 C5
Coeur d'Alene 144 C5
Coffeyville 153 A6
Coffin B. 134 B2
Coffin Bay Peninsula
134 B2
Coffs Harbour 135 B5
Cognac 88 D3
Cohuna 135 C4
Coiba, I. de 158 E3
Coig → 167 G3
Coihaique 167 F2
Coimbatore 115 P10
Coimbra Brazil 163 G7
Coimbra Portugal 86 B1

Coín 86 D3
Cojimies 162 C3
Colac 134 C3
Colatina 165 F5
Colbeck, C. 168 B17
Colchester 79 F7
Coleman 141 D8
Coleraine *Australia* 134 C3
Coleraine *U.K.* 79 D3
Coleridge, L. 137 E4
Colesberg 131 E5
Colhué Huapi, L. 167 F3
Colima 156 D4
Colinas 164 D5
Coll 78 C3
Collahuasi 163 H5
Collarenebri 135 A4
Collina, Passo di 90 B3
Collingwood 136 D5
Colmar 89 B7
Colo → 135 B5
Cologne = Köln 80 C4
Colombia ■ 162 C4
Colombo 115 R11
Colón 157 F9
Colonia Dora 166 B4
Colonsay 78 C3
Colorado □ 151 A10
Colorado → *Argentina* 167 D4
Colorado → *N. Amer.* 150 E5
Colorado Plateau 151 B7
Colorado Springs 146 F2
Columbia *Mo., U.S.A.* 147 F8
Columbia *S.C., U.S.A.* 155 B7
Columbia *Tenn., U.S.A.* 154 B4
Columbia → 144 C1
Columbia, C. 142 A7
Columbia, District of □ 149 E7
Columbia Basin 144 C4
Columbretes, Is. 87 C6
Columbus *Ga., U.S.A.* 154 C5
Columbus *Miss., U.S.A.* 154 C3
Columbus *Ohio, U.S.A.* 148 E4
Colville → 141 A4
Colville, C. 136 B6
Colwyn Bay 79 E5
Comácchio 90 B4
Comallo 167 E2
Comilla 113 F8
Comino, C. 91 D2
Committee B. 142 C5
Commonwealth B. 168 A14

Commoron Cr. → 135 A5
Como 90 B2
Como, L. di 90 B2
Comodoro Rivadavia 167 F3
Comoros ■ 123 H8
Compiègne 89 B5
Comrat 83 E9
Conara 134 D4
Concarneau 88 C2
Conceição da Barra 165 F6
Concepción *Bolivia* 163 G6
Concepción *Chile* 166 D2
Concepción *Paraguay* 166 A5
Concepción, L. 163 G6
Concepción del Oro 156 C4
Concepción del Uruguay 166 C5
Conchos → 156 B3
Concord *N.C., U.S.A.* 155 B7
Concord *N.H., U.S.A.* 149 C10
Concordia *Argentina* 166 C5
Concórdia *Brazil* 162 D5
Condamine 135 A5
Condeúba 165 E5
Condobolin 135 B4
Confuso → 134 A2
Congo (Brazzaville) = Congo ■ 128 E3
Congo (Kinshasa) = Congo, Dem. Rep. of the ■ 128 E4
Congo ■ 128 E3
Congo → 128 F2
Congo, Dem. Rep. of the ■ 128 E4
Conn, L. 79 D2
Connacht □ 79 E2
Connecticut □ 149 D9
Connecticut → 149 D9
Connemara 79 E2
Conran, C. 135 C4
Conselheiro Lafaiete 165 G5
Constance = Konstanz 80 E5
Constance, L. = Bodensee 89 C8
Constanța 92 B7
Constantine 126 A7
Constitución 166 D2
Contai 112 G6

Contamana 163 E4
Contas → 165 E6
Conway, L. 134 A2
Coober Pedy 134 A1
Cook, B. 167 H2
Cook, Mt. = Aoraki Mount Cook 137 E4
Cook Inlet 141 C4
Cook Is. ☑ 137 L14
Cook Strait 137 D6
Cooktown 133 D8
Coolabah 135 B4
Cooladdi 135 A4
Coolah 135 B4
Coolamon 135 B4
Cooma 135 C4
Coonabarabran 135 B4
Coonamble 135 B4
Coondapoor 115 N9
Cooninnie, L. 134 A2
Cooper Cr. → 134 A2
Cooroy 135 A5
Cootamundra 135 B4
Copenhagen = København 77 D8
Copiapó 166 B2
Copiapó → 166 B2
Coppermine → 140 B8
Coquimbo 166 C2
Corabia 92 C5
Coracora 163 G4
Coral Harbour 142 C5
Coral Sea L10
Corato 91 D6
Corby 79 E6
Corcubión 86 A1
Córdoba *Argentina* 166 C4
Córdoba *Spain* 86 D3
Córdoba, Sierra de 166 C4
Cordova 141 B5
Corfu = Kerkyra 93 E2
Coria 86 C2
Corigliano Cálabro 91 E6
Corinth = Korinthos 93 F4
Corinto 165 F5
Cork 79 F2
Çorlu 92 D6
Corner Brook 143 E8
Corneşti 83 E9
Cornwall 143 E6
Cornwall I. 142 B4
Cornwallis I. 142 B4
Corny Pt. 134 B2
Coro 162 A5
Coroatá 164 C5
Corocoro 163 G5
Coroico 163 G5
Coromandel 136 B6

Coronation Gulf 140 B8
Coronation I. 168 A4
Coronel 166 D2
Coronel Dorrego 166 D4
Coronel Suárez 166 D4
Corowa 135 C4
Corpus Christi 152 F5
Corrib, L. 79 E2
Corrientes 166 B5
Corrientes → 162 D4
Corrientes, C. *Colombia* 162 B3
Corrientes, C. *Mexico* 156 C3
Corriverton 162 B7
Corse □ 89 E8
Corse, C. 89 E8
Corsica = Corse □ 89 E8
Corsicana 153 C5
Corte 89 E8
Cortés, Mar de = California, G. de 156 B2
Çorum 118 B3
Corumbá 163 G7
Corunna = A Coruña 86 A1
Corvallis 144 D2
Cosenza 91 E6
Costa Rica ■ 158 E3
Cotabato 108 C2
Cotagaita 163 H5
Côte-d'Ivoire = Ivory Coast ■ 127 G4
Cotentin 88 B3
Cotonou 127 G6
Cotopaxi 162 D3
Cotswold Hills 79 F5
Cottbus 81 C8
Couedic, C. du 134 C2
Coulman I. 168 B15
Council Bluffs 147 E7
Courantyne → 162 B7
Coventry 79 E6
Covilhã 86 B2
Covington 148 E3
Cowal, L. 135 B4
Cowangie 134 C3
Cowell 134 B2
Cowra 135 B4
Coxim 165 F3
Cox's Bazar 113 G8
Cozumel, Isla 157 C7
Cracow = Kraków 82 C4
Cracow 135 A5
Cradock 131 E5
Craigavon 79 D3
Crailsheim 80 D6
Craiova 92 B5
Cranbrook 141 D8
Crateús 164 D5
Crato 164 D6

Crawley 79 F6
Crazy Mts. 145 C8
Crema 90 B2
Cremona 90 B3
Cres 90 B5
Crete = Kriti 93 G5
Créteil 88 B5
Creus, C. de 87 A7
Creuse → 88 C4
Crewe 79 E5
Criciúma 166 B7
Crimean Pen. = Krymskyy Pivostriv 85 D3
Crişul Negru → 82 E5
Crna → 92 D3
Crna Gora 92 C3
Croatia ■ 90 B6
Crocker, Banjaran 110 C5
Croker, C. 132 C5
Cromer 79 E7
Cromwell 137 F3
Crookston 135 B4
Cross Sound 141 C6
Crotone 91 E6
Crows Nest 135 A5
Crowsnest Pass 141 D8
Cruz Alta 166 B6
Cruz del Eje 166 C4
Cruzeiro do Sul 163 E4
Crystal Brook 134 B2
Csongrád 82 E5
Cuamba 131 A7
Cuando → 130 B4
Cuango = Kwango → 128 E3
Cuanza → 128 F2
Cuba ■ 158 B4
Cubango → 130 B4
Cúcuta 162 B4
Cuddalore 115 P11
Cuenca Ecuador 162 D3
Cuenca Spain 87 B5
Cuenca, Serranía de 87 C5
Cuernavaca 156 D5
Cuevas del Almanzora 87 D5
Cuevo 163 H6
Cuiabá 165 F2
Cuiabá → 165 F2
Cuito → 130 B4
Culcairn 135 C4
Culgoa → 135 A4
Culiacán 156 C3
Culion 108 B2
Cullarin Ra. 135 B4
Cullera 87 C5
Culuene → 165 E3
Culverden 137 E5
Cumaná 162 A6
Cumberland 149 E6

Cumberland Pen. 142 C7
Cumberland Plateau 148 F3
Cumberland Sd. 142 C7
Cumborah 135 A4
Cumbum 115 M11
Cummins 134 B2
Cumnock 135 B4
Cunene → 130 B2
Cúneo 90 B1
Cunnamulla 135 A4
Cupica, G. de 162 B3
Curaçao 159 D6
Curaray → 162 D4
Curiapo 162 B6
Curicó 166 C2
Curitiba 166 B7
Currabubula 135 B5
Currais Novos 164 D6
Curralinho 164 C4
Currie 134 C3
Curtea de Argeş 83 F7
Curtis Group 134 C4
Curuápanema → 164 C2
Curuçá 164 C4
Curup 111 E2
Cururupu 164 C5
Curuzú Cuatiá 165 B5
Cusco 163 F4
Cuttaburra → 135 A3
Cuttack 112 G5
Cuvier I. 136 B6
Cuxhaven 80 B5
Cuyo 108 B2
Cuzco = Cusco 163 F4
Cwmbran 79 F5
Cyclades = Kyklades 93 F5
Cygnet 134 D4
Cyprus ■ 118 D3
Cyrenaica = Barqa 124 C3
Czech Rep. ■ 82 D2
Częstochowa 82 C4

D

Da Hinggan Ling 103 B12
Da Lat 110 B3
Da Nang 110 A3
Da Qaidam 102 D7
Da Yunhe → 104 F3
Dabie Shan 106 B3
Dabo 111 E2
Dabola 127 F3
Dacca = Dhaka 113 F8
Dachau 81 D6
Dadanawa 162 C7
Dadra & Nagar Haveli □ 115 J8
Dadu 114 F5
Daegu 105 E8
Daejeon 105 D7

Daet 108 B2
Dagana 127 E2
Dagestan □ 85 E6
Dagupan 108 A2
Dahlak Kebir 121 D3
Dahod 115 H9
Daiō-Misaki 101 F5
Daisen 100 D7
Daisetsu-Zan 100 B8
Dakar 127 F2
Dakhla 126 D2
Dakhla, El Wâhât el 124 C4
Dalälven → 77 C9
Dalaman → 93 F7
Dalandzadgad 103 C8
Dālbandīn 114 E4
Dalby 135 A5
Dali 102 F8
Dalian 104 C4
Daliang Shan 102 F8
Dallas 153 C5
Dalmacija 90 C6
Dalmatia = Dalmacija 90 C6
Dalnegorsk 100 A4
Daloa 127 G4
Dalton 154 B5
Daly Waters 132 D5
Daman 115 J8
Damanhûr 124 B5
Damar 109 F3
Damaraland 130 C3
Damascus = Dimashq 118 D4
Damāvand 116 C3
Damāvand, Qolleh-ye 116 C3
Damba 128 F3
Dâmboviţa → 92 B6
Dāmghān 116 B3
Damiel 86 C4
Damietta = Ad Dammām 119 F7
Damoh 115 H11
Dampier 132 E2
Dampier, Selat 109 E4
Danbury 149 D9
Dandeldhura 112 C3
Dandeli 115 M9
Dandenong 135 C4
Dandong 105 B6
Dangrek, Phnom 110 B2
Danilov 84 B5
Dankhar Gompa 114 C11
Dannevirke 136 D7
Danube = Dunărea → 83 F9
Danville 155 A8
Danzhou 107 a
Danzig = Gdańsk 82 A4
Dar es Salaam 129 F7

Dārāb 116 D3
Daraj 124 B1
Darband 114 B8
Darbhanga 112 D5
Dardanelles = Çanakkale Boğazı 93 D6
Dârfûr 125 F3
Dargai 114 B7
Dargaville 136 A5
Darıca 92 D7
Darién, G. del 162 B3
Darjeeling = Darjiling 112 D7
Darjiling 112 D7
Darling → 134 B3
Darling Downs 135 A5
Darling Ra. 132 G2
Darlington 79 D6
Darłowo 82 A3
Darmstadt 80 D5
Darnah 124 B3
Darnley, C. 168 A10
Darnley B. 140 B7
Dart, C. 168 B18
Dartmoor 79 F5
Dartmouth 143 E7
Dartmouth, L. 135 A4
Darwha 115 J10
Darwin 132 C5
Dās 116 B3
Dashen, Ras 129 B7
Dasht → 114 G2
Daşoguz 97 E6
Datça 93 F6
Datia 115 G11
Datong 103 C10
Datu, Tanjung 111 D3
Datu Piang 108 C2
Daugava → 84 B1
Daugavpils 84 B2
Daulpur 114 F10
Dauphin 141 C9
Dauphiné 89 D6
Daurada, Costa 87 B6
Davangere 115 M9
Davao 108 C3
Davao G. 108 C3
Davenport 147 E9
David 158 E3
Davis Sea 168 A11
Davis Str. 138 C14
Davos 91 C8
Davyd Haradok 83 B8
Dawei = Tavoy 110 B1
Dawna Ra. 113 J12
Dawson, I. 167 G2
Dawson City 140 B6
Dax 88 E3
Daxian 103 E9
Daxue Shan 102 E8
Daylesford 134 C3
Dayr az Zawr 118 D5

Dayton 148 E3
Daytona Beach 155 E7
De Aar 130 E4
Dead Sea 119 E3
Deal I. 134 C4
Deán Funes 166 C4
Death Valley 150 B4
Debar 92 D3
Debre Markos 125 F6
Debrecen 82 E5
Decatur *Ala., U.S.A.* 154 B4
Decatur *Ill., U.S.A.* 147 F10
Deccan 115 L11
Děčín 82 C2
Dee → 78 C5
Deepwater 135 A5
Deer Lake 143 E8
Deggendorf 81 D7
Deh Bīd 116 D3
Dehibat 124 B1
Dehra Dun 114 D11
Dej 83 E6
Dekese 128 E4
Delano 150 C3
Delaware □ 149 E8
Delegate 135 C4
Delgado, C. 129 G8
Delgo 125 D5
Delhi 114 E10
Delice → 118 C3
Delicias 156 B3
Déline 140 B7
Delmenhorst 80 B5
Deloraine 134 D4
Delungra 135 A5
Delvinë 93 E3
Demanda, Sierra de la 86 A4
Dembidolo 125 G5
Demini → 162 D6
Demirci 93 E7
Demirköy 92 D6
Dempo 111 E2
Den Haag = 's-Gravenhage 80 B3
Den Helder 80 B3
Denali = McKinley, Mt. 141 B4
Dendang 111 E3
Denia 87 C6
Denial B. 134 B1
Deniliquin 135 C3
Denizli 118 C2
Denman Glacier 168 A11
Denmark ■ 77 E8
Denmark Str. 138 C17
Denov 97 F7
Denpasar 111 F5
Denton 152 C5
D'Entrecasteaux Is. 133 B9

Denver 146 F2
Deoghar 112 E6
Deolali 115 K8
Deoria 112 D4
Deosai Mts. 114 B9
Dera Ghazi Khan 114 D7
Dera Ismail Khan 114 D7
Derbent 85 E6
Derby *Australia* 132 D3
Derby *U.K.* 79 E6
Derg, L. 79 E2
Derry = Londonderry 79 D3
Des Moines 147 E8
Des Moines → 147 E9
Desaguadero → 163 G5
Dese 121 E2
Desna → 83 C10
Desolación, I. 167 G2
Despeñaperros, Paso 86 C4
Dessau 81 C7
D'Estrees B. 134 C2
Detmold 80 C5
Detroit 148 C4
Deutsche Bucht 80 A5
Deva 83 F6
Devakottai 115 Q11
Deventer 80 B4
Devon I. 142 B5
Devonport *Australia* 134 D4
Devonport *N.Z.* 136 B6
Dewas 115 H10
Deyhūk 116 C4
Deyyer 116 E2
Dezfūl 119 D7
Dezhneva, Mys 99 C16
Dezhou 104 D2
Dhahran = Aẓ Ẓahrān 119 F7
Dhaka 113 F8
Dhamtari 112 G3
Dhanbad 112 F6
Dhangarhi 112 C3
Dhankuta 112 D6
Dhar 115 H9
Dharmapuri 115 N11
Dhaulagiri 112 C4
Dhenkanal 112 G5
Dhrol 115 H7
Dhuburi 113 D7
Dhule 115 J9
Diafarabé 127 F5
Diamantina 165 F5
Diamantina → 134 A2
Diamantino 165 E2
Diamond Harbour 112 F7
Dibaya-Lubue 128 E3
Dibrugarh 113 D10
Didiéni 127 F4
Diefenbaker, L. 141 C9

Dieppe 88 B4
Digby 143 E7
Dighinala 113 F9
Digne-les-Bains 89 D7
Digos 108 C3
Digul → 109 F5
Dihang = Brahmaputra → 113 F7
Dijlah, Nahr → 119 E6
Dijon 89 C6
Dikson 96 B9
Dikti Oros 93 G5
Dili 109 F3
Dillingham 141 C4
Dilolo 128 G4
Dimashq 118 D4
Dimboola 134 C3
Dimitrovgrad *Bulgaria* 92 C5
Dimitrovgrad *Russia* 84 C9
Dinagat I. 108 B3
Dinajpur 113 E7
Dinan 88 B2
Dinant 80 C3
Dinar 118 C2
Dinār, Kūh-e 116 D2
Dinara Planina 90 B6
Dinard 88 B2
Dindigul 115 P11
Dingle 79 E1
Dingwall 78 C4
Dinosaur △ 145 F9
Diplog 108 C2
Dir 114 B7
Dire Dawa 121 F3
Dirfis Oros 93 E4
Dirranbandi 135 A4
Disa 115 G8
Disappointment, L. 132 E3
Disaster B. 135 C4
Discovery B. 134 C3
Disteghil Sar 114 A9
District of Columbia □ 149 E7
Distrito Federal □ 165 F4
Diu 115 J7
Divinópolis 165 G5
Divnoye 85 D5
Diyarbakır 118 C5
Djakarta = Jakarta 111 F3
Djambala 128 E2
Djanet 126 D7
Djelfa 126 B6
Djerba, Î. de 124 B1
Djerid, Chott 126 B7
Djibouti 121 E3
Djibouti ■ 121 E3
Djolu 128 D4
Djoum 128 D2

Djourab, Erg du 125 E2
Dmitriya Lapteva, Proliv 99 B12
Dnepropetrovsk = Dnipropetrovsk 85 D4
Dnieper = Dnipro → 85 D3
Dniester = Dnister → 83 E10
Dnipro → 85 D3
Dniprodzerzhynsk 85 D3
Dnipropetrovsk 85 D4
Dnister → 83 E10
Doba 125 G2
Doberai, Jazirah 109 E4
Dobo 109 F4
Doboj 90 B7
Dobrich 92 C5
Dobruja 92 B7
Dobrush 83 B10
Dodecanese = Dodekanisa 93 F6
Dodekanisa 93 F6
Dodge City 152 A3
Dodoma 129 F7
Doha = Ad Dawḥah 116 E2
Dohazari 113 F9
Doi 109 D3
Dois Irmãos, Sa. 165 D5
Dokdo = Liancourt Rocks 101 E2
Dolak, Pulau 109 F5
Dolbeau-Mistassini 143 E6
Dole 89 C6
Dolomiti 90 A3
Dolores 166 D5
Dolphin, C. 167 G5
Dolphin and Union Str. 140 B8
Dombarovskiy 97 D6
Dominica ■ 159 C7
Dominican Rep. ■ 159 C5
Domodóssola 90 A2
Domville, Mt. 135 A5
Don → *Russia* 85 D4
Don → *U.K.* 78 C5
Don Benito 86 C3
Donald 134 C3
Donau = Dunărea → 83 F9
Donauwörth 80 D6
Doncaster 79 E6
Dondo, Teluk 109 D2
Donegal 79 D2
Donets → 85 D5
Donetsk 85 D4
Donggala 109 E1
Dongguan 107 F2
Dongola 125 E5

Dongting Hu 106 C2
Dongying 104 D3
Donington, C. 134 B2
Donnelly's Crossing 136 A5
Donostia-San Sebastián 87 A5
Dora Báltea → 90 B2
Dorchester, C. 142 C6
Dordogne → 88 D3
Dordrecht 80 C3
Dori 127 F5
Dornbirn 80 E5
Doro, Kavo 93 E5
Dorohoi 83 E8
Döröö Nuur 102 B6
Dorrigo 135 B5
Dortmund 80 C4
Dos Bahías, C. 167 E3
Dos Hermanas 86 D3
Dosso 127 F6
Dothan 154 D5
Douai 89 A5
Douala 128 D1
Douarnenez 88 B1
Double Island Pt. 135 A5
Doubs → 89 C6
Doubtful Sd. 137 F2
Doubtless B. 136 A5
Douglas I. of Man 79 D4
Douglas U.S.A. 151 E8
Dourados 166 A6
Douro → 86 B1
Dover Australia 134 D4
Dover U.K. 79 F7
Dover, Str. of 79 F7
Dovrefjell 76 C7
Dowlat Yär 117 C6
Dowlatābād 116 D4
Drăgășani 92 B5
Dragichyn 83 B7
Dragoman, Prokhod 92 C4
Draguignan 89 E7
Drakensberg 131 E5
Drama 92 D5
Drammen 77 D8
Drava → 90 B7
Dresden 81 C7
Dreux 88 B4
Drin → 92 C2
Drina → 90 B7
Drobeta-Turnu Severin 92 B4
Drochia 83 D8
Drogheda 79 E3
Drohobych 83 D6
Dromedary, C. 135 C5
Dronning Maud Land 168 B7
Drumheller 141 C8
Drummond Pt. 134 B2

Drut → 83 B10
Drygalski I. 168 A11
Drysdale I. 134 B2
Dubăsari 83 E9
Dubăsari Vdkhr. 83 E9
Dubawnt → 140 B9
Dubawnt L. 140 B9
Dubayy 116 E3
Dubbo 135 B4
Dublin Ireland 79 E3
Dublin U.S.A. 155 C6
Dubno 83 C7
Dubovka 84 D5
Dubréka 127 G3
Dubrovnik 90 C7
Dubrovytsya 83 C8
Dudhi 112 E4
Dudinka 98 C6
Dugi Otok 90 B5
Duisburg 80 C4
Dukhān 116 E2
Duki 114 D6
Dulce → 166 C4
Duluth 147 B8
Dum Duma 113 D10
Dumaguete 108 C2
Dumai 111 D2
Dumaran 108 B1
Dumfries 79 D5
Dumyât 124 B5
Dún Laoghaire 79 E3
Duna = Dunărea → 83 F9
Dunakeszi 82 E4
Dunărea → 83 F9
Dunaújváros 82 E4
Dunback 137 F4
Dunbar 78 D5
Duncan 152 B5
Dund-Us 102 B6
Dundalk 79 D3
Dundee 78 C5
Dunedin 137 F4
Dunfermline 78 C5
Dungarvan 79 E3
Dungog 135 B5
Dungu 129 D5
Dunhuang 102 C6
Dunkerque 88 A5
Dunkirk = Dunkerque 88 A5
Dunolly 134 C3
Dunstan Mts. 137 F3
Durance → 89 E6
Durango 156 C4
Durazno 166 C5
Durban 131 D6
Düren 80 C4
Durgapur 112 F6
Durham U.K. 79 D6
Durham U.S.A. 155 B8
Durmitor 92 C2

Durrës 92 D2
Dursunbey 93 E7
Dushak 97 F7
Dushanbe 97 F7
Dusky Sd. 137 F2
Düsseldorf 80 C4
Dutch Harbor 141 C3
Duyun 103 F9
Dvina, Severnaya → 96 C5
Dwarka 115 H6
Dyer, C. 142 C7
Dyer Plateau 168 B3
Dyersburg 153 A9
Dymer 83 C10
Dzerzhinsk 84 B5
Dzhambul = Taraz 97 E8
Dzhankoy 85 D3
Działdowo 82 B5
Dzierżoniów 82 C3
Dzungarian Basin = Junggar Pendi 102 C5
Dzüünmod 103 B9
Dzyarzhynsk 83 B8
Dzyatlava 83 B7

E

Earnslaw, Mt. 137 F3
East Bengal 113 E7
East C. = Dezhneva, Mys 99 C16
East C. 136 B8
East China Sea 103 E13
East Falkland 167 G5
East Kilbride 78 D4
East London 131 E5
East Orange 149 D8
East St. Louis 147 F9
East Sea = Japan, Sea of 100 D4
East Timor ■ 109 F3
East Toorale 135 B4
Eastbourne N.Z. 137 D6
Eastbourne U.K. 79 F7
Eastern Desert = Es Sahrâ' Esh Sharqîya 124 C5
Eastern Ghats 115 N11
Eastmain 143 D6
Eastmain → 143 D6
Eau Claire 147 C9
Eau Claire, L. à l' 143 D6
Eberswalde-Finow 81 B7
Ebetsu 100 B7
Ebolowa 128 D2
Ebro → 87 B6
Eceabat 93 D6
Ech Chéliff 126 A6
Echizen 101 F5
Echo Bay 140 B8

Echuca 135 C3
Écija 86 D3
Eclipse Sd. 142 B6
Ecuador ■ 162 D3
Ed Debba 125 E5
Ed Dueim 125 F5
Eddystone Pt. 134 D4
Eden 135 C4
Eder → 80 C5
Edessa 93 D4
Edievale 137 F3
Edinburg 152 F4
Edinburgh 78 D5
Edineț 83 D8
Edirne 92 D6
Edithburgh 134 C2
Edmonton 141 C8
Edmundston 143 E7
Edremit 93 E6
Edremit Körfezi 93 E6
Edson 141 C8
Edward → 134 C3
Edward, L. 129 E5
Edward VII Land 168 C17
Edwards Plateau 152 D3
Égadi, Ísole 91 F4
Eger 82 E5
Egio 93 E4
Eglinton I. 142 B2
Egmont, C. 136 C5
Egmont △ 136 C6
Eğridir 118 C2
Eğridir Gölü 118 C2
Egypt ■ 124 C5
Eibar 87 A4
Eidsvold 135 A5
Eifel 80 C4
Eigg 78 C3
Eilat = Elat 119 E3
Eildon, L. 135 C4
Eindhoven 80 C3
Eire = Ireland ■ 79 E3
Eirunepé 163 E5
Eisenach 80 C6
Eisenerz 81 E8
Eivissa 87 C6
Ekaterinburg = Yekaterinburg 97 D7
Eketahuna 136 D6
Ekibastuz 97 D8
El Aaiún 126 C3
El Alamein 124 B4
El Bayadh 126 B6
El Calafate 167 G2
El Carmen 162 B3
El Centro 150 D5
El Cerro 163 G6
El Cuy 167 D3
El Diviso 162 C3
El Djouf 126 D4
El Dorado Ark., U.S.A. 153 C7

El Dorado *Kans., U.S.A.*
152 A5
El Dorado *Venezuela*
162 B6
El Escorial 86 B3
El Faiyûm 124 C5
El Fâsher 125 F4
El Fuerte 156 B3
El Gîza 124 C5
El Iskandarîya 124 B4
El Jadida 126 B4
El Khârga 124 C5
El Khartûm 125 E5
El Lucero 156 A3
El Maestrazgo 87 B5
El Mahalla el Kubra
124 B5
El Mansûra 124 B5
El Minyâ 124 C5
El Obeid 125 F5
El Odaiya 125 F4
El Oued 126 B7
El Paso 151 E9
El Prat de Llobregat
87 B7
El Puerto de Santa María
86 D2
El Qâhira 124 B5
El Salvador ■ 157 E7
El Suweis 124 C5
El Tigre 162 B6
El Turbio 167 G2
El Uqsur 124 C5
El Vigía 162 B4
El Wuz 125 E5
Elat 119 E3
Elâziğ 118 C4
Elba 90 C3
Elbasan 92 D3
Elbe → 81 B5
Elbert, Mt. 151 A9
Elbeuf 88 B4
Elbląg 82 A4
Elbrus 85 E5
Elburz Mts. = Alborz,
Reshteh-ye Kühhä-ye
116 B3
Elche 87 C5
Elda 87 C5
Elde → 81 B6
Eldoret 129 D7
Elefantes → 131 C6
Elektrostal 84 B4
Elephant I. 168 A4
Eleuthera I. 158 A4
Elgin *U.K.* 78 C5
Elgin *U.S.A.* 148 C1
Elgon, Mt. 129 D6
Eliase 109 F4
Elista 85 D5
Elizabeth *Australia*
134 B2

Elizabeth *U.S.A.* 149 D8
Elizabeth City 155 A9
Elizabethton 155 A6
Elk 82 B6
Elkhart 148 D3
Elkhovo 92 C6
Elko 144 F6
Ellef Ringnes I. 142 B3
Ellery, Mt. 135 C4
Ellesmere, L. 137 G5
Ellesmere I. 142 B6
Ellice Is. = Tuvalu ■
136 K12
Elliot Lake 143 C5
Elliston 134 B1
Elmore 135 C3
Elmshorn 80 B5
Eltham 136 C6
Eluru 112 J3
Elvas 86 C2
Ely 79 E7
eMalahleni 131 D5
Emāmrūd 116 B3
Embarcación 166 A4
Embetsu 100 A7
Embi 97 E6
Embi → 97 E6
Embrun 89 D7
Emden 80 B4
Emet 93 E7
Emi Koussi 125 E2
Emine, Nos 92 C6
Emissi, Tarso 124 D2
Emmen 80 B4
Empalme 156 B2
Empangeni 131 D6
Empedrado 166 B5
Ende 109 F2
Enderby Land 168 A9
Enewetak Atoll 136 H11
Enez 93 D6
Engaño, C. 108 A2
Engaru 100 A8
Engels 84 C6
Enggano 111 F2
England □ 79 E6
Englewood 146 F2
English Channel 79 F5
Enid 152 A5
Enna 91 F5
Ennedi 125 E3
Enngonia 135 A4
Ennis 79 E2

Enniskillen 79 D3
Enns → 81 D8
Enns → 81 D8
Enschede 80 B4
Ensenada 156 A1
Entebbe 129 D6
Entre Ríos □ 166 C5
Entroncamento 86 C1
Enugu 127 G7
Éolie, Ís. 91 E5
Épernay 89 B5
Ephesus 93 F6
Épinal 89 B7
Equatorial Guinea ■
128 D1
Er Rachidia 126 B5
Er Rahad 125 F5
Er Rif 126 A5
Erāwadī Myit =
Irrawaddy → 113 K10
Erbil = Arbīl 118 C6
Erciyaş Dağı 118 C3
Érd 82 E4
Erdek 93 D6
Erebus, Mt. 168 B15
Erechim 166 B6
Ereğli *Konya, Turkey*
118 C3
Ereğli *Zonguldak, Turkey*
118 B3
Eresma → 86 B3
Erfurt 81 C6
Ergani 118 C4
Érice 91 E4
Erie 149 C5
Erie, L. 148 C5
Erimanthos 93 F3
Erimo-Misaki 100 C8
Erlangen 81 D6
Ermenek 118 C3
Ermoupoli 93 F5
Erne, Lower L. 79 D3
Erode 115 P10
Eromanga 135 A3
Erramala Hills 115 M11
Errentería 87 A5
Erzgebirge 81 C7
Erzincan 118 C4
Erzurum 118 C5
Es Sahrâ' Esh Sharqîya
124 C5
Es Sînâ' 124 C5
Esan-Misaki 100 C7
Esashi *Hokkaidō, Japan*
100 A8
Esashi *Hokkaidō, Japan*
100 C7
Esbjerg 77 D7
Esch-sur-Alzette 89 B6
Escuinapa de Hidalgo
156 C3
Esenguly 97 F6

Eşfahān 116 C2
Esker Siding 143 D7
Eskilstuna 77 D9
Eskişehir 118 C2
Esla → 86 B2
Eslāmābād-e Gharb
118 D6
Eşme 93 E7
Esmeraldas 162 C3
Esperance 132 G3
Espichel, C. 86 C1
Espinhaço, Serra do
165 F5
Espírito Santo □ 165 G5
Espíritu Santo 136 L11
Espoo 77 C10
Esquel 167 E2
Esquina 166 C5
Essaouira 126 B4
Essen 80 C4
Essequibo → 162 B7
Esslingen 80 D5
Estados, I. de Los
167 G4
Estância 165 E6
Estevan 141 D9
Estonia ■ 77 G11
Estrela, Serra da 86 B2
Estremoz 86 C2
Estrondo, Serra do
164 D4
Esztergom 82 E4
Étampes 88 B5
Etawah 114 F11
eThekwini = Durban
131 D6
Ethiopia ■ 121 F2
Ethiopian Highlands
121 F2
Etna 91 F5
Etosha Pan 130 B3
Eucumbene, L. 135 C4
Eufaula 154 D5
Eugene 144 E2
Eugowra 135 B4
Eulo 135 A4
Euphrates = Furāt, Nahr
al → 119 E6
Eureka *Canada* 142 B5
Eureka *U.S.A.* 144 F1
Euroa 135 C4
Europa, Île 131 C8
Europa, Picos de 86 A3
Europa, Pt. 86 D3
Evans Head 135 A5
Evanston 148 D2
Evansville 148 F2
Everard, L. 134 B1
Everest, Mt. 112 C6
Everett 144 C2
Everglades △ 155 G7
Evia 93 E5

Évora **86 C2**
Évreux **88 B4**
Evros → **92 D6**
Évry **88 B5**
Ewo **128 E2**
Exaltación **163 F5**
Exeter **79 F5**
Exmoor **79 F5**
Exmouth **79 F5**
Extremadura □ **86 C2**
Eyasi, L. **129 E6**
Eyl **121 F4**
Eyre (North), L. **134 A2**
Eyre (South), L. **134 A2**
Eyre, L. **132 F6**
Eyre Mts. **137 F3**
Eyre Pen. **134 B2**
Ezhou **106 D3**
Ezine **93 E6**

F

F.Y.R.O.M. =
   Macedonia ■ **92 D3**
Fabriano **90 C4**
Fada **125 E3**
Fada-n-Gourma **127 F6**
Faddeyevskiy, Ostrov
   99 B12
Faenza **90 B3**
Færoe Is. = Føroyar ☑
   74 C4
Făgăraş **83 F7**
Fagnano, L. **167 G3**
Fahraj **117 D7**
Fair Isle **78 B6**
Fairbanks **141 B5**
Fairfield Ala., U.S.A.
   154 C4
Fairfield Calif., U.S.A.
   144 G2
Fairlie **137 F4**
Fairweather, Mt. **141 C6**
Faisalabad **114 D8**
Faizabad **112 D4**
Fakfak **109 E4**
Falaise **88 B3**
Falam **113 F9**
Falconara Maríttima
   90 C4
Falcone, C. del **90 D2**
Fălești **83 E8**
Falkland Is. ☑ **167 G5**
Falkland Sd. **167 G5**
Fall River **149 D10**
Falmouth **79 F4**
Fălticeni **83 E8**
Falun **77 C9**
Famagusta **118 D3**
Fano **90 C4**
Faradje **129 D5**
Farafangana **131 C9**
Farāh **114 C3**

Faranah **127 F3**
Farasān, Jazā'ir **121 D3**
Fareham **79 F6**
Farewell, C. **136 D5**
Farghona **97 E8**
Fargo **146 B6**
Farīmān **117 C4**
Farina **134 B2**
Faro Brazil **164 C2**
Faro Portugal **86 D2**
Farräshband **116 D3**
Fārs □ **116 D3**
Farsala **93 E4**
Fartak, Râs **119 E3**
Fāryāb □ **117 B6**
Fasā **116 D3**
Fasano **91 D6**
Fastiv **83 C9**
Fatagartuting, Tanjung
   109 E4
Fatehgarh **114 F11**
Fatehpur Raj., India
   114 F9
Fatehpur Ut. P., India
   112 E3
Favara **91 F4**
Favignana **91 F4**
Faxaflói **76 C1**
Faya-Largeau **125 E2**
Fayd **119 E5**
Fayetteville Ark., U.S.A.
   153 A6
Fayetteville N.C., U.S.A.
   155 B8
Fazilka **114 D9**
Fdérik **126 D3**
Feather → **144 G3**
Featherston **137 D6**
Fécamp **88 B4**
Fehmarn **81 A6**
Feilding **136 D6**
Feldkirch **80 E5**
Felipe Carrillo Puerto
   157 D7
Felixstowe **79 F7**
Fenoarivo Atsinanana
   131 B9
Fenyang **103 D10**
Feodosiya **85 D4**
Ferdows **116 C4**
Ferfer **121 F4**
Ferizaj **92 C3**
Ferkéssédougou **126 D3**
Fermo **90 C4**
Fermont **143 D5**
Fernando de Noronha
   164 C2
Fernando Póo = Bioko
   128 D1
Ferrara **90 B3**
Ferreñafe **163 E3**
Ferret, C. **88 D3**
Ferrol **86 A1**

Fès **126 B5**
Fetești **92 B6**
Fetlar **78 A6**
Feuilles → **142 D6**
Fezzan **124 C2**
Fianarantsoa **131 C9**
Fier **93 D2**
Figeac **88 D5**
Figueira da Foz **86 B1**
Figueres **87 A7**
Figuig **126 B5**
Fiji ■ **136 L12**
Filiatra **93 F3**
Filyos Çayı → **118 B3**
Fíngoè **131 A6**
Finike **118 C2**
Finland ■ **76 C11**
Finland, G. of **77 D11**
Finlay → **140 C7**
Finley **135 C4**
Finniss, C. **134 B1**
Fiora → **90 C3**
Fiordland △ **137 F2**
Firenze **90 C3**
Firozabad **114 F11**
Firozpur **114 D9**
Fīrūzābād **116 D3**
Fīrūzkūh **116 C3**
Fish → **130 D3**
Fishguard **79 E4**
Fisterra, C. **86 A1**
Fitz Roy **167 F3**
Fizi **129 E5**
Flagstaff **151 C7**
Flåm **76 C7**
Flaming Gorge Res.
   145 F9
Flamingo, Teluk **109 F5**
Flandre **80 C2**
Flathead L. **145 C7**
Flattery, C. **144 B1**
Flensburg **80 A5**
Flers **88 B3**
Flesko, Tanjung **109 D2**
Flin Flon **141 C9**
Flinders → **133 D7**
Flinders I. **134 C4**
Flinders Ranges **134 B2**
Flint **148 C4**
Flint I. **137 L15**
Florence = Firenze **90 C3**
Florence Ala., U.S.A.
   154 B4
Florence S.C., U.S.A.
   155 B8
Florence, L. **134 A2**
Flores **109 F2**
Flores Sea **109 F2**
Florești **83 E9**
Floriano **164 D5**

Florida, Straits of **158 B3**
Florina **93 D3**
Florø **76 C7**
Fluk **109 E3**
Fly → **133 B7**
Flying Fish, C. **168 B1**
Foça **93 E6**
Focșani **83 F8**
Fóggia **90 D6**
Föhr **80 A5**
Foix **88 E4**
Folda **76 B8**
Foligno **90 C4**
Folkestone **79 F7**
Fond du Lac **147 D10**
Fondi **90 D4**
Fongafale **136 K12**
Fonseca, G. de **157 E7**
Fontainebleau **89 B5**
Fontanay-le-Comte
   88 C3
Fonte Boa **162 D5**
Forbes **135 B4**
Fords Bridge **135 A4**
Forestier Pen. **134 D4**
Forfar **78 C5**
Forlì **90 B4**
Formentera **87 C6**
Formentor, C. de **87 C7**
Former Yugoslav
   Republic of Macedonia
   = Macedonia ■ **92 D3**
Fórmia **90 D4**
Formosa = Taiwan ■
   107 F6
Formosa **166 B5**
Formosa, Serra **165 E3**
Føroyar ☑ **74 C4**
Forsayth **133 D7**
Forst **81 C8**
Fort Albany **143 D5**
Fort Collins **146 E2**
Fort-de-France **159 D7**
Fort Dodge **147 D7**
Fort Good Hope **140 B7**
Fort Lauderdale **155 F7**
Fort Liard **140 B7**
Fort Macleod **141 D8**
Fort McPherson **140 B6**
Fort Myers **155 F7**
Fort Peck L. **145 C10**
Fort Pierce **155 F7**
Fort Providence **140 B8**
Fort Resolution **140 B8**
Fort Scott **153 A6**
Fort Shevchenko **97 E6**
Fort Simpson **140 B7**
Fort Smith Canada
   140 B8
Fort Smith U.S.A. **153 B6**
Fort Walton Beach
   154 D4
Fort Wayne **148 D3**

Fort William 78 C4
Fort Worth 152 C5
Fort Yukon 141 B5
Fortaleza 164 C6
Forür 116 E3
Foshan 107 F2
Fossano 90 B1
Fougères 88 B3
Foula 78 A5
Fourni 93 F6
Fouta Djallon 127 F3
Foveaux Str. 137 G3
Foxe Basin 142 C6
Foxe Chan. 142 C5
Foxe Pen. 142 C6
Foxton 136 D6
Foz do Iguaçu 166 B6
Franca 165 G4
Francavilla Fontana
　91 D6
France ■ 89 C5
Frances 134 C3
Franceville 128 E2
Franche-Comté □ 89 C6
Francistown 131 C5
Frankfurt Brandenburg,
　Germany 81 B8
Frankfurt Hessen,
　Germany 80 C5
Fränkische Alb 81 D6
Franklin B. 140 B7
Franklin I. 168 B15
Franklin Mts. 140 B7
Franklin Str. 140 A10
Frankston 135 C4
Frantsa Iosifa, Zemlya
　96 A6
Fraser → 141 D7
Fraser I. 135 A5
Fraserburgh 78 D6
Fray Bentos 166 C5
Fredericksburg 149 E7
Fredericton 143 E7
Frederikshavn 77 D8
Fredrikstad 77 D8
Free State □ 131 D5
Freeport Bahamas
　158 A4
Freeport U.S.A. 147 D10
Freetown 127 G3
Fregenal de la Sierra
　86 C2
Freiburg 80 E4
Freire 167 D2
Freising 81 D6
Freistadt 81 D8
Fréjus 89 E7
Fremont 150 B2
French Guiana ☑ 164 B3
French Polynesia ☑
　137 M16
French Riviera = Azur,
　Côte d' 89 E7

Fresco → 164 D3
Freshfield, C. 168 A14
Fresnillo 156 C4
Fresno 150 B3
Freycinet Pen. 134 D4
Fria, C. 130 B2
Frías 166 B3
Friedrichshafen 80 E5
Frobisher B. 142 C7
Frome → 134 A2
Frome, L. 134 B2
Frosinone 90 D4
Frutal 165 H4
Frýdek-Místek 82 D4
Fuchū 101 F3
Fuengirola 86 D3
Fuentes de Oñoro 86 B2
Fuerte → 156 B3
Fuerte Olimpo 163 H7
Fuerteventura 126 C3
Fuhai 102 B5
Fuji 101 F6
Fuji-San 101 F6
Fujian □ 107 E5
Fujiyama, Mt. = Fuji-San
　101 F6
Fukuchiyama 101 F4
Fukue-Shima 101 G1
Fukui 101 E5
Fukuoka 101 G2
Fukushima 101 E7
Fukuyama 101 F3
Fulda 80 C5
Fulda → 80 C5
Funabashi 101 F7
Funchal 126 B2
Fundación 162 A4
Fundão 86 B2
Fundy, B. of 143 E7
Funtua 127 F7
Furāt, Nahr al → 119 E6
Furneaux Group 134 D4
Fürstenwalde 81 B8
Fürth 80 D6
Fury and Hecla Str.
　142 C5
Fusagasugá 162 C4
Fushun 105 B5
Futuna 136 L12
Fuxin 104 A4
Fuyang 104 F1
Fuzhou 107 D5
Fyn 77 D8

G

Gaalkacyo 121 F4
Gabela 128 G2
Gabès 124 B1
Gabès, G. de 124 B1
Gabon ■ 128 E2
Gaborone 131 C5

Gabrovo 92 C5
Gachsārān 116 D2
Gadag 115 M9
Gadarwara 115 H11
Gadhada 115 J7
Gadsden 154 B4
Gadwal 115 L10
Gafsa 126 B7
Gag 109 D3
Gagnoa 127 G4
Gagnon 143 D7
Găgăuzia □ 83 E9
Galați 83 F9
Galatina 91 D7
Galdhøpiggen 76 C7
Galela 109 D3
Galesburg 147 E9
Galich 84 B5
Galicia □ 86 A2
Galilee, Sea of = Yam
　Kinneret 118 D3
Gállego → 87 B5
Gallegos → 167 G3
Gallinas, Pta. 162 A4
Gallipoli = Gelibolu 93 D6
Gallípoli 91 D6
Gällivare 76 B10
Galloway, Mull of 79 D4
Galveston 153 E6
Gálvez 166 C4
Galway 79 E2
Galway B. 79 E2
Gambia ■ 127 F2
Gambia → 127 F2
Gambier, Îs. 137 M17
Gambier Is. 134 C2
Gamboma 128 E3
Gan Jiang → 106 C4
Ganāveh 116 D2
Gäncä 85 E6
Ganda 130 A2
Gandak → 112 E5
Gandava 114 E5
Gander 143 E8
Gandhi Sagar 115 G9
Gandia 87 C5
Ganga → 113 F8
Ganganagar 114 E8
Gangaw 113 F10
Gangdisê Shan 112 B3
Ganges = Ganga →
　113 F8
Gangneung 105 D8
Gangtok 113 D7
Gani 109 E3

Gansu □ 102 D8
Ganta 127 G4
Gantheaume, C. 134 C2
Ganzhou 107 E3
Gaoua 127 F5
Gaoual 127 F3
Gap 89 D7
Gar 102 E3
Garabogazköl Aylagy
　97 E6
Garagum 97 F6
Garanhuns 164 D6
Garda, L. di 90 B3
Garden City 152 A3
Gardēz 114 C6
Gargliano → 90 D4
Garland 145 F7
Garmisch-Partenkirchen
　80 E6
Garmsār 116 C3
Garonne → 88 D3
Garoowe 121 F4
Garoua 125 G1
Garry, L. 140 B9
Garvie Mts. 137 F3
Gary 148 D2
Garzê 102 E8
Garzón 162 C3
Gascogne 88 E4
Gascogne, G. de 88 D2
Gascony = Gascogne
　88 E4
Gaspé 143 E7
Gaspésie, Pén. de la
　143 E7
Gastonia 155 B7
Gastre 167 E3
Gata, C. 87 D4
Gata, Sierra de 86 B2
Gateshead 79 D6
Gaväter 117 E5
Gavdos 93 G5
Gävle 77 C9
Gawilgarh Hills 115 J10
Gawler 134 B2
Gaxun Nur 102 C8
Gaya India 112 E5
Gaya Niger 127 F6
Gayndah 135 A5
Gaza 119 E3
Gaza Strip ■ 119 E3
Gaziantep 118 C4
Gcuwa 131 E5
Gdańsk 82 A4
Gdańska, Zatoka 82 A4
Gdov 84 B2
Gdynia 82 A4
Gebe 109 D3
Gebze 92 D7
Gedaref 125 F6
Gediz → 93 E6
Gedser 77 E8

Geelong **135 C3**
Geesthacht **80 B6**
Geidam **125 F1**
Gejiu **102 G8**
Gela **91 F5**
Gelibolu **93 D6**
Gelsenkirchen **80 C4**
Gemena **128 D3**
Gemerek **118 C4**
Gemlik **93 D7**
General Acha **166 D4**
General Alvear *B. Aires, Argentina* **166 D5**
General Alvear *Mendoza, Argentina* **166 D3**
General Belgrano **166 D5**
General Carrera, L. **167 F2**
General Juan Madariaga **166 D5**
General La Madrid **166 D4**
General MacArthur **108 B3**
General Pico **166 D4**
General Pinedo **166 B4**
General Santos **108 C3**
General Villegas **166 D4**
Geneva = Genève **80 E4**
Geneva, L. = Léman, L. **89 C7**
Genève **80 E4**
Genil → **86 D3**
Gennargentu, Mti. del **91 D2**
Genoa = Génova **90 B2**
Genoa **135 C4**
Génova **90 B2**
Génova, G. di **90 C2**
Gent **80 C2**
Genyem **109 E6**
Georga, Zemlya **96 A5**
George **130 E4**
George → **142 D7**
George, L. *N.S.W., Australia* **135 C4**
George, L. *S. Austral., Australia* **134 C3**
George Sound **137 F2**
George Town *Cayman Is.* **158 C3**
George Town *Malaysia* **110 C2**
George V Land **168 A14**
George VI Sound **168 B3**
Georgetown **162 B7**
Georgia □ **155 C6**
Georgia ■ **85 E5**
Georgian B. **143 E5**
Georgiyevsk **85 E5**
Gera **81 C7**
Geral de Goiás, Serra **165 E4**

Geraldton **132 F1**
Gerede **118 B3**
Gereshk **114 D4**
German Bight = Deutsche Bucht **80 A5**
Germany ■ **80 C6**
Germiston **131 D5**
Gernika-Lumo **87 A4**
Gerona = Girona **87 B7**
Geser **109 E4**
Getafe **86 B4**
Gettysburg **149 E7**
Getz Ice Shelf **168 B18**
Ghaghara → **112 E5**
Ghana ■ **127 G5**
Ghanzi **130 C4**
Ghardaïa **126 B6**
Gharm **97 F8**
Gharyān **124 B1**
Ghāt **124 D1**
Ghats, Eastern **115 N11**
Ghats, Western **115 N9**
Ghayl **119 G6**
Ghazal, Bahr el → *Chad* **125 F2**
Ghazal, Bahr el → *South Sudan* **125 G5**
Ghaziabad **114 E10**
Ghazipur **112 E4**
Ghaznī **114 C6**
Ghent = Gent **80 C2**
Ghowr □ **114 C4**
Ghugus **115 K11**
Ghūrīān **114 B2**
Gianitsa **93 D4**
Giarre **91 F5**
Gibeon **130 D3**
Gibraltar ☑ **86 D3**
Gibraltar, Str. of **86 E3**
Gibson Desert **132 E4**
Giessen **80 C5**
Gifu **101 F5**
Gíglio **91 C3**
Gijón **86 A3**
Gila → **150 D5**
Gilán □ **118 C7**
Gilbert Is. **136 J12**
Gilgandra **135 B4**
Gilgit **114 B9**
Gilles, L. **134 B2**
Gin Gin **135 A5**
Ginir **121 F3**
Giona, Oros **93 E4**
Giresun **118 B4**
Girga **124 C5**
Giridih **112 E6**
Girona **87 B7**
Girvan **78 D4**
Gisborne **136 C8**
Gisenyi **129 E5**
Gitega **129 E5**

Githio **93 F4**
Giurgiu **92 C5**
Giza = El Gîza **124 C5**
Gizab **114 C4**
Giżycko **82 A5**
Gjakovë **92 C3**
Gjirokastër **93 D3**
Gjoa Haven **140 B10**
Glace Bay **143 E8**
Gladstone *Queens., Australia* **135 E9**
Gladstone *S. Austral., Australia* **134 B2**
Glasgow **78 D4**
Glazov **96 D6**
Glen Canyon △ **151 B7**
Glen Innes **135 A5**
Glendale **150 C3**
Glenelg → **134 C3**
Glenmorgan **135 A4**
Glenorchy **134 D4**
Glenreagh **135 B5**
Glenrothes **78 C5**
Glens Falls **149 C9**
Gliwice **82 C4**
Głogów **82 C3**
Glomma → **77 C8**
Glorieuses, Îs. **131 A9**
Gloucester *Australia* **135 B5**
Gloucester *U.K.* **79 F5**
Glusk **83 B9**
Gmünd **81 D8**
Gmunden **81 E7**
Gniezno **82 B3**
Goa **115 M8**
Goalen Hd. **135 C5**
Goalpara **113 D8**
Goba **121 F2**
Gobabis **130 C3**
Gobi **103 C9**
Godavari → **112 J4**
Godavari Pt. **112 J4**
Godhra **115 H8**
Gods → **141 C10**
Gods L. **141 C10**
Godthåb = Nuuk **138 C14**
Goiânia **165 F4**
Goiás **165 F3**
Goio-Erê **166 A6**
Gojra **114 D8**
Gökçeada **93 D5**
Gökova Körfezi **93 F6**
Gokteik **113 F11**
Gold Coast **135 A5**
Golden B. **136 D5**
Golden Gate **144 H2**
Goldsboro **155 B9**
Goleniów **82 B2**
Golfo Aranci **90 D2**
Golspie **78 C5**

Goma **129 E5**
Gomera **126 C2**
Gómez Palacio **156 B4**
Gomogomo **109 F4**
Gomoh **112 F6**
Gonābād **116 C4**
Gonaïves **159 C5**
Gonbad-e Kāvūs **116 B3**
Gonda **112 D3**
Gonder **125 F6**
Gönen **93 D6**
Gonghe **102 D8**
Gongolgon **135 B4**
Good Hope, C. of **130 E3**
Goodooga **135 A4**
Goolgowi **135 B4**
Goondiwindi **135 A5**
Gop **115 H6**
Göppingen **80 D5**
Gorakhpur **112 D4**
Goražde **90 C7**
Gordon → **134 D4**
Gore *Ethiopia* **125 G6**
Gore *N.Z.* **137 G3**
Gorgān **116 B3**
Gorgona, I. **162 C3**
Goríźia **90 C6**
Gorkiy = Nizhniy Novgorod **84 B5**
Gorkovskoye Vdkhr. **84 B5**
Görlitz **81 C8**
Gorna Oryakhovitsa **92 C5**
Gorno-Altay □ **97 D9**
Gorno-Altaysk **97 D9**
Gornyy **100 A3**
Gorontalo **109 D2**
Gorzów Wielkopolski **82 B2**
Gosford **135 B5**
Goshogawara **100 C7**
Goslar **80 C6**
Gospič **90 B5**
Göta kanal **77 D9**
Göteborg **77 D8**
Gotha **80 C6**
Gothenburg = Göteborg **77 D8**
Gotland **77 D9**
Gotō-Rettō **101 G1**
Göttingen **80 C5**
Gouda **80 C3**
Gouin, Rés. **143 E6**
Goulburn **135 B4**
Governador Valadares **165 F5**
Goya **166 B5**
Goyang **105 D7**
Goyder Lagoon **134 A2**
Goyllarisquizga **163 F3**
Goz Beïda **125 F3**

Gozo **91 F5**
Graaff-Reinet **130 E4**
Gračac **90 B5**
Gracias a Dios, C. **158 D3**
Grado **86 A2**
Grafton **135 A5**
Graham Land **168 A3**
Grahamstown **131 E5**
Grajaú **164 D4**
Grajaú ➙ **164 C5**
Grampian Mts. **78 C4**
Grampians, The **134 C3**
Gran Canaria **126 C2**
Gran Chaco **166 B4**
Gran Paradiso **90 B1**
Gran Sasso d'Itália **90 C4**
Granada *Nic.* **157 E7**
Granada *Spain* **86 D4**
Granby **143 E6**
Grand Bahama I. **158 A4**
Grand Bassam **127 G5**
Grand ➙ = Da Yunhe ➙ **104 F3**
Grand Canyon **151 B6**
Grand Cayman **158 C3**
Grand Coulee Dam **144 C4**
Grand Falls **143 E7**
Grand Falls-Windsor **143 E8**
Grand Forks **146 B6**
Grand Island **146 E5**
Grand Rapids *Canada* **141 C10**
Grand Rapids *U.S.A.* **148 C3**
Grand St-Bernard, Col du **89 D7**
Grand Teton **145 E8**
Grande ➙ *Bolivia* **163 G6**
Grande ➙ *Bahia, Brazil* **165 E5**
Grande ➙ *Minas Gerais, Brazil* **165 G3**
Grande, B. **167 G3**
Grande, Rio ➙ **156 B5**
Grande Baleine ➙ **143 D6**
Granite City **147 F9**
Granity **137 D4**
Granja **164 C5**
Granollers **87 B7**
Grantham **79 E6**
Granville **88 B3**
Grasse **89 E7**
Graulhet **88 E4**
's-Gravenhage **80 B3**
Gravesend **135 A5**
Graz **81 E8**
Great Australian Bight **132 G4**

Great Barrier I. **136 B6**
Great Barrier Reef **133 D8**
Great Basin **144 G5**
Great Bear ➙ **140 B7**
Great Bear L. **140 B7**
Great Dividing Ra. **133 E8**
Great Falls **145 C8**
Great Inagua I. **158 B5**
Great Karoo **130 E4**
Great Lake **134 D4**
Great Ouse ➙ **79 E7**
Great Ruaha ➙ **129 F7**
Great Saint Bernard Pass = Grand St-Bernard, Col du **89 D7**
Great Salt L. **145 F7**
Great Salt Lake Desert **145 F7**
Great Sandy Desert **132 E3**
Great Slave L. **140 B8**
Great Smoky Mts. △ **155 B6**
Great Victoria Desert **132 F4**
Great Wall **103 D9**
Great Yarmouth **79 E7**
Greater Antilles **158 C5**
Greater Sunda Is. **111 F4**
Gredos, Sierra de **86 B3**
Greece ■ **93 E4**
Greeley **146 E2**
Greely Fd. **142 A5**
Green ➙ **151 A8**
Green Bay **148 B2**
Green C. **135 C4**
Greenland ☒ **138 C9**
Greenock **78 D4**
Greensboro **155 A8**
Greenville *Ala., U.S.A.* **154 D4**
Greenville *Miss., U.S.A.* **153 C8**
Greenville *N.C., U.S.A.* **155 B9**
Greenville *S.C., U.S.A.* **155 B6**
Greenwood *Miss., U.S.A.* **153 C8**
Greenwood *S.C., U.S.A.* **155 B6**
Gregory, L. **134 A2**
Greifswald **81 A7**
Greiz **81 C7**
Gremikha **96 C4**
Grenada ■ **159 D7**
Grenfell **135 B4**
Grenoble **89 D6**

Grey ➙ **137 E4**
Grey Ra. **135 A3**
Greymouth **137 E4**
Greytown **137 D6**
Griffin **155 C5**
Griffith **135 B4**
Grimsby **79 E6**
Gris-Nez, C. **88 A4**
Grise Fiord **142 B5**
Grójec **82 C5**
Groningen **80 B4**
Grootfontein **130 B3**
Grosser Arber **81 D7**
Grosseto **90 C3**
Grossglockner **81 E7**
Groznyy **85 E6**
Grudziądz **82 B4**
Gryazi **84 C4**
Gryazovets **96 D5**
Gua **112 F5**
Guadalajara *Mexico* **156 C4**
Guadalajara *Spain* **86 B4**
Guadalcanal **136 K11**
Guadalete ➙ **86 D2**
Guadalquivir ➙ **86 D2**
Guadalupe, Sierra de **86 C3**
Guadarrama, Sierra de **86 B4**
Guadeloupe ☒ **159 C7**
Guadiana ➙ **86 D2**
Guadix **86 D4**
Guafo, Boca del **167 E2**
Guaíra **166 A6**
Guaitecas, Is. **167 E2**
Guajará-Mirim **163 F5**
Guajira, Pen. de la **162 A4**
Gualeguaychú **166 C5**
Guam ☒ **136 H9**
Guamúchil **156 B3**
Guanajuato **156 C4**
Guandacol **166 B3**
Guane **158 B3**
Guangdong □ **107 F2**
Guangxi Zhuangzu Zizhiqu □ **103 G9**
Guangzhou **107 F2**
Guanipa ➙ **162 B6**
Guantánamo **158 B4**
Guantánamo B. **158 B5**
Guaporé ➙ **163 F5**
Guaqui **163 G5**
Guarapuava **166 B6**
Guarda **86 B2**
Guardafui, C. = Asir, Ras **121 E5**
Guasdualito **162 B4**
Guatemala **157 E6**
Guatemala ■ **157 D6**
Guaviare ➙ **162 C5**

Guaxupé **165 G4**
Guayaquil **162 D3**
Guayaquil, G. de **162 D2**
Guaymas **156 B2**
Guddu Barrage **114 E6**
Gudur **115 M11**
Guelph **148 C5**
Guéret **88 C4**
Guernica = Gernika-Lumo **87 A4**
Guernsey **79 G5**
Guidónia-Montecélio **90 C4**
Guijá **131 C6**
Guildford **79 F6**
Guilin **107 E1**
Guimarães **86 B1**
Guimaras □ **108 B2**
Guinea ■ **127 F3**
Guinea, Gulf of **123 F3**
Guinea-Bissau ■ **127 F3**
Guingamp **88 B2**
Güiria **162 A6**
Guiuan **108 B3**
Guiyang **103 F9**
Guizhou □ **103 F9**
Gujarat □ **115 H7**
Gujranwala **114 C9**
Gujrat **114 C9**
Gulbarga **115 L10**
Gulf, The = Persian Gulf **116 E2**
Gulgong **135 B4**
Güllük **93 F6**
Gülshat **97 E8**
Gulu **129 D6**
Gümüşhane **118 B4**
Gumzai **109 F4**
Guna **115 G10**
Gunnedah **135 B5**
Gunningbar Cr. ➙ **135 A4**
Gunsan **105 E7**
Guntakal **115 M10**
Guntur **112 J3**
Gunungapi **109 F3**
Gunungsitoli **111 D1**
Gunza **128 G2**
Gupis **114 A8**
Gurdaspur **114 C9**
Gurkha **112 C5**
Gurley **135 A4**
Gurupá **164 C3**
Gurupá, I. Grande de **164 C3**
Gurupi ➙ **164 C3**
Gusau **127 F7**
Güstrow **81 B7**
Gütersloh **80 C4**
Guthrie **152 B5**
Guwahati **113 D8**
Guyana ■ **162 B7**

Guyenne 88 D4
Guyra 135 B5
Gwa 113 J10
Gwabegar 135 B4
Gwādar 114 G3
Gwalior 114 F11
Gwanda 131 C5
Gwangju 105 E7
Gweru 131 B5
Gwydir → 135 A4
Gyaring Hu 102 E7
Gydanskiy Poluostrov 96 B8
Gyeongju 105 E8
Gympie 135 A5
Gyöngyös 82 E4
Győr 82 E3
Gyula 82 E5
Gyumri 85 E5

H

Haarlem 80 B3
Haast → 137 E3
Haboro 100 A7
Hachijō-Jima 101 G6
Hachinohe 100 C7
Hadarba, Ras 124 D6
Ḥadd, Ra's al 117 F4
Hadejia 127 F7
Hadera 118 D3
Ḥaḍramawt = 121 D4
Haeju 105 C6
Hafar al Bāṭin 119 E6
Hafizabad 114 C8
Haflong 113 E9
Hagen 80 C4
Hagerstown 149 E7
Hagi 101 F2
Hagondange 89 B7
Hague, C. de la 88 B3
Hague, The = 's-Gravenhage 80 B3
Haguenau 89 B7
Hai'an 107 a
Haicheng 105 B5
Haida Gwaii 140 C6
Haifa = Ḥefa 118 D3
Haikou 107 a
Ḥā'il 119 F5
Hailar 103 B11
Hailun 103 B13
Hailuoto 76 B10
Hainan □ 107 a
Hainan Str. = Qiongzhou Haixia 107 a
Haiphong 103 G9
Haiti ■ 159 C5
Haiya 125 E6
Hajdúböszörmény 82 E4
Haji Ibrahim 118 C6
Hajnówka 83 B6

Hakodate 100 C7
Hala 114 G6
Ḥalab 118 C4
Ḥalabjah 118 D6
Halaib 124 D6
Halberstadt 81 C6
Halcombe 136 D6
Halcon, Mt. 108 B2
Halden 77 D8
Haldia 112 F7
Haldwani 114 E11
Halfmoon Bay 137 G3
Halifax Canada 143 E7
Halifax U.K. 79 E6
Halīl → 116 E4
Hall Beach 142 C5
Hall Pen. 142 C7
Ḥallāniyat, Jazā'ir al 121 D6
Halle 81 C6
Hallett 134 B2
Halmahera 109 D3
Halmstad 77 D8
Ḥālūl 116 E3
Hamada 101 F3
Hamadān 118 D7
Ḥamāh 118 D4
Hamamatsu 101 F5
Hamar 76 C8
Hamburg 80 B5
Hämeenlinna 76 C10
Hameln 80 B5
Hamersley Ra. 132 E2
Hamhŭng 105 C7
Hami 102 C6
Hamilton Australia 134 C3
Hamilton Canada 143 E6
Hamilton N.Z. 136 B6
Hamilton U.K. 78 D4
Hamilton → 134 A2
Hamley Bridge 134 B2
Hamm 80 C4
Hammerfest 76 A10
Hammond 148 D2
Hampden 137 F4
Hampton 149 F7
Han Pijesak 90 B7
Han Shui → 106 B3
Hanamaki 100 C7
Hanau 80 C5
Handan 104 D1
Hangang → 105 D7
Hangzhou 106 B6
Hangzhou Wan 106 B6
Ḥanīsh 121 D3
Hankö 77 D10
Hanle 114 C11
Hanmer Springs 137 E5
Hanna 141 C8
Hannibal 147 F9

Hannover 80 B5
Hanoi 103 G9
Hanover = Hannover 80 B5
Hanover, I. 167 G2
Hansi 114 E9
Hanson, L. 134 B2
Hantsavichy 83 B8
Hanzhong 103 E9
Haora 112 F7
Haparanda 76 B10
Happy Valley-Goose Bay 143 D7
Hapur 114 E10
Ḥaql 119 E3
Har 109 F4
Har Hu 102 D7
Har Us Nuur 102 B6
Ḥaraḍ 119 F7
Harare 131 B6
Harbin 103 B13
Hardangerfjorden 76 C7
Hardy, Pen. 167 H3
Harer 121 F3
Hargeisa 121 F3
Hari → 111 E2
Haridwar 114 E11
Haringhata → 113 G7
Harīrūd → 114 A2
Harlingen 152 F5
Harlow 79 F8
Harney Basin 144 E4
Härnösand 76 C9
Harricana → 143 D6
Harris 78 C3
Harris, L. 134 B2
Harrisburg 149 E7
Harrogate 79 D6
Hart, L. 134 B2
Hartford 149 D9
Hartlepool 79 D6
Harvey 148 D2
Harwich 79 F7
Haryana □ 114 E10
Haryn → 83 B8
Harz 80 C6
Hasa 119 F7
Hassan 107 a
Hastings N.Z. 136 C7
Hastings U.K. 79 F7
Hastings U.S.A. 146 E5
Hastings Ra. 135 B5
Hatay 118 C4
Hatfield 134 B3
Hatgal 102 A8
Hathras 114 F11
Hatia 113 F8
Hattah 134 B3
Hatteras, C. 155 B10
Hattiesburg 153 D9
Hatvan 82 E4

Haugesund 77 D7
Hauraki G. 136 B6
Haut Atlas 126 B4
Havana = La Habana 158 B3
Havant 79 F6
Havel → 81 B7
Havelock 137 D5
Haverfordwest 79 F4
Havlíčkův Brod 82 D2
Havre 145 B9
Havre-St.-Pierre 143 D7
Havza 118 B3
Hawai'i □ 150 H12
Hawaiian Is. 150 H12
Hawea, L. 137 F3
Hawera 136 C6
Hawick 78 D5
Hawke B. 136 C7
Hawker 134 B2
Hay 135 B3
Hay River 140 B8
Hayes → 141 C10
Hayrabolu 92 D6
Haysyn 83 D9
Hayvoron 83 D9
Hazar 97 F6
Hazārān, Kūh-e 116 D4
Hazaribag 112 F5
Healesville 135 C4
Hearst 143 E5
Hebei □ 104 C2
Hebel 135 A4
Hebron = Al Khalīl 119 E3
Hebron 142 D7
Hechi 103 G9
Hechuan 103 D10
Heerlen 89 A6
Ḥefa 118 D3
Hefei 106 B4
Hegang 103 B14
Heidelberg 80 D5
Heihe 103 A13
Heilbronn 80 D5
Heilongjiang □ 103 B13
Heimaey 76 C1
Hekimhan 118 C4
Hekou 102 G8
Helena 145 C7
Helena -West Helena 153 B8
Helensville 136 B6
Helgoland 80 A4
Hellín 87 C5
Helmand □ 114 D3
Helmand → 114 D2
Helmsdale 78 B5
Helsingborg 77 D8
Helsinki 77 C11
Helwân 124 C5
Hemel Hempstead 79 F6
Henan □ 103 E10

Henares → 86 B4
Henashi-Misaki 100 C6
Henderson 155 A8
Hengyang 106 D2
Henrietta Maria, C.
  143 D5
Hentiyn Nuruu 103 B9
Henty 135 G4
Henzada 113 J10
Heraklion = Iraklio 93 G5
Herät 114 B3
Herceg-Novi 92 C2
Hereford 79 E5
Herford 80 B5
Herlen → 103 B11
Hermidale 135 B4
Hermosillo 156 B2
Hernád → 82 E5
's-Hertogenbosch 80 C3
Hessen □ 80 C5
Hexham 79 D5
Heywood 134 C3
Heze 104 E1
Hialeah 155 G7
Hibbing 147 B8
Hibbs B. 134 D4
Hickory 155 B7
Hicks, Pt. 135 C4
Hidalgo del Parral 156 B3
Higashiajima-San 101 E7
Higashiösaka 101 F4
High Point 155 B8
High River 141 C8
High Wycombe 79 F6
Hiiumaa 84 B1
Ḥijārah, Ṣaḥrā' al 119 E6
Ḥijāz 119 F4
Hikurangi Gisborne, N.Z.
  136 C7
Hikurangi Northland, N.Z.
  136 A6
Hildesheim 80 B5
Hillston 135 B4
Hilo 150 J13
Hilversum 80 B3
Himachal Pradesh □
  114 D10
Himalaya 112 C5
Himatnagar 115 H8
Himeji 101 F4
Himi 101 E5
Ḥimṣ 118 C3
Hindmarsh, L. 134 C3
Hindu Bagh 114 D5
Hindu Kush 114 B7
Hindupur 115 N10
Hinganghat 115 J11
Hingoli 115 K10
Hinojosa del Duque
  86 C3
Hirakud Dam 112 G4
Hiroo 100 B8

Hirosaki 100 C7
Hiroshima 101 F3
Hisar 114 E9
Hispaniola 159 C5
Hitachi 101 E7
Hjälmaren 77 D9
Hkakabo Razi 113 C11
Hkamti 113 E10
Hlyboka 83 D7
Ho Chi Minh City = Thanh
  Pho Ho Chi Minh
  110 B3
Hoai Nhon 110 B3
Hoare B. 142 C7
Hobart 134 D4
Hobbs Coast 168 B18
Hobyo 121 F4
Hodaka-Dake 101 E5
Hodgson 141 C10
Hódmezővásárhely 82 E5
Hodna, Chott el 126 A6
Hodonín 82 D3
Hoek van Holland 80 B3
Hof 81 C6
Hofsjökull 76 C2
Höfu 101 F2
Hogan Group 134 C4
Hoh Xil Shan 102 D5
Hohhot 103 C10
Hoi An 110 A3
Hokianga Harbour
  136 A5
Hokitika 137 E4
Hokkaidö □ 100 B8
Holbrook 135 C4
Holguín 158 B4
Holland = Netherlands ■
  80 B3
Hollywood 155 G7
Holman 140 A8
Holstebro 77 D7
Holyhead 79 E4
Homalin 113 E10
Hombori 127 E5
Home B. 142 C7
Homer 141 C4
Homyel 83 B10
Hon Chong 110 B2
Honbetsu 100 B8
Honduras ■ 157 E7
Honduras, G. de 157 D7
Hønefoss 77 C8
Honfleur 88 B4
Hong Kong □ 103 G10
Hongjiang 103 F9
Hongshui He → 103 G9
Hongze Hu 104 F3
Honiara 136 K10
Honolulu 150 H12
Honshū 101 F4
Hood, Mt. 144 D3
Hooghly = Hugli →
  112 G7

Hoorn 80 B3
Hoover Dam 150 B5
Hope, L. 134 A2
Hopedale 142 D7
Hopetoun 134 C3
Hopetown 130 D4
Hoquiam 144 C2
Horlick Mts. 168 C1
Horlivka 85 D4
Hormoz 116 E3
Hormoz, Jaz.-ye 116 E4
Hormozgän □ 116 E3
Hormuz, Str. of 116 E4
Horn 81 D8
Horn, Cape = Hornos, C.
  de 167 H3
Hornavan 76 B9
Hornos, C. de 167 H3
Horodenka 83 D7
Horodok Khmelnytskyy,
  Ukraine 83 D8
Horodok Lviv, Ukraine
  83 D6
Horokhiv 83 C7
Horqin Youyi Qianqi
  103 B12
Horqueta 166 A5
Horsham 134 C3
Horton → 140 B7
Hoshangabad 115 H10
Hoshiarpur 114 D9
Hospet 115 M10
Hoste, I. 167 H3
Hot Springs 153 B7
Hotan 102 D3
Hotazel 130 D4
Houhora Heads 136 A5
Houlton 149 A12
Houma 153 E8
Houston 153 E6
Hovd = Dund-Us 102 B6
Hövsgöl Nuur 102 A8
Howard 135 A5
Howe, C. 135 C5
Howitt, L. 134 A2
Howrah = Haora 112 F7
Höxter 80 C5
Hoy 78 B5
Høyanger 76 C7
Hoyerswerda 81 C8
Hpunan Pass 113 D11
Hradec Králové 82 C2
Hrodna 83 B6
Hrodzyanka 83 B9
Hrymayliv 83 D8
Hsenwi 113 F11
Hsinchu 107 E6
Hua Hin 110 B1
Huacho 163 F2
Huai He → 106 A5
Huai'an 104 F3
Huaibei 104 E2

Huainan 106 A4
Huaiyin 104 F3
Huallaga → 162 E3
Huambo 130 A3
Huancabamba 163 E3
Huancane 163 G5
Huancavelica 163 F3
Huancayo 163 F3
Huang He → 104 D3
Huangshan 106 C5
Huangshi 106 B3
Huánuco 163 E3
Huaraz 163 E3
Huarmey 163 F3
Huascarán, Nevado
  163 E3
Huasco 166 B2
Huatabampo 156 B3
Hubei □ 106 B2
Hubli 115 M9
Huddersfield 79 E6
Hudiksvall 76 C9
Hudson → 149 D8
Hudson Bay 142 C5
Hudson Mts. 168 B2
Hudson Str. 142 C7
Hue 110 A3
Huelva 86 D2
Huesca 87 A5
Hughenden 133 E7
Hugli → 112 G7
Huila, Nevado del 162 C3
Huinca Renancó 166 C4
Huize 102 F8
Huizhou 107 F3
Hukawng Valley 113 D11
Ḥulayfā' 119 F5
Hull = Kingston upon Hull
  79 E6
Hull 143 E6
Hulun Nur 103 B11
Humahuaca 166 A3
Humaitá 163 E6
Humber → 79 E6
Humboldt 141 C9
Humboldt → 144 F4
Hume, L. 135 C4
Hün 124 C2
Húnaflói 76 B1
Hunan □ 106 D2
Hunedoara 83 F6
Hungary ■ 82 E4
Hungerford 135 A3
Hüngnam 105 D7
Hunsrück 80 D4
Hunter I. 134 D3
Hunter Ra. 135 B5
Hunterville 136 C6
Huntington 148 E4
Huntington Beach
  150 D3
Huntly N.Z. 136 B6

Huntly *U.K.* **78 C5**
Huntsville *Canada* **143 E6**
Huntsville *U.S.A.* **154 B4**
Huonville **134 D4**
Huron, L. **148 B4**
Hurunui → **137 E5**
Húsavík **76 B2**
Huşi **83 E9**
Hutchinson **152 A5**
Hutton, Mt. **135 A4**
Huwaki **109 F3**
Huzhou **106 B6**
Hvar **90 C6**
Hwang Ho = Huang
  He → **104 D3**
Hwange **131 B5**
Hyargas Nuur **102 B6**
Hyderabad *India* **115 L11**
Hyderabad *Pakistan*
  114 G6
Hydra **93 F4**
Hyères **89 E7**
Hyères, Îs. d' **89 E7**
Hyūga **101 G2**

I

I-n-Gall **127 E7**
Iaco → **163 E5**
Ialomiţa → **92 B6**
Iaşi **83 E8**
Iba **108 A2**
Ibadan **127 G6**
Ibagué **162 C3**
Ibar → **92 C3**
Ibarra **162 C3**
Ibiá **165 F4**
Ibiapaba, Sa. da **164 C5**
Ibiza = Eivissa **87 C6**
Ibonma **109 E4**
Ibotirama **165 E5**
Ibu **109 D3**
Ibusuki **101 H2**
Ica **163 F3**
Iça → **162 D5**
Içana **162 C5**
İçel **118 C3**
Iceland ■ **76 B2**
Ichchapuram **112 H5**
Ichihara **101 F7**
Ichilo → **163 G6**
Ichinomiya **101 F5**
Ichinoseki **100 D7**
Içoguz **97 E6**
Idaho □ **145 D7**
Idaho Falls **145 E7**
Idar-Oberstein **80 D4**
Idfû **124 D5**
Idi **110 C1**
Idiofa **128 E3**
Idlib **118 D4**
Ierapetra **93 G5**
Iesi **90 C4**

Ife **127 G6**
Iforas, Adrar des **126 E6**
Igarapava **165 G4**
Igarka **96 C9**
Iglésias **91 E2**
Iglulik **142 C5**
İğneada Burnu **92 D7**
Igoumenitsa **93 E3**
Iguaçu → **166 B6**
Iguaçu, Cat. del **166 B6**
Iguala **156 D5**
Igualada **87 B6**
Iguatu **164 D6**
Iharana **131 A10**
Ihosy **131 C9**
Iida **101 F5**
Iisalmi **76 C11**
Ijebu-Ode **127 G6**
IJsselmeer **80 B3**
Ikaria **93 F6**
Ikeda **101 F3**
Ikela **128 E4**
Iki **101 G1**
Ikopa → **131 B9**
Ilagan **108 A2**
Ilam **118 D6**
Iława **82 B4**
Ile → **97 E8**
Île-de-France □ **88 B5**
Ilebo **128 E4**
Ilesha **127 G6**
Ilhéus **165 E6**
Iligan **108 C2**
Illana B. **108 C2**
Illapel **166 C2**
Iller → **80 D5**
Illimani, Nevado **163 G5**
Ilmen, Ozero **84 B3**
Ilo **163 G4**
Iloilo **108 B2**
Ilorin **127 G6**
Imabari **101 F3**
Imandra, Ozero **96 C4**
Imari **101 G1**
Imatra **76 C11**
imeni Ismail Samani, Pik
  97 F8
Imeri, Serra **162 C5**
Imi **121 F3**
Ímola **90 B3**
Imperatriz **164 D4**
Impéria **90 C2**
Imperial Dam **150 D5**
Impfondo **128 D3**
Imphal **113 E9**
Imuruan B. **108 B1**
In Salah **126 C6**
Ina **101 F5**
Inangahua **137 D4**
Inanwatan **109 E4**
Iñapari **163 F5**
Inari **76 B11**

Inarijärvi **76 B11**
Inca **87 C7**
İnce Burun **118 B3**
Incheon **105 D7**
İncirliova **93 F6**
Incomáti → **131 D6**
Indalsälven → **76 C9**
Indaw **113 E11**
Independence *Kans.,
  U.S.A.* **153 A6**
Independence *Mo.,
  U.S.A.* **147 F7**
India ■ **115 J10**
Indian → **155 F7**
Indiana □ **148 D3**
Indianapolis **148 E2**
Indigirka → **99 B13**
Indira Gandhi Canal
  114 F8
Indonesia ■ **111 E4**
Indore **115 H9**
Indravati → **112 H3**
Indre → **88 C4**
Indus → **115 G5**
İnebolu **118 B3**
Ingham **135 A5**
Inglewood *Queens.,
  Australia* **135 A5**
Inglewood *Vic., Australia*
  134 C3
Inglewood *N.Z.* **136 C6**
Ingolstadt **81 D6**
Ingraj Bazar **112 E7**
Ingrid Christensen Coast
  168 A10
Inhambane **131 C7**
Inharrime **131 C7**
Inhulec **85 D3**
Inírida → **162 C5**
Injune **135 A4**
Inland Kaikoura Ra.
  137 D5
Inle L. **113 G11**
Inn → **81 D7**
Innamincka **134 A3**
Inner Hebrides **78 C3**
Inner Mongolia = Nei
  Mongol Zizhiqu □
  103 C10
Innsbruck **81 E6**
Inongo **128 E3**
Inowrocław **82 B4**
Insein **113 J11**
International Falls **147 A8**
Inukjuak **142 D6**
Inútil, B. **167 G2**
Inuvik **140 B6**
Invercargill **137 G3**
Inverell **135 A5**
Invergordon **78 C4**
Inverness **78 C4**
Inverurie **78 C5**
Investigator Group
  134 B1

Investigator Str. **134 C2**
Inya **97 D9**
Inza **84 C6**
Ioannina **93 E3**
Ionian Is. = Ionioi Nisoi
  93 E3
Ionian Sea **91 F6**
Ionioi Nisoi **93 E3**
Ios **93 F6**
Iowa □ **147 D8**
Iowa City **147 E9**
Ipameri **165 F4**
Ipatinga **165 F5**
Ipiales **162 C3**
Ipixuna **163 E4**
Ipoh **110 D2**
Ippy **128 C4**
İpsala **92 D6**
Ipswich *Australia* **135 A5**
Ipswich *U.K.* **79 E7**
Ipu **164 C5**
Iqaluit **142 C7**
Iquique **163 H4**
Iquitos **162 D4**
Iracoubo **164 A3**
Iraklio **93 G5**
Iran ■ **116 C3**
Iran, Pegunungan **111 D4**
Īrānshahr **117 E5**
Irapuato **156 C4**
Iraq ■ **118 D5**
Ireland ■ **79 E3**
Irian Jaya = Papua □
  109 E5
Iringa **129 F7**
Iriri → **164 C3**
Irish Sea **79 E4**
Irkutsk **98 D8**
Irō-Zaki **101 F6**
Iron Baron **134 B2**
Iron Knob **134 B2**
Ironwood **147 B9**
Irpin **83 C10**
Irrara Cr. → **135 A4**
Irrawaddy → **113 K10**
Irrawaddy, Mouths of the
  113 K10
Irtysh → **96 C7**
Irún **87 A5**
Irvine **78 D4**
Irymple **134 B3**
Isabela **108 C2**
Ísafjörður **76 B1**
Isahaya **101 G2**
Isar → **81 D7**
Íschia **91 D4**
Ise-Wan **101 F5**
Isère → **89 D6**
Isérnia **90 D5**
Isfahan = Eşfahān
  116 C2
Ishikari-Gawa → **100 B7**

Ishikari-Wan **100 B7**
Ishim ⇥ **97 D8**
Ishinomaki **100 D7**
Ishkoman **114 A8**
Isil Kul **97 D8**
Isiro **129 D5**
İskenderun **118 C4**
Iskür ⇥ **92 C5**
Islamabad **114 C8**
Island L. **141 C10**
Island Lagoon **134 B2**
Islands, B. of **136 A6**
Islay **78 D3**
Isle ⇥ **88 D3**
Isle of Wight □ **79 F6**
Ismâ'îlîya **119 E3**
Isparta **118 C2**
Íspica **91 F5**
Israel ■ **118 E3**
Issoire **89 D5**
İstanbul **92 D7**
İstanbul Boğazı **92 D7**
Istiea **93 E4**
Istra **90 B4**
Istres **89 E6**
Itaberaba **165 E5**
Itabira **165 F5**
Itabuna **165 E6**
Itaipú, Represa de
166 B6
Itaituba **164 C2**
Itajaí **166 B7**
Italy ■ **90 C4**
Itapecuru Mirim **164 C5**
Itaperuna **165 G5**
Itapicuru ⇥ *Bahia, Brazil*
165 E6
Itapicuru ⇥ *Maranhão,
Brazil* **164 C5**
Itapipoca **164 C6**
Itaquí **166 B5**
Ithaki **93 E3**
Itō **101 F6**
Itonamas ⇥ **163 F6**
Ituiutaba **165 F4**
Itumbiara **165 F4**
Iturbe **166 A3**
Itzehoe **80 B5**
Ivanava **83 B7**
Ivanhoe **135 B3**
Ivano-Frankivsk **83 D7**
Ivanovo **84 B5**
Ivory Coast ■ **127 G4**
Ivrea **90 B1**
Ivujivik **142 C6**
Iwaizumi **100 D7**
Iwaki **101 E7**
Iwakuni **101 F3**
Iwamizawa **100 B7**
Iwanai **100 B7**
Iwata **101 F5**

Iwate-San **100 D7**
Iwo **127 G6**
Ixiamas **163 F5**
Izhevsk **96 D6**
İzmayil **83 F9**
İzmir **93 E6**
İznik Gölü **93 D7**
Izu-Shotō **101 F7**
Izumi-Sano **101 F4**
Izumo **101 F3**
Izyaslav **83 C8**

J

Jabalpur **115 H11**
Jablah **118 D4**
Jablonec nad Nisou
82 C2
Jaboatão **164 D6**
Jaca **87 A5**
Jacareí **166 A7**
Jackson *Mich., U.S.A.*
148 C3
Jackson *Miss., U.S.A.*
153 C8
Jackson *Tenn., U.S.A.*
154 B3
Jackson B. **137 E3**
Jacksons **137 E4**
Jacksonville *Fla., U.S.A.*
155 D7
Jacksonville *Ill., U.S.A.*
147 F9
Jacksonville *N.C., U.S.A.*
155 B9
Jacmel **159 C5**
Jacobabad **114 E6**
Jacobina **165 E5**
Jacundá ⇥ **164 C3**
Jade Mt. = Yü Shan
103 G12
Jaén *Peru* **163 E3**
Jaén *Spain* **86 D4**
Jaffa = Tel Aviv-Yafo
118 D3
Jaffa, C. **134 C2**
Jaffna **115 Q12**
Jagadhri **114 D10**
Jagdalpur **112 H3**
Jagodina **92 B3**
Jagraon **114 D9**
Jagtial **115 K11**
Jaguariaíva **166 A7**
Jaguaribe ⇥ **164 C6**
Jahrom **116 D3**
Jailolo **109 D3**
Jailolo, Selat **109 D3**
Jaipur **114 F9**
Jakarta **111 F3**
Jalālābād **114 B7**
Jalgaon **115 J9**
Jalna **115 K9**
Jalón ⇥ **87 B5**

Jalpaiguri **113 D7**
Jaluit L. **136 J11**
Jamaica ■ **158 C4**
Jamalpur *Bangla.* **113 E7**
Jamalpur *India* **112 E6**
Jamanxim ⇥ **164 C2**
Jambi **111 E2**
Jambongan, Pulau
110 C5
James ⇥ **146 D6**
James B. **143 D5**
James Ross I. **168 A4**
Jamestown *Australia*
134 B2
Jamestown *N. Dak.,
U.S.A.* **146 B5**
Jamestown *N.Y., U.S.A.*
149 C6
Jamkhandi **115 L9**
Jammu **114 C9**
Jammu & Kashmir □
114 B10
Jamnagar **115 H7**
Jamshedpur **112 F6**
Jand **114 C8**
Jandaq **116 C3**
Jandowae **135 A5**
Janesville **147 D10**
Janjanbureh **127 F3**
Januária **165 F5**
Jaora **115 H9**
Japan ■ **101 F5**
Japan, Sea of **100 D4**
Japurá ⇥ **162 D5**
Jaqué **162 B3**
Jarama ⇥ **86 B4**
Jari ⇥ **164 C3**
Jarvis I. **137 K15**
Jarwa **112 D4**
Jāsk **116 E4**
Jasper **154 C4**
Jászberény **82 E4**
Jataí **165 F3**
Jaú **165 G4**
Jauja **163 F3**
Jaunpur **112 E4**
Java = Jawa **111 F3**
Java Sea **111 E3**
Jawa **111 F3**
Jaya, Puncak **109 E5**
Jayanti **113 D7**
Jayapura **109 E6**
Jayawijaya, Pegunungan
109 E5
Jaynagar **112 D6**
Jebel, Bahr el ⇥ **125 G5**
Jedburgh **78 D5**
Jedda = Jiddah **119 C3**
Jefferson City **147 F8**
Jega **127 F6**
Jeju **105 F7**
Jeju-do **105 F7**

Jelenia Góra **82 C2**
Jelgava **84 B1**
Jena **81 C6**
Jeonju **105 E7**
Jeparit **134 C3**
Jequié **165 E5**
Jequitinhonha **165 F5**
Jequitinhonha ⇥ **165 F6**
Jérémie **158 C5**
Jerez de la Frontera
86 D2
Jerez de los Caballeros
86 C2
Jerilderie **135 C4**
Jersey **79 G5**
Jersey City **149 D8**
Jerusalem **119 E3**
Jervis B. **135 C5**
Jessore **113 F7**
Jeypore **112 H4**
Jhal Jhao **114 F4**
Jhalawar **115 G10**
Jhang Maghiana **114 D8**
Jhansi **115 G11**
Jharsuguda **112 G5**
Jhelum **114 C8**
Jhelum ⇥ **114 D8**
Jhunjhunun **114 E9**
Jiamusi **103 B14**
Ji'an **106 D3**
Jiangmen **107 F2**
Jiangsu □ **104 F4**
Jiangxi □ **106 D4**
Jiangyin **106 B6**
Jiaozhou **104 D4**
Jiaxing **106 B6**
Jiayi **107 F4**
Jiddah **119 G4**
Jido **113 C10**
Jieyang **107 F4**
Jihlava **82 D2**
Jihlava ⇥ **82 D3**
Jijiga **121 F3**
Jilin **103 C13**
Jima **125 G6**
Jiménez **156 B4**
Jinan **104 D2**
Jindabyne **135 C4**
Jindřichův Hradec **82 D2**
Jingdezhen **106 C4**
Jinggu **102 G8**
Jingmen **106 B2**
Jingzhou **106 B2**
Jinhua **106 C5**
Jining
  *Nei Monggol Zizhiqu,
  China* **103 C10**
Jining *Shandong, China*
104 E2
Jinja **129 D6**
Jinnah Barrage **114 C7**
Jinxi **104 B4**
Jinzhong **103 D10**

Jinzhou 104 B4
Jiparaná → 163 E6
Jipijapa 162 D2
Jiroft 116 D4
Jiu → 92 C4
Jiujiang 106 C3
Jiuquan 102 D7
Jixi 103 B14
Jizzax 97 E7
Joaçaba 166 B6
João Pessoa 164 D7
Joaquín V. González
166 B4
Jodhpur 114 F8
Joensuu 76 C11
Johannesburg 131 D5
Johnson City 155 A6
Johnstown 149 D6
Johor Bahru 111 D2
Joinville 166 B7
Joinville I. 168 A4
Joliet 148 D1
Joliette 143 E6
Jolo 108 C2
Jones Sound 142 B5
Jonesboro 153 B8
Jönköping 77 D8
Jonquière 143 E6
Joplin 153 A6
Jordan ■ 119 E4
Jorhat 113 D10
Jorong 111 E4
Jos 127 G7
Jotunheimen 76 C7
Jowzjān □ 117 B6
Juan de Fuca, Str of.
144 B1
Juan Fernández, Arch. de
161 G3
Juàzeiro 165 D5
Juàzeiro do Norte 164 D6
Juba → 121 G3
Juby, C. 126 C3
Juchitán de Zaragoza
157 D7
Juiz de Fora 165 G5
Juli 163 G5
Juliaca 163 G4
Jullundur 114 D9
Jumilla 87 C5
Jumla 112 C4
Jumna = Yamuna →
112 E3
Junagadh 115 J7
Jundiaí 166 A7
Juneau 141 D6
Junee 135 B4
Junggar Pendi 102 C5
Junín 166 C4
Junín de los Andes
167 D2
Jūniyah 118 D3

Jur → 125 G4
Jura 78 D4
Jura, Mts. du 89 C7
Juruá → 162 D5
Juruena → 163 E7
Juruti 164 C2
Justo Daract 166 C3
Juventud, I. de la 158 B3
Jwaneng 130 C4
Jylland 77 D7
Jyväskylä 76 C11

K

K2 114 B10
Kabaena 109 F2
Kabala 127 G3
Kabale 129 E6
Kabalo 129 F5
Kabanjahe 111 D1
Kabardino-Balkaria □
85 E5
Kabasalan 108 C2
Kabompo → 130 A4
Kabongo 129 F5
Kabūd Gonbad 116 B4
Kābul 114 B6
Kābul → 114 C8
Kaburuang 109 D3
Kabwe 131 A5
Kachchh, Gulf of 115 H6
Kachchh, Rann of
115 G6
Kachin □ 113 D11
Kachīry 97 D8
Kaçkar 85 E5
Kadan Kyun 110 B1
Kadapa 115 M11
Kadina 134 B2
Kadoma 131 B5
Kadugli 125 F4
Kaduna 127 F7
Kaédi 127 E3
Kaesŏng 105 D7
Kāf 119 E4
Kafanchan 127 G7
Kafue → 131 B5
Kaga Bandoro 128 C3
Kağızman 118 B5
Kagoshima 101 H2
Kahayan → 111 E4
Kahnūj 116 E4
Kahramanmaraş 118 C4
Kahurangi △ 137 D5
Kai, Kepulauan 109 F4
Kai Besar 109 F4
Kai Kecil 109 F4
Kaiapoi 137 E5
Kaieteur Falls 162 B7
Kaifeng 104 E1
Kaikohe 136 A5
Kaikoura 137 E5

Kaimana 109 E4
Kaimanawa Mts. 136 C6
Kainji Res. 127 F6
Kaipara Harbour 136 B6
Kaironi 109 E4
Kairouan 124 A1
Kaiserslautern 80 D4
Kaitaia 136 A5
Kaitangata 137 G3
Kajaani 76 C11
Kajabbi 133 D6
Kajo Kaji 125 H5
Kakamega 129 D6
Kakanui Mts. 137 F4
Kakhovka 85 D3
Kakhovske Vdskh. 85 D3
Kakinada 112 J4
Kalaallit Nunaat =
Greenland ☒ 138 C9
Kalabagh 114 C7
Kalabahi 109 F2
Kalach 84 C5
Kaladan → 113 G9
Kalahari 130 C4
Kalakan 99 D9
Kalamata 93 F4
Kalamazoo 148 D3
Kalan 118 C4
Kalao 109 F2
Kalaotoa 109 F2
Kalat 114 E5
Kalce 90 B5
Kale 93 F7
Kalegauk Kyun 113 K11
Kalemie 129 F5
Kalewa 113 F10
Kalgoorlie-Boulder
132 G3
Kaliakra, Nos 92 C7
Kalianda 111 F3
Kalibo 108 B2
Kalima 129 E5
Kalimantan 111 E4
Kálimnos 93 F6
Kaliningrad 84 C1
Kalinkavichy 83 B9
Kalispell 145 B6
Kalisz 82 C4
Kallsjön 76 C11
Kalmar 77 D9
Kalmykia □ 85 D6
Kalocsa 82 E4
Kaluga 84 C4
Kalush 83 D7
Kalutara 115 R11
Kama → 97 D6
Kamaishi 100 D7
Kamarān 121 D3
Kamchatka, Poluostrov
99 D13
Kamchatka Pen. =
Kamchatka, Poluostrov
99 D13

Kamchiya → 92 C6
Kamen 97 D9
Kamen-Rybolov 100 A3
Kamenjak, Rt 90 B4
Kamensk Uralskiy 97 D7
Kamin-Kashyrskyy 83 C7
Kamina 129 F5
Kamloops 141 C7
Kampala 129 D6
Kampar → 111 D2
Kampen 80 B3
Kampong Cham 110 B3
Kampong Chhnang
110 B2
Kampong Saom 110 B2
Kampot 110 B2
Kampuchea =
Cambodia ■ 110 B3
Kamrau, Teluk 109 E4
Kamui-Misaki 100 B7
Kamyanets-Podilskyy
83 D8
Kamyanka-Buzka 83 C7
Kamyshin 84 C6
Kanaaupscow 143 D6
Kanagi 100 C7
Kananga 128 F4
Kanash 84 B6
Kanazawa 101 E5
Kanchanaburi 110 B1
Kanchenjunga 112 D7
Kanchipuram 115 N11
Kandahār 114 D4
Kandalaksha 76 B12
Kandangan 111 E5
Kandi 127 F6
Kandla 115 H7
Kandos 135 B4
Kandy 115 R12
Kangaroo I. 134 C2
Kangāvar 118 D7
Kangean, Kepulauan
111 F5
Kanggye 105 B7
Kangiqsualujjuaq 142 D7
Kangiqsujuaq 142 C6
Kangirsuk 142 D7
Kangto 113 D9
Kaniapiskau, L. =
Caniapiscau, L. 143 D7
Kanin, Poluostrov 96 C5
Kanin Nos, Mys 96 C5
Kaniva 134 C3
Kankakee 148 D1
Kankan 127 F4
Kanker 112 G3
Kannapolis 155 B5
Kannauj 114 F11
Kannod 115 H10
Kannur 115 P9
Kannyakumari 115 Q10
Kano 127 F7

Kanowit 111 D4
Kanoya 101 H2
Kanpetlet 113 G9
Kanpur 112 D3
Kansas □ 146 F5
Kansas City *Kans., U.S.A.*
  147 F7
Kansas City *Mo., U.S.A.*
  147 F7
Kansk 98 D7
Kanye 131 C5
Kaohsiung 107 F6
Kaolack 127 F2
Kapan 85 F6
Kapanga 128 F4
Kapfenberg 81 E8
Kapiri Mposhi 131 A5
Kāpīsā □ 117 C7
Kapit 111 D4
Kapiti I. 137 D6
Kapoeta 125 H5
Kaposvár 82 E3
Kaptai L. 113 F9
Kapuas → 111 E3
Kapuas Hulu,
  Pegunungan 111 D4
Kapunda 134 B2
Kapuni 136 C6
Kaputar, Mt. 135 B5
Kara 96 C7
Kara Kum = Garagum
  97 F6
Kara Sea 96 B8
Karabiğa 93 D6
Karabük 118 B3
Karaburun 93 E6
Karacabey 93 D7
Karacasu 93 F7
Karachi 115 G5
Karad 115 L9
Karaganda = Qaraghandy
  97 E8
Karaikal 115 P11
Karaikkudi 115 P11
Karakalpakstan =
  Qoraqalpoghistan □
  97 E6
Karakelong 108 D3
Karakitang 109 D3
Karakol 97 E8
Karalon 98 D9
Karaman 118 C3
Karamay 102 B4
Karambu 111 F5
Karamea Bight 137 D4
Karasino 96 C9
Karasuk 97 D8
Karatsu 101 G2
Karawanken 90 A5

Karbalā' 119 D6
Karcag 82 E5
Karditsa 93 E3
Karelia □ 76 C12
Kargasok 97 D9
Kargat 97 D9
Kargil 114 B10
Kariba, L. 131 B5
Kariba Dam 131 B5
Kariba Gorge 131 B5
Karimata, Kepulauan
  111 E3
Karimata, Selat 111 E3
Karimnagar 115 K11
Karimunjawa, Kepulauan
  111 F4
Karin 121 E4
Karkinitska Zatoka 85 D3
Karlovac 90 B5
Karlovo 92 C5
Karlovy Vary 82 C1
Karlsbad = Karlovy Vary
  82 C1
Karlskrona 77 D9
Karlsruhe 80 D5
Karlstad 77 D8
Karnal 114 E10
Karnali → 112 C3
Karnataka □ 115 N10
Kärnten □ 81 E7
Karonga 129 F6
Karoonda 134 C2
Karora 125 E6
Karpathos 93 G6
Kars 118 B5
Karsakpay 97 E7
Karufa 109 E4
Karungu 129 E6
Karviná 82 D4
Karwar 115 M9
Kasai → 128 E3
Kasama 129 G6
Kasandra Kolpos 93 D4
Kasaragod 115 N9
Kasba L. 140 B9
Kasempa 131 A5
Kasenga 129 G5
Kāshān 116 C2
Kashgar = Kashi 102 D3
Kashi 102 D3
Kashk-e Kohneh 114 B3
Kāshmar 116 C4
Kasimov 84 C5
Kasiruta 109 E3
Kasongo 129 E5
Kasongo Lunda 128 F3
Kasos 93 G6
Kassalâ 125 E6
Kassel 80 C5
Kastamonu 118 B3
Kasur 114 D9
Katanga □ 129 F4

Katangi 115 J11
Katerini 93 D4
Katha 113 E11
Kathiawar 115 H7
Kathmandu 112 D5
Katihar 112 E6
Katima Mulilo 130 B4
Katiola 127 G4
Katmandu = Kathmandu
  112 D5
Katoomba 135 B5
Katowice 82 C4
Katsina 127 F7
Kattegat 77 D8
Kaua'i 150 G11
Kaunas 84 C1
Kavala 92 D5
Kavalerovo 100 A4
Kavīr, Dasht-e 116 C3
Kaw 164 B3
Kawagoe 101 F6
Kawaguchi 101 F6
Kawardha 112 G3
Kawasaki 101 F6
Kawasi 109 E3
Kawawachikamach
  143 D7
Kawerau 136 C7
Kawhia 136 C6
Kawhia Harbour 136 C6
Kawio, Kepulauan
  108 D3
Kaya 127 F5
Kayah □ 113 H11
Kayan → 111 D5
Kayeli 109 E3
Kayes 127 F3
Kayin □ 113 H11
Kayoa 109 D3
Kayseri 118 C3
Kazachye 99 B11
Kazakhstan ■ 97 E7
Kazan 84 B6
Kazanlǎk 92 C5
Kāzerūn 116 D2
Kazym → 96 C7
Kea 93 F5
Kebnekaise 76 B9
Kebri Dehar 121 F3
Kecskemét 82 E4
Kediri 111 F4
Keetmanshoop 130 D3
Kefalonia 93 E3
Kefamenanu 109 F2
Keffi 127 G7
Keflavík 76 C1
Keighley 79 E6
Keimoes 130 D4
Keith 134 C2
Kekri 114 G9
Kells 79 E3
Kelowna 141 D8

Kelso 137 F3
Kem 96 C4
Kema 109 D3
Kemah 118 C4
Kemerovo 97 D9
Kemi 76 B10
Kemijärvi 76 B11
Kemijoki → 76 B10
Kemp Land 168 A9
Kempsey 135 B5
Kempten 80 E6
Kendal 111 F4
Kendall 135 B5
Kendari 109 E2
Kendawangan 111 E4
Kendrapara 112 G6
Kenema 127 G3
Keng Tawng 113 G12
Keng Tung 113 G12
Kenitra 126 B4
Kennewick 144 C4
Kenogami → 143 D5
Kenosha 148 C2
Kent Group 134 C4
Kent Pen. 140 B9
Kentaū 97 E7
Kentucky □ 148 F3
Kentville 143 E7
Kenya ■ 129 D7
Kenya, Mt. 129 E7
Kepi 109 F5
Kerala □ 115 P10
Kerang 134 C3
Kerch 85 D4
Kericho 129 E7
Kerinci 111 E2
Kerkyra 93 E2
Kermadec Is. 136 M13
Kermadec Trench
  137 N13
Kermān 116 D4
Kermānshāh 118 D6
Kerrobert 141 C9
Kerzaz 126 C5
Keşan 92 D6
Kesennuma 100 D7
Kestenga 96 C4
Ket → 97 D9
Ketapang 111 E4
Ketchikan 141 C6
Kętrzyn 82 A5
Key West 158 B3
Khabarovsk 99 E11
Khābūr → 118 D5
Khairpur 114 F6
Khakassia □ 98 D6
Khalkhāl 118 C7
Khalmer Yu 96 C7
Khalturin 84 B6
Khalūf 120 C6
Khambhat 115 H8
Khambhat, G. of 115 J8

Khamir **121 D3**
Khānābād **117 B7**
Khānaqīn **118 D6**
Khandwa **115 J10**
Khanewal **114 D7**
Khanka, L. **100 A3**
Khanty-Mansiysk **97 C7**
Khapcheranga **98 E9**
Kharagpur **112 F6**
Kharan Kalat **114 E4**
Kharānaq **116 C3**
Kharda **115 K9**
Khargon **115 J9**
Khārk, Jazīreh-ye **119 E7**
Kharkiv **84 D4**
Kharkov = Kharkiv **84 D4**
Kharovsk **84 B5**
Kharta **92 D7**
Khartoum = El Khartûm **125 E5**
Khasan **100 B2**
Khāsh **114 E2**
Khashm el Girba **125 F6**
Khaskovo **92 D5**
Khatanga **98 B8**
Khatanga → **98 B8**
Khaybar, Ḥarrat **119 F5**
Khed Brahma **115 G8**
Khemmarat **110 A3**
Khenchela **126 A7**
Kherson **85 D3**
Kheta → **98 B8**
Khilok **98 D9**
Khíos = Chios **93 E6**
Khmelnik **83 D8**
Khmelnytskyy **83 D8**
Khmer Rep. =
Cambodia ■ **110 B3**
Khodoriv **83 D7**
Kholm *Afghan.* **117 B6**
Kholm *Russia* **84 B3**
Khomeyn **116 C2**
Khon Kaen **110 A2**
Khorramābād **118 D7**
Khorramshahr **119 E7**
Khotyn **83 D8**
Khouribga **126 B4**
Khowst **114 C6**
Khoyniki **83 C9**
Khũgīānī **114 D4**
Khŭjand **97 E7**
Khukhan **110 B2**
Khulna **113 F7**
Khulna □ **113 F7**
Khūr **116 C4**
Khushab **114 C8**
Khust **83 D6**
Khuzdar **114 F5**
Khvor **116 C3**

Khvormūj **116 D2**
Khvoy **118 C6**
Khyber Pakhtunkhwa □
114 B8
Khyber Pass **114 B7**
Kiama **135 B5**
Kiamba **108 C2**
Kibombo **129 E5**
Kibwezi **129 E7**
Kicking Horse Pass
141 C8
Kidal **127 E6**
Kidnappers, C. **136 C7**
Kiel **80 A6**
Kiel Canal = Nord-
Ostsee-Kanal **80 A5**
Kielce **82 C5**
Kieler Bucht **80 A6**
Kiev = Kyyiv **83 C10**
Kiffa **127 E3**
Kifrī **118 D6**
Kigali **129 E6**
Kigoma-Ujiji **129 E5**
Kii-Sanchi **101 F5**
Kikinda **92 B3**
Kikládhes = Kyklades
93 F5
Kikwit **128 E3**
Kilcoy **135 A5**
Kilifi **129 F7**
Kilimanjaro **129 E7**
Kilis **118 C4**
Kiliya **83 F9**
Kilkenny **79 E3**
Kilkís **93 D4**
Killarney *Australia* **135 A5**
Killarney *Ireland* **79 E2**
Killeen **152 E5**
Killini **93 F4**
Kilmarnock **78 D4**
Kilmore **135 C4**
Kilosa **129 F7**
Kilrush **79 E2**
Kilwa Kivinje **129 F7**
Kimaam **109 F5**
Kimba **134 B2**
Kimberley *Australia*
132 D4
Kimberley *S. Africa*
130 D4
Kimch'aek **105 B8**
Kimmirut **142 C7**
Kimry **84 B4**
Kinabalu, Gunung
110 C5
Kindia **127 F3**
Kindu **129 E5**
Kineshma **84 B5**
King George B. **167 G4**
King George I. **168 A4**
King George Is. **143 D5**
King I. **134 C3**
King William I. **140 B10**

Kingaroy **135 A5**
Kingoonya **134 B2**
Kings Canyon △ **150 B3**
King's Lynn **79 E7**
Kingscote **134 C2**
Kingsport **155 A6**
Kingston *Canada* **143 E6**
Kingston *Jamaica* **158 C4**
Kingston *N.Z.* **137 F3**
Kingston South East
134 C2
Kingston upon Hull **79 E6**
Kingstown **159 D7**
Kingsville **152 F5**
Kınık **93 E6**
Kinkala **128 E2**
Kinleith **136 C6**
Kinngait **142 C6**
Kinsale **79 F2**
Kinshasa **128 E3**
Kiparissia **93 F3**
Kiparissiakos Kolpos
93 F3
Kipushi **131 A5**
Kirghizia = Kyrgyzstan ■
97 E8
Kiribati ■ **136 K12**
Kırıkkale **118 C3**
Kirillov **84 B4**
Kiritimati **137 J15**
Kirkcaldy **78 C5**
Kirkcudbright **79 D4**
Kirkland Lake **143 E5**
Kırklareli **92 D6**
Kirkūk **118 D6**
Kirkwall **78 B5**
Kirov **96 D5**
Kirovohrad **85 D3**
Kirovskiy **100 A3**
Kirsanov **84 D4**
Kırşehir **118 C3**
Kirthar Range **114 F5**
Kiruna **76 B10**
Kiryū **101 E6**
Kisangani **129 D5**
Kisar **109 F3**
Kiselevsk **97 D9**
Kishanganj **112 D7**
Kishangarh **114 F7**
Kishb, Ḥarrat al **119 G5**
Kishinev = Chişinău
83 E9
Kishtwar **114 C9**
Kisii **129 E6**
Kiskőrös **82 E4**
Kiskunfélegyháza **82 E4**
Kiskunhalas **82 E4**
Kislovodsk **85 E5**
Kismaayo **121 H3**
Kiso-Gawa → **101 F5**
Kissidougou **127 G3**

Kisumu **129 E6**
Kita **127 F4**
Kitaibaraki **101 E7**
Kitakyūshū **101 G2**
Kitale **129 D7**
Kitami **100 B8**
Kitchener **143 E5**
Kittakittaooloo, L. **134 A2**
Kitui **129 E7**
Kitwe **131 A5**
Kivertsi **83 C7**
Kivu, L. **129 E5**
Kızıl Irmak → **85 E4**
Kızlyar **85 E6**
Kladno **82 C2**
Klagenfurt **81 E8**
Klaipėda **84 B1**
Klamath Falls **144 E3**
Klamath Mts. **144 F2**
Klang **111 D2**
Klarälven → **77 C8**
Klatovy **82 D1**
Klerksdorp **131 D5**
Klodzko **82 C3**
Klondike **140 B6**
Klouto **127 G6**
Kluane, L. **140 B6**
Kluang **111 D2**
Kluczbork **82 C4**
Klyetsk **83 B8**
Knossos **93 G5**
Knox Coast **168 A12**
Knoxville **155 B6**
Koba **109 E4**
Kobarid **90 A4**
Kōbe **101 F4**
København **77 D8**
Koblenz **80 C4**
Kobryn **83 B7**
Kocaeli **85 E2**
Kočani **92 D4**
Koch Bihar **113 D7**
Kochi *India* **115 Q10**
Kōchi *Japan* **101 G3**
Kodiak **141 C4**
Kodiak I. **141 C4**
Kofiau **109 E3**
Koforidua **127 G5**
Kōfu **101 F6**
Kogon **97 F7**
Kohat **114 C7**
Kohima **113 E10**
Kohkīlūyeh va Būyer
Aḥmadi □ **116 D2**
Kohler Ra. **168 B1**
Kokas **109 E4**
Koko Kyunzu **113 K9**
Koko Nur = Qinghai Hu
102 D8
Kokomo **148 D2**
Kökshetaū **97 D7**
Koksoak → **142 D7**

Kokstad 131 E5
Kola 109 F4
Kola Pen. = Kolskiy
  Poluostrov 76 B13
Kolaka 109 E2
Kolar 115 N11
Kolar Gold Fields
  115 N11
Kolasib 113 E9
Kolayat 114 F8
Kolguyev, Ostrov 96 C5
Kolhapur 115 L9
Kolín 82 C2
Kolkata 113 F7
Kollam 115 Q10
Köln 80 C4
Koło 82 B4
Kołobrzeg 82 A2
Kolomna 84 B4
Kolomyya 83 D7
Kolonodale 109 E2
Kolpashevo 97 D9
Kolpino 84 B3
Kolskiy Poluostrov
  76 B13
Kolwezi 129 G5
Kolyma → 99 C13
Komatsu 101 E5
Komi □ 96 C6
Komodo 109 F1
Komoran, Pulau 109 F5
Komotini 92 D5
Komsomolets, Ostrov
  98 A7
Kon Tum 110 B3
Konar □ 114 B7
Konch 114 G11
Kondoa 129 E7
Kondoz 117 B7
Köneurgench 97 E6
Kong 127 G5
Kong, Koh 110 B2
Konglu 113 D11
Kongolo 129 F5
Konin 82 B4
Konjic 90 C6
Konosha 96 C5
Konotop 84 C3
Konqi He → 102 C6
Końskie 82 C5
Konstanz 80 E5
Kontagora 127 F7
Konya 118 C3
Konya Ovası 118 C3
Koonibba 134 B1
Koorawatha 135 B4
Kootenay L. 141 D8
Kopaonik 92 C3
Koper 90 B4
Kopi 134 B2
Koprivnica 90 A6
Kopychyntsi 83 D7

Korab 92 D3
Korçë 93 D3
Korčula 90 C6
Kordestān □ 118 D6
Kordofân 125 F4
Korea, North ■ 105 B7
Korea, South ■ 105 D7
Korea Bay 105 C6
Korea Strait 105 E8
Korets 83 C8
Korhogo 127 G4
Korinthiakos Kolpos
  93 E4
Korinthos 93 F4
Kōriyama 101 E7
Koro 127 G4
Korogwe 129 F7
Koror 108 C4
Körös → 82 E5
Korosten 83 C9
Korostyshev 83 C9
Kortrijk 80 C2
Kos 93 F6
Kościan 82 B3
Kosciuszko, Mt. 135 C4
Kosha 124 D5
Koshiki-Rettō 101 H1
Košice 82 D5
Kosovo ■ 92 C3
Kôstî 125 F5
Kostopil 83 C8
Kostroma 84 B5
Kostrzyn 82 B2
Koszalin 82 A3
Kota 115 G9
Kota Belud 110 C5
Kota Bharu 110 C5
Kota Kinabalu 110 C5
Kota Tinggi 111 D2
Kotaagung 111 F2
Kotabaru 111 E5
Kotabumi 111 E2
Kotamobagu 109 D2
Kotelnich 84 B6
Kotelnyy, Ostrov 99 B11
Kotka 77 C11
Kotlas 96 C5
Kotor 92 C2
Kotovsk 83 E9
Kotri 114 G6
Kotturu 115 M10
Kotzebue 141 B3
Koudougou 127 F5
Kouilou → 128 E2
Koula Moutou 128 E2
Koumra 125 G2
Kousseri 125 F1
Kouvola 76 C11
Kovel 83 C7
Kovrov 84 B5
Köyceğiz 93 F7

Kozan 118 C3
Kozani 93 D3
Kozhikode 115 P9
Kozyatyn 83 D9
Kra, Kho Khot 110 B1
Kragujevac 92 B3
Krakatoa = Rakata, Pulau
  111 F3
Kraków 82 C4
Kraljevo 92 C3
Kramatorsk 85 D4
Kranj 90 A5
Kraśnik 82 C6
Krasnoarmeysk 97 D5
Krasnodar 85 D4
Krasnoperekopsk 85 D3
Krasnoselkup 96 C9
Krasnoturinsk 96 D7
Krasnoyarsk 98 D7
Krasnyy Luch 85 D4
Krasnyy Yar 85 D6
Kratie 110 B3
Krau 109 E6
Krefeld 80 C4
Kremen 90 B5
Kremenchuk 84 D3
Kremenchuksk Vdskh.
  84 D3
Kremenets 83 C7
Krems 81 D8
Kribi 128 D1
Krishna → 112 K3
Krishnanagar 113 F7
Kristiansand 77 D7
Kristiansund 76 C7
Kriti 93 G5
Krk 90 B5
Kronprins Olav Kyst
  168 A9
Kronshtad 84 B2
Kroonstad 131 D5
Kropotkin 85 D5
Krotoszyn 82 C3
Krung Thep = Bangkok
  110 B2
Krupki 83 A9
Kruševac 92 C3
Krychaw 83 B10
Krymskyy Pivostriv 85 D3
Kryvyy Rih 85 D3
Ksar el Kebir 126 B4
Kuala Kubu Bharu
  111 D2
Kuala Lipis 111 D2
Kuala Lumpur 111 D2
Kuala Sepetang 110 D2
Kuala Terengganu
  110 C2
Kualajelai 111 E4
Kualakapuas 111 E4
Kualakurun 111 E4
Kualapembuang 111 E4

Kualasimpang 111 D1
Kuandang 109 D2
Kuantan 111 D2
Kuban → 85 D4
Kuching 111 D4
Kuda 115 H7
Kudat 110 C5
Kudymkar 96 D6
Kufstein 81 E7
Kugluktuk 140 B8
Küh-e Sorkh 116 C4
Kühak 114 F3
Kühpāyeh 116 C3
Kuito 130 A3
Kuji 100 C7
Kukës 92 C3
Kula 93 E7
Kulasekarappattinam
  115 Q11
Kulen 110 B2
Külob 97 F7
Kulunda 97 D8
Kulwin 134 C3
Kuma → 85 E6
Kumagaya 101 E6
Kumai 111 E4
Kumamba, Kepulauan
  109 E5
Kumamoto 101 G2
Kumanovo 92 C3
Kumara 137 E4
Kumasi 127 G5
Kumba 128 D1
Kumbakonam 115 P11
Kumbarilla 135 A5
Kumon Bum 113 D11
Kungur 97 D6
Kunlong 113 F12
Kunlun Shan 102 D5
Kunming 102 F8
Kuopio 76 C11
Kupa → 90 B6
Kuqa 102 C4
Kür → 85 E6
Kurdistan 118 D5
Kürdzhali 92 D5
Kure 101 F3
Kurgan 97 D7
Kurigram 113 E7
Kuril Is. = Kurilskiye
  Ostrova 99 E12
Kurilskiye Ostrova
  99 E12
Kurnool 115 L11
Kurow 137 F4
Kurri Kurri 135 B5
Kursk 84 C4
Kuruktag 102 C5
Kuruman 130 D4
Kurume 101 G2
Kuş Gölü 93 D6
Kuşadası 93 F6

Kushimoto 101 G4
Kushiro 100 B9
Kushtia 113 F7
Kuskokwim B. 141 C3
Kütahya 118 C5
Kutaisi 85 E5
Kutno 82 B4
Kutu 128 E3
Kutum 125 F3
Kuujjuaq 142 D7
Kuujjuarapik 143 D6
Kuusamo 76 B11
Kuwait = Al Kuwayt
  119 E7
Kuwait ■ 119 E6
Kuybyshev = Samara
  84 C7
Kuybyshev 97 D8
Kuybyshevskoye Vdkhr.
  84 B6
Kuyumba 98 C7
Kuzey Anadolu Dağları
  118 B3
Kuznetsk 84 C6
Kvarner 90 B5
Kvarnerič 90 B5
Kwajalein 136 J11
Kwakoegron 164 A2
KwaMashu 131 D6
Kwando �~ 130 B4
Kwango �~ 128 E3
Kwatisore 109 E4
KwaZulu Natal □ 131 D6
Kwekwe 131 B5
Kwidzyn 82 B4
Kwoka 109 E4
Kyabra Cr. ➛ 135 A3
Kyabram 135 C4
Kyancutta 134 B2
Kyaukpadaung 113 G10
Kyaukpyu 113 H9
Kyaukse 113 G11
Kyklades 93 F5
Kyneton 135 C3
Kyō-ga-Saki 101 F4
Kyoga, L. 129 D6
Kyogle 135 A5
Kyonpyaw 113 J10
Kyōto 101 F4
Kyrenia 118 D3
Kyrgyzstan ■ 97 E8
Kystatyam 98 C10
Kythira 93 F4
Kythnos 93 F5
Kyunhla 113 F10
Kyūshū 101 G2
Kyustendil 92 C4
Kyusyur 98 B10
Kyyiv 83 C10
Kyyivske Vdskh. 83 C10
Kyzyl Kum 97 E7
Kyzyl-Kyya 97 E8

L

La Alcarria 87 B4
La Asunción 162 A6
La Banda 166 B4
La Carlota 166 C4
La Ceiba 157 D7
La Cocha 166 B3
La Crosse 147 D9
La Grande ➛ 143 D6
La Grange 154 C5
La Guaira 162 A5
La Habana 158 B3
La Línea de la
  Concepción 86 D3
La Mancha 87 C4
La Palma 126 C2
La Palma del Condado
  86 D2
La Paragua 162 B6
La Paz Entre Ríos,
  Argentina 166 C5
La Paz San Luis,
  Argentina 166 C3
La Paz Bolivia 163 G5
La Paz Mexico 156 C2
La Pedrera 162 D3
La Plata 166 D5
La Quiaca 166 A3
La Rioja 166 B3
La Rioja □ 87 A4
La Robla 86 A3
La Roche-sur-Yon 88 C3
La Rochelle 88 C3
La Roda 87 C4
La Romana 159 C6
La Serena 166 B2
La Seu d'Urgell 87 A6
La Seyne-sur-Mer 89 E6
La Spézia 90 B2
La Tortuga, I. 159 D6
La Tuque 143 E6
La Unión 167 E2
La Urbana 162 B5
La Vall d'Uixó 87 C5
La Vega 159 C5
Labé 127 F3
Laboulaye 166 C4
Labrador 143 D7
Labrador City 143 D7
Labrador Sea 142 D8
Lábrea 163 E6
Labuan, Pulau 110 C5
Labuha 109 E3
Labuhanbajo 109 F2
Labuk, Telok 110 C5
Labyrinth, L. 134 B2
Labytnangi 96 C7
Lac La Biche 141 C8
Lacanau 88 D3
Laccadive Is. =
  Lakshadweep Is.
  94 G9

Lacepede B. 134 C2
Lachlan ➛ 135 B3
Lacombe 141 C8
Ladakh Ra. 114 B10
Lādīz 117 D5
Ladoga, L. =
  Ladozhskoye Ozero
  76 C12
Ladozhskoye Ozero
  76 C12
Ladysmith 131 D5
Lae 133 B8
Lafayette 153 D7
Lafia 127 G7
Lages 166 B6
Laghmān □ 117 C7
Laghouat 126 B6
Lagonoy G. 108 B2
Lagos Nigeria 127 G6
Lagos Portugal 86 D1
Laguna 166 B7
Lagunas 162 E3
Lahad Datu 108 C1
Lahad Datu, Telok
  108 D1
Lahat 111 E2
Lahewa 111 D1
Lāhījān 118 C7
Lahn ➛ 80 C4
Lahore 114 D9
Lahti 76 C11
Laï 125 G2
Lairg 78 B4
Laizhou 104 D3
Lake Cargelligo 135 B4
Lake Charles 153 D7
Lake City 155 D6
Lake Worth 155 F7
Lakeland 155 E7
Lakes Entrance 135 C4
Lakewood 148 D5
Lakonikos Kolpos 93 F4
Lakor 109 F3
Lakota 127 G4
Lakshadweep Is. 94 G9
Lalaghat 113 E9
L'Albufera 87 C5
Lalín 86 A1
Lamaing 113 K11
Lamas 163 E3
Lambaréné 128 E2
Lamego 86 B2
Lameroo 134 C3
Lamia 93 E4
Lamon B. 108 B2
Lampa 163 G4
Lampedusa 91 G4
Lampione 91 G4
Lampung □ 111 F2
Lamu 129 E8
Läna'i 150 H12

Lanak La 114 B11
Lancaster U.K. 79 D5
Lancaster U.S.A. 149 D7
Lancaster Sd. 142 B5
Lanciano 90 C5
Landeck 80 E6
Landes 88 D3
Landi Kotal 114 B7
Land's End 79 F4
Landshut 81 D7
La'nga Co 112 B3
Langjökull 76 C2
Langkawi, Pulau 110 C1
Langkon 110 C5
Langreo 86 A3
Langres 89 C6
Langres, Plateau de
  89 C6
Langsa 110 D1
Languedoc 89 E5
Lannion 88 B2
Lansdowne 135 B5
Lansing 148 C3
Lanusei 91 E2
Lanzarote 126 C3
Lanzhou 103 D8
Laoag 108 A2
Laoang 108 B3
Laon 89 B5
Laos ■ 110 A3
Lappland 76 B10
Lâpseki 93 D6
Laptev Sea 98 B10
L'Áquila 90 C4
Lār 116 E3
Laramie 146 E2
Larantuka 109 F2
Larat 109 F4
Laredo 152 F4
Lariang 109 E1
Larisa 93 E4
Larnaca 118 D3
Larne 79 D4
Larrimah 132 D5
Larsen Ice Shelf 168 A3
Larvik 77 D8
Las Anod 121 F4
Las Cruces 151 D9
Las Flores 166 D5
Las Lajas 166 D2
Las Lomitas 166 A4
Las Palmas de Gran
  Canaria 126 C2
Las Plumas 167 E3
Las Varillas 166 C4
Las Vegas 150 B5
Lash-e Joveyn 114 D2
Lashio 113 F11
Lassen Pk. 144 F3
Lastoursville 128 E2
Lastovo 90 C6
Latacunga 162 D3

Latina 90 D4
Latrobe 134 D4
Latvia ■ 84 B1
Lauchhammer 81 C7
Launceston 134 D4
Laurel 153 D9
Lauria 91 D5
Lausanne 80 E4
Laut 110 D3
Laut Kecil, Kepulauan 111 E5
Laval 88 B3
Lavrio 93 F5
Lawas 110 D5
Lawele 109 F2
Lawrence N.Z. 137 F3
Lawrence U.S.A. 147 F7
Lawton 152 B4
Layla 119 G6
Lazio □ 90 C4
Lazo 100 B3
Le Creusot 89 C6
Le Havre 88 B4
Le Mans 88 C4
Le Mont-St-Michel 88 B3
Le Puy-en-Velay 89 D5
Le Touquet-Paris-Plage 88 A4
Le Tréport 88 A4
Le Verdon-sur-Mer 88 D3
Leavenworth 147 F7
Lebak 108 C2
Lebanon ■ 118 D3
Łębork 82 A3
Lebrija 86 D2
Lebu 166 D2
Lecce 91 D7
Lecco 90 B2
Lech → 80 D6
Lechang 107 E2
Łęczyca 82 B4
Leeds 79 E6
Leer 80 B4
Leeton 135 B4
Leeuwarden 80 B3
Leeuwin, C. 132 G2
Leeward Is. 159 C7
Lefkada 93 E3
Leganés 86 B4
Legazpi 108 B2
Legionowo 82 B5
Legnago 90 B3
Legnica 82 C3
Leh 114 B10
Leicester 79 E6
Leiden 80 B3
Leie → 80 C2
Leine → 80 B5
Leinster □ 79 E3
Leipzig 81 C7
Leiria 86 C1
Leitrim 79 D2

Leleque 167 E2
Léman, L. 89 C7
Lemhi Ra. 145 D7
Lena → 98 B10
Leninsk 85 D6
Leninsk-Kuznetskiy 97 D9
Lenmalu 109 E4
Lens 89 A5
Lentini 91 F5
Leoben 81 E8
León Mexico 156 C4
León Nic. 157 E7
León Spain 86 A3
León, Montes de 86 A2
Leongatha 135 C4
Leova 83 E9
Lerwick 78 A6
Les Cayes 158 C5
Les Sables-d'Olonne 88 C3
Lesbos 93 E6
Leskovac 92 C3
Lesotho ■ 131 D5
Lesozavodsk 100 A3
Lesser Antilles 159 D7
Lesser Sunda Is. 109 F2
Leszno 82 C3
Lethbridge 141 D8
Leti, Kepulauan 109 F3
Leticia 162 D4
Letpadan 113 J10
Letpan 113 H10
Letterkenny 79 D3
Leuser, Gunung 111 D1
Leuven 80 C3
Levanger 76 C8
Levin 136 D6
Lévis 143 E6
Levka Oros 93 G5
Lewis 78 B3
Lewisporte 143 E8
Lewiston Idaho, U.S.A. 144 C5
Lewiston Maine, U.S.A. 149 B10
Lexington Ky., U.S.A. 148 E3
Lexington N.C., U.S.A. 155 B7
Leyte 108 B2
Lezhë 92 D2
Lhasa 102 F6
Lhazê 102 D3
L'Hermite, I. 167 H3
Lhokkruet 110 D1
Lhokseumawe 110 C1
L'Hospitalet de Llobregat 87 B7
Liancourt Rocks 101 E2
Lianga 108 C3
Lianyungang 104 E3

Liaodong Bandao 104 C5
Liaodong Wan 104 B4
Liaoning □ 104 B5
Liaoyang 105 B5
Liaoyuan 105 A6
Liard → 140 D2
Libenge 128 D3
Liberal 152 A3
Liberec 82 C2
Liberia ■ 127 G4
Lîbîya, Sahrâ' 124 C4
Libobo, Tanjung 109 E3
Libourne 88 D3
Libreville 128 D1
Libya ■ 124 C2
Libyan Desert = Lîbîya, Sahrâ' 124 C4
Licantén 166 D2
Licata 91 F4
Lichinga 131 A7
Lida 83 B7
Liechtenstein ■ 80 E5
Liège 80 C3
Lienz 81 E7
Liepāja 84 B1
Liffey → 79 E3
Lifford 79 D3
Lightning Ridge 135 A4
Liguria □ 90 B2
Ligurian Sea 90 C2
Lijiang 102 F8
Likasi 129 G5
Lille 89 A5
Lillehammer 76 C8
Lilongwe 131 A6
Liloy 108 C2
Lim → 90 C7
Lima Indonesia 109 E3
Lima Peru 163 F3
Lima U.S.A. 148 D3
Lima → 86 B1
Limassol 118 D3
Limay Mahuida 166 D3
Limbang 110 D5
Limbe 128 D1
Limburg 80 C5
Limeira 165 G4
Limerick 79 E2
Limfjorden 77 D7
Limnos 93 E5
Limoges 88 D4
Limón 158 E3
Limousin □ 88 D4
Limoux 88 E5
Limpopo → 131 D6
Limuru 129 E7
Linares Chile 166 D2
Linares Mexico 156 C5
Linares Spain 86 C4
Linchuan 105 D6
Lincoln Argentina 166 C4
Lincoln N.Z. 137 E5

Lincoln U.K. 79 E6
Lincoln U.S.A. 147 E6
Linden 162 B7
Lindesnes 77 D7
Lindi 129 F7
Lindos 93 F7
Lingayen 108 A2
Lingayen G. 108 A2
Lingen 80 B4
Lingga 111 E2
Lingga, Kepulauan 111 E2
Linguère 127 E2
Linhai 106 C6
Linhares 165 F5
Linköping 77 D9
Linosa 91 G4
Linqing 104 D1
Lins 165 G4
Linxia 102 D8
Linyi 104 E3
Linz 81 D8
Lion, G. du 89 E6
Lipa 108 B2
Lípari 91 E5
Lipetsk 84 C4
Lipovets 83 D9
Lippe → 80 C4
Liptrap, C. 135 C4
Lira 129 D6
Lisala 128 D4
Lisboa 86 C1
Lisbon = Lisboa 86 C1
Lisburn 79 D3
Lisieux 88 B4
Liski 84 C4
Lismore 135 A5
Lister, Mt. 168 B15
Liston 135 A5
Listowel 79 E2
Litani → 118 D3
Lithgow 135 B5
Lithino, Akra 93 G5
Lithuania ■ 84 B1
Litoměřice 82 C2
Little Barrier I. 136 B6
Little Missouri → 146 B3
Little River 137 E5
Little Rock 153 B7
Liuwa Plain 130 A4
Liuzhou 103 G9
Livadia 93 E4
Liverpool Canada 143 E7
Liverpool U.K. 79 E5
Liverpool Ra. 135 B5
Livingstone 131 B5
Livny 84 C4
Livorno 90 C3
Ljubljana 90 A5
Llancanelo, Salina 166 D3

Llanelli 79 F4
Llanes 86 A3
Llano Estacado 152 C2
Llanos 162 C4
Lleida 87 B6
Liria 87 C5
Llobregat → 87 B7
Lloret de Mar 87 B7
Llucmajor 87 C7
Llullaillaco, Volcán 166 A3
Loa → 166 A2
Lobatse 131 D5
Lobería 166 D5
Lobito 130 A2
Locarno 89 C8
Loches 88 C4
Lock 134 B2
Lodhran 114 E7
Lodi Italy 90 B3
Lodi U.S.A. 144 G3
Lodja 128 E4
Lodwar 129 D7
Łódź 82 C4
Lofoten 76 B9
Logan 145 F8
Logan, Mt. 140 B5
Logone → 125 F2
Logroño 87 A4
Lohardaga 112 F5
Loikaw 113 H11
Loir → 88 C3
Loire → 88 C2
Loja Ecuador 162 D3
Loja Spain 86 D3
Lokitaung 129 D7
Lokkan tekojärvi 76 B11
Lokoja 127 G7
Lom 92 C4
Lomami → 128 D4
Lombárdia □ 90 B2
Lomblen 109 F2
Lombok 111 F5
Lomé 127 G6
Lomela 128 E4
Lomela → 128 E4
Lomond, L. 78 C4
Lompobatang 109 F1
Łomża 82 B6
Loncoche 167 D2
Londa 115 M9
London Canada 143 E5
London U.K. 79 F6
Londonderry 79 D3
Londonderry, C. 132 C4
Londonderry, I. 167 H2
Londrina 166 A6
Long Beach 150 D3
Long I. Bahamas 158 B4
Long I. U.S.A. 149 D9
Long Xuyen 110 B3
Longford Australia 134 D4

Longford Ireland 79 E3
Longiram 111 E5
Longnawan 111 D4
Longreach 133 E7
Longview Tex., U.S.A. 153 C6
Longview Wash., U.S.A. 144 C2
Longyan 107 E4
Lons-le-Saunier 89 C6
Lop Nur 102 C6
Lopez, C. 128 E1
Lora → 114 D4
Lora, Hāmūn-i- 114 E4
Lora Cr. → 134 A2
Lora del Río 86 D3
Lorain 141 D4
Loralai 114 D6
Lorca 87 D5
Lord Howe I. 136 N10
Lord Howe Rise 136 N11
Lorestān □ 118 D6
Loreto 164 D4
Lorient 88 C2
Lorne 134 C3
Lorraine □ 89 B7
Los Alamos 151 C9
Los Andes 166 C2
Los Angeles Chile 166 D2
Los Angeles U.S.A. 150 C3
Los Blancos 166 A4
Los Hermanos, Is. 162 A6
Los Mochis 156 B3
Los Roques, Is. 162 A5
Los Testigos, Is. 162 A6
Los Vilos 166 C2
Lošinj 90 B5
Lot → 88 D4
Lota 166 D2
Loubomo 128 E2
Louga 127 E2
Lougheed I. 142 B3
Louis Trichardt 131 C5
Louis XIV, Pte. 143 D6
Louisiade Arch. 133 C9
Louisiana □ 153 D8
Louisville 148 E3
Loulé 86 D1
Lourdes 88 E3
Louth Australia 135 B4
Louth U.K. 79 E6
Lovech 92 C5
Lowell 149 C10
Lower California = Baja California 156 A1
Lower Hutt 137 D6
Lower Saxony = Niedersachsen □ 80 B5

Lower Tunguska = Tunguska, Nizhnyaya → 98 C6
Lowestoft 79 E7
Lowgar □ 117 C7
Łowicz 82 B4
Loxton 134 B3
Loyalty Is. = Loyauté, Îs. 136 M11
Loyauté, Îs. 136 M11
Loyew 83 C10
Luachimo 128 F4
Lualaba → 129 D5
Lu'an 106 B4
Luanda 128 F2
Luangwa → 131 A6
Luanshya 131 A5
Luapula → 129 F5
Luarca 86 A2
Luau 128 G4
Lubang Is. 108 B2
Lubango 130 A2
Lubbock 152 C3
Lübeck 81 B6
Lubin 82 C3
Lublin 83 C6
Lubukinggau 111 E2
Lubuksikaping 111 D2
Lubumbashi 131 A5
Lubutu 129 E5
Lucca 90 C3
Lucena Phil. 108 B2
Lucena Spain 86 D3
Lucerne = Luzern 89 C8
Luckenwalde 81 B7
Lucknow 112 D3
Lüda = Dalian 104 C4
Lüderitz 130 D3
Ludhiana 114 D9
Ludwigsburg 80 D5
Ludwigshafen 80 D5
Lufira → 129 F5
Lufkin 153 D6
Luga 84 B2
Lugano 89 C8
Lugo Italy 90 B3
Lugo Spain 86 A2
Lugoj 83 F5
Luhansk 85 D4
Luís Correia 164 C5
Luitpold Coast 168 B5
Luiza 128 F4
Lukanga Swamp 131 A5
Lukenie → 128 E3
Łuków 83 C6
Lulua → 128 E4
Lumbala N'guimbo 130 A4

Lumsden 137 F3
Lumut, Tanjung 111 E3
Lund 77 D8
Lundazi 131 A6
Lundu 111 D3
Lüneburg 80 B6
Lüneburger Heide 80 B6
Lunéville 89 B7
Lunglei 113 F9
Luni 114 G8
Luni → 115 G7
Luninyets 83 B8
Luofu 129 E5
Luoyang 103 E10
Lurgan 79 D3
Lusaka 131 B5
Lusambo 128 E4
Lushnjë 93 D2
Lutherstadt Wittenberg 81 C7
Luton 79 F6
Łutsel K'e 140 B8
Lutsk 83 C7
Lützow Holmbukta 168 A8
Luuq 121 G3
Luwuk 109 E2
Luxembourg 89 B7
Luxembourg ■ 80 D4
Luxor = El Uqsur 124 C5
Luza 84 A6
Luzern 89 C8
Luzhou 103 F9
Luziânia 165 F4
Luzon 108 A2
Lviv 83 D7
Lvov = Lviv 83 D7
Lyakhavichy 83 B8
Lyakhovskiye, Ostrova 99 B12
Lydenburg 131 D6
Lydia 93 E7
Lyell 137 D5
Lyepyel 84 C2
Łyna → 82 A5
Lynchburg 149 F6
Lynd Ra. 135 A4
Lyndhurst 134 B3
Lynn Lake 141 C9
Lyon 89 D6
Lyonnais 89 D6
Lysychansk 85 D4
Lyttelton 137 E5
Lyubertsy 84 B4
Lyuboml 83 C7

M

Ma'ān 119 E3
Ma'anshan 106 B5
Ma'arrat an Nu'mān 118 D2
Maas → 80 C3
Maastricht 89 A6

McAllen 152 F4
Macapá 164 B3
Macau *Brazil* 164 D6
Macau *China* 107 F2
M'Clintock Chan. 140 A9
M'Clure Str. 142 B2
McComb 153 D8
MacDonnell Ranges
  132 E5
Macedonia □ 93 D4
Macedonia ■ 92 D3
Maceió 165 D6
Macerata 90 C4
Macfarlane, L. 134 B2
Macgillycuddy's Reeks
  79 F2
McGregor Ra. 134 A3
Mach 114 E5
Machala 162 D3
Machakos 129 E7
Machilipatnam 112 J3
Machiques 162 A4
Machu Picchu 163 F4
Macintyre → 135 A5
Mackay 133 E8
Mackay, L. 132 E4
Mackenzie → 140 B6
Mackenzie King I. 142 B2
Mackenzie Mts. 140 B6
McKinley, Mt. 141 B4
Macksville 135 B5
Maclean 135 A5
Maclear 131 E5
Macleay → 135 B5
McMurdo Sd. 168 B15
Mâcon *France* 89 C6
Macon *U.S.A.* 155 C6
McPherson Ra. 135 A5
Macquarie Harbour
  134 D4
MacRobertson Land
  168 B10
Macumba → 134 A2
Madadeni 131 D6
Madang 133 B8
Madaripur 113 F8
Madauk 113 J11
Madaya 113 F11
Maddalena 90 D2
Madeira 126 B2
Madeira → 162 D7
Madeleine, Îs. de la
  143 E7
Madha 115 L9
Madhya Pradesh □
  115 H10
Madikeri 115 N9
Madimba 128 E3

Madingou 128 E2
Madison 147 D10
Madiun 111 F4
Madras = Chennai
  115 N12
Madre, L. 153 F5
Madre, Sierra 108 A2
Madre de Dios → 163 F5
Madre de Dios, I. 167 G1
Madre Occidental, Sierra
  156 B3
Madrid 86 B4
Madurai 115 Q11
Madurantakam 115 N11
Mae Sot 110 A1
Maebashi 101 E6
Maevatanana 131 B9
Mafeteng 131 D5
Maffra 135 C4
Mafia I. 129 F7
Mafra *Brazil* 166 B7
Mafra *Portugal* 86 C1
Magadan 99 D13
Magallanes, Estrecho de
  167 G2
Magangué 162 B4
Magdalena *Argentina*
  166 D5
Magdalena *Bolivia*
  163 F6
Magdalena → 162 A4
Magdeburg 81 B6
Magelang 111 F4
Magellan's Str. =
  Magallanes, Estrecho
  de 167 G2
Maggiore, L. 90 B2
Magnetic Pole (North)
  142 A2
Magnetic Pole (South)
  168 A13
Magnitogorsk 97 D6
Maguarinho, C. 164 C4
Magwe 113 G10
Mahābād 118 C6
Mahabo 131 C8
Mahajanga 131 B9
Mahakam → 111 E5
Mahalapye 131 C5
Maḥallāt 116 C2
Mahanadi → 112 G6
Maharashtra □ 115 J10
Mahbubnagar 115 L10
Mahdia 124 A1
Mahenge 129 F7
Maheno 137 F4
Mahesana 115 H8
Mahia Pen. 136 C7
Mahilyow 83 B10
Mahinerangi, L. 137 F3
Mai-Ndombe, L. 128 E3
Maicuru → 164 C3

Maidstone 79 F7
Maiduguri 125 F1
Maikala Ra. 112 G3
Main → 80 D5
Maine 88 C3
Maingkwan 113 D11
Mainit, L. 108 C3
Mainland *Orkney, U.K.*
  78 B5
Mainland *Shet., U.K.*
  78 A6
Mainz 80 C5
Maipú 166 D5
Maiquetía 162 A5
Mairabari 113 D9
Maitland *N.S.W., Australia*
  135 B5
Maitland *S. Austral.,
  Australia* 134 B2
Maizuru 101 F4
Majene 109 E1
Majorca = Mallorca
  87 C7
Majuro 136 J12
Makale 109 E1
Makassar 109 F1
Makassar, Selat 109 E1
Makgadikgadi Salt Pans
  131 C5
Makhachkala 85 E6
Makian 109 D3
Makīnsk 97 D8
Makiyivka 85 D4
Makkah 119 G4
Makó 82 E5
Makokou 128 D2
Makrai 115 H10
Makran 117 E5
Makran Coast Range
  114 G4
Mākū 118 C6
Makurazaki 101 H2
Makurdi 127 G7
Malabar Coast 115 P9
Malacca, Straits of
  110 D1
Maladzyechna 83 A8
Málaga 86 D3
Malagasy Rep. =
  Madagascar ■ 131 C9
Malakal 125 G5
Malakand 114 B7
Malang 111 F4
Malanje 128 F3
Mälaren 77 D9
Malargüe 166 D3
Malaryta 83 C7
Malatya 118 C4
Malawi ■ 131 A6
Malawi, L. 131 A6
Malay Pen. 110 C2
Malaybalay 108 C3

Malåyer 118 D7
Malaysia ■ 110 D4
Malazgirt 118 C5
Malbooma 134 B1
Malbork 82 A4
Malden I. 137 K15
Maldives ■ 94 H9
Maldonado 166 C6
Maleas, Akra 93 F4
Malegaon 115 J9
Malema 131 A7
Malha 125 E4
Mali ■ 127 E5
Mali → 113 E11
Maliku 109 E2
Malili 109 E2
Malin Hd. 78 D3
Malindi 129 E8
Malino 109 D2
Malita 108 C3
Malkara 92 D6
Mallacoota Inlet 135 C4
Mallaig 78 C4
Mallawi 124 C5
Mallorca 87 C7
Mallow 79 E2
Malmö 77 D8
Malolos 108 B2
Malpelo, I. de 162 C2
Malta ■ 91 G5
Maltahöhe 130 C3
Maluku 109 E3
Malvan 115 L8
Malvinas, Is. = Falkland
  Is. ☑ 167 G5
Malyn 83 C9
Malyy Lyakhovskiy,
  Ostrov 99 B12
Mamanguape 164 D6
Mamasa 109 E1
Mamberamo → 109 E5
Mambilima Falls 129 G5
Mamburao 108 B2
Mamoré → 163 F5
Mamou 127 F3
Mamuju 109 E1
Man 127 G4
Man, I. of 79 D4
Man Na 113 F11
Manacapuru 162 D6
Manacor 87 C7
Manado 109 D2
Managua 157 E7
Manakara 131 C9
Manama = Al Manāmah
  116 E2
Mananjary 131 C9
Manapouri 137 F2
Manapouri, L. 137 F2
Manas 102 C5
Manas → 113 D8
Manaus 162 D7

Manchester *U.K.* 79 E5
Manchester *U.S.A.*
149 C10
Mand ➔ 116 D3
Mandal 77 D7
Mandala, Puncak 109 E6
Mandalay 113 F11
Mandalī 118 D6
Mandar, Teluk 109 E1
Mandaue 108 B2
Mandi 114 D10
Mandimba 131 A7
Mandioli 109 E3
Mandla 112 F3
Mandritsara 131 B9
Mandsaur 115 G9
Mandvi 115 H6
Mandya 115 N10
Manfalût 124 C5
Manfredónia 90 D5
Mangalia 92 C7
Mangalore 115 N9
Mangaweka 136 C6
Manggar 111 E3
Manggawitu 109 E4
Mangghystaū Tübegi
97 E6
Mangkalihat, Tanjung
109 D1
Mangnai 102 D6
Mango 127 F6
Mangoche 131 A7
Mangoky ➔ 131 C8
Mangole 109 E3
Mangonui 136 A5
Mangueira, L. da 166 C6
Manica 131 B6
Manicoré 163 E6
Manicouagan ➔ 143 E7
Manicouagan, Rés.
143 D7
Manīfah 119 F7
Manihiki 137 L14
Manila 108 B2
Manila B. 108 B2
Manilla 135 B5
Manipur □ 113 E9
Manipur ➔ 113 F10
Manisa 93 E6
Manitoba □ 141 C10
Manitoba, L. 141 C10
Manitoulin I. 143 E5
Manitowoc 148 B2
Manizales 162 B3
Manjhand 114 G6
Manjra ➔ 115 K10
Manmad 115 J9
Manna 111 E2
Mannahill 134 B3
Mannar 115 Q11
Mannar, G. of 115 Q11

Mannar I. 115 Q11
Mannheim 80 D5
Mannum 134 B2
Manokwari 109 E4
Manono 129 F5
Manosque 89 E6
Manresa 87 B6
Mansa 129 G5
Mansel I. 142 C5
Mansfield *Australia*
135 C4
Mansfield *U.K.* 79 E6
Mansfield *U.S.A.* 148 D4
Manta 162 D2
Mantalingajan, Mt.
110 C5
Mantes-la-Jolie 88 B4
Manthani 115 K11
Mántova 90 B3
Manú 163 F4
Manuel Alves ➔ 165 E4
Manui 109 E2
Manukau 136 B6
Manych-Gudilo, Ozero
85 D5
Manzai 114 C7
Manzanares 86 C4
Manzanillo *Cuba* 158 B4
Manzanillo *Mexico*
156 D4
Manzhouli 103 B11
Mao *Chad* 125 F2
Maó *Spain* 87 C8
Maoke, Pegunungan
109 E5
Maoming 107 G1
Mapam Yumco 112 B3
Mapia, Kepulauan
109 D4
Mapuera ➔ 162 D7
Maputo 131 D6
Maqat 97 E6
Maqnā 119 E3
Maquela do Zombo
128 F3
Maquinchao 167 E3
Mar Chiquita, L. 166 C4
Mar del Plata 166 D5
Mar Menor 87 D5
Maraã 162 D5
Marabá 164 D4
Maracá, I. de 164 B3
Maracaibo 162 A4
Maracaibo, L. de 162 B4
Maracay 162 A5
Maradi 127 F7
Marāgheh 118 C6
Marāh 119 F6
Marajó, I. de 164 C4
Marand 118 C6
Maranguape 164 C6
Maranhão □ 164 D4

Maranoa ➔ 135 A4
Marañón ➔ 162 D4
Marão 131 C6
Maratua 109 D1
Marbella 86 D3
Marburg 80 C5
Marche 88 C4
Marchena 86 D3
Mardan 114 B8
Mardin 118 C5
Margarita, I. de 162 A6
Margaritovo 100 B4
Margate 79 F7
Marghilon 97 E8
Mārgow, Dasht-e 114 D3
Mari El □ 84 B6
Maria I. 134 D4
Maria van Diemen, C.
136 A5
Mariana Trench 136 H9
Maribor 90 A5
Marie Byrd Land 168 B18
Mariental 130 C3
Mariinsk 97 D9
Marília 165 G3
Marín 86 A1
Marinduque 108 B2
Maringá 166 A6
Marion 153 A9
Mariscal Estigarribia
163 H6
Maritimes, Alpes 89 D7
Mariupol 85 D4
Marīvān 118 D6
Marka 121 G3
Markham, Mt. 168 C15
Marks 84 C6
Marla 134 A1
Marmagao 115 M8
Marmara 93 D6
Marmara Denizi 92 D7
Marmaris 93 F7
Marmolada, Mte. 90 A3
Marne ➔ 88 B5
Maroantsetra 131 B9
Marondera 131 B6
Maroni ➔ 164 A3
Maroochydore 135 A5
Maroona 134 C3
Maroua 125 F1
Marovoay 131 B9
Marquesas, Îs. 137 K17
Marrakech 126 B4
Marrawah 134 D3
Marree 134 A2
Marrowie Cr. ➔ 135 B4
Marrupa 131 A7
Marsá Matrûh 124 B4
Marsabit 129 D7
Marsala 91 F4
Marsden 135 B4
Marseille 89 E6

Marshall 153 C6
Marshall Is. ■ 136 J12
Marshalltown 147 D8
Martaban 113 J11
Martaban, G. of 113 J11
Martapura
    *Kalimantan Selatan,
    Indonesia* 111 E4
Martapura
    *Sumatera Selatan,
    Indonesia* 111 E2
Martigues 89 E6
Martinborough 137 D6
Martinique ☑ 159 D7
Martinsville 155 A8
Marton 136 D6
Martos 86 D4
Marudi 111 D4
Maruf 114 D5
Marugame 101 F3
Marwar 114 G8
Mary 97 F7
Maryborough *Queens.,
    Australia* 135 A5
Maryborough *Vic.,
    Australia* 134 C3
Maryland □ 149 E7
Marystown 143 E8
Masaka 129 E6
Masalembo, Kepulauan
111 F4
Masalima, Kepulauan
111 F5
Masamba 109 E2
Masan 105 E8
Masandam, Ra's 116 E4
Masasi 129 G7
Masaya 157 E7
Masbate 108 B2
Mascara 126 A6
Masela 109 F3
Maseru 131 D5
Mashābih 119 F44
Mashhad 116 F4
Mâshkel, Hāmūn-i-
114 E3
Mashki Chāh 114 E3
Mashonaland 131 B6
Masindi 129 D6
Masjed Soleyman 119 E7
Mask, L. 79 E2
Maskin 116 F4
Masoala, Tanjon' i
131 B10
Mason City 147 D8
Masqat 117 F4
Massa 90 B3
Massachusetts □ 149 C9
Massakory 125 F2
Massangena 131 C6
Massena 149 B8
Massenya 125 F2

Massif Central **89 D5**
Massinga **131 C7**
Masson I. **168 A11**
Masterton **137 D6**
Mastuj **114 A8**
Mastung **114 E5**
Masty **83 B7**
Masuda **101 F2**
Masvingo **131 C6**
Matabeleland **131 B5**
Matadi **128 F2**
Matagalpa **157 E7**
Matagami **143 E6**
Matagami, L. **143 E6**
Matak **111 D3**
Matam **127 E3**
Matamoros *Coahuila, Mexico* **156 B4**
Matamoros *Tamaulipas, Mexico* **156 B5**
Ma'ṭan às Sarra **124 D3**
Matane **143 E7**
Matanzas **158 B3**
Mataram **111 F5**
Matarani **163 G4**
Mataró **87 B7**
Mataura **137 G3**
Matehuala **156 C4**
Matera **91 D6**
Mathraki **93 E2**
Mathura **114 F10**
Mati **108 C3**
Matiri Ra. **137 D5**
Mato Grosso □ **165 E3**
Mato Grosso, Planalto do **165 F3**
Mato Grosso do Sul □ **165 F3**
Matosinhos **86 B1**
Maṭruḥ **117 F4**
Matsue **101 F3**
Matsumae **100 C7**
Matsumoto **101 E6**
Matsusaka **101 F5**
Matsuyama **101 G3**
Mattagami → **143 D5**
Mattancheri **115 Q10**
Matthews Ridge **162 B6**
Matucana **163 F3**
Maturín **162 D7**
Mau Ranipur **115 G11**
Maubeuge **89 A5**
Maude **135 B3**
Maudin Sun **113 K10**
Maués **162 D7**
Mauganj **112 E3**
Maui **150 H12**
Maumere **109 F2**
Maun **130 B4**
Maungmagan Kyunzu **113 K11**
Mauritania ■ **127 E3**

Mauritius ■ **123 H9**
Mawkmai **113 G11**
Mawlaik **113 F10**
Mawson Coast **168 A10**
Mayaguana I. **159 B5**
Mayagüez **159 C6**
Maydena **134 D4**
Mayenne → **88 C3**
Maykop **85 E5**
Mayo **140 B6**
Mayon Volcano **108 B2**
Mayor I. **136 B7**
Mayotte ☑ **131 A9**
Mayu **109 D3**
Mazabuka **131 B5**
Mazagão **164 C3**
Mazán **162 D4**
Māzandarān □ **116 B3**
Mazar-e Sharīf **117 B6**
Mazara del Vallo **91 F4**
Mazarrón **87 D5**
Mazaruni → **162 B7**
Mazatlán **156 C3**
Māzhān **116 D4**
Mazīnān **116 B4**
Mazoe → **131 B6**
Mazurski, Pojezierze **82 B5**
Mazyr **83 C9**
Mbabane **131 D6**
Mbaïki **128 D3**
Mbala **129 F6**
Mbale **129 D6**
Mbalmayo **128 D2**
Mbandaka **128 D3**
Mbanza Congo **128 F2**
Mbanza Ngungu **128 F2**
Mbarara **129 E6**
Mbeya **129 F6**
Mbini = Río Muni □ **128 D2**
Mbombela **131 D6**
Mbour **127 F2**
Mbuji-Mayi **128 F4**
Mdantsane **131 E5**
Mead, L. **150 B5**
Mearim → **164 C5**
Meaux **89 B5**
Mecca = Makkah **119 G4**
Mechelen **80 C3**
Mecheria **126 B5**
Mecklenburg **81 B6**
Mecklenburger Bucht **81 A6**
Medan **111 D1**
Medanosa, Pta. **167 F3**
Médéa **126 A6**
Medellín **162 B3**
Medford **144 E2**
Medgidia **92 B7**
Medicine Bow Mts. **145 F10**

Medicine Hat **141 C8**
Medina = Al Madīnah **119 F4**
Medina del Campo **86 B3**
Medina Sidonia **86 D3**
Medinipur **112 F6**
Mediterranean Sea **122 C5**
Médoc **88 D3**
Medveditsa → **84 D5**
Medvezhyegorsk **96 C4**
Meekatharra **132 F2**
Meerut **114 E10**
Megara **93 F4**
Meghalaya □ **113 E8**
Meighen I. **142 B4**
Meiktila **113 G10**
Meissen **81 C7**
Meizhou **107 E4**
Mejillones **166 A2**
Mekhtar **114 D6**
Meknès **126 B4**
Mekong → **110 C3**
Mekongga **109 E2**
Melagiri Hills **115 N10**
Melaka **111 D2**
Melanesia **136 K10**
Melbourne *Australia* **135 C3**
Melbourne *U.S.A.* **155 E7**
Mélèzes → **142 D6**
Melfort **141 C9**
Melilla **87 E4**
Melitopol **85 D4**
Melk **81 D8**
Melo **166 C6**
Melolo **109 F2**
Melrose **135 B4**
Melun **89 B5**
Melville **141 C9**
Melville I. *Australia* **132 C5**
Melville I. *Canada* **142 B2**
Melville Pen. **142 C5**
Memboro **109 F1**
Memel = Klaipéda **84 B1**
Memmingen **80 E6**
Mempawah **111 D3**
Memphis *Tenn., U.S.A.* **154 B3**
Memphis *Tex., U.S.A.* **152 B3**
Ménaka **127 E6**
Mendawai → **111 E4**
Mende **89 D5**
Mendocino, C. **144 F1**
Mendoza **166 C2**
Mene Grande **162 B4**
Menemen **93 E6**
Menggala **111 E3**
Mengzi **102 G8**
Menindee **134 B3**

Menindee L. **134 B3**
Meningie **134 C2**
Menominee **148 B2**
Menongue **130 A3**
Menorca **87 C7**
Mentawai, Kepulauan **111 E1**
Menton **89 E7**
Meppel **80 B4**
Merano **90 A3**
Merauke **109 F6**
Merbein **134 B3**
Merced **150 B2**
Mercedes *B. Aires, Argentina* **166 C5**
Mercedes *Corrientes, Argentina* **166 B5**
Mercedes *San Luis, Argentina* **166 C3**
Mercedes *Uruguay* **166 C5**
Mercer **136 B6**
Mercy, C. **142 C7**
Meredith, C. **167 G4**
Mergui Arch. = Myeik Kyunzu **110 B3**
Mérida *Mexico* **157 C7**
Mérida *Spain* **86 C2**
Mérida *Venezuela* **162 B4**
Meridian **154 C3**
Merirumã **164 B3**
Merriwa **135 B5**
Merseburg **81 C6**
Mersin = İçel **118 C3**
Mersing **111 D2**
Merthyr Tydfil **79 F5**
Mértola **86 D2**
Meru **129 D7**
Mesa **151 D7**
Meshgin Shahr **118 C6**
Mesolongi **93 E3**
Mesopotamia = Al Jazirah **118 D5**
Messina **91 E5**
Messina, Str. di **91 E5**
Messini **93 F4**
Messiniakos Kolpos **93 F4**
Meta → **162 B5**
Meta Incognita Pen. **142 C7**
Metairie **153 E8**
Metán **166 B4**
Methven **137 E4**
Metlakatla **141 C6**
Metz **89 B7**
Meulaboh **111 D1**
Meureudu **110 C1**
Meuse → **89 A6**
Mexiana, L. **164 C4**
Mexicali **156 A1**
Mexico ■ **156 C4**

México, Ciudad de **156 D5**
Mexico, G. of **157 B7**
Meymaneh **114 B4**
Mezen **96 C5**
Mezen → **96 C5**
Mézenc, Mt. **89 D6**
Mezőkövesd **82 E5**
Mezőtúr **82 E5**
Mhow **115 H9**
Miami **155 G7**
Miami Beach **155 G7**
Miāndowāb **118 C6**
Miandrivazo **131 B9**
Miāneh **118 C6**
Mianwali **114 C7**
Miass **97 D7**
Michigan □ **148 C3**
Michigan, L. **148 C2**
Michurin **92 C6**
Michurinsk **84 C5**
Micronesia **136 H11**
Micronesia, Federated States of ■ **136 J10**
Middelburg **130 E5**
Middlesbrough **79 D6**
Midi, Canal du → **88 E4**
Midland **152 D3**
Midyat **118 C5**
Midzör **92 C4**
Międzychód **82 B2**
Międzyrzec Podlaski **83 C6**
Mielec **82 C5**
Mieres **86 A3**
Mikines **93 F4**
Mikonos = Mykonos **93 F5**
Milagro **162 D3**
Milano **90 B2**
Milâs **93 F6**
Milazzo **91 E5**
Mildura **134 B3**
Miles **135 A5**
Miletus **93 F6**
Milford Haven **79 F4**
Milford Sd. **137 F2**
Milford Sound **137 F2**
Mill I. **168 A12**
Millau **89 D5**
Millicent **134 C3**
Millinocket **149 B11**
Millmerran **135 A5**
Milos **93 F5**
Milparinka **134 A3**
Milton **137 G3**
Milton Keynes **79 E6**
Milwaukee **148 C2**
Min Jiang → *Fujian, China* **107 E5**
Min Jiang → *Sichuan, China* **103 F8**

Mīnā' al Aḥmadī **119 E7**
Mīnā Su'ud **119 E7**
Minamata **101 G2**
Minamiaizu **101 E6**
Minamisōma **101 E7**
Minas **166 C5**
Minas Gerais □ **165 F4**
Minbu **113 G10**
Mindanao **108 C2**
Mindanao Sea = Bohol Sea **108 C2**
Mindanao Trench **108 B3**
Minden **80 B5**
Mindiptana **109 F6**
Mindoro **108 B2**
Mindoro Str. **108 B2**
Mingäçevir Su Anbarı **85 E6**
Mingin **113 F10**
Minho **86 B1**
Minna **127 G7**
Minneapolis **147 C8**
Minnesota □ **147 B7**
Minnipa **134 B2**
Miño → **86 B1**
Minorca = Menorca **87 C7**
Minot **146 A4**
Minsk **84 C2**
Mińsk Mazowiecki **82 B5**
Mintaka Pass **114 A9**
Minto, L. **142 D6**
Minutang **113 C11**
Mira **90 B4**
Mirabello, Kolpos **93 G5**
Miraj **115 L9**
Miram Shah **114 C7**
Miramichi **143 E7**
Miranda **165 G2**
Miranda de Ebro **87 A4**
Miranda do Douro **86 B2**
Miri **110 D4**
Mirim, L. **166 C6**
Mirpur Khas **114 G6**
Mirzapur **112 E4**
Mish'āb, Ra's al **119 E7**
Mishan **103 B14**
Miskolc **82 D5**
Misool **109 E4**
Miṣrātah **124 B2**
Missinaibi → **143 D5**
Mississippi □ **153 C9**
Mississippi → **153 E9**
Mississippi River Delta **153 E9**
Missoula **145 C7**
Missouri □ **147 F8**
Missouri → **147 F9**
Mistassini, L. **143 D6**
Mitchell *Australia* **135 A4**
Mitchell *U.S.A.* **146 D5**
Mitchell → **133 D7**

Mitilini **93 E6**
Mito **101 E7**
Mitrovicë **92 C3**
Mittagong **135 B5**
Mitú **162 C4**
Mitumba, Mts. **129 F5**
Mitwaba **129 F5**
Miyake-Jima **101 F6**
Miyako **100 D7**
Miyakonojō **101 H2**
Miyazaki **101 H2**
Mizdah **124 B1**
Mizoram □ **113 F9**
Mjosa **76 C8**
Mladá Boleslav **82 C2**
Mława **82 B5**
Mljet **90 C6**
Mmabatho **131 D5**
Mo i Rana **76 B8**
Moa **109 F3**
Mobaye **128 D4**
Mobayi **128 D4**
Mobile **154 D3**
Moçambique **131 B8**
Mochudi **131 C5**
Mocimboa da Praia **129 G8**
Mocoa **162 C3**
Mocuba **131 B7**
Modane **89 D7**
Módena **90 B3**
Modesto **150 B2**
Módica **91 F5**
Modimolle **131 C5**
Moe **135 C4**
Moengo **164 A3**
Mogadishu = Muqdisho **121 G4**
Mogami-Gawa → **100 D7**
Mogaung **113 E11**
Mogok **113 F11**
Mohács **82 F4**
Moḥammadābād **116 B4**
Mohyliv-Podilskyy **83 D8**
Moisie → **143 D7**
Mojave Desert **150 C4**
Moji das Cruzes **166 A7**
Mokai **135 C4**
Mokau **136 C6**
Mokokchung **113 D10**
Mokopane **131 C5**
Mokpo **105 E7**
Mokra Gora **92 C3**
Molchanovo **97 D9**
Moldavia = Moldova ■ **83 E9**
Molde **76 C7**
Moldoveanu, Vf. **83 F7**
Molepolole **131 C5**
Molfetta **90 D6**

Moline **147 E9**
Mollendo **163 G4**
Moloka'i **150 H12**
Molong **135 B4**
Molopo → **130 D4**
Molu **109 F4**
Molucca Sea **109 E2**
Moluccas = Maluku **109 E3**
Moma **131 B7**
Mombasa **129 E7**
Mombetsu **100 A8**
Momchilgrad **92 D5**
Mompós **162 B4**
Mona Passage **159 C6**
Monaco ■ **89 E7**
Monahans **152 D2**
Moncayo, Sierra del **87 B5**
Mönchengladbach **80 C4**
Monchique **86 D1**
Monclova **156 B4**
Moncton **143 E7**
Mondego → **86 B1**
Mondeodo **109 E2**
Mondovì **90 B1**
Monforte de Lemos **86 A2**
Mong Hsat **113 G12**
Mong Kung **113 G11**
Mong Nai **113 G11**
Mong Ton **113 G12**
Mong Yai **113 F12**
Mongalla **125 G5**
Mongo **125 F2**
Mongolia ■ **103 B8**
Mongu **130 B4**
Monkoto **128 E4**
Monópoli **91 D6**
Monroe *La.*, *U.S.A.* **153 C7**
Monroe *N.C.*, *U.S.A.* **155 B7**
Monrovia **127 G3**
Mons **80 C2**
Monse **109 E2**
Mont-de-Marsan **88 E3**
Mont-Laurier **143 E6**
Mont-St-Michel, Le **88 B3**
Montalbán **87 B5**
Montana □ **92 C4**
Montana □ **145 C9**
Montargis **89 C5**
Montauban **88 D4**
Montbéliard **89 C7**
Montceau-les-Mines **89 C6**
Monte Alegre **164 C3**
Monte Azul **165 F5**
Monte-Carlo **90 C1**
Monte Caseros **166 C5**

Monte Comán 166 C3
Monte Santu, C. di 91 D2
Montecristo 90 C3
Montego Bay 158 C4
Montélimar 89 D6
Montemorelos 156 B5
Montenegro ■ 92 C2
Montepuez 131 B7
Monterey 150 B2
Montería 162 B3
Monterrey 156 B4
Montes Claros 165 F5
Montesilvano 90 C5
Montevideo 166 C5
Montgomery 154 C4
Montilla 86 D3
Montluçon 89 C5
Montmorillon 88 C4
Montoro 86 C3
Montpellier 89 E5
Montréal 143 E6
Montrose U.K. 78 C5
Montrose U.S.A. 151 A9
Montserrat ☑ 159 C7
Monywa 113 F10
Monza 90 B2
Monze 131 B5
Monze, C. 115 G5
Monzón 87 B6
Moonie 135 A5
Moonie ➝ 135 A4
Moonta 134 B2
Moose Jaw 141 C9
Moosomin 141 C9
Moosonee 143 D5
Mopti 127 F5
Moquegua 163 G4
Mora 76 C8
Moradabad 114 E11
Morafenobe 131 B8
Moramanga 131 B9
Moratuwa 115 R11
Morava ➝ Serbia 92 B3
Morava ➝ Slovak Rep.
  82 D3
Morawhanna 162 B7
Moray Firth 78 C5
Morden 141 D10
Mordvinia ☐ 84 C5
Moree 135 A4
Morelia 156 D4
Morella 87 B5
Morena, Sierra 86 C3
Moreton I. 135 A5
Morgan City 153 E8
Morioka 100 D7
Morlaix 88 B2
Mornington 135 C4
Mornington, I. 167 F1
Moro G. 108 C2
Morocco ■ 126 B4
Morogoro 129 F7

Morombe 131 C8
Morón 158 B4
Morón de la Frontera
  86 D3
Morondava 131 C8
Morotai 109 D3
Moroto 129 D6
Morphou 118 D3
Morrinhos 165 F4
Morrinsville 136 B6
Morristown 155 A6
Morshansk 84 C5
Mortlake 134 C3
Morundah 135 B4
Moruya 135 C5
Morvan 89 C6
Morven 135 A4
Morwell 135 C4
Moscos Is. 110 B1
Moscow = Moskva 84 B4
Moscow 144 C5
Mosel ➝ 89 A7
Mosgiel 137 F4
Moshi 129 E7
Mosi-oa-Tunya = Victoria
  Falls 131 B5
Mosjøen 76 B8
Moskva 84 B4
Mosonmagyaróvár 82 E3
Mosquera 162 C3
Moss Vale 135 B5
Mossburn 137 F3
Mosselbaai 130 E4
Mossendjo 128 E2
Mossgiel 135 B3
Mossoró 164 D6
Most 82 C1
Mostaganem 126 A6
Mostar 90 C6
Mostardas 166 C6
Mostyska 83 D6
Mosul = Al Mawşil
  118 C5
Motihari 112 D5
Motril 86 D4
Motueka 137 D5
Motueka ➝ 137 D5
Moudros 93 E5
Mouila 128 E2
Moulamein 135 C3
Moulins 89 C5
Moulmein 113 J11
Moundou 125 G2
Mount Aspiring △ 137 F3
Mount Barker 134 C2
Mount Cook 137 E4
Mount Gambier 134 C3
Mount Hope N.S.W.,
  Australia 135 B4
Mount Hope S. Austral.,
  Australia 134 B2

Mount Isa 133 E6
Mount Lofty Ranges
  134 B2
Mount Maunganui
  136 B7
Mount Perry 135 A5
Moura Brazil 162 D6
Moura Portugal 86 C2
Mourdi, Dépression du
  125 E3
Moussoro 125 F2
Moutong 109 D2
Moyale 129 D7
Moyen Atlas 126 B4
Moyo 111 F5
Moyyero ➝ 98 C8
Moyynty 98 E8
Mozambique ■ 131 B7
Mozambique Chan.
  123 H8
Mozdok 85 E5
Mpanda 129 F6
Mpika 131 A6
Mpumalanga 129 F7
Mthatha 131 E5
Mu Us Shamo 103 D9
Muar 111 D2
Muarabungo 111 E2
Muaraenim 111 E2
Muarajuloi 111 E4
Muarakaman 111 E5
Muaratebo 111 E2
Muaratembesi 111 E2
Muarateweh 111 E4
Mubi 125 F1
Muckadilla 135 A4
Mucuri 165 F6
Mudanjiang 103 C13
Mudanya 93 D7
Mudgee 135 B4
Mufulira 131 A5
Mugi 101 G4
Muğla 93 F7
Mugu 112 C4
Muhammad Qol 124 D6
Mühlhausen 80 C6
Mühlig Hofmann fjell
  168 B7
Mukacheve 83 D6
Mukah 111 D4
Mukden = Shenyang
  105 B5
Mukomuko 111 E2
Muktsar 114 D9
Mula 87 C5
Mulanje, Mt. 131 B7
Mulchén 166 D2
Mulde ➝ 81 C7
Mulhacén 86 D4
Mulhouse 89 C7
Mull 78 C4
Mullengudgery 135 B4

Muller, Pegunungan
  111 D4
Mullingar 79 E3
Mullumbimby 135 A5
Multan 114 D7
Mumbai 115 K8
Muna 109 F2
Munabao 113 H9
München 81 D6
Muncie 148 D3
Münden 80 C5
Mundo Novo 165 E5
Mungallala 135 A4
Mungallala Cr. ➝ 135 A4
Mungbere 129 D5
Munger 112 E6
Munich = München
  81 D6
Muñoz Gamero, Pen.
  167 G2
Münster 80 C4
Munster ☐ 79 E2
Muntok 111 E3
Muqdisho 121 G4
Murallón, Cerro 167 F2
Murang'a 129 E7
Murashi 84 B6
Muratlı 92 D6
Murchison ➝ 132 F1
Murchison, Mt. 168 B15
Murchison Falls 129 D6
Murcia 87 C5
Murcia ☐ 87 D5
Mureș ➝ 92 A3
Murfreesboro 154 B4
Murgap 97 F8
Murgon 135 A5
Müritz 81 B7
Murmansk 76 B12
Murom 84 B5
Muroran 100 B7
Muroto 101 G4
Muroto-Misaki 101 G4
Murray ➝ 134 C2
Murray Bridge 134 C2
Murrumbidgee ➝
  134 B3
Murrumburrah 135 B4
Murrurundi 135 B5
Murtoa 134 C3
Murwara 112 F3
Murwillumbah 135 A5
Murzüq 124 C1
Murzüq, Idehān 124 D1
Mürzzuschlag 81 E8
Muş 118 C5
Mûsa, Gebel 119 E3
Musa Khel 114 D6
Mûsa Qal'eh 114 C4
Musala Bulgaria 92 C4
Musala Indonesia 111 D1
Muscat = Masqat 117 F4

Muscatine 147 E9
Musgrave Ranges 132 F5
Mushie 128 E3
Musi → 111 E2
Musina 131 C6
Muskogee 153 B6
Musoma 129 E6
Mussoorie 114 D11
Mustafakemalpaşa 93 D7
Mustang 112 C4
Musters, L. 167 F3
Muswellbrook 135 B5
Mût *Egypt* 124 C4
Mut *Turkey* 118 C3
Mutare 131 B6
Muting 109 F6
Mutoray 98 C8
Mutsu 100 C7
Mutsu-Wan 100 C7
Muynak 97 E6
Muzaffarabad 114 B8
Muzaffargarh 114 D7
Muzaffarnagar 114 E10
Muzaffarpur 112 D5
Muzhi 96 C7
Mvuma 131 B6
Mwanza *Dem. Rep. of the Congo* 129 F5
Mwanza *Tanzania* 129 E6
Mweka 128 E4
Mweru, L. 129 F5
Mwinilunga 130 A4
My Tho 110 B3
Myanaung 113 H10
Myanmar = Burma ■ 113 G11
Myaungmya 113 J10
Mycenæ = Mikines 93 F4
Myeik Kyunzu 110 B1
Myingyan 113 G10
Myitkyina 113 E11
Mykolayiv 85 D3
Mykonos 93 F5
Mymensingh 113 E8
Mýrdalsjökull 76 C2
Mysia 93 E6
Mysore = Karnataka □ 115 N10
Mysore 115 N10
Myszków 82 C4
Mytishchi 84 B4

N

Naab → 81 D7
Nababeep 130 D3
Naberezhnyye Chelny 97 D6
Nabeul 124 A1
Nabire 109 E5
Nābulus 118 D3
Nacala 131 A8
Nachingwea 129 G7

Nacogdoches 153 D6
Nacozari de García 156 A3
Nadiad 115 H8
Nadüshan 116 C3
Nadvirna 83 D7
Nadym 96 C8
Nadym → 96 C8
Nafpaktos 93 E3
Nafplio 93 F4
Nafud Desert = An Nafūd 119 E5
Naga 108 B2
Nagaland □ 113 E10
Nagano 101 E6
Nagaoka 101 E6
Nagaon 113 D9
Nagappattinam 115 P11
Nagar Parkar 115 G7
Nagasaki 101 G1
Nagaur 114 F8
Nagercoil 115 Q10
Nagîneh 116 C4
Nagorno-Karabakh □ 97 E5
Nagoya 101 F5
Nagpur 115 J11
Nagykanizsa 82 E3
Nagykőrös 82 E4
Naha 101 F13
Nahāvand 118 D7
Nain *Canada* 142 D7
Nā'īn *Iran* 116 C3
Nairn 78 C5
Nairobi 129 E7
Najafābād 116 C2
Najd 119 F5
Najibabad 114 E11
Najin 105 A9
Nakashibetsu 100 B9
Nakhodka 99 E11
Nakhon Phanom 110 A2
Nakhon Ratchasima 110 B2
Nakhon Sawan 110 A2
Nakhon Si Thammarat 110 C2
Nakina 143 D5
Nakuru 129 E7
Nal → 114 G4
Nalchik 85 E5
Nalgonda 115 L11
Nallamalai Hills 115 M11
Nam Co 102 E6
Nam-Phan 110 B3
Namak, Daryācheh-ye 116 C3
Namak, Kavir-e 116 C4
Namaland 130 D3
Namangan 97 E8

Namapa 131 A7
Namber 109 E4
Nambour 135 A5
Nambucca Heads 135 B5
Namib Desert 130 C2
Namibe 130 B2
Namibia ■ 130 C3
Naminüs = Lubango 130 A2
Namlea 109 E3
Namoi → 135 B4
Nampa 144 E5
Namp'o 105 C6
Nampō-Shotō 101 H7
Nampula 131 B7
Namrole 109 E3
Namse Shankou 112 C4
Namtu 113 F11
Namur 80 C3
Nanaimo 141 D7
Nanango 135 A5
Nanao 101 E5
Nanchang 106 C3
Nanchong 103 E9
Nancy 89 B7
Nanda Devi 114 D11
Nanded 115 K10
Nandewar Ra. 135 B5
Nandurbar 115 J9
Nandyal 115 M11
Nanga-Eboko 128 D2
Nanga Parbat 114 B9
Nangapinoh 111 E4
Nangarhār □ 114 B7
Nangatayap 111 E4
Nanjing 106 A5
Nanking = Nanjing 106 A5
Nanning 103 G9
Nanping 106 D5
Nansen Sd. 142 A4
Nantes 88 C3
Nantong 106 A6
Nantucket I. 149 D10
Nanuque 165 F5
Nanusa, Kepulauan 108 D3
Nanyang 103 E10
Nanyuki 129 D7
Nao, C. de la 87 C6
Napa 144 G2
Napier 136 C7
Naples = Nápoli 91 D5
Naples 155 F7
Napo → 162 D4
Nápoli 91 D5
Nara 127 E4
Naracoorte 134 C3
Naradhan 135 B4
Narasapur 112 J3

Narathiwat 110 C2
Narayanganj 113 F8
Narayanpet 115 L10
Narbonne 89 E5
Nardò 93 D2
Narew → 82 B5
Narin 114 A6
Narmada → 115 J8
Narodnaya 96 C6
Narooma 135 C5
Narrabri 135 B4
Narran → 135 A4
Narrandera 135 B4
Narromine 135 B4
Narsimhapur 115 H11
Narva 84 B2
Narvik 76 B9
Naryan-Mar 96 C6
Narym 97 D9
Naryn 97 E8
Naseby 137 F4
Naser, Buheirat en 124 D5
Nashville 154 A4
Nasik 115 K8
Nasirabad 114 F9
Nassau 158 A4
Nassau, B. 167 H3
Nasser, L. = Naser, Buheirat en 124 D5
Natal *Brazil* 164 D6
Natal *Indonesia* 111 D1
Naţanz 116 C2
Natashquan 143 D7
Natashquan → 143 D7
Natchez 153 D8
Nathalia 135 C4
Nathdwara 115 G8
Natitingou 127 F6
Natkyizin 113 K11
Natron, L. 129 E7
Natuna Besar, Kepulauan 111 D3
Natuna Selatan, Kepulauan 111 D3
Naturaliste, C. 134 D4
Naumburg 81 C6
Nauru ■ 136 K11
Nauta 162 D4
Nautanwa 112 D4
Navahrudak 83 B7
Navalmoral de la Mata 86 C3
Navarino, I. 167 H3
Navarra □ 87 A5
Nävodari 92 B7
Navoi 97 E7
Navojoa 156 B3
Navsari 115 J8
Nawabshah 114 F6
Nawakot 112 D5
Nawalgarh 114 F9

Nawāsīf, Ḥarrat 119 G5
Naxçivan 85 F6
Naxos 93 F5
Nāy Band 116 E3
Nayoro 100 A8
Nazas → 156 B4
Nazilli 93 F7
Ndalatando 128 F2
Ndélé 128 C4
Ndjamena 125 F1
Ndola 131 A5
Neagh, Lough 79 D3
Neales → 134 A2
Near Is. 141 C1
Neath 79 F5
Nebine Cr. → 135 A4
Nebraska □ 146 E5
Nébrodi, Monti 91 F5
Neckar → 80 D5
Necochea 166 D5
Neepawa 141 C10
Neftçala 118 C7
Negele 121 F2
Negombo 115 M11
Negotin 92 B4
Negro → Argentina
166 D3
Negro → Brazil 162 D6
Negro → Uruguay
166 C5
Negros 108 C2
Nei Mongol Zizhiqu □
103 C10
Neijiang 103 F8
Neiva 162 C3
Nellore 115 M11
Nelson Canada 141 D8
Nelson N.Z. 137 D5
Nelson → 141 C10
Nelson, C. 134 C3
Nelson, Estrecho 167 G2
Nelson Lakes △ 137 D5
Néma 127 E4
Nemunas → 84 B1
Nemuro 100 B9
Nemuro-Kaikyō 100 B9
Nenagh 79 E2
Nenjiang 103 B13
Nepal ■ 112 D5
Nepalganj 112 C3
Neretva → 90 C6
Ness, L. 78 C4
Nestos → 92 D5
Netherlands ■ 80 B3
Netherlands Antilles =
ABC Islands 159 D6
Nettilling L. 142 C6
Neubrandenburg 81 B7
Neumünster 80 A5
Neunkirchen 80 D4
Neuquén 166 D3
Neuruppin 81 B7

Neustrelitz 81 B7
Neva → 84 B3
Nevada □ 144 G5
Nevers 89 C5
Nevertire 135 B4
Nevinnomyssk 85 E5
Nevşehir 118 C3
New Amsterdam 162 B7
New Bedford 149 D10
New Bern 155 B9
New Brighton 137 E5
New Britain Papua N. G.
136 K10
New Britain U.S.A.
149 D9
New Brunswick □
143 E7
New Caledonia ⊠
136 M11
New Delhi 114 E10
New England Ra. 135 B5
New Forest △ 79 F6
New Glasgow 143 E7
New Hampshire □
149 C10
New Haven 149 D9
New Hebrides =
Vanuatu ■ 136 L11
New Ireland 136 K10
New Jersey □ 149 E9
New Liskeard 143 E6
New London 149 D9
New Mexico □ 151 C9
New Norfolk 134 D4
New Orleans 153 E8
New Plymouth 136 C6
New Providence 158 A4
New Siberian Is. =
Novosibirskiye Ostrova
99 B12
New South Wales □
135 B4
New York 149 D9
New York □ 149 C8
New Zealand ■ 136 D7
Newark 149 D8
Newburgh 149 D8
Newbury 79 F6
Newcastle 135 B5
Newcastle-upon-Tyne
79 D6
Newfoundland &
Labrador □ 143 D8
Newman 132 E2
Newport I. of W., U.K.
79 F6
Newport Newport, U.K.
79 F5
Newport U.S.A. 149 D10
Newport News 149 F7
Newquay 79 F4
Newry 79 D3

Neya 84 B5
Neyrīz 116 D3
Neyshābūr 116 B4
Ngabang 111 D3
Ngabordamlu, Tanjung
109 F4
Nganglong Kangri
112 A3
Ngaoundéré 128 C2
Ngapara 137 F4
Ngoring Hu 102 E7
Nguigmi 125 F1
Nha Trang 110 B3
Nhill 134 C3
Niagara Falls Canada
143 E6
Niagara Falls U.S.A.
149 C6
Niah 111 D4
Niamey 127 F6
Nias 111 D1
Nicaragua ■ 157 E7
Nicaragua, L. de 157 E7
Nicastro 91 E6
Nice 89 E7
Nichinan 101 H2
Nicobar Is. 95 H11
Nicosia 118 D3
Nicoya, Pen. de 157 F7
Niedersachsen □ 80 B5
Nienburg 80 B5
Nieuw Amsterdam
164 A2
Nieuw Nickerie 164 A2
Niğde 118 C3
Niger ■ 127 E7
Niger → 127 G7
Nigeria ■ 127 G7
Nightcaps 137 F3
Nii-Jima 101 F6
Niigata 101 E6
Ni'ihau 150 H10
Niitsu 101 E6
Nijmegen 80 C3
Nikiniki 109 F2
Nikolayevsk 84 C6
Nikopol 85 D3
Nīkshahr 117 E5
Nikšić 92 C2
Nīl, Nahr en → 124 B5
Nīl el Abyad → 125 E5
Nīl el Azraq → 125 E5
Nile = Nīl, Nahr en →
124 B5
Nimach 115 G9
Nîmes 89 E6
Nimmitabel 135 C4
Nīmrūz □ 117 D5
Nīnawá 118 C5
Nindigully 135 A4
Nineveh = Nīnawá
118 C5

Ningbo 106 C6
Ningxia Huizu Zizhiqu □
103 D9
Niobrara → 146 D5
Nioro du Sahel 127 E4
Niort 88 C3
Nipawin 141 C9
Nipigon, L. 143 E5
Nipissing, L. 143 E6
Niquelândia 165 E4
Nirmal 115 K11
Nirmali 112 D6
Niš 92 C3
Nişāb Si. Arabia 119 E6
Nişāb Yemen 121 E4
Niterói 165 G5
Niue ☑ 137 L14
Niut 111 D4
Nivernais 89 C5
Nizamabad 115 K11
Nizamghat 113 C10
Nizhnevartovsk 97 C8
Nizhniy Novgorod 84 B5
Nizhniy Tagil 97 D6
Nizhyn 84 C3
Nkhotakota 131 A6
Nkongsamba 128 D1
Nmai → 113 E11
Noakhali 113 F8
Nobeoka 101 G2
Nocera Inferiore 91 D5
Nogales Mexico 156 A2
Nogales U.S.A. 151 E7
Nōgata 101 G2
Noginsk 98 C7
Noires, Mts. 88 B2
Noirmoutier, Î. de 88 C2
Nojima-Zaki 101 F6
Nok Kundi 114 E3
Nola 128 D3
Nome 141 B3
Nong Khai 110 A2
Nord-Ostsee-Kanal
80 A5
Norderney 80 B4
Norderstedt 80 B5
Nordfriesische Inseln
80 A5
Nordhausen 80 C6
Nordkapp 76 A11
Nordrhein-Westfalen □
80 C4
Nordvik 98 B9
Norfolk 149 F7
Norfolk I. 136 M11
Norilsk 98 C6
Norman 152 B5
Norman Wells 140 B7
Normandie 88 B4
Normandy = Normandie
88 B4
Normanton 133 D7
Norquinco 167 E2

Norrköping 77 D9
Norrland 76 C9
Norseman 132 G3
North, C. 143 E7
North Battleford 141 C9
North Bay 143 E6
North Bend 144 E1
North C. 136 A5
North Cape = Nordkapp 76 A11
North Carolina □ 155 B7
North Channel 79 D4
North Dakota □ 146 B4
North East Frontier Agency = Arunachal Pradesh □ 113 C10
North I. 136 B5
North Korea ■ 105 B7
North Lakhimpur 113 D10
North Magnetic Pole 142 A2
North Minch 78 B4
North Ossetia-Alaniya □ 85 E5
North Platte 146 E4
North Platte → 146 E4
North Saskatchewan → 141 C8
North Sea 78 D8
North Taranaki Bight 136 C6
North Thompson → 141 C7
North Uist 78 B4
North West C. 132 E1
North West Frontier = Khyber Pakhtunkhwa □ 114 B8
North West Highlands 78 C4
North West River 143 D7
Northampton 79 E6
Northern Circars 112 J4
Northern Ireland □ 79 D3
Northern Marianas ☑ 136 H9
Northern Sporades = Voreíos Sporades 93 E4
Northern Territory □ 132 D5
Northland □ 136 A5
Northumberland, C. 134 C3
Northumberland Str. 143 E7
Northwest Territories □ 140 B9
Norton Sd. 141 B3
Norway ■ 76 C8
Norway House 141 C10
Norwegian B. 142 B5

Norwegian Sea 74 B5
Norwich 79 E7
Noshiro 100 C7
Noṣratābād 117 D4
Nossob → 130 D4
Notre Dame B. 143 E8
Nottaway → 143 D6
Nottingham 79 E6
Nottingham I. 142 C6
Nouâdhibou 126 D2
Nouâdhibou, Râs 126 D2
Nouakchott 127 E2
Nouméa 136 M11
Nova Friburgo 165 G5
Nova Iguaçu 165 G5
Nova Iorque 164 D5
Nova Scotia □ 143 E7
Nova Venécia 165 F5
Nova Zagora 92 C5
Novara 90 B2
Novaya Ladoga 84 A3
Novaya Lyalya 97 D7
Novaya Zemlya 96 B6
Novgorod = Velikiy Novgorod 84 B3
Novhorod-Siverskyy 84 C3
Novi Lígure 90 B2
Novi Pazar 92 C3
Novi Sad 92 B2
Novo Mesto 90 B5
Novoaltaysk 97 D9
Novocherkassk 85 D5
Novohrad-Volynskyy 83 C7
Novokachalinsk 100 A3
Novokuybyshevsk 84 C6
Novokuznetsk 97 D9
Novomoskovsk 84 C4
Novorossiysk 85 E4
Novorybnoye 98 B8
Novoselytsya 83 D8
Novoshakhtinsk 85 D4
Novosibirsk 97 D9
Novosibirskiye Ostrova 99 B12
Novotroitsk 97 D6
Novouzensk 84 C6
Novovolynsk 83 C7
Novska 90 B6
Novyy Port 96 C8
Nowa Sól 82 C2
Nowra 135 B5
Nowshera 114 B8
Nowy Targ 82 D5
Nowy Tomyśl 82 B3
Noyon 89 B5
Nsanje 131 B7
Nubian Desert = Nûbîya, Es Sahrâ en 124 D5

Nûbîya, Es Sahrâ en 124 D5
Nuboai 109 E5
Nueltin L. 140 B10
Nueva Rosita 156 B4
Nuéve de Julio 166 D4
Nuevitas 158 B4
Nuevo, G. 167 E4
Nuevo Laredo 156 B5
Nugget Pt. 137 G3
Nuhaka 136 C7
Nukey Bluff 134 B2
Nuku'alofa 137 M13
Nukus 97 E6
Nullarbor Plain 132 G4
Numalla, L. 135 A3
Numan 125 G1
Numazu 101 F6
Numfoor 109 E4
Numurkah 135 C4
Nunavut □ 142 C5
Nuneaton 79 E6
Nunivak I. 141 B3
Nunkun 114 C10
Núoro 91 D2
Nuremberg = Nürnberg 81 D6
Nuriootpa 134 B2
Nürnberg 81 D6
Nusa Tenggara Barat □ 111 F5
Nusa Tenggara Timur □ 109 F2
Nushki 114 E5
Nuuk 138 C14
Nuwakot 112 C4
Nuweveldberge 130 E4
Nuyts Arch. 134 B1
Nyahururu 129 D7
Nyaingêntanglha Shan 102 F5
Nyâlâ 125 F3
Nyasa, L. = Malawi, L. 131 A6
Nyasvizh 83 B8
Nyda 96 C8
Nyíregyháza 83 E5
Nymagee 135 B4
Nyngan 135 B4
Nysa 82 C3
Nysa → 82 B2
Nyurba 98 C9
Nzega 129 E6
Nzérékoré 127 G4
Nzeto 128 F2

O

Ō-Shima 101 F6
Oahe, L. 146 C4
O'ahu 150 H12
Oak Ridge 155 A5
Oakey 135 A5
Oakland 150 B1

Oamaru 137 F4
Oates Land 168 A15
Oaxaca 156 D5
Ob → 96 C7
Oba 143 E6
Oban 78 C4
Oberhausen 80 C4
Oberon 135 B4
Obi, Kepulauan 109 E3
Óbidos 164 C2
Obihiro 100 B8
Obilatu 109 E3
Obo 129 C5
Obozerskiy 96 C5
Obskaya Guba 96 C8
Obuasi 127 G5
Ocala 155 E6
Ocaña 86 C4
Occidental, Cordillera 162 C5
Oceanside 150 D4
Ocniţa 83 D8
Ōda 101 F3
Odate 100 C7
Odawara 101 F6
Ödemiş 93 E7
Odense 77 D8
Oder → 81 B8
Odesa 85 D3
Odessa = Odesa 85 D3
Odessa 152 D2
Odienné 127 G4
Odintsovo 84 B4
Odisha □ 112 G5
Odzi 131 B6
Oeiras 164 D5
Ofanto → 90 D6
Offa 127 G6
Offenbach 80 C5
Offenburg 80 D4
Oga 100 D6
Oga-Hantō 100 D6
Ōgaki 101 F5
Ogasawara Gunto 95 F16
Ogbomosho 127 G6
Ogden 145 F7
Ogdensburg 149 B8
Óglio → 90 B3
Ogooué → 128 E1
Ohai 137 F2
Ohakune 136 C6
Ohanet 126 C7
Ohata 100 C7
Ohau, L. 137 F3
Ohio □ 148 D4
Ohio → 148 F1
Ohře → 82 C2
Ohrid 92 D3
Ohridsko Jezero 93 D3
Oise → 88 B5
Ōita 101 G2
Oiticica 164 D5

Ojos del Salado, Cerro
  166 B3
Oka → 96 D5
Okaba 109 F5
Okahandja 130 C3
Okanogan → 144 B4
Okara 114 D8
Okavango Delta 130 B4
Okayama 101 F3
Okazaki 101 F5
Okeechobee, L. 155 F7
Okefenokee Swamp
  155 D6
Okhotsk, Sea of 99 D12
Oki-Shotō 101 E3
Okinawa-Jima 103 F13
Oklahoma □ 152 B5
Oklahoma City 152 B5
Okmulgee 153 B6
Oksibil 109 E6
Oktyabrskoy Revolyutsii,
  Ostrov 98 B7
Okuru 137 E3
Okushiri-Tō 100 B6
Öland 77 D9
Olary 134 B3
Olavarría 166 D4
Oława 82 C3
Ólbia 90 D2
Old Crow 140 B6
Oldenburg 80 B5
Oldham 79 E5
Olekma → 99 C10
Olekminsk 99 C10
Oleksandriya 83 C8
Olenek 98 C9
Olenek → 98 B10
Oléron, Î. d' 88 D3
Oleśnica 82 C3
Olevsk 83 C8
Olhão 86 D2
Olinda 164 D7
Olivenza 86 C2
Ollagüe 163 H5
Olomouc 82 D3
Olongapo 108 B2
Olot 87 A7
Olsztyn 82 B5
Olt → 92 C5
Oltenița 92 B6
Olympos Oros 93 D4
Olympia Greece 93 F3
Olympia U.S.A. 144 C2
Olympic Mts. 144 C2
Olympus, Mt. = Olympos
  Oros 93 D4
Om → 97 D8
Omagh 79 D3
Omaha 147 E7
Oman ■ 120 C6
Oman, G. of 117 E4
Omaruru 130 C3

Omate 163 G4
Ombai, Selat 109 F2
Omboué 128 E1
Ombrone → 90 C3
Omdurmân 125 E5
Ometepec 156 D5
Omo → 125 G6
Omsk 97 D8
Ōmu 100 A8
Omul, Vf. 83 F7
Omuramba Omatako →
  130 B4
Ōmuta 101 G2
Onda 87 C5
Ondangwa 130 B3
Öndörhaan 103 B10
Onega 96 C4
Onega, L. = Onezhskoye
  Ozero 76 C13
Oneşti 83 E8
Onezhskoye Ozero
  76 C13
Ongarue 136 C6
Onilahy → 131 C8
Onitsha 127 G7
Ontario □ 143 E5
Ontario, L. 149 C7
Oodnadatta 134 A2
Oostende 80 C2
Opala 128 E4
Opava 82 D3
Opole 82 C3
Oporto = Porto 86 B1
Opotiki 136 C7
Opua 136 A6
Opunake 136 C5
Oradea 83 E5
Örafajökull 76 C2
Orai 114 G11
Oral 84 C7
Oran 126 A5
Orange Australia 135 B4
Orange France 89 D6
Orange U.S.A. 153 D7
Orange → 130 D3
Orange, C. 164 B3
Orangeburg 155 C7
Oranienburg 81 B7
Orapa 131 C5
Oras 108 B3
Orbetello 90 C3
Orbost 135 C4
Orchila, I. 162 A5
Ordos = Mu Us Shamo
  103 D9
Ordu 118 B4
Örebro 77 D9
Oregon □ 144 E3
Orekhovo-Zuyevo 84 B4
Orel 84 C4
Ören 93 F6
Orenburg 97 D6

Orepuki 137 G2
Orfanos Kolpos 93 D5
Orgaz 86 C4
Orhaneli 93 E7
Orhangazi 93 D7
Orhei 83 E9
Orhon Gol → 103 A9
Oriental, Cordillera
  162 B4
Orihuela 87 C5
Orinoco → 162 B6
Orissa = Odisha □
  112 G5
Oristano 91 E2
Oristano, G. di 91 E2
Orizaba 156 D5
Orizaba, Pico de 156 D5
Orkney Is. 78 B5
Orlando 155 E7
Orléanais 88 C5
Orléans 88 C4
Ormara 114 G4
Ormoc 108 B2
Ormond 136 C7
Örnsköldsvik 76 C9
Orocué 162 C4
Oroqen Zizhiqi 153 A13
Oroquieta 108 C2
Orosháza 82 E5
Ororoo 134 B2
Orsha 84 C3
Orsk 97 D6
Orşova 92 B4
Ortaca 93 F7
Ortegal, C. 86 A2
Orthez 88 E3
Ortigueira 86 A2
Ortles 90 A3
Ortón → 163 F5
Orūmīyeh 118 C6
Orūmīyeh, Daryācheh-ye
  118 C6
Oruro 163 G5
Oruzgān □ 114 C5
Orvieto 90 C4
Oryakhovo 92 C4
Ōsaka 101 F4
Ōsaki 100 D7
Osh 97 E8
Oshakati 130 B3
Oshawa 143 E6
Oshkosh 146 E3
Oshogbo 127 G6
Oshwe 128 E3
Osijek 90 B7
Osizweni 131 D6
Oskarshamn 77 D9
Öskemen 97 E9
Oslo 77 D8
Oslofjorden 77 D8
Osmanabad 115 K10
Osmaniye 118 C4

Osnabrück 80 B5
Osorno 167 E2
Ossa, Mt. 134 D4
Ossa, Oros 93 E4
Ostend = Oostende
  80 C2
Oster 83 C10
Österdalälven → 76 C8
Östersund 76 C8
Ostfriesische Inseln
  80 B4
Ostrava 82 D4
Ostróda 82 B4
Ostroh 83 C8
Ostrołęka 82 B5
Ostrów Mazowiecka
  82 B5
Ostrów Wielkopolski
  82 C3
Ostrowiec-Świętokrzyski
  82 C5
Ostuni 91 D6
Osuna 86 D3
Oswego 149 C7
Otago □ 137 F3
Otago Harbour 137 F4
Otaki 136 D6
Otaru 100 B7
Otavalo 162 C3
Otjiwarongo 130 C3
Otoineppu 100 A8
Otorohanga 136 C6
Otranto 93 D2
Otranto, C. d' 93 D2
Otranto, Str. of 93 D2
Ōtsu 101 F4
Ottawa 143 E6
Ottawa Is. 142 D5
Ottumwa 147 E8
Oturkpo 127 G7
Otway, B. 167 G2
Otway, C. 134 C3
Otwock 82 B5
Ouachita Mts. 153 B6
Ouagadougou 127 F5
Ouallene 126 D6
Ouarga 126 B7
Ouarzazate 126 B4
Oubangi → 128 E3
Oudtshoorn 130 E4
Ouessant, Î. d' 88 B1
Ouesso 128 D3
Ouezzane 126 B4
Oujda 126 B5
Oulu 76 B11
Oulujärvi 76 C11
Oulujoki → 76 B11
Oum Chalouba 125 E3
Oum Hadjer 125 F2
Ounianga Sérir 125 E3
Ourense 86 A2
Ouricuri 164 D5

Ouro Prêto 165 G5
Outaouais → 143 E6
Outer Hebrides 78 C3
Outjo 130 C3
Ouyen 134 C3
Ovalle 166 C2
Ovamboland 130 B3
Oviedo 86 A3
Ovruch 83 C9
Owaka 137 G3
Owase 101 F5
Owbeh 114 B3
Owen Sound 143 E5
Owen Stanley Ra. 133 B8
Owo 127 G7
Owyhee → 144 E5
Oxford N.Z. 137 E5
Oxford U.K. 79 F6
Oxnard 150 C3
Oxus = Amudarya →
  97 E6
Oya 111 D4
Oyama 101 E6
Oyem 128 D2
Oyo 127 G6
Ozamiz 108 C2
Ozark Plateau 153 A8
Ózd 82 D5

P

Pa-an 113 J11
Paarl 130 E3
Pab Hills 114 F5
Pabianice 82 C4
Pabna 113 E7
Pacaja → 164 C3
Pacaraima, Sa. 162 C6
Pacasmayo 163 E3
Pachpadra 114 G8
Pachuca 156 C5
Padaido, Kepulauan
  109 E5
Padang 111 E2
Padangpanjang 111 E2
Padangsidempuan
  111 D1
Paderborn 80 C5
Pádova 90 B3
Padua = Pádova 90 B3
Paducah 148 F1
Paeroa 136 B6
Pag 90 B5
Pagadian 108 C2
Pagai Selatan, Pulau
  111 E2
Pagai Utara, Pulau
  111 E2
Pagalu = Annobón
  123 G4
Pagastikos Kolpos 93 E4
Pagatan 111 E5
Pahiatua 136 D6

Päijänne 76 C11
Painan 111 E2
Painted Desert 151 C7
País Vasco □ 87 A4
Paisley 78 D4
Paita 162 E2
Pajares, Puerto de 86 A3
Pakistan ■ 114 E7
Pakokku 113 G10
Paktiā □ 114 C6
Pakxe 110 A3
Pala 125 G2
Palagruža 90 C6
Palakkad 115 P10
Palam 115 K10
Palampur 114 C10
Palana 134 C4
Palanan 108 A2
Palanan Pt. 108 A2
Palangkaraya 111 E4
Palani Hills 115 P10
Palanpur 115 G8
Palapye 131 C5
Palau ■ 108 C4
Palawan 110 C5
Palayankottai 115 Q10
Paleleh 109 D2
Palembang 111 E2
Palencia 86 A3
Palermo 91 E4
Palestine 153 D6
Paletwa 113 G9
Pali 114 G8
Palikir 136 J10
Paliouri, Akra 93 E4
Palitana 115 J7
Palk Bay 115 Q11
Palk Strait 115 Q11
Palm Springs 150 D4
Palma, B. de 87 C7
Palma de Mallorca 87 C7
Palmares 164 D6
Palmas, C. 127 H4
Pálmas, G. di 91 E2
Palmeira dos Índios
  165 D6
Palmer 141 B5
Palmer Arch. 168 A3
Palmer Land 168 B3
Palmerston 137 F4
Palmerston North 136 D6
Palmi 91 E5
Palmira 162 C3
Palopo 109 E2
Palos, C. de 87 D5
Palu Indonesia 109 E1
Palu Turkey 118 C5
Pamiers 88 E4
Pamir 97 F8
Pamlico Sd. 155 B10
Pampa 152 B3
Pampanua 109 E2

Pampas Argentina
  166 D4
Pampas Peru 163 F4
Pamplona 162 B4
Pamplona-Iruña 87 A5
Panaji 115 M8
Panamá 157 F9
Panama ■ 158 E4
Panamá, G. de 158 E4
Panama Canal 158 E4
Panama City 154 D5
Panão 163 E3
Panay 108 B2
Panay, G. 108 B2
Pančevo 92 B3
Pandan 108 B2
Pandharpur 115 L9
Panevėžys 84 B1
Pangani 129 F7
Pangkajene 109 E1
Pangkalanbrandan
  111 D1
Pangkalanbuun 111 E4
Pangkalpinang 111 E3
Pangnirtung 142 C7
Pangutaran Group
  108 C2
Panjgur 114 F4
Panjin 104 B5
Panjnad Barrage 114 E7
Panorama 166 A6
Pantar 109 F2
Pante Macassar 109 F2
Pantelleria 91 F3
Paoua 128 C3
Pápa 82 E3
Papakura 136 B6
Papantla 156 C5
Papar 110 C5
Paparoa △ 137 E4
Papeete 137 L16
Papua □ 109 E5
Papua New Guinea ■
  136 K9
Papudo 166 C2
Papun 113 H11
Pará □ 164 C3
Paracatu 165 F4
Paracel Is. 110 A4
Parachilna 134 B2
Paradip 112 G6
Parado 109 F1
Paragua → 162 B6
Paraguaçu → 165 E6
Paraguaná, Pen. de
  162 A4
Paraguarí 166 B5
Paraguay ■ 166 A5
Paraguay → 166 B5
Paraíba □ 164 D6
Parakou 127 G6
Paramaribo 164 A2

Paraná Argentina 166 C4
Paraná Brazil 165 E4
Paraná □ 166 A6
Paraná → 166 C5
Paranaguá 166 B7
Paranaíba 165 F3
Paranaíba → 165 G3
Paranapanema →
  166 A6
Parang Maguindanao,
  Phil. 108 C2
Parang Sulu, Phil. 108 C2
Parângul Mare, Vf. 83 F6
Paraparaumu 136 D6
Parbhani 115 K10
Parchim 81 B6
Pardo → Bahia, Brazil
  165 F6
Pardo → Mato Grosso,
  Brazil 165 G3
Pardubice 82 C2
Parecis, Serra dos
  163 F7
Parepare 109 E1
Parga 93 E3
Pariaguán 162 B6
Parigi 109 E2
Parika 162 B7
Parima, Serra 162 C6
Parinari 162 D4
Parintins 164 C3
Pariparit Kyun 113 K9
Paris France 88 B5
Paris U.S.A. 153 C6
Park Range 145 G10
Parkersburg 148 E5
Parkes 135 B4
Parla 86 B4
Parma 90 B3
Parnaguá 165 E5
Parnaíba 164 C5
Parnaíba → 164 C5
Parnassos 93 E4
Pärnu 84 B1
Paroo → 135 B3
Paros 93 F5
Parral 166 D2
Parry Is. 142 B3
Parry Sound 143 E6
Partinico 91 E4
Paru → 164 C3
Parvān □ 114 B6
Parvatipuram 112 H4
Pas, The 141 C9
Pasadena Calif., U.S.A.
  150 C3
Pasadena Tex., U.S.A.
  153 E6
Pascagoula 153 D9
Pascani 83 E8
Paschimbanga □ 112 F7
Pasco 144 C4

Pašman 90 C5
Pasni 114 G3
Paso de Indios 167 E3
Passau 81 D7
Passero, C. 91 F5
Passo Fundo 166 B6
Passos 165 G4
Pastaza → 162 D3
Pasto 162 C3
Patagonia 167 F3
Patan 115 H8
Patani 109 D3
Patchewollock 134 C3
Patea 136 C6
Paternò 91 F5
Paterson 149 D8
Pathankot 114 C9
Patiala 114 D10
Patkai Bum 113 D10
Patmos 93 F6
Patna 112 E5
Patos, L. dos 166 C6
Patos de Minas 165 F4
Patquía 166 C3
Patra 93 E3
Patraikos Kolpos 93 E3
Patrocínio 165 F4
Pattani 110 C2
Patuakhali 113 F8
Pau 88 E3
Pauk 113 G10
Paulistana 164 D5
Paulo Afonso 165 D6
Pavia 90 B2
Pavlodar 97 D8
Pavlohrad 85 D4
Pavlovo 84 B5
Pavlovsk 84 C5
Pawtucket 149 D10
Paxi 90 B3
Payakumbuh 111 E2
Payne L. 142 D6
Paysandú 166 C5
Paz, B. de la 156 C2
Pazar 118 B5
Pazardzhik 92 C5
Pécs 82 E4
Pedder, L. 134 D4
Pedirka 134 A2

Pedra Azul 165 F5
Pedreiras 164 C5
Pedro Afonso 165 D4
Pedro Juan Caballero
  166 A5
Peebinga 134 B3
Peel → Australia 135 B5
Peel → Canada 140 B6
Peera Peera Poolanna L.
  134 A2
Pegasus Bay 137 E5
Pegu 113 J11
Pegu Yoma 113 H10
Pehuajó 166 D4
Peine 80 B6
Peixe 165 E4
Pejë 92 C3
Pekalongan 111 F3
Pekanbaru 111 D2
Pekin = Beijing 104 C2
Pelagie, Is. 91 G4
Pelaihari 111 E4
Peleaga, Vf. 83 F6
Peleng 109 E2
Peljesac 90 C6
Pelly → 140 B6
Pelly Bay 142 C5
Pelopónnesos □ 93 F4
Pelorus Sd. 137 D5
Pelotas 166 C6
Pelvoux, Massif du 89 D7
Pemangsiantar 111 D1
Pemba 131 A8
Pemba I. 129 F7
Pembroke Canada
  143 E6
Pembroke U.K. 79 F4
Penápolis 166 A6
Peñarroya-Pueblonuevo
  86 C3
Peñas, C. de 86 A3
Peñas, G. de 167 F2
Pend Oreille, L. 144 C5
Pendembu 127 G3
Pendleton 144 D4
Penedo 165 E6
Penguin 134 D4
Peniche 86 C1
Penida, Nusa 111 F5
Peninsular Malaysia □
  111 D2
Penmarch, Pte. de 88 C1
Pennines 79 D5
Pennsylvania □ 149 D7
Penny Str. 142 B4
Penola 134 C3
Penong 132 G5
Penrhyn 137 K15
Penrith 135 B5
Pensacola 154 D4
Pensacola Mts. 168 C4

Penshurst 134 C3
Penticton 141 D8
Pentland Firth 78 B5
Penza 84 C6
Penzance 79 F4
Peoria 147 E10
Perabumulih 111 E2
Perche, Collines du
  88 B4
Perdido, Mte. 87 A6
Pereira 162 C3
Pereyaslav-Khmelnytskyy
  84 C3
Pergamino 166 C4
Péribonka → 143 E6
Perico 166 A3
Périgueux 88 D4
Perijá, Sierra de 162 B4
Perlas, Arch. de las
  158 E4
Pernambuco □ 165 D6
Pernatty Lagoon 134 B2
Pernik 92 C4
Perpignan 89 E5
Persepolis 116 D3
Pershotravensk 83 C8
Persia = Iran ■ 116 C3
Persian Gulf 116 E2
Perth Australia 132 G2
Perth U.K. 78 C5
Perth Amboy 149 D8
Peru ■ 162 C3
Perúgia 90 C4
Pervomaysk 85 D3
Pervouralsk 97 D6
Pésaro 90 C4
Pescara 90 C5
Peshawar 114 B7
Peshkopi 92 D3
Pesqueira 164 D6
Petah Tiqwa 118 D3
Petauke 131 A6
Peter I. Øy 168 A2
Peter's River Australia
  134 B2
Peterborough Canada
  143 E6
Peterborough U.K. 79 E6
Petersburg Alaska, U.S.A.
  141 C6
Petersburg Va., U.S.A.
  149 F7
Petitsikapau L. 143 D7
Petlad 115 H8
Peto 157 C7
Petone 137 D6
Petra Velikogo, Zaliv
  100 B3
Petrich 92 D4
Petrolândia 165 D6
Petrolina 165 D5

Petropavl 97 D7
Petropavlovsk-
  Kamchatskiy 99 D13
Petrópolis 165 G5
Petroşani 83 F6
Petrovaradin 92 B2
Petrovsk 84 C6
Petrozavodsk 76 C12
Peureulak 110 D1
Pforzheim 80 D5
Phagwara 114 D9
Phalodi 114 F8
Phan Rang-Thap Cham
  110 B3
Phangan, Ko 110 C2
Phangnga 110 C1
Phatthalung 110 C2
Phetchabun 110 A2
Philadelphia 149 E8
Philippine Trench =
  Mindanao Trench
  108 C3
Philippines ■ 108 B2
Phillip I. 135 C4
Phitsanulok 110 A2
Phnom Penh 110 B2
Phoenix 151 D6
Phra Nakhon Si
  Ayutthaya 110 B2
Phuket 110 C1
Piacenza 90 B2
Pian Cr. → 135 B4
Pianosa 90 C3
Piatra Neamţ 83 E8
Piauí □ 164 D5
Piave → 90 B4
Pibor Post 125 G3
Picardie □ 89 B5
Pichilemu 166 C2
Pico Truncado 167 F3
Picton Australia 135 B5
Picton N.Z. 137 D6
Picún Leufú 167 D3
Piedmont = Piemonte □
  90 B1
Piedras, R. de las →
  163 F5
Piedras Negras 156 B4
Pielinen 76 C11
Piemonte □ 90 B1
Piet Retief 131 D6
Pietermaritzburg 131 D6
Pietrosul, Vf. Maramureş,
  Romania 83 E7
Pietrosul, Vf. Suceava,
  Romania 83 E7
Pigüe 166 D4
Piła 82 B3
Pilar 166 B5
Pilcomayo → 166 B5
Pilibhit 114 E11
Pilica → 82 C5

Pilos 93 F3
Pimba 134 B2
Pimenta Bueno 163 F6
Pimentel 163 E3
Pinang 110 C2
Pinar del Río 158 B3
Pınarhisar 92 D6
Pińczów 82 C5
Pindos Oros 93 E3
Pindus Mts. = Pindos
  Oros 93 E3
Pine Bluff 153 B7
Pinega → 96 C5
Pinerolo 90 B1
Pines, Akra 93 D5
Ping → 110 A2
Pingdong 103 G12
Pingliang 103 D9
P'ingtung 107 F6
Pingxiang
  *Guangxi Zhuangzu,
  China* 103 G9
Pingxiang *Jiangxi, China*
  106 D6
Pinhel 86 B2
Pini 111 D1
Pinios → 93 E4
Pinnaroo 134 C3
Pinrang 109 E1
Pinsk 83 B8
Pintados 163 H5
Pinyug 84 A6
Piombino 90 C3
Pioner, Ostrov 98 B7
Piorini, L. 162 D6
Piotrków Trybunalski
  82 C4
Pīp 117 E5
Piquiri → 166 A6
Piracicaba 166 A7
Piracuruca 164 C5
Piræus = Pireas 93 F4
Pirané 166 B5
Pirapora 165 F5
Pireas 93 F4
Pirgos 93 F3
Pirin Planina 92 D4
Piripiri 164 C5
Pirmasens 80 D4
Pirot 92 C4
Piru 109 E3
Pisa 90 C3
Pisagua 163 G4
Pisco 163 F3
Pishan 102 D3
Pising 109 F2
Pistóia 90 C3
Pisuerga → 86 B3
Pitarpunga L. 134 B3
Pitcairn I. 137 M17
Piteå 76 B10

Piteşti 92 B5
Pithapuram 112 J4
Pittsburg 153 A6
Pittsburgh 149 D5
Pittsworth 135 A5
Piura 162 E2
Placentia 143 E8
Placentia B. 143 E8
Plainview 152 B3
Plaka, Akra 93 G6
Plasencia 86 B2
Plastun 100 A5
Plata, Río de la →
  166 C5
Plátani → 91 F4
Platte → 147 F7
Plauen 81 C7
Plei Ku 110 B3
Plenty, B. of 136 B7
Pleven 92 C5
Pljevlja 92 C2
Płock 82 B4
Plöckenstein 81 D7
Ploieşti 92 B6
Plovdiv 92 C5
Plumtree 131 C5
Plymouth 79 F4
Plzeň 82 D1
Po → 90 B4
Pobedy, Pik 97 E8
Pocatello 145 E7
Poços de Caldas 165 G4
Podgorica 92 C2
Podilska Vysochyna
  83 D8
Podolsk 84 B4
Poh 109 E2
Pohang 105 D8
Pohnpei 136 J10
Poinsett, C. 168 A12
Pointe-à-Pitre 159 C7
Pointe-Noire 128 E2
Poitiers 88 C4
Poitou 88 C3
Pokaran 114 F7
Pokataroo 135 A4
Polan ■ 117 E5
Poland ■ 82 B5
Polatsk 84 B2
Police 82 B2
Poligiros 93 D4
Polillo Is. 108 B2
Pollachi 115 P10
Polnovat 96 C7
Polokwane 131 C5
Polonne 83 C8
Poltava 84 D3
Polunochnoye 96 C7
Polynesia 137 L15
Pombal 86 C1
Pomézia 90 D4
Pomorskie, Pojezierze
  82 B3

Ponca City 152 A5
Ponce 159 C6
Pond Inlet 142 B6
Pondicherry =
  Puducherry 115 P11
Ponferrada 86 A2
Ponnani 115 P9
Ponta Grossa 166 B6
Ponta Porã 166 A5
Pontarlier 89 C7
Pontchartrain, L. 153 D8
Ponte Nova 165 G5
Pontevedra 86 A1
Pontiac 148 C4
Pontianak 111 E3
Pontine Mts. = Kuzey
  Anadolu Dağları
  118 B3
Pontivy 88 B2
Pontoise 88 B5
Ponziane, Ísole 91 D4
Poochera 134 B1
Poole 79 F6
Poona = Pune 115 K8
Pooncarie 134 B3
Poopelloe L. 135 B3
Poopó, L. de 163 G5
Popayán 162 C3
Popilta L. 134 B3
Popio L. 134 B3
Poplar Bluff 153 A8
Popocatépetl, Volcán
  156 D5
Popokabaka 128 F3
Porbandar 115 J6
Porcupine → 141 B5
Pordenone 90 B4
Pori 76 C10
Porlamar 162 A6
Poroshiri-Dake 100 B8
Porpoise B. 168 A13
Port Alberni 141 D7
Port Angeles 144 B2
Port Arthur *Australia*
  134 D4
Port Arthur *U.S.A.* 153 E7
Port-au-Prince 159 C5
Port Augusta 134 B2
Port Broughton 134 B2
Port-Cartier 143 D7
Port Chalmers 137 F4
Port Darwin 167 G5
Port Davey 134 D4
Port Dickson 111 D2
Port Elizabeth 131 E5
Port Fairy 134 C3
Port-Gentil 128 E1
Port Harcourt 127 H7
Port Hawkesbury 143 E7
Port Hedland 132 E2
Port Hope Simpson
  143 D8
Port Huron 148 C4

Port Kenny 134 B1
Port Lincoln 134 B2
Port Loko 127 G3
Port Louis 123 J9
Port MacDonnell 134 C3
Port Macquarie 135 B5
Port Moresby 133 E7
Port Nolloth 130 D3
Port of Spain 159 D7
Port Pegasus 137 G2
Port Phillip B. 135 C3
Port Pirie 134 B2
Port Said = Bûr Sa'îd
  124 B5
Port Shepstone 131 E6
Port Sudan = Bûr Sûdân
  125 E6
Port Talbot 79 F5
Port-Vendres 89 E5
Port Vila 136 L11
Port Wakefield 134 B2
Porta Orientalis 92 B4
Portadown 79 D3
Portage la Prairie
  141 D10
Portalegre 86 C2
Portbou 87 A7
Portile de Fier 92 B4
Portimão 86 D1
Portland *N.S.W., Australia*
  135 B4
Portland *Vic., Australia*
  134 C3
Portland *Maine, U.S.A.*
  149 C10
Portland *Oreg., U.S.A.*
  144 D2
Portland B. 134 C3
Portlaoise 79 E3
Porto 86 B1
Pôrto Alegre 166 C6
Porto de Moz 164 C3
Porto Empédocle 91 F4
Porto Esperança 163 G7
Porto Franco 164 C4
Porto Mendes 166 A6
Porto Murtinho 163 H7
Porto Nacional 165 E4
Porto-Novo 127 G6
Porto Santo, I. de 126 B2
Porto Seguro 165 F6
Porto Tórres 90 D2
Porto União 166 B6
Porto-Vecchio 89 F8
Porto Velho 163 E6
Porto Walter 163 E4
Portoferráio 90 C3
Portoscuso 91 E2
Portoviejo 162 D2
Portree 78 C3
Portsmouth *U.K.* 79 F6
Portsmouth *U.S.A.*
  149 F7

Porttipahdan tekojärvi
76 B11
Portugal ■ 86 C1
Porvenir 167 G2
Posadas 166 B5
Poso 109 E2
Posse 165 E4
Possession I. 168 B15
Postmasburg 130 D4
Postojna 90 B5
Potchefstroom 131 D5
Potenza 91 D5
Poteriteri, L. 137 G2
Poti 85 E5
Potomac → 149 E7
Potosí 163 G5
Pototan 108 B2
Potrerillos 166 B3
Potsdam 81 B7
Poughkeepsie 149 D9
Považská Bystrica 82 D4
Poverty B. 136 C8
Póvoa de Varzim 86 B1
Powder → 146 B2
Powell, L. 151 B7
Poyang Hu 106 C4
Požarevac 92 B3
Poznań 82 B3
Pozo Almonte 163 H5
Pozoblanco 86 C3
Pozzuoli 91 D5
Prachuap Khirikhan
110 B1
Prado 165 F6
Prague = Praha 82 C2
Praha 82 C2
Prainha 164 C3
Prainha Nova 163 E6
Prapat 111 D1
Prata 165 F4
Prato 90 C3
Pravia 86 A2
Praya 111 F5
Preobrazheniye 100 B3
Preparis North Channel
113 K9
Preparis South Channel
113 K9
Přerov 82 D3
Preservation Inlet 137 G2
Presidencia Roque Saenz
Peña 166 B4
Presidente Epitácio
165 G3
Presidente Prudente
165 G3
Prespansko Jezero
93 D3
Presque Isle 149 A11
Preston 79 E5
Pretoria 131 D5
Preveza 93 E3
Příbram 82 D2

Prichard 154 D3
Prieska 130 D4
Prilep 92 D3
Prime Seal I. 134 D4
Prince Albert 141 C9
Prince Albert Mts.
168 B15
Prince Albert Pen.
140 A8
Prince Albert Sd. 140 A8
Prince Alfred, C. 142 B1
Prince Charles I. 142 C6
Prince Charles Mts.
168 B10
Prince Edward I. □
143 E7
Prince of Wales I.
140 A10
Prince Patrick I. 142 B2
Principe da Beira 163 F6
Prins Harald Kyst 168 B8
Prinsesse Astrid Kyst
168 B7
Prinsesse Ragnhild Kyst
168 B8
Pripet Marshes 83 B9
Prishtinë 92 C3
Priština = Prishtinë 92 C3
Privas 89 D6
Privolzhskaya
Vozvyshennost 84 C6
Prizren 92 C3
Proddatur 115 M11
Progreso 157 C7
Prokopyevsk 97 D9
Prokuplje 92 C3
Prome 113 H10
Propriá 165 E6
Prosna → 82 B3
Prostějov 82 D3
Proston 135 A5
Provence 89 E6
Providence 149 D10
Providencia, I. de 158 D3
Provins 89 B5
Provo 145 F8
Pruszków 82 B5
Prut → 83 F9
Pruzhany 83 B7
Prydz B. 168 A10
Pryluky 84 C3
Prypyat → 83 C10
Psara 93 E5
Psiloritis, Oros 93 G5
Pskov 84 B2
Ptsich → 83 B9
Puán 166 D4
Pucallpa 163 E4
Puducherry 115 P11
Pudukkottai 115 P11
Puebla 156 D5
Pueblo 146 F2
Puelches 166 D3

Puente Alto 166 C2
Puente-Genil 86 D3
Puerto Aisén 167 F2
Puerto Ayacucho 162 B5
Puerto Barrios 157 D7
Puerto Bermúdez 163 F4
Puerto Bolívar 162 D3
Puerto Cabello 162 A5
Puerto Cabezas 158 D3
Puerto Carreño 162 B5
Puerto Chicama 163 E3
Puerto Coig 167 G3
Puerto Cortés 157 D7
Puerto Cumarebo 162 A5
Puerto Deseado 167 F3
Puerto Heath 163 F5
Puerto La Cruz 162 A6
Puerto Leguízamo
162 D4
Puerto Lobos 167 E3
Puerto Madryn 167 E3
Puerto Maldonado
163 F5
Puerto Montt 167 E2
Puerto Natales 167 G2
Puerto Páez 162 B5
Puerto Pinasco 166 A5
Puerto Plata 159 C5
Puerto Princesa 108 C1
Puerto Rico ☑ 159 C6
Puerto Santa Cruz
167 G3
Puerto Sastre 163 H7
Puerto Suárez 163 G7
Puerto Wilches 162 B4
Puertollano 86 C3
Pueyrredón, L. 167 F2
Pugachev 84 C6
Puget Sound 144 C2
Puigcerdà 87 A6
Pukaki, L. 137 F4
Pukapuka 137 L14
Pukekohe 136 B6
Pula 90 B4
Pulandian 104 C4
Puławy 82 C5
Pullman 144 C5
Pulog, Mt. 108 A2
Pultusk 82 B5
Puná, I. 162 D2
Punakaiki 137 E4
Punakha Dzong 113 D7
Punata 163 G5
Punch 114 C9
Pune 115 K8
Puning 107 F4
Punjab □ India 114 D9
Punjab □ Pakistan
114 D8
Puno 163 G4
Punta Alta 166 D4
Punta Arenas 167 G2
Punta del Díaz 166 B2

Puntarenas 158 E3
Punto Fijo 162 A4
Puquio 163 F4
Pur → 96 C8
Puracé, Vol. 162 C3
Puri 112 H5
Purnia 112 E6
Purukcahu 111 E4
Puruliya 112 F6
Purus → 162 D6
Pusan = Busan 105 E8
Pushkino 84 C6
Putao 113 D11
Putaruru 136 C6
Putian 107 F5
Putignano 91 D6
Puting, Tanjung 111 E4
Putorana, Gory 98 C7
Puttalam 115 Q11
Puttgarden 81 A6
Putumayo → 162 D5
Putussibau 111 D4
Puvirnituq 142 C6
Puy-de-Dôme 89 D5
Pwllheli 79 E4
Pyapon 113 J10
Pyasina → 98 B6
Pyatigorsk 85 E5
Pyetrikaw 83 B9
Pyinmana 113 H11
P'yŏngyang 105 C6
Pyrénées 87 A6
Pyu 113 H11

Q

Qā'emshahr 116 B3
Qaidam Pendi 102 D6
Qal'at al Akhḍar 119 E4
Qalāt-i-Ghilzai 117 C6
Qamruddin Karez 114 D6
Qandahār = Kandahār
114 D4
Qandyaghash 97 E6
Qapshaghay 97 E8
Qarabutaq 97 E7
Qaraghandy 97 E8
Qaraghayly 97 E8
Qarataü
Ongtüstik Qazaqstan,
Kazakhstan 97 E7
Qarataü Zhambyl,
Kazakhstan 97 E8
Qarazhal 97 E8
Qardho 121 F4
Qarqan He → 102 D6
Qarqaraly 97 E8
Qarshi 97 F7
Qaşr-e Qand 117 C5
Qasr Farâfra 124 C4
Qatar ■ 116 E2
Qattâra, Munkhafed el
124 C4
Qāyen 116 C4

Qazvīn 118 C7
Qena 124 C5
Qeshm 116 E4
Qikiqtarjuaq 142 C7
Qila Saifullāh 114 D6
Qilian Shan 102 D7
Qingdao 104 D4
Qinghai □ 102 D7
Qinghai Hu 102 D8
Qinhuangdao 104 C3
Qinzhou 103 G9
Qiongzhou Haixia 107 a
Qiqihar 103 B12
Qitai 102 C5
Qom 116 C2
Qomolangma Feng =
  Everest, Mt. 112 C6
Qomsheh 116 C2
Qoraqalpoghistan □
  97 E6
Qostanay 97 D7
Quambatook 134 C3
Quambone 135 B4
Quang Ngai 110 A3
Quanzhou 107 E5
Quaqtaq 142 C7
Quartu Sant'Élena 91 E2
Quba 85 E6
Qūchān 116 B4
Queanbeyan 135 C4
Québec 143 E6
Québec □ 143 E6
Queen Alexandra Ra.
  168 C15
Queen Charlotte Is. =
  Haida Gwaii 140 C6
Queen Charlotte Sd.
  141 C7
Queen Elizabeth Is.
  138 B9
Queen Mary Land
  168 B11
Queen Maud G. 140 B9
Queen Maud Mts.
  168 C16
Queenscliff 135 C3
Queensland □ 133 E7
Queenstown Australia
  134 D4
Queenstown N.Z. 137 F3
Queenstown S. Africa
  131 E5
Queimades 165 E6
Quelimane 131 B7
Querétaro 156 C4
Quetta 114 D5
Quezon City 108 B2
Qui Nhon 110 B3
Quibaxe 128 F2
Quibdó 162 B3
Quiberon 88 C2
Quilán, C. 167 E2
Quillabamba 163 F4

Quillagua 163 H5
Quillota 166 C2
Quilon = Kollam 115 Q10
Quilpie 135 A3
Quimilí 166 B4
Quimper 88 B1
Quimperlé 88 C2
Quincy 147 F9
Quines 166 C3
Quintanar de la Orden
  86 C4
Quirindi 135 B5
Quissanga 131 A8
Quito 162 D3
Quixadá 164 C6
Qulan 97 E8
Qulsary 97 E6
Qünghirot 97 E6
Quorn 134 B2
Qŭqon 97 E8
Quseir 124 C5
Quzhou 106 C5
Qyzylorda 97 E7

R

Raahe 76 C10
Raba 109 F1
Rába → 82 E3
Rabat Malta 91 G5
Rabat Morocco 126 B4
Rabaul 136 K10
Rābigh 119 G4
Râbniţa 83 E9
Race, C. 143 E8
Rach Gia 110 B3
Racine 148 C2
Rădăuţi 83 E7
Radekhiv 83 C7
Radom 82 C5
Radomsko 82 C4
Radomyshl 83 C9
Radstock, C. 134 B1
Rae 140 B8
Rae Bareli 112 D3
Rae Isthmus 142 C5
Raetihi 136 C6
Rafaela 166 C4
Rafḩā 119 E5
Rafsanjān 116 D4
Ragachow 83 B10
Ragama 115 R11
Raglan 136 B6
Ragusa 91 F5
Raha 109 E2
Rahimyar Khan 114 E7
Raichur 115 L10
Raigarh 112 G4
Railton 134 D4
Rainier, Mt. 144 C3
Raipur 112 G3
Ra'is 119 G4
Raj Nandgaon 112 G3
Raja, Ujung 111 D1

Raja Ampat, Kepulauan
  109 E3
Rajahmundry 112 J3
Rajang → 111 D4
Rajapalaiyam 115 Q10
Rajasthan □ 114 F8
Rajgarh 115 G10
Rajkot 115 H7
Rajpipla 115 J8
Rajshahi 113 E7
Rakaia 137 E5
Rakaia → 137 E5
Rakan, Ra's 116 E2
Rakaposhi 114 A9
Rakata, Pulau 111 F3
Rakhiv 83 D7
Rakitnoye 100 A4
Rakiura △ 137 G2
Raleigh 155 B8
Ramanathapuram
  115 Q11
Rame Hd. 135 C4
Ramechhap 112 D6
Ramgarh Jharkhand, India
  112 F5
Ramgarh Raj., India
  114 F7
Râmnicu Sărat 83 F8
Râmnicu Vâlcea 83 F7
Rampur 114 E11
Rampur Hat 112 E6
Ramree I. 113 H9
Ramtek 115 J11
Ranaghat 113 F7
Ranau 110 C5
Rancagua 166 C2
Ranchi 112 F5
Randers 77 D8
Rangaunu B. 136 A5
Rangia 113 D8
Rangiora 137 E5
Rangitaiki → 136 B7
Rangitata → 137 E4
Rangoon 113 J11
Rangoon → 113 J11
Rangpur 113 E7
Ranibennur 115 M9
Raniganj 112 F6
Raniwara 115 G8
Rankin Inlet 140 B10
Rankins Springs 135 B4
Ranohira 131 C9
Ranong 110 C1
Ransiki 109 E4
Rantauprapat 111 D1
Rantemario 109 E1
Rapa 137 M16
Rapallo 90 B2
Räpch 117 E4
Raper, C. 142 C7
Rapid City 146 C3
Rarotonga 137 M14

Ra's al Khaymah 116 E4
Ra's aţ Tib 91 F3
Rasht 118 C7
Rat Islands 141 C1
Ratangarh 114 E9
Rathenow 81 B7
Ratlam 115 H9
Ratnagiri 115 L8
Raukumara Ra. 136 C7
Rauma 76 C10
Raurkela 112 F5
Rausu-Dake 100 A9
Rava-Ruska 83 C6
Rāvar 116 D4
Ravenna 90 B4
Ravensburg 80 E5
Ravi → 114 D7
Rawalpindi 114 C8
Rawene 136 A5
Rawlins 145 F10
Rawson 167 E3
Ray, C. 143 E8
Rayadurg 115 M10
Rayagada 112 H4
Raz, Pte. du 88 B1
Razāzah, Buḩayrat ar
  119 D5
Razgrad 92 C6
Razim, Lacul 92 B7
Ré, Î. de 88 C3
Reading U.K. 79 F6
Reading U.S.A. 149 D8
Realicó 166 D4
Rebi 109 F4
Rebiana 124 D3
Rebun-Tō 100 A9
Rechytsa 83 B10
Recife 164 D7
Reconquista 166 B5
Recreo 166 B3
Red → 153 D8
Red Cliffs 134 B3
Red Deer 141 C8
Red River of the North →
  141 D10
Red Sea 120 C2
Redcar 79 D6
Redcliffe 135 A5
Redding 144 F2
Redditch 79 E6
Redon 88 C2
Redondela 86 A1
Redwood City 150 B1
Ree, L. 79 E3
Reefton 137 E4
Regensburg 81 D7
Réggio di Calábria 91 E5
Réggio nell'Emília 90 B3
Reghin 83 E7
Regina 141 C9
Rehoboth 130 C3
Rehovot 118 E3

Reichenbach 81 C7
Reidsville 155 A8
Reigate 79 F6
Reims 89 B6
Reina Adelaida, Arch.
  167 G2
Reindeer L. 141 C9
Reinga, C. 136 A5
Reinosa 86 A3
Remanso 165 D5
Remarkable, Mt. 134 B2
Remeshk 117 E4
Rendsburg 80 A5
Rengat 111 E2
Reni 83 F9
Renmark 134 B3
Rennes 88 B3
Reno 144 G4
Reno → 90 B4
Republican → 146 F6
Repulse Bay 142 C5
Requena Peru 162 E4
Requena Spain 87 C5
Resistencia 166 B5
Reşiţa 83 F5
Resolute 142 B4
Resolution I. Canada
  142 C7
Resolution I. N.Z. 137 F2
Rethimno 93 G5
Réunion ☑ 123 J9
Reus 87 B6
Reutlingen 80 D5
Reval = Tallinn 84 B1
Revelstoke 141 C8
Revillagigedo, Is. de
  156 D2
Rewa 112 E3
Rewari 114 E10
Rey Malabo 128 D1
Reykjavík 76 C1
Reynosa 156 B5
Rhein → 80 C4
Rhein-Main-Donau-Kanal
  81 D6
Rheine 80 B4
Rheinland-Pfalz ☐ 80 C4
Rhine = Rhein → 80 C4
Rhode Island ☐ 149 D10
Rhodes 93 F7
Rhodopi Planina 92 D5
Rhön 80 C5
Rhondda 79 F5
Rhône → 89 E6
Rhum = Rùm 78 C3
Riachão 164 D4
Riasi 114 C9
Riau ☐ 111 E2
Riau, Kepulauan ☐
  111 E2
Ribadeo 86 A2
Ribeirão Prêto 165 G4

Riberalta 163 F5
Riccarton 137 E5
Richards Bay 131 D6
Richland 144 C4
Richmond N.Z. 137 D5
Richmond Calif., U.S.A.
  144 H2
Richmond Va., U.S.A.
  149 F7
Richmond Ra. 135 A5
Ridder 97 D9
Ried 81 D7
Riesa 81 C7
Rieti 90 C4
Rīga 84 B1
Riga, G. of 84 B1
Rīgestān 114 D4
Rigolet 142 D8
Riiser-Larsen-halvøya
  168 A8
Rijeka 90 B5
Rimah, Wadi ar →
  119 F5
Rímini 90 B4
Rimouski 143 E7
Rinca 109 F1
Rinconada 166 A3
Rinjani, Gunung 111 F5
Rio Branco Brazil 163 E5
Río Branco Uruguay
  166 C6
Río Cuarto 166 C4
Rio de Janeiro 165 G5
Rio do Sul 166 B7
Río Gallegos 167 G3
Río Grande Argentina
  167 G3
Rio Grande Brazil 166 C6
Río Grande → 156 B5
Río Grande de
  Santiago → 156 C3
Rio Grande do Norte ☐
  164 D6
Rio Grande do Sul ☐
  166 B6
Río Largo 165 D6
Río Mulatos 163 G5
Río Muni ☐ 128 D2
Río Negro 166 B7
Rio Verde 165 F3
Riobamba 162 D3
Ríohacha 162 A4
Ríosucio Caldas,
  Colombia 162 B3
Ríosucio Choco,
  Colombia 162 B3
Rishiri-Tō 100 A7
Riva del Garda 90 B3
Rivadavia 166 B2
Rivera 166 C5
Riverside 150 D4
Riverton Australia 134 B2

Riverton N.Z. 137 G2
Riviera = Azur, Côte d'
  89 E7
Riviera di Levante 90 B2
Riviera di Ponente 90 B2
Rivière-du-Loup 143 E7
Rivne 83 C8
Rívoli 90 B1
Rivoli B. 134 C3
Riyadh = Ar Riyāḍ 119 F6
Rize 118 B5
Rizhao 104 E3
Rizzuto, C. 91 E6
Roanne 89 C6
Roanoke 149 F6
Robbins I. 134 D4
Robertson I. 168 A4
Robertstown 134 B2
Roberval 143 E6
Robinvale 134 B3
Roboré 163 G7
Robson, Mt. 141 C8
Roca, C. da 86 C1
Rocas, Atol das 164 C7
Rocha 166 C6
Rochefort 88 D3
Rochester Minn., U.S.A.
  147 C8
Rochester N.Y., U.S.A.
  149 C7
Rock, The 135 C4
Rock Hill 155 B7
Rock Island 147 E9
Rock Springs 145 F9
Rockefeller Plateau
  168 C18
Rockford 147 D10
Rockhampton 133 E9
Rocky Mount 155 B9
Rocky Mts. 140 C7
Rod 114 E3
Rodez 89 D5
Ródhos = Rhodes 93 F7
Rodney, C. 136 B6
Roes Welcome Sd.
  142 C5
Rogagua, L. 163 F5
Rogatyn 83 D7
Rogoaguado, L. 163 F5
Rohri 114 F6
Rohtak 114 E10
Roi Et 110 A2
Rojo, C. 156 C5
Rokan → 111 D2
Rolândia 166 A6
Roma Australia 135 A4
Roma Italy 90 D4
Romaine → 143 D7
Roman 83 E8
Romang 109 F3
Romania ■ 92 B5
Romans-sur-Isère 89 D6

Romblon 108 B2
Rome = Roma 90 D4
Rome 154 B5
Romorantin-Lanthenay
  88 C4
Roncador, Serra do
  165 E3
Ronda 86 D3
Rondônia ☐ 163 F6
Rondonópolis 165 F3
Ronge, L. la 141 C9
Ronne Ice Shelf 168 B3
Roorkee 114 E10
Roosevelt → 163 E6
Roosevelt I. 168 B16
Roquetas de Mar 87 D4
Roraima ☐ 162 C6
Roraima, Mt. 162 B6
Rosa, Monte 89 D7
Rosario Argentina 166 C4
Rosário Brazil 164 C5
Rosario Mexico 156 C3
Rosario Paraguay 166 A5
Rosario de la Frontera
  166 B3
Rosário do Sul 166 C6
Roscommon 79 E2
Roseau Dominica 159 C7
Roseau U.S.A. 147 A7
Rosebery 134 D4
Roseburg 144 E2
Rosenheim 81 E7
Roses, G. de 87 A7
Rosetown 141 C9
Roseville 144 G3
Rosewood 135 A5
Rosignano Marittimo
  90 C3
Rosignol 162 B7
Roşiori de Vede 92 B5
Roslavl 84 C3
Ross Australia 134 D4
Ross N.Z. 137 E4
Ross I. 168 B15
Ross Ice Shelf 168 C16
Ross Sea 168 B15
Rossano 91 E6
Rosslare 79 E3
Rosso 127 E2
Rossosh 84 C4
Rostock 81 A7
Rostov Don, Russia
  85 D4
Rostov Yaroslavl, Russia
  84 B4
Roswell 152 C1
Rotherham 79 E6
Roto 135 B4
Rotondo, Mte. 89 E8
Rotoroa, L. 137 D5
Rotorua 136 C7
Rotorua, L. 136 C7

Rotterdam 80 C3
Rottweil 80 D5
Rotuma 136 L12
Roubaix 89 A5
Rouen 88 B4
Round Mt. 135 B5
Roussillon 89 E5
Rouyn-Noranda 143 E6
Rovaniemi 76 B11
Rovereto 90 B3
Rovigo 90 B3
Rovinj 90 B4
Rowena 135 A4
Roxas 108 B2
Roxburgh 137 F3
Royal Leamington Spa
  79 E6
Royan 88 D3
Rozdilna 83 E10
Rozhyshche 83 C7
Rtishchevo 84 C5
Ruahine Ra. 136 C7
Ruapehu 136 C6
Ruapuke I. 137 G3
Rub' al Khālī 120 D4
Rubio 162 B4
Rubtsovsk 97 D9
Rudall 134 B2
Rudolfa, Ostrov 96 A6
Rufiji → 129 F7
Rufino 166 C4
Rugby 79 E6
Rügen 81 A7
Ruhr → 80 C4
Rukwa, L. 129 F6
Rùm 78 C3
Rumāḥ 119 F6
Rumania = Romania ■
  92 B5
Rumbek 125 G4
Rumia 82 A4
Rumoi 100 B7
Runanga 137 E4
Runaway, C. 136 B7
Rundu 130 B3
Ruoqiang 102 D5
Rupa 113 D9
Rupat 111 D2
Rupert → 143 D6
Rurrenabaque 163 F5
Ruse 92 C4
Russas 164 C6
Russellkonda 112 H5
Russia ■ 95 C10
Rustavi 85 E6
Rustenburg 131 D5
Ruteng 109 F2
Ruvuma → 129 G8
Ruwenzori 129 D5
Rwanda ■ 129 E6
Ryazan 84 C4
Ryazhsk 84 C5
Rybinsk 84 B4

Rybinskoye Vdkhr. 84 B4
Rylstone 135 B4
Ryōtsu 100 D6
Rypin 82 B4
Ryūkyū-Rettō 103 F13
Rzeszów 82 C5
Rzhev 84 B3

S

Sa Dec 110 B3
Sa'ādat Shahr 116 D3
Saale → 81 C6
Saalfeld 81 C6
Saar → 89 B7
Saarbrücken 80 D4
Saaremaa 84 B1
Šabac 92 B2
Sabadell 87 B7
Sabah □ 110 C5
Sabalān, Kūhhā-ye
  118 C6
Sabalana, Kepulauan
  109 F1
Sábanalarga 162 A4
Sabang 110 C1
Saberania 109 E5
Sabhā 124 C1
Sabinas 156 B4
Sabinas Hidalgo 156 B4
Sablayan 108 B2
Sable, C. Canada 143 E7
Sable, C. U.S.A. 158 A3
Sable I. 143 E8
Sabrina Coast 168 A12
Sabulubek 111 E1
Sabzevār 116 B4
Săcele 83 F7
Sachsen □ 81 C7
Sachsen-Anhalt □ 81 C7
Sacramento 144 G3
Sacramento → 144 G3
Sacramento Mts.
  151 D10
Sadd el Aali 124 D5
Sado 100 E6
Safi 126 B4
Safid Kūh 114 B3
Saga 101 G2
Sagar 115 M9
Sagarmatha = Everest,
  Mt. 112 C6
Saginaw 148 C4
Sagua la Grande 158 B3
Sagunt 87 C5
Sahagún 86 A3
Sahand, Küh-e 118 C6
Sahara 126 D6
Saharanpur 114 E10
Saharien, Atlas 126 B6
Sahiwal 114 D8
Sa'id Bundās 125 G3
Saidpur 113 E7

Saidu Sharif 114 B8
Saigon = Thanh Pho Ho
  Chi Minh 110 B3
Saikhoa Ghat 113 D10
Saiki 101 G2
Sailolof 109 E4
Saimaa 76 C11
St. Andrews 78 C5
St. Anthony 143 D8
St. Arnaud 134 C3
St-Augustin 143 D8
St. Augustine 155 E7
St. Austell 79 F4
St-Brieuc 88 B2
St. Catharines 149 C6
St-Chamond 89 D6
St. Christopher-Nevis =
  St. Kitts & Nevis ■
  159 C7
St. Cloud 147 C7
St. Croix 159 C7
St-Denis 88 B5
St-Dizier 89 B6
St. Elias, Mt. 140 B5
St-Étienne 89 D6
St-Flour 89 D5
St-Gaudens 88 E4
St. George 135 A4
St-Georges 164 B3
St. George's 159 D7
St. George's Channel
  79 F3
St. Georges Hd. 135 C5
St. Gotthard P. = San
  Gottardo, P. del 89 C8
St. Helena 123 H3
St. Helena B. 130 E3
St. Helens 134 D4
St. Helier 79 G5
St-Hyacinthe 143 E6
St-Jean, L. 143 E6
St. John 143 E7
St. John's Antigua & B.
  159 C7
St. John's Canada
  143 E8
St. Johns → 155 D7
St. Joseph 147 F7
St. Joseph, L. 143 D4
St. Kilda 78 C2
St. Kitts & Nevis ■
  159 C7
St-Laurent du Maroni
  164 A3
St. Lawrence → 143 E7
St. Lawrence, Gulf of
  143 E7
St. Lawrence I. 141 B2
St-Lô 88 B3
St-Louis 127 E2
St. Louis 147 F9
St. Lucia ■ 159 D7
St-Malo 88 B2

St-Marc 159 C5
St. Mary Pk. 134 B2
St. Marys 134 D4
St-Mathieu, Pte. 88 B1
St-Nazaire 88 C2
St-Omer 88 A5
St. Paul 147 C8
St. Peter Port 79 G5
St. Petersburg =
  Sankt-Peterburg 84 B3
St. Petersburg 155 F6
St-Pierre-et-Miquelon ☑
  143 E8
St-Quentin 89 B5
St-Tropez 89 E7
St. Vincent, G. 134 C2
Saintes 88 D3
Saintonge 88 D3
Saipan 136 H9
Sairang 113 F9
Saitama 101 F6
Sajama 163 G5
Sajószentpéter 82 D5
Sakākah 119 E5
Sakakawea, L. 146 B4
Sakarya 118 B2
Sakata 100 D6
Sakhalin 99 D12
Sakon Nakhon 110 A2
Sala 77 D9
Sala Consilina 91 D5
Saladillo 166 D5
Salado → B. Aires,
  Argentina 166 D5
Salado → La Pampa,
  Argentina 166 D3
Salado → Santa Fe,
  Argentina 166 C4
Salaga 127 G5
Salālah 121 D5
Salamanca Chile 166 C2
Salamanca Spain 86 B3
Salamina 93 F4
Salar de Atacama 166 A3
Salar de Uyuni 163 H5
Salaverry 163 E3
Salawati 109 E4
Salayar 109 F2
Saldanha 130 E3
Sale Australia 135 C4
Salé Morocco 126 B4
Salekhard 96 C7
Salem India 115 P11
Salem U.S.A. 144 D2
Salerno 91 D5
Salgótarján 82 D4
Salihli 93 E7
Salihorsk 83 B8
Salima 131 A6
Salina Italy 91 E5
Salina U.S.A. 146 F6
Salina Cruz 157 D5
Salinas Brazil 165 F5

Salinas *Ecuador* **162 D2**
Salinas *U.S.A.* **150 B2**
Salinas Grandes **166 C3**
Salinópolis **164 C4**
Salisbury *Australia* **134 B2**
Salisbury *U.K.* **79 F6**
Salisbury *U.S.A.* **155 B7**
Salisbury I. **142 C6**
Salluit **142 C6**
Salmās **118 C6**
Salmon → **144 D5**
Salmon River Mts. **145 D6**
Salon-de-Provence **89 E6**
Salonica = Thessaloniki **93 D4**
Salonta **82 E5**
Salsk **85 D5**
Salso → **91 F4**
Salt L. **134 B3**
Salt Lake City **145 F8**
Salta **166 A3**
Saltillo **156 B4**
Salto **166 C5**
Salto → **90 C4**
Salton Sea **150 D5**
Salûm **124 B4**
Salur **112 H4**
Salvador **165 E6**
Salvador, El ■ **157 E7**
Salween → **113 J11**
Salyan **85 F6**
Salzach → **81 D7**
Salzburg **81 E7**
Salzgitter **80 B6**
Salzwedel **81 B6**
Samales Group **108 C2**
Samangān □ **117 B7**
Samani **100 B8**
Samar **108 B3**
Samara **84 C7**
Samarinda **111 E5**
Samarkand = Samarqand **97 F7**
Samarqand **97 F7**
Sāmarrā' **118 D5**
Sambalpur **112 G5**
Sambar, Tanjung **111 E4**
Sambas **111 D3**
Sambhal **114 E11**
Sambhar **114 F9**
Sambiase **91 E6**
Sambir **83 D6**
Samoa ■ **137 L13**
Samokov **92 C4**
Samos **93 F6**
Samothraki **93 D5**
Sampit **111 E4**
Sampit, Teluk **111 E4**
Samsun **118 B4**
Samui, Ko **110 C2**

Samut Prakan **110 B2**
Samut Songkhram **110 B2**
San **127 F5**
San Agustin, C. **108 C3**
San Andrés, I. de **158 D3**
San Andrés Tuxtla **157 D5**
San Angelo **152 D3**
San Antonio *Chile* **166 C2**
San Antonio *U.S.A.* **152 E4**
San Antonio, C. **166 D5**
San Antonio Oeste **167 E4**
San Benedetto del Tronto **90 C4**
San Bernardino **150 C4**
San Bernardino Str. **108 B2**
San Bernardo **166 C2**
San Bernardo, I. de **162 B3**
San Borja **163 F5**
San Buenaventura = Ventura **150 C3**
San Carlos *Argentina* **166 C3**
San Carlos *Chile* **166 D2**
San Carlos *Phil.* **108 B2**
San Carlos *Amazonas, Venezuela* **162 C5**
San Carlos *Cojedes, Venezuela* **162 B5**
San Carlos de Bariloche **167 E2**
San Carlos del Zulia **162 B4**
San Cristóbal *Argentina* **166 C4**
San Cristóbal *Venezuela* **162 B4**
San Cristóbal de las Casas **157 D6**
San Diego **150 D4**
San Diego, C. **167 G3**
San Felipe *Chile* **166 C2**
San Felipe *Venezuela* **162 A5**
San Fernando *Chile* **166 C2**
San Fernando *La Union, Phil.* **108 A2**
San Fernando *Pampanga, Phil.* **108 A2**
San Fernando *Spain* **86 D2**
San Fernando *Trin. & Tob.* **159 D7**
San Fernando de Apure **162 B5**
San Fernando de Atabapo **162 C5**

San Francisco *Argentina* **166 C4**
San Francisco *U.S.A.* **150 B1**
San Francisco de Macorís **159 C5**
San Gottardo, P. del **89 C8**
San Ignacio *Bolivia* **163 G6**
San Ignacio *Paraguay* **166 B5**
San Ildefonso, C. **108 A2**
San Javier **163 G6**
San Joaquin → **150 A2**
San Jorge, G. **167 F3**
San José *Costa Rica* **158 E3**
San Jose *Mind. Occ., Phil.* **108 B2**
San Jose *Nueva Ecija, Phil.* **108 A2**
San Jose *U.S.A.* **150 B2**
San José de Chiquitos **163 G6**
San José de Jáchal **166 C3**
San José de Mayo **166 C5**
San José del Guaviare **162 C4**
San Juan *Argentina* **166 C3**
San Juan *Puerto Rico* **159 C6**
San Juan → **158 D3**
San Juan de los Morros **162 B5**
San Juan Mts. **151 B9**
San Justo **166 C4**
San Lorenzo **162 C3**
San Lorenzo, Mte. **167 F2**
San Lucas **163 H5**
San Lucas, C. **156 C2**
San Luis **166 C3**
San Luis Obispo **150 C2**
San Luis Potosí **156 C4**
San Marino **90 C4**
San Marino ■ **90 C4**
San Martín, L. **167 F2**
San Matías **163 G7**
San Matías, G. **167 E4**
San Miguel **157 E7**
San Miguel → **163 F6**
San Miguel de Tucumán **166 B3**
San Nicandro Gargánico **90 D5**
San Nicolás de los Arroyos **166 C4**
San Pedro **127 H4**

San Pedro de las Colonias **156 B4**
San Pedro de Macorís **159 C6**
San Pedro del Paraná **166 B5**
San Pedro Sula **157 D7**
San Pietro **91 E2**
San Rafael *Argentina* **166 C3**
San Rafael *U.S.A.* **144 H2**
San Remo **90 C1**
San Roque *Argentina* **166 B5**
San Roque *Spain* **86 D3**
San Rosendo **166 D2**
San Salvador **157 E7**
San Salvador de Jujuy **166 A4**
San Salvador I. **158 B5**
San Sebastián = Donostia-San Sebastián **87 A5**
San Sebastián **167 G3**
San Severo **90 D5**
San Valentin, Mte. **167 F2**
San Vicente de Cañete **163 F3**
San Vicente de la Barquera **86 A3**
Şan'ä' **121 D3**
Sana → **90 B6**
Sanaga → **128 D1**
Sanana **109 E3**
Sanandaj **118 D6**
Sancti Spíritus **158 B4**
Sancy, Puy de **89 D5**
Sandakan **110 C5**
Sandanski **92 D4**
Sanday **78 B5**
Sandía **163 F5**
Sandıklı **118 C2**
Sandoa **128 F4**
Sandomierz **82 C3**
Sandusky **148 D4**
Sandy C. **134 D3**
Sandy L. **141 C10**
Sanford *Fla., U.S.A.* **155 E7**
Sanford *N.C., U.S.A.* **155 B8**
Sanford, Mt. **141 B5**
Sanga → **128 D3**
Sangamner **115 K9**
Sangar **99 C10**
Sangeang **109 F1**
Sangerhausen **81 C6**
Sanggau **111 D4**
Sangihe, Pulau **109 D3**
Sangkapura **111 F4**
Sangli **115 L9**
Sangmélima **128 D2**

Sangre de Cristo Mts. 152 A1
Saniklauq 143 D6
Sanjo 101 E6
Sankt Gallen 89 C8
Sankt Moritz 89 C8
Sankt-Peterburg 84 B3
Sankt Pölten 81 D8
Sankuru → 128 E4
Sanliurfa 118 C4
Sanlúcar de Barrameda 86 D2
Sanmenxia 103 E10
Sanming 107 D4
Sanmu 101 F4
Sant Antoni de Portmany 87 C6
Sant Feliu de Guíxols 87 B7
Sant Jordi, G. de 87 B6
Santa Ana Bolivia 163 F5
Santa Ana El Salv. 157 E7
Santa Ana U.S.A. 150 M10
Santa Barbara 150 C3
Santa Catalina I. 150 D3
Santa Catarina □ 166 B7
Santa Clara 158 B4
Santa Clotilde 162 D4
Santa Coloma de Gramenet 87 B7
Santa Cruz Bolivia 163 G6
Santa Cruz Phil. 108 B2
Santa Cruz U.S.A. 150 B1
Santa Cruz → 167 G3
Santa Cruz de Tenerife 126 C2
Santa Cruz do Sul 166 B6
Santa Cruz Is. 136 L11
Santa Fé Argentina 166 C4
Santa Fe U.S.A. 151 C10
Santa Filomena 165 D4
Santa Inés, I. 167 G2
Santa Isabel 166 D3
Santa Isabel do Morro 165 E3
Santa Lucia Range 150 C2
Santa Maria Brazil 166 B6
Santa Maria U.S.A. 150 C2
Santa María → 156 A3
Santa Maria da Vitória 165 E5
Santa Maria di Léuca, C. 93 E2
Santa Marta 162 A4

Santa Marta, Sierra Nevada de 162 A4
Santa Rosa La Pampa, Argentina 166 D4
Santa Rosa San Luis, Argentina 166 C3
Santa Rosa Brazil 166 B6
Santa Rosa U.S.A. 144 G2
Santa Vitória do Palmar 166 C6
Santai 103 E8
Santana, Coxilha de 166 C5
Santana do Livramento 166 C5
Santander 86 A4
Santarém Brazil 164 C3
Santarém Portugal 86 C1
Santiago Chile 166 C2
Santiago → 162 D3
Santiago de Compostela 86 A1
Santiago de Cuba 158 C4
Santiago de los Caballeros 159 C5
Santiago del Estero 166 B4
Santo Amaro 165 E6
Santo Ângelo 166 B6
Santo Antônio do Leverger 165 F2
Santo Domingo 159 C6
Santo Tomás 163 F4
Santo Tomé 166 B5
Santoña 86 A4
Santorini 93 F5
Santos 166 A7
Sanya 107 a
São Bernardo do Campo 165 G4
São Borja 166 B5
São Carlos 166 A7
São Cristóvão 165 E6
São Domingos 165 E4
São Francisco 165 F5
São Francisco → 165 E6
São Francisco do Sul 166 B7
São Gabriel 166 C6
São João da Madeira 86 B1
São João del Rei 165 G5
São João do Araguaia 164 D4
São João do Piauí 164 D5
São José do Rio Preto 165 G4
São Leopoldo 166 B6
São Lourenço 165 G4

São Lourenço → 165 F2
São Luís 164 C5
São Marcos → 165 F4
São Marcos, B. de 164 C5
São Mateus 165 F6
São Paulo 166 A7
São Roque, C. de 164 D6
São Sebastião, I. de 166 A7
São Tomé & Príncipe ■ 123 F4
São Vicente, C. de 86 D1
Saône → 89 D6
Saonek 109 E4
Saparua 109 E3
Sapele 127 G7
Saposoa 163 E3
Sapporo 100 B7
Sapulpa 153 B5
Saqqez 118 C6
Sar-e Pol 117 B6
Sar Planina 92 C3
Sarāb 118 C6
Saragossa = Zaragoza 87 B5
Saraguro 162 D3
Sarajevo 90 C7
Saran, Gunung 111 E4
Sarangani B. 108 C3
Sarangani Is. 108 C3
Sarangarh 112 G4
Saransk 84 C6
Sarapul 97 D6
Sarasota 155 F6
Saratov 84 C6
Sarāvān 117 E5
Saravane 110 A3
Sarawak □ 111 D4
Saray 92 D6
Sarayköy 93 F7
Sarbāz 117 E5
Sarbīsheh 117 C4
Sarda → 112 D3
Sardarshahr 114 E9
Sardegna □ 91 D2
Sardinia = Sardegna □ 91 D2
Sardis 93 E7
Sargodha 114 C8
Sarh 125 G2
Sārī 116 B3
Sangöl 93 E7
Sankamış 118 B5
Sarikei 111 D4
Sariwŏn 105 C6
Sark 79 G5
Şarköy 93 D6
Sarlat-la-Canéda 88 D4
Sarmi 109 E5
Sarmiento 167 F3
Sarnia 143 E5
Sarolangun 111 E2

Saronikos Kolpos 93 F4
Sarre = Saar → 89 B7
Sarreguemines 89 B7
Sarthe → 88 C3
Sarvestän 116 D3
Sary-Tash 97 F8
Saryshaghan 97 E8
Sasaram 112 E5
Sasebo 101 G1
Saser Kangri 114 B10
Saskatchewan □ 141 C9
Saskatchewan → 141 C9
Saskatoon 141 C9
Saskylakh 98 B9
Sasovo 84 C5
Sassandra 127 H4
Sassandra → 127 H4
Sássari 91 D2
Sassnitz 81 A7
Sassuolo 90 B3
Sasyk, Ozero 83 F9
Sata-Misaki 101 H2
Satadougou 127 F3
Satara 115 L8
Satmala Hills 115 J9
Satna 112 E3
Sátoraljaújhely 82 D5
Satpura Ra. 115 J10
Satsuma-Sendai 101 H2
Satu Mare 83 E6
Satui 111 E5
Saturnina → 163 F7
Sauðarkrókur 76 B2
Saudi Arabia ■ 119 F6
Sauerland 80 C4
Sault Ste. Marie Canada 143 E5
Sault Ste. Marie U.S.A. 148 A5
Saumlaki 109 F4
Saumur 88 C3
Saunders, C. 137 F4
Saurimo 128 F4
Sava → 92 B3
Savalou 127 G6
Savannah 155 C7
Savannah → 155 C7
Savannakhet 110 A2
Save → 131 C6
Säveh 118 D7
Savelugu 127 G5
Savoie □ 89 D7
Savona 90 B2
Savonlinna 76 C11
Savoy = Savoie □ 89 D7
Sawahlunto 111 E2
Sawai 109 E3
Sawai Madhopur 114 F10
Sawatch Range 151 A9
Sawu 109 F2
Sawu Sea 109 F2

Saxony = Sachsen □
  81 C7
Sayán 163 F3
Sayan, Zapadnyy 98 D7
Saydā 118 D3
Sayghān 117 C6
Sayhūt 121 D5
Saylac 121 E3
Sazanit 93 D2
Sázava → 82 D2
Sazin 114 B8
Scandicci 90 C3
Scandinavia 76 C8
Scarborough 79 D6
Schaffhausen 89 C8
Schelde → 80 C3
Schenectady 149 C9
Schiermonnikoog 80 B4
Schio 90 B3
Schleswig 80 A5
Schleswig-Holstein □
  80 A5
Schouten I. 134 D4
Schwäbische Alb 80 D5
Schwaner, Pegunungan
  111 E4
Schwarzwald 80 D5
Schwedt 81 B8
Schweinfurt 80 C6
Schwerin 81 B6
Schwyz 89 C8
Sciacca 91 F4
Scilla 91 E5
Scilly, Isles of 79 G3
Scone 135 B5
Scotland □ 78 C4
Scott Glacier 168 A12
Scottsbluff 146 E3
Scottsdale 134 D4
Scranton 149 D8
Scunthorpe 79 E6
Seaspray 135 C4
Seattle 144 C2
Sebastopol = Sevastopol
  85 E3
Şebinkarahisar 118 B4
Sebuku 111 E5
Sebuku, Teluk 111 D5
Secretary I. 137 F2
Secunderabad 115 L11
Sedalia 147 F8
Sedan 89 B6
Seddon 137 D6
Seddonville 137 D5
Sédhiou 127 F2
Sedova, Pik 96 B6
Seferihisar 93 E6
Segamat 111 D2
Segesta 91 F4
Seget 109 E4
Ségou 127 F4
Segovia 86 B3
Segre → 87 B6

Séguéla 127 G4
Segura → 87 C5
Sehore 115 H10
Seinäjoki → 76 C10
Seine → 88 B4
Sekayu 111 E2
Sekondi-Takoradi 127 H5
Selaru 109 F4
Selçuk 93 F6
Sele → 91 D5
Selebi-Phikwe 131 C5
Selenge Mörön →
  103 A9
Seletan, Tanjung 111 E4
Sélibabi 127 E3
Selîma, El Wâhât el
  124 D4
Selkirk 141 C10
Selkirk Mts. 141 C8
Selma 155 B8
Selpele 109 E4
Selu 109 F4
Selva 166 B4
Selvas 163 E5
Seman → 93 D2
Semarang 111 F4
Semey 97 D9
Semirara Is. 108 B2
Semitau 111 D4
Semmering P. 81 E8
Semnān 116 C3
Semporna 108 D1
Semuda 111 E4
Sena Madureira 163 E5
Senador Pompeu 164 D6
Senanga 131 B4
Sendai 100 D7
Sendai-Wan 100 D7
Senegal ■ 127 F3
Sénégal → 127 E2
Senhor-do-Bonfim
  165 E5
Senigállia 90 C4
Senj 90 B5
Senja 76 B9
Senlis 89 B5
Senmonorom 110 B3
Sens 89 B5
Senta 92 B3
Seongnam 105 D7
Seoul 105 D7
Sept-Îles 143 D7
Sequoia △ 150 B3
Seram 109 E3
Seram Sea 109 E3
Serasan 111 D3
Serbia ■ 92 B3
Serdar 97 F6
Serdobsk 84 C5
Seremban 111 D2
Sergipe □ 165 E6
Sergiyev Posad 84 B4
Seria 110 D4

Serian 111 D4
Serifos 93 F5
Sermata 109 F3
Serov 96 D7
Serowe 131 C5
Serpukhov 84 C4
Serres 92 D4
Serrinha 165 E6
Serua 109 F4
Serui 109 E5
Sesepe 109 E3
Setana 100 B6
Sète 89 E5
Sete Lagoas 165 F5
Sétif 126 A7
Setonaikai 101 F3
Settat 126 B4
Setúbal 86 C1
Setúbal, B. de 86 C1
Sevana Lich 85 E6
Sevastopol 85 E3
Sevem → Canada
  143 D5
Sevem → U.K. 79 F5
Severnaya Zemlya 98 B7
Severnyye Uvaly 84 B6
Severo-Yeniseyskiy
  98 C7
Severodvinsk 96 C4
Sevilla 86 D2
Sevlievo 92 C5
Seward 141 B5
Seward Peninsula
  141 B3
Sewer 109 F4
Seychelles ■ 94 J7
Seyðisfjörður 76 B3
Seymour 135 C4
Sfântu Gheorghe 83 F7
Sfax 124 B1
Shaanxi □ 103 E9
Shaba = Katanga □
  129 F4
Shabeelle → 121 G3
Shache 102 D3
Shackleton Ice Shelf
  168 A11
Shackleton Inlet 168 C15
Shadrinsk 97 D7
Shahdād 116 D4
Shahdād, Namakzār-e
  116 D4
Shahdadkot 114 F5
Shahgarh 114 F6
Shahjahanpur 114 F11
Shahrig 114 D5
Shajapur 115 H10
Shakhty 85 D5
Shakhunya 84 B6
Shaki 127 G6
Shalqar 97 E6
Shām, Bādiyat ash
  119 D4

Shām, J. ash 116 F4
Shamīl 116 E4
Shammar, Jabal 119 F5
Shamo, L. 125 G6
Shan □ 113 G12
Shandong □ 104 E3
Shandong Bandao
  104 D4
Shangani → 131 B5
Shanghai 106 B6
Shangqiu 104 E1
Shangrao 106 C4
Shangri-La = Zhongdian
  102 F7
Shangshui 103 E10
Shannon 136 D6
Shannon → 79 E2
Shantou 107 F4
Shanxi □ 103 D10
Shaoguan 107 E2
Shaoxing 106 C6
Shaoyang 106 D1
Shaqra' 119 F6
Shari 100 B9
Sharjah = Ash Shāriqah
  116 E3
Sharon 148 D5
Sharya 84 B6
Shashi 103 E10
Shasta, Mt. 144 F2
Shatt al Arab 119 E7
Shawinigan 143 E6
Shaykh, J. ash 118 D3
Shchūchīnsk 97 D8
Sheboygan 148 C2
Sheffield 79 E6
Shekhupura 114 D8
Shelby 155 B8
Shelbyville 154 B4
Shellharbour 135 B5
Shenandoah → 149 E7
Shendam 127 G7
Shendī 125 E5
Shenyang 105 B5
Shenzhen 107 F3
Sheopur Kalan 114 G10
Shepetivka 83 C8
Shepparton 135 C4
Sherbro I. 127 G3
Sherbrooke 143 E6
Sheridan 145 D10
Sherman 153 C5
Shetland Is. 78 A6
Shibām 121 D4
Shibata 101 E6
Shibecha 100 B9
Shibetsu 100 A8
Shīeli 97 E7
Shijiazhuang 104 C1
Shikarpur 114 F6
Shikoku □ 101 G3
Shikotsu-Ko 100 B7
Shiliguri 112 D7

Shillong 113 E8
Shimanto 101 G3
Shimla 114 D10
Shimoga 115 N9
Shimonoseki 101 G2
Shīndand 114 C3
Shingū 101 G4
Shinyanga 129 E6
Shio-no-Misaki 101 G4
Shipchenski Prokhod
  92 C5
Shīr Kūh 116 D3
Shiragami-Misaki 100 C7
Shīrāz 116 D3
Shire → 131 B7
Shiriya-Zaki 100 C7
Shīrvān 116 B4
Shivpuri 115 G10
Shiyan 106 A1
Shizuoka 101 F6
Shklow 83 A10
Shkodër 92 C2
Shkumbini → 93 D2
Shmidta, Ostrov 98 A7
Shoshone Mts. 144 G5
Shreveport 153 C7
Shrewsbury 79 E5
Shrirampur 112 F7
Shū 97 E8
Shuangliao 105 A5
Shuangyashan 103 B14
Shule 102 D3
Shumagin Is. 141 C4
Shumen 92 C6
Shunān 101 F2
Shuqrā' 121 E4
Shūr → 116 D3
Shurugwi 131 B6
Shūsf 117 D5
Shūshtar 119 D7
Shwebo 113 F10
Shwegu 113 E11
Shweli → 113 F11
Shymkent 97 E7
Shyok 114 B11
Shyok → 114 B9
Si Sa Ket 110 A2
Siahan Range 114 F4
Siak Sri Indrapura
  111 D2
Sialkot 114 C9
Siam = Thailand ■
  110 A2
Sian = Xi'an 103 E9
Siantan 111 D3
Siargao I. 108 C3
Siasi 108 C2
Siau 109 D3
Šiauliai 84 B1
Šibenik 90 C5
Siberia 98 C8
Siberut 111 E1
Sibi 114 E5

Sibirtsevo 100 A3
Sibiti 128 E2
Sibiu 83 F7
Sibolga 111 D1
Sibsagar 113 D10
Sibu 111 D4
Sibuco 108 C2
Sibuguey B. 108 C2
Sibut 128 C3
Sibutu 108 D1
Sibutu Passage 108 D1
Sibuyan I. 108 B2
Sibuyan Sea 108 B2
Sichuan □ 102 E8
Sicilia 91 F5
Sicuani 163 F4
Siddipet 115 K11
Sidi-bel-Abbès 126 A5
Sidi Ifni 126 C3
Sidley, Mt. 168 B18
Sidra = Surt 124 B2
Siedlce 83 B6
Sieg → 80 C4
Siegen 80 C5
Siemreab 110 B2
Siena 90 C3
Sieradz 82 C4
Sierra Colorada 167 E3
Sierra Gorda 166 A3
Sierra Leone ■ 127 G3
Sierra Madre Occidental
  156 B3
Sierra Nevada Spain
  86 D4
Sierra Nevada U.S.A.
  144 G3
Sifnos 93 F5
Sighetu-Marmaţiei 83 E6
Sigli 110 C1
Siglufjörður 76 B2
Sigsig 162 D3
Sigüenza 87 B4
Siguiri 127 F4
Sikar 114 F9
Sikasso 127 F4
Sikhote Alin, Khrebet
  99 E11
Sikhote Alin Ra. = Sikhote
  Alin, Khrebet 99 E11
Sikinos 93 F5
Sikkim □ 112 D7
Sil → 86 A2
Silchar 113 E9
Silesia = Śląsk 82 C3
Silgarhi Doti 112 C3
Silghat 113 D9
Silifke 118 C3
Siling Co 102 E5
Silistra 92 B6
Silivri 92 D7
Sillajhuay, Cordillera
  163 G5
Simav 93 E7

Simbirsk = Ulyanovsk
  84 C6
Simeria 83 F6
Simeulue 111 D1
Simferopol 85 E3
Simi 93 F6
Simikot 112 C3
Simla = Shimla 114 D10
Simpson Desert 132 F6
Simpson Pen. 142 C5
Sina Dhago 121 F4
Sinabang 111 D1
Sinai = Es Sînâ' 124 C5
Sinai, Mt. = Mûsa, Gebel
  119 E3
Sincelejo 162 B3
Sincorá, Serra do 165 E5
Sind Sagar Doab 114 D7
Sindangan 108 C2
Sindh □ 114 F6
Sines 86 D1
Sines, C. de 86 D1
Singa 125 F5
Singapore ■ 111 D2
Singaraja 111 F5
Singida 129 E6
Singkang 109 E2
Singkawang 111 D3
Singleton 135 B5
Sinjai 109 F2
Sinjär 118 C5
Sinkat 125 E6
Sinkiang = Xinjiang Uygur
  Zizhiqu □ 102 C5
Sinni → 91 D6
Sinop 118 B3
Sintang 111 D4
Sintra 86 C1
Siocon 108 C2
Siófok 82 E4
Sioux City 147 D6
Sioux Falls 146 D6
Sioux Lookout 141 C10
Siping 105 A6
Sipura 111 E1
Siquijor 108 C2
Siracusa 91 F5
Sirajganj 113 E7
Siret → 83 F9
Sīrjān 116 D3
Sirohi 115 G8
Sironj 115 G10
Sirsa 114 E9
Sirte = Surt 124 B2
Sisak 90 B7
Sisophon 110 B2
Sīstān 117 D5
Sīstān, Daryācheh-ye
  117 D5
Sīstān va Balūchestān □
  117 E5
Sitapur 112 D3
Sitges 87 B6

Sitia 93 G6
Sitka 141 C6
Sittang Myit → 113 J11
Sittwe 113 G9
Siuri 112 F6
Sivas 118 C4
Siverek 118 C4
Sivrihisar 118 C2
Sîwa 124 C4
Siwalik Range 112 D4
Siwan 112 D5
Sjælland 77 D8
Skadarsko Jezero 92 C2
Skagen 77 D8
Skagerrak 77 D7
Skagway 141 C6
Skala-Podilska 83 D8
Skalat 83 D7
Skardu 114 B9
Skarżysko-Kamienna
  82 C5
Skeena → 140 C6
Skegness 79 E7
Skeleton Coast 130 C2
Skellefteå 76 C10
Skellefteälven → 76 C10
Skiathos 93 E4
Skien 77 D7
Skierniewice 82 C5
Skikda 126 A7
Skole 83 D6
Skopelos 93 E4
Skopje 92 C3
Skvyra 83 D9
Skye 78 C3
Skyros 93 E5
Śląsk 82 C3
Slatina 92 B5
Slave → 140 B8
Slavgorod 97 D8
Slavonski Brod 90 B7
Slavuta 83 C8
Slavyanka 100 B2
Slawharad 83 B10
Sleaford B. 134 B2
Sleeper Is. 142 D5
Sligo 79 D2
Sliven 92 C3
Slobodskoy 84 B7
Slobozia 92 B6
Slonim 83 B7
Slough 79 F6
Slovak Rep. ■ 82 D4
Slovenia ■ 90 B5
Slovenské Rudohorie
  82 D4
Slovyansk 85 D4
Sluch → 83 C8
Słupsk 82 A3
Slutsk 83 B8
Smallwood Res. 143 D7
Smarhon 83 A8
Smederevo 92 B3

Smithton 134 D4
Smoky Bay 134 B1
Smolensk 84 C3
Smolikas, Oros 93 D3
Smolyan 92 D5
Smyrna = İzmir 93 E6
Snake → 144 C4
Snake I. 135 C4
Snake River Plain 145 E7
Sneek 80 B3
Sněžka 82 C2
Snøhetta 76 C7
Snowdon 79 E4
Snowtown 134 B2
Snowy → 135 C4
Snowy Mts. 135 C4
Snyatyn 83 D7
Snyder 152 C3
Sobat → 125 G5
Sobral 164 C5
Soc Trang 110 C3
Sochi 85 E4
Société, Îs. de la 137 L15
Socompa, Portezuelo de 166 A3
Socotra 121 E5
Söderhamn 76 C9
Sodiri 125 F4
Sofia → 131 B9
Sofiya 92 C5
Sogamoso 162 B4
Sognefjorden 76 C7
Sohâg 124 C5
Soissons 89 B5
Sokal 83 C7
Söke 93 F6
Sokhumi 85 E5
Sokodé 127 G6
Sokol 84 B5
Sokółka 83 B6
Sokołów Podlaski 83 B6
Sokoto 127 G6
Sol, Costa del 86 D3
Solander I. 137 G2
Solano 108 A2
Solapur 115 L9
Soledad 162 B6
Soligalich 84 B5
Solikamsk 96 D6
Solingen 80 C4
Sologne 88 C4
Solok 111 E2
Solomon Is. ■ 136 K10
Solomon Sea 133 B9
Solon 103 B12
Solor 109 F2
Šolta 90 C6
Solţānābād 116 B4
Solţānīyeh 118 C7
Solunska Glava 92 D3
Solwezi 131 A5
Sōma Japan 100 E7

Soma Turkey 93 E6
Somalia ■ 121 F4
Somaliland □ 121 E4
Sombor 92 B2
Sombrerete 156 C4
Somerset I. 140 A10
Someş → 83 E6
Somme → 88 A4
Somosierra, Puerto de 86 B4
Somport, Túnel de 88 E3
Sóndrio 90 A2
Sonepur 112 G4
Song Cau 110 B3
Songea 129 G7
Songhua Hu 105 A7
Songhua Jiang → 103 B14
Songkhla 110 C2
Songo 131 B6
Songpan 102 E8
Sonipat 114 E10
Sono → 165 D4
Sonora → 156 B2
Sonsonate 157 E7
Sopi 109 D3
Sopot 82 A4
Sopron 82 E3
Sorel 164 C4
Soria 87 B4
Soroca 83 D9
Sorocaba 166 A7
Sorong 109 E4
Soroti 129 D6
Sørøya 76 A10
Sorsogon 108 B2
Sosnowiec 82 C4
Souanké 128 D2
Soudas, Ormos 93 G5
Sŏul = Seoul 105 D7
Sources, Mt. aux 131 D5
Soure 164 C4
Souris → 141 D10
Sousa 164 C6
Sousse 124 A1
South Africa ■ 130 E4
South Australia □ 134 B2
South Bend 148 D2
South Carolina □ 155 C7
South China Sea 110 C4
South Dakota □ 146 C4
South East C. 134 D4
South Horr 129 D7
South I. 137 E3
South Invercargill 137 G3
South Korea ■ 105 D7
South Magnetic Pole 168 A13
South Nahanni → 140 B7

South Orkney Is. 168 A4
South Platte → 146 E4
South Pole 168 C
South Ronaldsay 78 B5
South Saskatchewan → 141 C9
South Shetland Is. 168 A4
South Shields 79 D6
South Sudan ■ 125 G4
South Taranaki Bight 136 C6
South Uist 78 C3
South West C. Australia 134 D4
South West C. N.Z. 137 G2
Southampton 79 F6
Southampton I. 142 C5
Southbridge 137 E5
Southend-on-Sea 79 F7
Southern Alps 137 E4
Southern Indian L. 141 C10
Southern Ocean 168 A9
Southern Uplands 78 D5
Southland □ 137 F3
Southport 135 A5
Sovetsk Kaliningrad, Russia 84 B1
Sovetsk Kirov, Russia 84 B6
Soweto 131 D5
Sozh → 83 C10
Spain ■ 86 C4
Spalding 134 B2
Spanish Town 158 C4
Spartanburg 155 B7
Sparti 93 F4
Spartivento, C. Calabria, Italy 91 F6
Spartivento, C. Sard., Italy 91 E2
Spassk-Dalniy 100 A3
Spatha, Akra 93 G4
Spencer, C. 134 C2
Spencer G. 134 B2
Spenser Mts. 137 E5
Spey → 78 C5
Speyer 80 D5
Split 90 C6
Spokane 144 C5
Spoleto 90 C4
Sporyy Navolok, Mys 96 B7
Spratly Is. 110 C4
Spree → 81 B7
Springfield N.Z. 137 E4
Springfield Ill., U.S.A. 147 F10
Springfield Mass., U.S.A. 149 C9

Springfield Mo., U.S.A. 153 A7
Springfield Ohio, U.S.A. 148 E4
Springfield Oreg., U.S.A. 144 D2
Springs 131 D5
Sre Ambel 110 C2
Srebrenica 90 B7
Sredinnyy Khrebet 99 D14
Śrem 82 B3
Sremska Mitrovica 92 B2
Sri Lanka ■ 115 R12
Srikakulam 112 H4
Srinagar 114 B9
Stade 80 B5
Stafford 79 E5
Stakhanov 85 D4
Stalowa Wola 83 C6
Stamford 149 D7
Stanke Dimitrov 92 C4
Stanley Australia 134 D4
Stanley Falk. Is. 167 G5
Stanovoy Khrebet 99 D10
Stanthorpe 135 A5
Stara Planina 92 C4
Stara Zagora 92 C5
Starachowice 82 C5
Staraya Russa 84 B3
Starbuck I. 137 K15
Stargard Szczeciński 82 B2
Staritsa 84 B3
Starogard Gdański 82 B4
Starokonstyantyniv 83 D8
Staryy Chartoriysk 83 C7
Staryy Oskol 84 D4
State College 149 D7
Statesville 155 B7
Stavanger 77 D7
Staveley 137 E4
Stavropol 85 D5
Stawell 134 C3
Stefansson Bay 168 A9
Steiermark □ 81 E8
Steinkjer 76 C8
Stendal 81 B6
Stephens Creek 134 B3
Stephenville 143 C8
Sterlitamak 97 D6
Stettin = Szczecin 82 B2
Stettiner Haff 81 B8
Stettler 141 C8
Steubenville 148 D5
Stevenage 79 F6
Stevenson → 134 A2
Stewart → 140 B6
Stewart, I. 167 G2
Stewart I. 137 G2
Steyr 81 D8

Stillwater *N.Z.* **137 E4**
Stillwater *U.S.A.* **152 A5**
Stînga Nistrului □ **83 E9**
Štip **92 D4**
Stirling **78 C5**
Stockerau **81 D9**
Stockholm **77 D9**
Stockport **79 E5**
Stockton **150 B2**
Stockton-on-Tees **79 D6**
Stoeng Treng **110 B3**
Stoke-on-Trent **79 E5**
Stokes Pt. **134 D3**
Stolac **90 C6**
Stolbovoy, Ostrov **98 B11**
Stolin **83 C8**
Stonehaven **78 C5**
Stony Tunguska = Tunguska, Podkamennaya → **98 C7**
Stora Lulevatten **76 B9**
Storavan **76 B9**
Store Bælt **77 D8**
Storm B. **134 D4**
Stormberge **131 E5**
Stornoway **78 B3**
Storozhynets **83 D7**
Storsjön **76 C8**
Storuman **76 B9**
Stowbtsy **83 B8**
Strahan **134 D4**
Stralsund **81 A7**
Stranraer **79 D4**
Strasbourg **89 B7**
Stratford *Canada* **148 C5**
Stratford *N.Z.* **136 C6**
Strathalbyn **134 C2**
Straubing **81 D7**
Streaky B. **134 B1**
Streaky Bay **134 B1**
Strezhevoy **97 C8**
Strimonas → **93 D4**
Strómboli **91 E5**
Stronsay **78 B5**
Stroud Road **135 B5**
Strumica **92 D4**
Stryy **83 D6**
Strzelecki Cr. → **134 A2**
Stuart Ra. **134 A1**
Stuttgart **80 D5**
Suakin **125 E6**
Subansiri → **113 D9**
Subi **111 D3**
Subotica **82 E4**
Suceava **83 E8**
Sucre **163 G5**
Sudan ■ **125 E4**
Sudbury **143 E5**
Sudd **125 G4**

Sudeten Mts. = Sudety **82 C3**
Sudety **82 C3**
Sudirman, Pegunungan **109 E5**
Sueca **87 C5**
Suez = El Suweis **124 C5**
Şuḩār **116 E4**
Sühbaatar **103 A9**
Suhl **80 C6**
Suihua **103 B13**
Suizhou **106 B2**
Sukadana **111 E3**
Sukagawa **101 E7**
Sukaraja **111 E4**
Sukhona → **96 C5**
Sukkur **114 F6**
Sukkur Barrage **114 F6**
Sukumo **101 G3**
Sula, Kepulauan **109 E3**
Sulaiman Range **114 D6**
Sulawesi **109 E2**
Sulawesi Sea = Celebes Sea **109 D2**
Sulima **127 G3**
Sulina **83 F9**
Sullana **162 D2**
Sultanpur **112 D4**
Sulu Arch. **108 C2**
Sulu Sea **108 C2**
Sulūq **124 B3**
Sulzberger Ice Shelf **168 B17**
Sumalata **109 D2**
Sumatera **111 D2**
Sumba **109 F1**
Sumba, Selat **109 F1**
Sumbawa **111 F5**
Sumbawa Besar **111 F5**
Sumbe **128 G2**
Summerside **143 E7**
Šumperk **82 D3**
Sumqayit **85 E6**
Sumter **155 C7**
Sumy **84 C3**
Sunbury **135 C3**
Sunda, Selat **111 F3**
Sundarbans **113 G7**
Sundargarh **112 F5**
Sunderland **79 D6**
Sundsvall **76 C9**
Sungaigerong **111 E2**
Sungailiat **111 E3**
Sungaipakning **111 D2**
Sungaipenuh **111 E2**
Sungurlu **118 B3**
Sunnyvale **150 B1**
Suntar **98 C9**
Supaul **112 D6**
Superior **147 B8**
Superior, L. **143 E5**
Suphan Dağı **118 C5**
Supiori **109 E5**

Suqian **104 F3**
Şūr *Lebanon* **118 D3**
Şūr *Oman* **117 F4**
Sura → **84 B6**
Surabaya **111 F4**
Surakarta **111 F4**
Surat *Australia* **135 A4**
Surat *India* **115 J8**
Surat Thani **110 C1**
Suratgarh **114 E8**
Surgut **97 C8**
Surigao **108 C3**
Suriapet **115 L11**
Suriname ■ **164 B2**
Suriname → **164 A2**
Surt **124 B2**
Surt, Khalīj **124 B2**
Surtsey **76 C1**
Suruga-Wan **101 F6**
Süsangerd **119 E7**
Susanville **144 F3**
Susquehanna → **149 E7**
Susques **166 A3**
Susunu **109 E4**
Susurluk **93 E7**
Sutherland **130 E4**
Sutherland Falls **137 F2**
Sutlej → **114 E7**
Suttsu **100 B7**
Suva **136 L12**
Suva Planina **92 C4**
Suwałki **83 A6**
Suwarrow Is. **137 L14**
Suweis, Khalīg el **124 C5**
Suwon **105 D7**
Suzdal **84 B5**
Suzhou **106 B6**
Suzu **101 E5**
Suzu-Misaki **101 E5**
Svealand **77 D9**
Sverdrup Chan. **142 B4**
Sverdrup Is. **142 B4**
Svishtov **92 C3**
Svislach **83 B7**
Svyetlahorsk **83 B9**
Swakopmund **130 C2**
Swan Hill **134 C3**
Swansea **79 F5**
Swaziland ■ **131 D6**
Sweden ■ **77 D9**
Sweetwater **152 C3**
Swellendam **130 E4**
Świdnica **82 C3**
Świdnik **83 C6**
Świebodzin **82 B2**
Świecie **82 B4**
Swift Current **141 C9**
Swindon **79 F6**
Świnoujście **82 B2**
Switzerland ■ **89 C8**
Sydney *Australia* **135 B5**
Sydney *Canada* **143 E7**
Syktyvkar **96 C6**

Sylhet **113 E8**
Sylt **80 A5**
Sym **97 C9**
Syracuse **149 C7**
Syrdarya → **97 E12**
Syria ■ **118 D4**
Syrian Desert = Shām, Bādiyat ash **119 D4**
Syzran **84 C6**
Szczecin **82 B2**
Szczecinek **82 B3**
Szczytno **82 B5**
Szechuan = Sichuan □ **102 E8**
Szeged **82 E5**
Székesfehérvár **82 E4**
Szekszárd **82 E4**
Szentes **82 E5**
Szolnok **82 E5**
Szombathely **82 E3**

T

Tabacal **166 A4**
Tabaco **108 B2**
Ṭābah **119 F5**
Tabas *Khorāsān, Iran* **117 C5**
Tabas *Yazd, Iran* **116 C4**
Tabatinga, Serra da **165 E5**
Tablas I. **108 B2**
Table B. **130 E3**
Table Mt. **130 E3**
Tábor **82 D2**
Tabora **129 F6**
Tabou **127 H4**
Tabrīz **118 C6**
Tabūk **119 E4**
Tacheng **102 B4**
Tacloban **108 B2**
Tacna **163 G4**
Tacoma **144 C2**
Tacuarembó **166 C4**
Tademaït, Plateau du **126 C6**
Tadjoura **121 E3**
Tadmor **137 D5**
Tadzhikistan = Tajikistan ■ **97 F8**
Taegu = Daegu **105 E8**
Taejŏn = Daejeon **105 D7**
Tafalla **87 A5**
Tafermaar **109 F4**
Taft **108 B3**
Taftan **114 E2**
Taftān, Kūh-e **117 D5**
Taga Dzong **113 D7**
Taganrog **85 D4**
Tagbilaran **108 C2**
Tagliamento → **90 B4**
Taguatinga **165 E5**
Tagum **108 C3**
Tagus = Tejo → **86 C1**

Tahakopa 137 G3
Tahan, Gunung 110 D2
Tahat 126 D7
Täherī 116 E3
Tahiti 137 L16
Tahoe, L. 144 G3
Tahoua 127 F7
Tahta 124 C5
Tahulandang 109 D3
Tahuna 109 D3
Tai'an 104 D2
T'aichung 107 E6
Taieri → 137 G4
Taihape 136 C6
Tailem Bend 134 C2
Taimyr Peninsula =
   Taymyr, Poluostrov
   98 B7
Tain 78 C4
T'ainan 107 F6
T'aipei 107 E6
Taiping 110 D2
Taitao, Pen. de 167 F1
T'aitung 107 F6
Taiwan ■ 107 F6
Taiwan Strait 107 E5
Taiyuan 103 D10
Taizhou 106 C6
Ta'izz 121 E3
Tajikistan ■ 97 F8
Tak 110 A1
Takada 101 E6
Takaka 137 D5
Takamatsu 101 F4
Takaoka 101 E5
Takapuna 136 B6
Takasaki 101 E6
Takayama 101 E5
Takengon 110 D1
Takeo 110 B2
Takeshima = Liancourt
   Rocks 101 E2
Täkestän 118 D7
Takhār □ 117 B7
Takikawa 100 B7
Taklamakan 102 D4
Talara 162 D2
Talas 97 E8
Talaud, Kepulauan
   108 D3
Talavera de la Reina
   86 C3
Talayan 108 C2
Talbragar → 135 B4
Talca 166 D2
Talcahuano 166 D2
Talcher 112 G5
Taldyqorghan 97 E8
Tälesh, Kühhä-ye 118 C7
Tali Post 125 G5
Talibon 108 B2
Taliwang 111 F5

Tall 'Afar 118 C5
Talladega 154 C4
Talladega 154 C4
Tallahassee 155 D5
Tallangatta 135 C4
Tallinn 84 B1
Taloyoak 140 B10
Taltal 166 B2
Talwood 135 A4
Talyawalka Cr. →
   134 B3
Tama Abu, Banjaran
   111 D5
Tamale 127 G5
Tamanrasset 126 D7
Tambacounda 127 F3
Tambelan, Kepulauan
   111 D3
Tambo de Mora 163 F3
Tambora 111 F5
Tambov 84 C5
Tâmega → 86 B1
Tamenglong 113 E9
Tamgak, Adrar 127 E7
Tamil Nadu □ 115 P10
Tampa 155 F6
Tampere 76 C10
Tampico 156 C5
Tamsagbulag 103 B11
Tamu 113 E10
Tana → Kenya 129 E8
Tana → Norway 76 A11
Tana, L. 125 F6
Tanabe 101 G4
Tanahbala 111 E1
Tanahgrogot 111 E5
Tanahjampea 109 F2
Tanahmasa 111 E1
Tanahmerah 109 F6
Tanami Desert 132 D5
Tanana → 141 B4
Tananarive =
   Antananarivo 131 B9
Tánaro → 90 B2
Tanch'ŏn 105 B8
Tandag 108 C3
Tandil 166 D5
Tando Adam 114 G6
Tandou L. 134 B3
Taneatua 136 C7
Tanezrouft 126 D6
Tanga 129 F7
Tanganyika, L. 129 F5
Tanger 126 A4
Tanggula Shan 102 E6
Tangier = Tanger 126 A4
Tangshan 104 C3
Tanimbar, Kepulauan
   109 F4
Tanjay 108 C2
Tanjung 111 E5
Tanjungbalai 111 D1

Tanjungbatu 111 D5
Tanjungpandan 111 E3
Tanjungpinang 111 D2
Tanjungredeb 111 D5
Tanjungselor 111 D5
Tanout 127 F7
Tanta 124 B5
Tanunda 134 B2
Tanzania ■ 129 F6
Taolanaro 131 D9
Taoudenni 126 D5
Taourirt 126 B4
Tapa 84 B1
Tapachula 156 D6
Tapah 110 D2
Tapajós → 164 C3
Tapaktuan 111 D1
Tapanui 137 F3
Tapauá → 163 E6
Tapeta 127 G4
Tapirapecó, Serra
   162 C6
Tapti → 115 J8
Tapuae-o-Uenuku
   137 D5
Tapul Group 108 C2
Taquari → 163 G7
Tara Australia 135 A5
Tara Russia 97 D8
Tara → 92 C2
Tarābulus Lebanon
   118 D3
Tarābulus Libya 124 B1
Tarakan 111 D5
Taranaki □ 136 C6
Taranaki, Mt. 136 C6
Tarancón 87 B4
Táranto 91 D6
Táranto, G. di 91 D6
Tarapacá 162 D5
Tararua Ra. 136 C6
Tarashcha 83 D10
Tarauacá 163 E4
Tarauacá → 163 E5
Tarawa 136 J12
Tarawera 136 C7
Tarawera, L. 136 C7
Taraz 97 E8
Tarazona 87 B5
Tarbagatay, Khrebet
   97 E9
Tarbela Dam 114 B8
Tarbes 88 E4
Tarcoola 134 B1
Tarcoon 135 B4
Taree 135 B5
Tarfaya 126 C2
Târgovişte 92 B5
Târgu Jiu 83 F6
Târgu Mureş 83 E7
Tarifa 86 D3
Tarija 166 A4
Tariku → 109 E5
Tarim He → 102 D5
Tarim Pendi 102 C4
Taritatu → 109 E5

Tarkhankut, Mys 85 D3
Tarko Sale 96 C8
Tarkwa 127 G5
Tarlac 108 A2
Tarma 163 F3
Tarn → 88 D4
Tarnobrzeg 82 C5
Tarnów 82 C5
Tarnowskie Góry 82 C4
Taroom 135 A4
Taroudannt 126 B4
Tarragona 87 B6
Tarsus 118 C3
Tartagal 166 A4
Tartu 84 B2
Ţarţūs 118 D3
Tarutung 111 D1
Tash-Kömür 97 E8
Tashkent = Toshkent
   97 E7
Tashtagol 97 D9
Tasman B. 137 D5
Tasman Mts. 137 D5
Tasman Pen. 134 D4
Tasmania □ 134 D4
Tatabánya 82 E4
Tatarbunary 83 F9
Tatarsk 97 D8
Tatarstan □ 97 D6
Tateyama 101 F6
Tathra 135 C4
Tatnam, C. 143 D4
Tatry 82 D4
Tatvan 118 C5
Taubaté 166 A7
Tauern 81 E7
Taumarunui 136 C6
Taumaturgo 163 E4
Taungdwingyi 113 G10
Taunggyi 113 G11
Taungup 113 H10
Taunton 79 F5
Taunus 80 C5
Taupo 136 C7
Taupo, L. 136 C6
Tauranga 136 B7
Tauranga Harb. 136 B7
Taurianova 91 E6
Taurus Mts. = Toros
   Dağları 118 C3
Tavda 97 D7
Tavda → 97 D7
Tavira 86 D2
Tavoy 110 B1
Tawau 110 D5
Tawi-tawi I. 108 C2
Tay → 78 C5
Tayabamba 163 E3
Taygetos Oros 93 F4
Taylakova 97 D8
Taymä 119 F4
Taymyr, Oz. 98 B8

Taymyr, Poluostrov
98 B7
Taytay **108 B1**
Taz ⇥ **96 C8**
Taza **126 B5**
Tazovskiy **96 C8**
Tbilisi **85 E5**
Tchad = Chad ■ **125 E2**
Tchad, L. **125 F1**
Tchibanga **128 E2**
Tczew **82 A4**
Te Anau, L. **137 F2**
Te Aroha **136 B6**
Te Awamutu **136 C6**
Te Kuiti **136 C6**
Te Puke **136 B7**
Te Waewae B. **137 G2**
Tebakang **111 D4**
Tébessa **126 A7**
Tebicuary ⇥ **166 B5**
Tebingtinggi **111 D1**
Tecuci **92 B6**
Tefé **162 D6**
Tegal **111 F3**
Tegucigalpa **157 E7**
Tehachapi **150 C3**
Teheran = Tehrān **116 C2**
Tehoru **109 E3**
Tehrān **116 C2**
Tehuantepec **157 D5**
Tehuantepec, G. de
157 D5
Tehuantepec, Istmo de
157 D6
Tejen **97 F7**
Tejo ⇥ **86 C1**
Tekapo, L. **137 E4**
Tekeli **97 E8**
Tekirdağ **92 D6**
Tekkali **112 H5**
Tel Aviv-Yafo **118 D3**
Tela **157 D7**
Telangana □ **115 K11**
Telavi **85 E6**
Teles Pires ⇥ **163 E7**
Telford **79 E5**
Telsen **167 E3**
Teluk Intan **111 D2**
Telukbutun **111 D3**
Telukdalam **111 D1**
Tema **127 G5**
Temerloh **111 D2**
Temir **97 E6**
Temirtau *Kazakhstan*
97 D8
Temirtau *Russia* **97 D9**
Tempe **151 D7**
Temple **152 D5**
Temuco **166 D2**
Temuka **137 F4**
Tenali **112 J3**
Tenaro, Akra **93 F4**
Tenasserim **110 B1**

Tenda, Colle di **90 B1**
Tendaho **121 E3**
Tenerife **126 C2**
Tengah, Kepulauan
111 F5
Tengchong **102 G7**
Tenggarong **111 E5**
Tengiz Köli **97 D7**
Tengzhou **104 E2**
Tenkasi **115 Q10**
Tennessee □ **154 B4**
Tennessee ⇥ **148 F1**
Tenom **110 C5**
Tenterfield **135 A5**
Teófilo Otoni **165 F5**
Tepa **109 F3**
Tepic **156 C4**
Teplice **82 C1**
Ter ⇥ **87 A7**
Téramo **90 C4**
Terang **134 C3**
Terebovlya **83 D7**
Terek ⇥ **85 E6**
Teresina **164 D5**
Terewah, L. **135 A4**
Teridgerie Cr. ⇥ **135 B4**
Términi Imerese **91 F4**
Termiz **97 F7**
Térmoli **90 C5**
Ternate **109 D3**
Terney **100 A5**
Terni **90 C4**
Ternopil **83 D7**
Terowie **134 B2**
Terracina **90 D4**
Terralba **91 E2**
Terrassa **87 B7**
Terre Haute **148 E2**
Terschelling **80 B3**
Teruel **87 B5**
Teryaweynya L. **134 B3**
Teshio **100 A7**
Teshio-Gawa ⇥ **100 A7**
Tesiyn Gol ⇥ **102 A6**
Teslin **140 B6**
Tessalit **126 D6**
Tetas, Pta. **166 A2**
Tete **131 B6**
Teterev ⇥ **83 C10**
Teteven **92 C5**
Tetiyev **83 D9**
Tétouan **126 A4**
Tetovo **92 C3**
Teuco ⇥ **166 B4**
Teun **109 F3**
Teutoburger Wald **80 B5**
Tevere ⇥ **90 D4**
Tewantin **135 A5**
Texarkana **153 C6**
Texas □ **152 D4**
Texas City **153 E6**

Texel **80 B3**
Teyvareh **117 C6**
Tezpur **113 D9**
Thabana Ntlenyana
131 D5
Thabazimbi **131 C5**
Thailand ■ **110 A2**
Thailand, G. of **110 B2**
Thakhek **110 A2**
Thal **114 C7**
Thalassery **115 P9**
Thallon **135 A4**
Thames **136 B6**
Thames ⇥ **79 F7**
Thandwe **113 H10**
Thane **115 K8**
Thanh Pho Ho Chi Minh
110 B3
Thanjavur **115 P11**
Thar Desert **114 F7**
Tharad **115 G7**
Thargomindah **135 A3**
Tharrawaddy **113 J10**
Thasos **93 D5**
Thaton **113 J11**
Thatta **115 G5**
Thaungdut **113 E10**
Thayetmyo **113 H10**
Thazi **113 G11**
The Bahamas ■ **158 A4**
The Gambia ■ **127 F2**
The Gulf = Persian Gulf
116 E2
The Hague =
's-Gravenhage **80 B3**
The Pas **141 C9**
The Wash **79 E8**
Thebes = Thiva **93 E4**
Theebine **135 A5**
Thermopylæ **93 E4**
Thessaloniki **93 D4**
Thessaloniki Kolpos
93 D4
Thetford **79 E7**
Thetford Mines **143 E6**
Thevenard **134 B1**
Thiel Mts. **168 C2**
Thiers **89 D5**
Thiès **127 F2**
Thika **129 E7**
Thimphu **113 D7**
Thionville **89 B7**
Thira = Santorini **93 F5**
Thiruvananthapuram
115 Q10
Thistle I. **134 C2**
Thiva **93 E4**
Þjórsá ⇥ **76 C1**
Thohoyandou **131 C6**
Thomas, L. **134 A2**
Thomasville *Ga.*, *U.S.A.*
155 D6

Thomasville *N.C.*, *U.S.A.*
155 B7
Thompson **141 C10**
Thrace **92 D6**
Three Gorges Dam
106 B1
Three Hummock I.
134 D3
Three Points, C. **127 H5**
Thrissur **115 P10**
Thunder Bay **143 E5**
Thung Song **110 C1**
Thunkar **113 D8**
Thüringer Wald **80 C6**
Thurles **79 E3**
Thurso **78 B5**
Thurston I. **168 B2**
Tian Shan **102 C3**
Tianjin **104 C2**
Tianmen **106 B2**
Tianshui **103 E9**
Tiaret **126 A6**
Tiber = Tevere ⇥ **90 D4**
Tiberias, L. = Yam
Kinneret **118 D3**
Tibesti **124 D2**
Tibet = Xizang Zizhiqu □
102 E5
Tibooburra **134 A3**
Tiburón, I. **156 B2**
Ticino ⇥ **90 B2**
Tiddim **113 F9**
Tidjikja **127 E3**
Tidore **109 D3**
Tieling **105 A5**
Tien Shan = Tian Shan
102 C3
Tientsin = Tianjin **104 C2**
Tierra de Campos **86 A3**
Tierra del Fuego, I.
Grande de **167 G3**
Tiétar ⇥ **86 C2**
Tifu **109 E3**
Tighina **83 E9**
Tigre ⇥ **162 D4**
Tigris = Dijlah, Nahr ⇥
119 E6
Tigyaing **113 F11**
Tijuana **156 A1**
Tikamgarh **115 G11**
Tikhoretsk **85 D5**
Tikrīt **118 D5**
Tiksi **98 B10**
Tilamuta **109 D2**
Tilburg **80 C3**
Tilos **93 F6**
Tilpa **135 B3**
Timaru **137 F4**
Timbuktu = Tombouctou
127 E5
Timimoun **126 C6**
Timiris, Râs **127 E2**

Timişoara 82 F5
Timmins 143 E5
Timok → 92 B4
Timor 109 F2
Timor Leste = East
  Timor ■ 109 F3
Tinaca Pt. 108 C3
Tindouf 126 C4
Tingo María 163 B3
Tinian 136 H9
Tinogasta 166 B3
Tinos 93 F5
Tintinara 134 C3
Tioman, Pulau 111 D2
Tipperary 79 E2
Tīrān 116 C2
Tiranë 92 B2
Tiraspol 83 E9
Tire 93 E6
Tirebolu 85 E4
Tiree 78 C3
Tirich Mir 114 A7
Tîrnavos 93 E4
Tirodi 115 J11
Tirol □ 80 E6
Tirso → 91 E2
Tiruchchirappalli 115 P11
Tirunelveli 115 Q10
Tirupati 115 N11
Tiruppur 115 P10
Tiruvannamalai 115 N11
Tisa → 92 B3
Tisdale 141 C9
Tit-Ary 98 B10
Titicaca, L. 163 G5
Titule 129 D5
Tivaouane 127 F2
Tívoli 90 D7
Tiwī 117 F4
Tizi-Ouzou 126 A6
Tlaxiaco 156 D5
Tlemcen 126 B5
Toamasina 131 B9
Toay 166 D4
Toba Kakar 114 D6
Tobago 159 D7
Tobelo 109 D3
Tobermory 78 C3
Toboali 111 E3
Toboli 109 E2
Tobol → 97 D7
Tobolsk 97 D7
Tobruk = Tubruq 124 B3
Tocantinópolis 165 E4
Tocantins □ 165 E4
Tocantins → 164 C4
Tocumwal 135 C4
Tocuyo → 162 A5
Todeli 109 E2
Todos os Santos, B. de
  165 E6
Togian, Kepulauan
  109 E2

Togliatti 84 C6
Togo ■ 127 G6
Toinya 125 G4
Tokala 109 E2
Tōkamachi 101 E6
Tokanui 137 G3
Tokarahi 137 F4
Tokat 118 B4
Tokdo = Liancourt Rocks
  101 E2
Tokelau Is. ☑ 137 K13
Tokmak 97 E8
Tokushima 101 F4
Tōkyō 101 F6
Tolaga Bay 136 C8
Toledo Spain 86 C3
Toledo U.S.A. 148 D4
Toledo, Montes de 86 C3
Toliara 131 C8
Tolima 162 C3
Tolitoli 109 D2
Tolo, Teluk 109 E2
Toluca 156 D5
Tomakomai 100 B7
Tomar 86 C1
Tomaszów Mazowiecki
  82 C4
Tombouctou 127 E5
Tombua 130 B2
Tomelloso 86 C4
Tomini 109 D2
Tomini, Teluk 109 E2
Tomsk 97 D9
Tonantins 162 D5
Tondano 109 D2
Tonekābon 116 B2
Tonga ■ 137 L13
Tonga Trench 137 L13
Tongariro △ 136 C6
Tongchuan 103 D9
Tonghua 105 B6
Tongjiang 103 B14
Tongliao 104 A5
Tongling 106 B4
Tongoy 166 C2
Tongsa Dzong 113 D8
Tongue → 146 B2
Tonk 114 F9
Tonkin, G. of 103 H9
Tonlé Sap 110 B2
Toompine 135 A3
Toora 135 C4
Toowoomba 135 A5
Topeka 147 F7
Topolobampo 156 B3
Torata 163 G4
Torbalı 93 E6
Torbat-e Heydārīyeh
  116 C4
Torbat-e Jām 117 C5
Torbay □ 79 F5
Tordesillas 86 B3

Torgau 81 C7
Torino 90 B1
Torit 125 H5
Tormes → 86 B2
Torneälven → 76 B10
Torneträsk 76 B9
Tornio 76 E12
Tornquist 166 D4
Toro, Cerro del 166 B3
Toronto 143 E6
Toropets 84 B3
Tororo 129 D6
Toros Dağları 118 C3
Torre de Moncorvo 86 B2
Torre del Greco 91 D5
Torrejón de Ardoz 86 B4
Torrelavega 86 A3
Torremolinos 86 D3
Torrens, L. 134 B2
Torrent 87 C5
Torreón 156 B4
Torres Vedras 86 C1
Torrevieja 87 D5
Tórshavn 74 C4
Tortosa 87 B6
Tortosa, C. 87 B6
Torūd 116 C3
Toruń 82 B4
Tosa-Wan 101 G3
Toscana □ 90 C3
Toshkent 97 E7
Tostado 166 B4
Tosya 118 B3
Totma 84 A5
Totten Glacier 168 A12
Tottenham 135 B4
Tottori 101 F4
Toubkal, Djebel 126 B4
Tougan 127 F5
Touggourt 126 B7
Toul 89 B6
Toulon 89 E6
Toulouse 88 E4
Toummo 124 D1
Toungoo 113 H11
Touraine 88 C4
Tourcoing 89 A5
Touriñán, C. 86 A1
Tournai 80 C2
Tournon-sur-Rhône
  89 D6
Tours 88 C4
Towada 100 C7
Towada-Ko 100 C7
Townsville 133 D8
Tōya-Ko 100 B7
Toyama 101 E5
Toyama-Wan 101 E5
Toyohashi 101 F5
Toyooka 101 F4
Toyota 101 F5
Tozeur 126 B7

Trabzon 118 B4
Trafalgar, C. 86 D2
Trail 141 D8
Tralee 79 E2
Trancas 166 B3
Trang 110 C1
Trangan 109 F4
Trangie 135 B4
Trani 90 D6
Transantarctic Mts.
  168 C3
Transilvania 83 F7
Transnistria = Stînga
  Nistrului □ 83 E9
Trápani 91 E4
Traralgon 135 C4
Trasimeno, L. 90 C4
Traun 81 D8
Travemünde 81 B6
Travers, Mt. 137 E5
Travnik 90 B6
Trébbia → 90 B2
Trebíč 82 D2
Trebinje 90 C7
Treinta y Tres 166 C6
Trelew 167 E3
Tremp 87 A6
Trenque Lauquen 166 D4
Trent → 79 E6
Trento 90 A3
Trenton 149 D8
Tres Arroyos 166 D4
Três Lagoas 165 G3
Tres Montes, C. 167 F1
Tres Puntas, C. 167 F3
Três Rios 165 G5
Treviso 90 B4
Triabunna 134 D4
Trida 135 B4
Trier 80 D4
Trieste 90 B4
Triglav 90 A4
Trikala 93 E3
Trikora, Puncak 109 E5
Trinidad Bolivia 163 F6
Trinidad Cuba 158 B3
Trinidad Uruguay 166 C5
Trinidad U.S.A. 152 A1
Trinidad & Tobago ■
  159 D7
Trinity → 153 E6
Trinity B. 143 E8
Trinity Range 144 F4
Trinkitat 125 E6
Tripoli = Tarābulus
  Lebanon 118 D3
Tripoli = Tarābulus Libya
  124 B1
Tripoli 93 F4
Tripura □ 113 F8
Trivandrum =
  Thiruvananthapuram
  115 Q10

Troglav 90 C6
Trois-Rivières 143 E6
Troitsko Pechorsk 96 C6
Trollhättan 77 D8
Tromsø 76 B9
Tronador, Mte. 167 E2
Trondheim 76 C8
Trondheimsfjorden 76 C8
Trout L. 140 B7
Trouville-sur-Mer 88 B4
Troy Turkey 93 E6
Troy Ala., U.S.A. 154 D5
Troy N.Y., U.S.A. 149 C9
Troyes 89 B6
Trudovoye 100 B3
Trujillo Honduras 157 D7
Trujillo Peru 163 E3
Trujillo Spain 86 C3
Trujillo Venezuela 162 B4
Truk 136 J10
Trundle 135 B4
Truro Canada 143 E7
Truro U.K. 79 F4
Truskavets 83 D6
Trutnov 82 C2
Tsaratanana 131 B9
Tsetserleg 102 B8
Tshabong 130 D4
Tshane 130 C4
Tshela 128 E2
Tshikapa 128 F4
Tshwane = Pretoria
  131 D5
Tsiigehtchic 140 B6
Tsimlyanskoye Vdkhr.
  85 D5
Tsingtao = Qingdao
  104 D4
Tskhinvali 85 E5
Tsna → 84 C5
Tsuchiura 101 E7
Tsugaru-Kaikyō 100 C7
Tsumeb 130 B3
Tsuruga 101 F5
Tsuruoka 100 D6
Tsushima 101 F1
Tsuyama 101 F4
Tsyelyakhany 83 B7
Tual 109 F4
Tuamotu, Îs. 137 L16
Tuamotu Ridge 137 M17
Tuao 108 A2
Tuapse 85 E4
Tuatapere 137 G2
Tubarão 166 B7
Tübingen 80 D5
Tubruq 124 B3
Tubuaï, Îs. 137 M16
Tucacas 162 A5
Tucson 151 D7
Tucumcari 152 B2
Tucupita 162 B6
Tucuruí 164 C4

Tucuruí, Represa de
  164 C4
Tudela 87 A5
Tudmur 118 D4
Tuguegarao 108 A2
Tui 86 A1
Tukangbesi, Kepulauan
  109 F2
Tuktoyaktuk 140 B6
Tukuyu 129 F6
Tula 84 C4
Tülak 117 C5
Tulcán 162 C3
Tulcea 83 F9
Tulchyn 83 D9
Tulita 140 B7
Tullamore Australia
  135 B4
Tullamore Ireland 79 E3
Tulle 88 D4
Tulsa 153 A6
Tuluá 162 C3
Tumaco 162 C3
Tumatumari 162 B7
Tumba, L. 128 E3
Tumbarumba 135 C4
Tumbes 162 D2
Tumby Bay 134 B2
Tumeremo 162 B6
Tumkur 115 N10
Tump 114 F3
Tumpat 110 C2
Tumu 127 F5
Tumucumaque, Serra
  164 B3
Tumut 135 C4
Tuncurry 135 B5
Tundzha → 92 D6
Tungabhadra →
  115 M11
Tunguska, Nizhnyaya →
  98 C6
Tunguska,
  Podkamennaya →
  98 C7
Tunis 122 A1
Tunisia ■ 122 B1
Tunja 162 B4
Tunuyán → 166 C3
Tupelo 154 B3
Tupinambarana, I.
  162 D7
Tupiza 166 A3
Tupungato, Cerro 166 C3
Túquerres 162 C3
Tura 98 C8
Turabah 119 E5
Türān 116 C4
Turayf 119 E4
Turek 82 B4
Türgovishte 92 C6
Turgutlu 93 E6

Turhal 118 B4
Turia → 87 C5
Turiaçu 164 C4
Turiaçu → 164 C4
Turin = Torino 90 B1
Turkana, L. 129 D7
Turkestan = Türkistan
  97 E7
Turkey ■ 118 C3
Türkistan 97 E7
Türkmenabat 97 F7
Türkmenbashi 97 E6
Turkmenistan ■ 97 F6
Turks & Caicos Is. ☑
  159 B5
Turku 77 C10
Turnagain, C. 136 D7
Turneffe Is. 157 D7
Turnhout 80 C3
Turnu Măgurele 92 C5
Turnu Roşu, P. 83 F7
Turpan 102 C5
Turpan Pendi 102 C5
Turukhansk 98 C6
Tuscaloosa 154 C4
Tuscany = Toscana □
  90 C3
Tuticorin 115 Q11
Tutóia 164 C5
Tutong 110 D4
Tutrakan 92 B6
Tuttlingen 80 E5
Tutuala 109 F3
Tutuila 137 L13
Tutume 131 C5
Tuvalu ■ 136 K12
Tuxpan 156 C5
Tuxtla Gutiérrez 157 D6
Tuz Gölü 118 C3
Tūz Khurmātū 118 D6
Tuzla 92 B7
Tver 84 B4
Tweed Heads 135 A5
Twin Falls 145 E6
Twofold B. 135 C4
Tyachiv 83 D6
Tychy 83 C5
Tyler 153 C6
Tyre = Sūr 118 D3
Tyrol = Tirol □ 80 E6
Tyrrell → 134 C3
Tyrrell, L. 134 C3
Tyrrhenian Sea 91 E4
Tyumen 97 D7
Tzaneen 131 C6

U

U.S.A. = United States of
  America ■ 139 F10
U.S. Virgin Is. ☑ 159 C7
Uatumã → 162 D7
Uaupés 162 D5
Uaupés → 162 C5

Ubá 165 G5
Ubaitaba 165 E6
Ubauro 114 E6
Ube 101 G2
Úbeda 86 C4
Uberaba 165 F4
Uberlândia 165 F4
Ubon Ratchathani
  110 A2
Ubort → 83 B9
Ubundu 129 E5
Ucayali → 162 D4
Uchiura-Wan 100 B7
Udagamandalam
  115 P10
Udaipur 115 G8
Udaipur Garhi 112 D6
Udgir 115 K10
Udhampur 114 C9
Údine 90 A4
Udmurtia □ 96 D6
Udon Thani 110 A2
Udupi 115 N9
Uele → 129 D4
Uelzen 80 B6
Ufa 97 D6
Ugab → 130 C2
Ugalla → 129 F6
Uganda ■ 129 D6
Ugljan 90 B5
Uíge 128 F2
Uinta Mts. 145 F8
Uitenhage 131 E5
Ujjain 115 H9
Ujung Pandang =
  Makassar 109 F1
Ukhrul 113 E10
Ukhta 96 C6
Ukraine ■ 85 D3
Ulaanbaatar 103 B9
Ulaangom 102 A6
Ulaanjirem 103 B9
Ulan Bator = Ulaanbaatar
  103 B9
Ulan Ude 98 D8
Ulcinj 92 D2
Ulhasnagar 115 K8
Uliastay 102 B7
Ulladulla 135 C5
Ullapool 78 C4
Ulleungdo 105 D9
Ulm 80 D5
Ulmarra 135 A5
Ulsan 105 E8
Ulster □ 79 D3
Ulubat Gölü 93 D7
Uludağ 93 D7
Ulungur He → 102 B5
Uluru 132 F5
Ulutau 97 E7
Ulverstone 134 D4
Ulyanovsk 84 C6

Umala 163 G5
Uman 83 D10
Umaria 112 F3
Umarkot 115 G6
Umbrella Mts. 137 F3
Umeå 76 C10
Umeälven ➔ 76 C10
Umera 109 E3
Umlazi 131 E6
Umm al Qaywayn 116 E3
Umm Lajj 119 F4
Umm Ruwaba 125 F5
Umnak I. 141 C3
Umniati ➔ 131 B5
Umuarama 165 G3
Umzimvubu 131 E5
Una ➔ 90 B6
Unalaska 141 C3
Uncía 163 G5
Underbool 134 C3
Ungarie 135 B4
Ungarra 134 B2
Ungava, Pén. d' 142 C5
Ungava B. 142 D7
Ungheni 83 E8
Unimak I. 141 C3
União da Vitória 166 B6
United Arab Emirates ■
116 F3
United Kingdom ■ 79 D5
United States of
America ■ 139 F10
Unnao 112 D3
Unst 78 A6
Ünye 118 B4
Upata 162 B6
Upemba, L. 129 F5
Upington 130 D4
Upper Hutt 137 D6
Upper Volta = Burkina
Faso ■ 127 F5
Uppsala 77 D9
Ur 119 E6
Ural = Zhayyq ➔ 97 E6
Ural 135 B4
Ural Mts. = Uralskie Gory
96 D6
Uralla 135 B5
Uralsk = Oral 84 C7
Uralskie Gory 96 D6
Uray 97 C7
Urbana 148 D1
Urbino 90 C4
Urbión, Picos de 87 A4
Urcos 163 F4
Urewera △ 136 C7
Urfa = Sanliurfa 118 C4
Urganch 97 E7
Uribia 162 A4
Urla 93 E6
Urmia = Orūmīyeh
118 C6

Urubamba ➔ 163 F4
Urucará 162 D7
Uruçuí 164 D5
Uruguai ➔ 166 B6
Uruguaiana 166 B5
Uruguay ■ 166 C5
Uruguay ➔ 166 C5
Urumchi = Ürümqi
102 C5
Ürümqi 102 C5
Ürzhar 97 E9
Usakos 130 C3
Usedom 81 B8
Ushibuka 101 G2
Üshtöbe 97 E8
Ushuaia 167 G3
Usman 84 C4
Uspallata, P. de 166 C3
Ussuriysk 99 E11
Ust-Ishim 97 D8
Ust-Kuyga 99 B11
Ust-Olenek 98 B10
Ust-Port 96 C9
Ust-Tsilma 96 C6
Ústí nad Labem 82 C2
Ústica 91 E4
Ustinov = Izhevsk 96 D6
Ustyurt Plateau 97 E6
Usu 102 C4
Usumacinta ➔ 157 D6
Uta 109 E5
Utah □ 145 G8
Utiariti 163 F7
Utica 149 C8
Utrecht 80 B3
Utrera 86 D3
Utsunomiya 101 E6
Uttar Pradesh □ 114 F11
Uttaradit 110 A2
Uusikaupunki 77 C10
Uvat 97 D7
Uvinza 129 F6
Uvira 129 E5
Uvs Nuur 102 A6
Uwajima 101 G3
Uyuni 163 H5
Uzbekistan ■ 97 E7
Uzerche 88 D4
Uzh ➔ 83 C10
Uzhhorod 83 D6
Užice 92 C2
Uzunköprü 92 D6

V

Vaal ➔ 130 D4
Vaasa 76 C10
Vác 82 E4
Vadakara 115 P9
Vadodara 115 H8
Vadsø 76 D13

Vaduz 89 C8
Vahsel B. 168 B5
Vakh ➔ 97 C8
Val-d'Or 143 E6
Valahia 92 B5
Valandovo 92 D4
Valcheta 167 E3
Valdayskaya
Vozvyshennost 84 B3
Valdepeñas 86 C4
Valdés, Pen. 167 E4
Valdez 141 B5
Valdivia 167 D2
Valdosta 155 D6
Valença 92 B5
Valença do Piauí 164 D5
Valence 89 D6
Valencia Spain 87 C5
Valencia Venezuela
162 A5
Valencia □ 87 C5
Valencia, G. de 87 C6
Valencia de Alcántara
86 C2
Valencia I. 79 F1
Valenciennes 89 A5
Valentim, Sa. do 164 D5
Valera 162 B4
Valjevo 92 B2
Valkenswaard 80 C3
Valladolid Mexico 157 C7
Valladolid Spain 86 B3
Valle de la Pascua
162 B5
Valledupar 162 A4
Vallejo 144 G2
Vallenar 166 B2
Valletta 91 G5
Valls 87 B6
Valognes 88 B3
Valozhyn 83 A8
Valparaíso 166 C2
Vals, Tanjung 109 F5
Valsad 115 J8
Valverde del Camino
86 D2
Van 118 C5
Van, L. = Van Gölü
118 C5
Van Gölü 118 C5
Van Rees, Pegunungan
109 E5
Vanadzor 85 E5
Vancouver Canada
141 D7
Vancouver U.S.A. 144 D2
Vancouver I. 141 D7
Vanderhoof 141 C7
Vangaindrano 131 C9
Vännäs 76 C9
Vannes 88 C2
Vanrhynsdorp 130 E3
Vantaa ➔ 77 C11

Vanua Levu 136 L12
Vanuatu ■ 136 L11
Vapnyarka 83 D9
Varanasi 112 E4
Varangerfjorden 76 A11
Varaždin 90 A6
Varberg 77 D8
Vardak □ 117 C7
Varese 90 B2
Varna 92 C6
Varzaneh 116 C3
Vasa Barris ➔ 165 E6
Vasilevichi 83 B9
Västerås 77 D9
Västerdalälven ➔ 76 C8
Västervik 77 D9
Vasto 90 C5
Vasylkiv 83 C10
Vatican City ■ 90 D4
Vatnajökull 76 C2
Vatra-Dornei 83 E7
Vättern 77 D8
Vawkavysk 83 B7
Vaygach, Ostrov 96 C6
Vedea ➔ 92 C5
Vega 76 B8
Vegreville 141 C8
Vejer de la Frontera
86 D3
Velebit Planina 90 B5
Veles 92 D3
Vélez-Málaga 86 D3
Vélez Rubio 87 D4
Velhas ➔ 165 F5
Velika Kapela 90 B5
Velikaya ➔ 84 B2
Veliki Ustyug 84 A6
Velikiy Novgorod 84 B3
Velikiye Luki 84 B3
Veliko Tŭrnovo 92 C5
Velikonda Range
115 M11
Velletri 90 D4
Vellore 115 N11
Venado Tuerto 166 C4
Vendée □ 88 C3
Vendôme 88 C4
Venézia 90 B4
Venézia, G. di 90 B4
Venezuela ■ 162 B5
Venezuela, G. de 162 A4
Vengurla 115 M8
Venice = Venézia 90 B4
Venkatapuram 112 H3
Ventotene 91 D4
Ventoux, Mt. 89 D6
Ventspils 84 B1
Venturaí ➔ 162 C5
Ventura 150 C3
Venus B. 135 C4
Vera Argentina 166 B4
Vera Spain 87 D5

Veracruz 156 **D5**
Veraval 115 **J7**
Verbánia 90 **B2**
Vercelli 90 **B2**
Verde � 167 **E3**
Verden 80 **B5**
Verdun 89 **B6**
Vereeniging 131 **D5**
Verga, C. 127 **F3**
Veria 93 **D4**
Verín 86 **B2**
Verkhnevilyuysk 98 **C10**
Verkhniy Baskunchak 85 **D6**
Verkhoyansk 99 **C11**
Verkhoyanskiy Khrebet 99 **C10**
Vermont □ 149 **C9**
Vernon Canada 141 **C8**
Vernon U.S.A. 152 **B4**
Verona 90 **B3**
Versailles 88 **B5**
Vert, C. 127 **F2**
Verviers 80 **C3**
Veselovskoye Vdkhr. 85 **D5**
Vesoul 89 **C7**
Vesterålen 76 **B9**
Vestfjorden 76 **B8**
Vesuvio 91 **D5**
Veszprém 82 **E3**
Vettore, Mte. 90 **C4**
Vezhen 92 **C5**
Viacha 163 **G5**
Viamão 166 **C6**
Viana 164 **C5**
Viana do Alentejo 86 **C2**
Viana do Castelo 86 **B1**
Vianópolis 165 **F4**
Viaréggio 90 **C3**
Vibo Valéntia 91 **E6**
Vic 87 **B7**
Vicenza 90 **B3**
Vichy 89 **C5**
Vicksburg 153 **C8**
Victor 115 **J7**
Victor Harbor 134 **C2**
Victoria Canada 141 **D7**
Victoria Chile 166 **D2**
Victoria □ 134 **C3**
Victoria, L. Africa 129 **E6**
Victoria, L. Australia 134 **B3**
Victoria, Mt. 113 **G9**
Victoria de Durango = Durango 156 **C4**
Victoria Falls 131 **B5**
Victoria I. 140 **A8**
Victoria Ld. 168 **B14**
Victorica 166 **D3**
Vicuña 166 **C2**
Vidin 92 **C4**

Vidisha 115 **H10**
Viedma 167 **E4**
Viedma, L. 167 **F2**
Vienna = Wien 81 **D9**
Vienne 89 **D6**
Vienne � 88 **C4**
Vientiane 110 **A2**
Vierzon 88 **C5**
Vietnam ■ 110 **A3**
Vigan 108 **A2**
Vigévano 90 **B2**
Vigia 164 **C4**
Vigo 86 **A1**
Vijayawada 112 **J3**
Víjosë � 93 **D2**
Vikna 76 **C8**
Vila do Bispo 86 **D1**
Vila Franca de Xira 86 **C1**
Vila Nova de Gaia 86 **B1**
Vila Real Portugal 86 **B2**
Vila-Real Spain 87 **C5**
Vila Real de Santo António 86 **D2**
Vila Velha 165 **G5**
Vilagarcía de Arousa 86 **A1**
Vilanculos 131 **C7**
Vilanova i la Geltrú 87 **B6**
Vileyka 83 **A8**
Vilhelmina 76 **C9**
Vilhena 163 **F6**
Vilkitskogo, Proliv 98 **B8**
Villa Angela 166 **B4**
Villa Bella 163 **F5**
Villa de María 166 **B4**
Villa Dolores 166 **C3**
Villa Hayes 166 **B5**
Villa María 166 **C4**
Villa Mazán 166 **B3**
Villa Montes 166 **A4**
Villa Ocampo 166 **B5**
Villacarrillo 86 **C4**
Villach 81 **E7**
Villaguay 166 **C5**
Villahermosa 157 **D6**
Villajoyosa 87 **C5**
Villalba 86 **A2**
Villanueva de la Serena 86 **C3**
Villarrica Chile 167 **D2**
Villarrica Paraguay 166 **B5**
Villarrobledo 87 **C4**
Villavicencio 162 **C4**
Villaviciosa 86 **A3**
Villazón 166 **A3**
Villena 87 **C5**
Villeneuve-d'Ascq 89 **A5**
Villeneuve-sur-Lot 88 **D4**
Villingen-Schwenningen 80 **D5**

Vilnius 84 **C2**
Vilyuy � 99 **C10**
Vilyuysk 99 **C10**
Viña del Mar 166 **C2**
Vinarós 87 **B6**
Vindhya Ra. 115 **H10**
Vineland 149 **E8**
Vinkovci 90 **B7**
Vinnytsya 83 **D9**
Viqueque 109 **F3**
Virac 108 **B2**
Viramgam 115 **H8**
Virden 141 **D9**
Vire 88 **B3**
Vírgenes, C. 167 **G3**
Virgin Is. (British) ☑ 159 **C7**
Virgin Is. (U.S.) ☑ 159 **C7**
Virginia 131 **D5**
Virginia □ 149 **F6**
Virginia Beach 149 **F8**
Virovitica 90 **B6**
Virudunagar 115 **Q10**
Vis 90 **C6**
Visalia 150 **B3**
Visayan Sea 108 **B2**
Visby 77 **D3**
Viscount Melville Sd. 142 **B3**
Višegrad 90 **C7**
Viseu Brazil 164 **C4**
Viseu Portugal 86 **B2**
Vishakhapatnam 112 **J4**
Viso, Mte. 90 **B1**
Viterbo 90 **C4**
Viti Levu 136 **L12**
Vitigudino 86 **B2**
Vitória 165 **G5**
Vitória da Conquista 165 **E5**
Vitoria-Gasteiz 87 **A4**
Vitsyebsk 84 **B3**
Vittória 91 **F5**
Vittório Véneto 90 **B4**
Vivero 86 **A2**
Vize 92 **D6**
Vizianagaram 112 **H4**
Vladikavkaz 85 **E5**
Vladimir 84 **B5**
Vladivostok 99 **E11**
Vlissingen 80 **C2**
Vlorë 93 **D2**
Vltava � 82 **C2**
Vogelsberg 80 **C5**
Voghera 90 **B2**
Vohimena, Tanjon' i 131 **D9**
Voi 129 **E7**
Voiron 89 **D6**
Vojvodina □ 92 **B2**
Volga � 85 **D6**

Volga Hts. = Privolzhskaya Vozvyshennost 84 **C6**
Volgodonsk 85 **D5**
Volgograd 85 **D5**
Volgogradskoye Vdkhr. 84 **C6**
Volkhov � 84 **A3**
Volochanka 98 **B7**
Volodymyr-Volynskyy 83 **C7**
Vologda 84 **B4**
Volos 93 **E4**
Volovets 83 **D6**
Volsk 84 **C6**
Volta, L. 127 **G6**
Volta Redonda 165 **G5**
Volterra 90 **C3**
Volturno � 90 **D4**
Volzhskiy 85 **D5**
Voreios Sporades 93 **E4**
Vorkuta 96 **C7**
Voronezh 84 **C4**
Vosges 89 **B7**
Vostok I. 137 **L15**
Vouga � 86 **B1**
Voznesensk 85 **D3**
Vrangelya, Ostrov 99 **B15**
Vranje 92 **C3**
Vratsa 92 **C4**
Vrbas � 90 **B6**
Vršac 92 **B3**
Vryburg 130 **D4**
Vryheid 131 **D6**
Vukovar 90 **B7**
Vulcan 83 **F6**
Vulcanești 83 **F9**
Vulcano 91 **E5**
Vung Tau 110 **B3**
Vyatka = Kirov 96 **D5**
Vyatskiye Polyany 84 **B7**
Vyazma 84 **B3**
Vyborg 96 **C3**
Vychegda � 96 **C5**
Vychodné Beskydy 83 **D5**
Vylkove 83 **F9**
Vynohradiv 83 **D6**
Vyshniy Volochek 84 **B3**
Vyškov 82 **D3**

W

Waal � 80 **C3**
Wabash � 148 **F1**
Waco 152 **B5**
Wad Hamid 125 **E5**
Wad Medanî 125 **F5**
Waddington, Mt. 141 **C7**
Waddy Pt. 135 **A5**
Wadi Halfa 124 **D5**
Wafangdian 104 **C4**
Wafrah 119 **E6**

Wager B. 142 C5
Wagga Wagga 135 C4
Waghete 109 E5
Wah 114 C8
Wahai 109 E3
Waiau → 137 E5
Waibeem 109 E4
Waigeo 109 E4
Waihi 136 B6
Waihou → 136 B6
Waikabubak 109 F1
Waikaremoana, L.
136 C7
Waikari 137 E5
Waikerie 134 B2
Waikokopu 136 C7
Waikouaiti 137 F4
Waimakariri → 137 E5
Waimate 137 F4
Wainganga → 115 K11
Waingapu 109 F2
Waiouru 136 C6
Waipara 137 E5
Waipawa 136 C7
Waipiro 136 C8
Waipoua Forest 136 A5
Waipu 136 A6
Waipukurau 136 D7
Wairakei 136 C6
Wairarapa, L. 137 D6
Wairoa 136 C7
Waitaki → 137 F4
Waitangi 136 A6
Waitara 136 C6
Waitomo Caves 136 C6
Waiuku 136 B6
Wajima 101 E5
Wajir 129 D8
Wakasa-Wan 101 F4
Wakatipu, L. 137 F3
Wakayama 101 F4
Wakefield 137 D5
Wakkanai 100 A7
Wakool 135 C3
Wakool → 134 C3
Wakre 109 E4
Wałbrzych 82 C3
Walcha 135 B5
Wales □ 79 E4
Walgett 135 A4
Walgreen Coast 168 B1
Walla Walla 144 C4
Wallachia = Valahia
92 B5
Wallal 135 A4
Wallaroo 134 B2
Wallis & Futuna, Îs. ☑
136 L13
Wallowa Mts. 144 D5
Wallumbilla 135 A4

Walvis Bay 130 C2
Wamba 129 D5
Wamena 109 E5
Wamulan 109 E3
Wana 114 C6
Wanaaring 135 A3
Wanaka 137 F3
Wanaka, L. 137 F3
Wandoan 135 A4
Wanganella 135 C3
Wanganui 136 C6
Wangaratta 135 C4
Wangary 134 B2
Wangerooge 80 B4
Wangiwangi 109 F2
Warangal 115 L11
Waratah 134 D4
Waratah B. 135 C4
Warburton 135 C4
Warburton → 134 A2
Ward 137 D6
Ward → 135 A4
Wardha 115 J11
Wardha → 115 K11
Warialda 135 A5
Warkopi 109 E4
Warner Mts. 144 F3
Warracknabeal 134 C3
Warragul 135 C4
Warrego → 135 B4
Warren Australia 135 B4
Warren U.S.A. 148 C4
Warri 127 G7
Warrina 134 A2
Warrington U.K. 79 E5
Warrington U.S.A.
154 D4
Warrnambool 134 C3
Warsaw = Warszawa
82 B5
Warszawa 82 B5
Warta → 82 B2
Waru 109 E4
Warwick 135 A5
Wasatch Ra. 145 F8
Wash, The 79 E7
Washim 115 J10
Washington 149 E7
Washington □ 144 C3
Washington, Mt. 149 B10
Wasian 109 E4
Wasior 109 E4
Wasiri 109 F3
Waskaganish 143 D6
Wasserkuppe 80 C5
Watampone 109 E2
Waterbury 149 D9
Waterford 79 E3
Waterloo 147 D8
Watertown 149 C8
Waterville 149 B11
Watford 79 F6

Watrous 141 C9
Watsa 129 D5
Watson Lake 140 B7
Watsonville 150 B2
Wattiwarriganna Cr. →
134 A2
Watubela, Kepulauan
109 E4
Wau 125 G4
Wauchope 135 B5
Waukegan 148 C2
Waukesha 148 C1
Wausau 147 C10
Wauwatosa 148 C2
Waverley 136 C6
Wāw al Kabīr 124 C2
Waxahachie 153 C5
Waycross 155 D6
Wazirabad 114 C9
We 110 C1
Weda 109 D3
Weda, Teluk 109 D3
Weddell I. 167 G4
Weddell Sea 168 A4
Wedderburn 134 C3
Wee Waa 135 B4
Weiden 81 D7
Weifang 104 D3
Weihai 104 D5
Weimar 81 C6
Weipa 133 C7
Weir → 135 A4
Wejherowo 82 A4
Welkom 131 D5
Wellesley Is. 132 D6
Wellington Australia
135 B4
Wellington N.Z. 137 D6
Wellington, I. 167 F1
Wellington, L. 135 C4
Wellington Chan. 142 B4
Wels 81 D8
Welshpool 79 E5
Wemindji 143 D6
Wenatchee 144 C3
Wenchi 127 G5
Wendesi 109 E4
Wensu 102 C4
Wentworth 134 B3
Wenut 109 E4
Wenzhou 106 D6
Weri 109 E4
Werra → 80 C5
Werrimull 134 B3
Werris Creek 135 B5
Weser → 80 B5
West Bank ■ 118 D3
West Bengal =
Paschimbanga □
112 F7
West Falkland 167 G4
West Ice Shelf 168 A11

West Palm Beach 155 F7
West Pt. 134 C2
West Virginia □ 148 E5
West Wyalong 135 B4
Westall, Pt. 134 B1
Westbury 134 D4
Westerland 80 A5
Western Australia □
132 F3
Western Ghats 115 N9
Western Sahara ■
126 D3
Western Samoa =
Samoa ■ 137 L13
Westerwald 80 C4
Westland △ 137 E4
Westland Bight 137 E4
Weston-super-Mare
79 F5
Westport Ireland 79 E2
Westport N.Z. 137 D4
Westray 78 B5
Wetar 109 F3
Wetaskiwin 141 C8
Wetzlar 80 C5
Wexford 79 E3
Weyburn 141 D9
Weymouth 79 F5
Wha Ti 140 B8
Whakaari 136 B7
Whakatane 136 B7
Whale Cove 140 B10
Whales, B. of 168 B16
Whangamata 136 B6
Whangamomona 136 C6
Whanganui △ 136 C6
Whangarei 136 A6
Whangarei Harb. 136 A6
Wheeling 148 D5
White → Ark., U.S.A.
153 C8
White → Ind., U.S.A.
148 E2
White Cliffs 134 B3
White Nile = Nîl el
Abyaḍ → 125 E5
White Russia = Belarus ■
84 C2
White Sea = Beloye More
76 B13
Whitecliffs 137 E4
Whitehaven 79 D5
Whitehorse 140 B6
Whitemark 134 D4
Whitianga 136 B6
Whitney, Mt. 150 B3
Whittlesea 135 C4
Wholdaia L. 140 B9
Whyalla 134 B2
Wichita 152 A5
Wichita Falls 152 C4
Wick 78 B5

Wickham, C. **134 C3**
Wicklow Mts. **79 E3**
Wieluń **82 C4**
Wien **81 D9**
Wiener Neustadt **81 E9**
Wiesbaden **80 C5**
Wight, I. of **79 F6**
Wilcannia **134 B3**
Wildspitze **80 E6**
Wilhelm, Mt. **133 B8**
Wilhelm II Coast **168 A11**
Wilhelmshaven **80 B5**
Wilkes-Barre **149 D8**
Willandra Creek →
  135 B4
Willemstad **159 D6**
William Creek **134 A2**
Williams Lake **141 C7**
Williamsburg **149 F7**
Williamsport **149 D8**
Williamstown **135 C3**
Williston **146 A3**
Willunga **134 C2**
Wilmington *Australia*
  134 B2
Wilmington *Del., U.S.A.*
  149 E8
Wilmington *N.C., U.S.A.*
  155 B9
Wilpena Cr. → **134 B2**
Wilson **155 B9**
Wilsons Promontory
  135 C4
Wimmera → **134 C3**
Winchester **79 F6**
Wind River Range **145 E9**
Windhoek **130 C3**
Windsor *Australia* **135 B5**
Windsor *Canada* **143 E5**
Wingham **135 B5**
Winisk → **143 D5**
Winnipeg **143 D10**
Winnipeg, L. **141 C10**
Winnipegosis L. **141 C9**
Winona **147 C9**
Winston-Salem **155 A7**
Winterthur **89 C8**
Winton *Australia* **133 E7**
Winton *N.Z.* **137 G3**
Wirrulla **134 B1**
Wisconsin □ **147 C10**
Wisła → **82 A4**
Wismar **81 B6**
Witbank = eMalahleni
  131 D5
Wittenberge **81 B6**
Włocławek **82 B4**
Włodawa **83 C6**
Wokam **109 F4**
Wolfsberg **81 E8**
Wolfsburg **81 B6**

Wolin **82 B2**
Wollaston, Is. **167 H3**
Wollaston Pen. **140 B8**
Wollongong **135 B5**
Wondai **135 A5**
Wongalarroo L. **135 B3**
Wŏnsan **105 C7**
Wonthaggi **135 C4**
Woodend **135 C3**
Woodland **144 G3**
Woodroffe, Mt. **132 F5**
Woods, L. of the **141 D10**
Woodstock **143 E7**
Woodville **136 D6**
Woolamai, C. **135 C4**
Woolgoolga **135 B5**
Woomera **134 B2**
Worcester *S. Africa*
  130 E3
Worcester *U.K.* **79 E5**
Worcester *U.S.A.*
  149 C10
Workington **79 D5**
Worms **80 D5**
Worthing **79 F6**
Wosi **109 E3**
Wowoni **109 E2**
Wrangel I. = Vrangelya,
  Ostrov **99 B15**
Wrangell **141 C6**
Wrangell Mts. **141 B5**
Wrath, C. **78 B4**
Wrexham **79 E5**
Wrigley **140 B7**
Wrocław **82 C3**
Września **82 B3**
Wu Jiang → **103 F9**
Wuhan **106 B3**
Wuhu **106 B5**
Wukari **127 G7**
Wuliaru **109 F4**
Wuntho **113 F10**
Wuppertal **80 C4**
Würzburg **80 D5**
Wutongqiao **102 F8**
Wuwei **102 D8**
Wuxi **106 B6**
Wuyi Shan **106 D4**
Wuzhong **103 D9**
Wuzhou **107 F1**
Wyandotte **148 C4**
Wyandra **135 A4**
Wyangala, L. **135 B4**
Wyara, L. **135 A3**
Wycheproof **134 C3**
Wyndham *Australia*
  132 D4
Wyndham *N.Z.* **137 G3**
Wynyard **134 D4**
Wyoming □ **145 E10**
Wyong **135 B5**

X

Xaafuun **121 E5**
Xaafuun, Ras **121 E5**
Xai-Xai **131 D6**
Xainza **102 E5**
Xalapa **156 D5**
Xangongo **130 B3**
Xankändi **85 F6**
Xanthi **92 D5**
Xapuri **163 F5**
Xátiva **87 C5**
Xi Jiang → **107 F2**
Xiaguan **102 F8**
Xiamen **107 E5**
Xi'an **103 E9**
Xiang Jiang → **107 C2**
Xiangfan **106 A2**
Xianggang = Hong
  Kong □ **103 G10**
Xiangtan **106 D2**
Xiantao **106 B2**
Xiao Hinggan Ling
  103 B13
Xiaoshan **106 B6**
Xichang **102 F8**
Xigazê **102 F5**
Xing'an **107 E1**
Xinghua **104 F3**
Xingu → **164 C3**
Xining **102 D8**
Xinjiang Uygur Zizhiqu □
  102 C5
Xintai **104 E2**
Xinxiang **103 D10**
Xinyang **106 A3**
Xique-Xique **165 E5**
Xiva **97 E7**
Xixabangma Feng
  112 C5
Xixón = Gijón **86 A3**
Xizang Zizhiqu □ **102 E5**
Xuanhua **104 B1**
Xúquer → **87 C5**
Xuzhou **104 E2**

Y

Ya'an **102 F8**
Yaapeet **134 C3**
Yablonovyy Khrebet
  98 D9
Yacheng **107 a**
Yacuiba **166 A4**
Yadgir **115 L10**
Yahuma **128 D4**
Yakima **144 C3**
Yakovlevka **100 A3**
Yakumo **100 B3**
Yakutat **141 C6**
Yakutsk **99 C10**
Yala **110 C2**
Yalinga **128 C4**

Yalong Jiang → **102 F8**
Yalova **92 D7**
Yalta **85 E3**
Yalu Jiang → **105 C6**
Yam Kinneret **118 D3**
Yamagata **100 D7**
Yamaguchi **101 F2**
Yamal, Poluostrov **96 B8**
Yamba **135 A5**
Yambio **125 H4**
Yambol **92 C6**
Yamdena **109 F4**
Yamethin **113 G11**
Yamma Yamma, L.
  134 A3
Yamoussoukro **127 G4**
Yampil **83 D9**
Yamuna → **112 E3**
Yamzho Yumco **102 F6**
Yana → **99 B11**
Yanbu 'al Baḥr **119 F4**
Yancheng **104 F4**
Yanco Cr. → **135 C4**
Yandoon **113 J10**
Yangambi **128 D4**
Yangjiang **107 G1**
Yangon = Rangoon
  113 J11
Yangquan **103 D10**
Yangshan **106 B7**
Yangtse = Chang
  Jiang → **106 B6**
Yangtze Kiang = Chang
  Jiang → **106 B6**
Yangzhou **106 A5**
Yanji **105 A8**
Yanqi **102 C5**
Yantabulla **135 A4**
Yantai **104 D4**
Yaoundé **128 D2**
Yapen **109 E5**
Yapen, Selat **109 E5**
Yaqui → **156 B2**
Yar-Sale **96 C8**
Yaraka **133 E7**
Yaransk **84 B6**
Yaremcha **83 D7**
Yarensk **96 C5**
Yarí → **162 D4**
Yarkhun → **114 A8**
Yarmouth **143 E7**
Yaroslavl **84 B4**
Yarram **135 C4**
Yarraman **135 A5**
Yarras **135 B5**
Yartsevo **98 C7**
Yaselda **83 B8**
Yasinya **83 D7**
Yass **135 B4**
Yatağan **93 F7**
Yathkyed L. **140 B10**
Yatsushiro **101 G2**

Yavari ➜ 162 D4
Yavatmal 115 J11
Yavoriv 83 D6
Yawatahama 101 G3
Yazd 116 D3
Yazdān 117 C5
Yazoo ➜ 153 C8
Yebyu 113 K12
Yecla 87 C5
Yegros 166 B5
Yei 125 H5
Yekaterinburg 97 D7
Yelarbon 135 A5
Yelets 84 C4
Yell 78 A6
Yellow = Huang He ➜ 104 D3
Yellow Sea 105 E5
Yellowhead Pass 141 C8
Yellowknife 140 B8
Yellowstone ➜ 146 B3
Yellowstone △ 145 D9
Yelsk 83 C9
Yemen ■ 121 D4
Yenangyaung 113 G10
Yenda 135 B4
Yenice 93 E6
Yenisey ➜ 96 B9
Yeniseysk 98 D7
Yeniseyskiy Zaliv 96 B9
Yenyuka 99 D10
Yeola 115 J9
Yeovil 79 F5
Yerbent 97 F6
Yerevan 85 E5
Yershov 84 C6
Yessey 98 C8
Yeu, Î. d' 88 C2
Yevpatoriya 85 D3
Yeysk 85 D4
Yibin 103 F8
Yichang 106 B1
Yichun 103 B13
Yıldız Dağları 92 D6
Yinchuan 103 D9
Yingkou 104 B5
Yining 102 C4
Yinmabin 113 F10
Yishan 103 G9
Yiwu 106 C6
Yixing 106 B5
Yiyang 106 C2
Yog Pt. 108 B2
Yogyakarta 111 F4
Yokadouma 128 D2
Yokkaichi 101 F5
Yokohama 101 F6
Yokosuka 101 F6
Yola 125 G1
Yonago 101 F3
Yong'an 107 E4
Yongzhou 107 D1
Yonibana 127 G3

Yonkers 149 D9
Yonne ➜ 89 B5
York U.K. 79 E6
York U.S.A. 149 E7
York, C. 133 C7
Yorke Pen. 134 B2
Yorkton 141 C9
Yosemite △ 150 B3
Yoshkar Ola 84 B6
Youghal 79 F3
Young 135 B4
Younghusband, L. 134 B2
Younghusband Pen. 134 C2
Youngstown 148 D5
Yozgat 118 C3
Ysyk-Köl 97 E8
Yu Jiang ➜ 103 G10
Yü Shan 103 G12
Yuan Jiang ➜ 106 C1
Yuba City 144 G3
Yübetsu 100 A8
Yucatán, Canal de 157 C7
Yucatán, Península de 157 D7
Yueyang 106 C2
Yukon ➜ 141 B3
Yukon Territory □ 140 B6
Yukta 98 C8
Yuma 150 D5
Yumen 102 D7
Yungas 163 G5
Yunnan □ 102 G8
Yunta 134 B2
Yurga 97 D9
Yurihonjō 100 D7
Yurimaguas 163 E3
Yushu 102 E7
Yuzhno-Sakhalinsk 99 E12
Yvetot 88 B4

Z

Zāb al Kabīr ➜ 118 C5
Zāb aş Şaghīr ➜ 118 D5
Zābol □ 117 D6
Zābolī 117 E5
Zabrze 82 C4
Zacatecas 156 C4
Zadar 90 B5
Zadetkyi Kyun 110 C1
Zafra 86 C2
Żagań 82 C2
Zagazig 124 B5
Zagreb 90 B6
Zägros, Kühhä-ye 116 C2
Zagros Mts. = Zagros, Kühhä-ye 116 C2
Zähedän 117 D5
Zahlah 118 D3

Zaïre = Congo ➜ 128 F2
Zaječar 92 C4
Zākhū 118 C5
Zakinthos = Zakynthos 93 F3
Zakynthos 93 F3
Zalaegerszeg 82 E3
Zalău 83 E6
Zalew Wiślany 82 A4
Zalingei 125 F3
Zalishchyky 83 D7
Zambeze ➜ 131 B7
Zambezi 130 A4
Zambia ■ 131 B5
Zamboanga 108 C2
Zamora Mexico 156 D4
Zamora Spain 86 B3
Zamość 83 C6
Zanesville 148 E4
Zanjān 118 C7
Zante = Zakynthos 93 F3
Zanzibar 129 F7
Zaouiet Reggâne 126 C6
Zaoyang 106 A2
Zaozhuang 104 E2
Západné Beskydy 82 D4
Zaporizhzhya 85 D4
Zara 118 C4
Zaragoza 87 B5
Zarand 116 D4
Zaranj 114 D2
Zaria 127 F7
Zaruma 162 D3
Zaskar Mts. 114 C10
Zavāreh 116 C3
Zawiercie 82 C4
Zāyandeh ➜ 116 C3
Zaysan 97 E9
Zaysan Köli 97 E9
Zbarazh 83 D7
Zdolbuniv 83 C8
Zduńska Wola 82 C4
Zeebrugge 80 C2
Zeehan 134 D4
Zeitz 81 C7
Zelenograd 84 B4
Zemun 92 B3
Zenica 90 B6
Žepče 90 B7
Żêzere ➜ 86 C1
Zgorzelec 82 C2
Zhabinka 83 B7
Zhambyl = Taraz 97 E7
Zhangaqazaly 97 E7
Zhangjiagang 106 B6
Zhangjiakou 104 B1
Zhangye 102 D8
Zhangzhou 107 E4
Zhanjiang 107 G1
Zhanyi 102 F8
Zhaoqing 107 F2

Zhaotong 102 F8
Zharkent 97 E8
Zhashkiv 83 D10
Zhayylma 97 D7
Zhayyq ➜ 97 E6
Zhejiang □ 106 C6
Zhengzhou 103 E10
Zhenjiang 106 A5
Zhezqazghan 97 E7
Zhigansk 98 C10
Zhilinda 98 B9
Zhitomir = Zhytomyr 83 C9
Zhlobin 83 B10
Zhmerynka 83 D9
Zhob 114 D6
Zhodzina 83 A9
Zhongdian 102 F7
Zhongshan 107 F2
Zhovkva 83 C6
Zhu Jiang ➜ 107 F2
Zhuhai 107 F2
Zhumadian 106 A3
Zhuzhou 106 D2
Zhytomyr 83 C9
Zibo 104 D3
Zielona Góra 82 C2
Zigong 103 F8
Ziguéy 125 F2
Ziguinchor 127 F2
Zile 118 B3
Zillah 124 C2
Zimbabwe ■ 131 B5
Zimnicea 92 C5
Zinder 127 F7
Zion △ 151 B6
Zirreh, Gowd-e 114 E3
Zlatograd 92 D5
Zlatoust 97 D6
Zlín 82 D3
Zmeinogorsk 97 D9
Znojmo 82 D3
Zolochiv 83 D7
Zomba 131 B7
Zongo 128 D3
Zonguldak 118 B2
Zorritos 162 D2
Zouar 124 D2
Zouîrât 126 D3
Zrenjanin 92 B3
Żufār 120 D5
Zug 89 C8
Zugspitze 80 E6
Zumbo 131 B6
Zunyi 103 F9
Zürich 89 C8
Zuwārah 124 B1
Zvishavane 131 C6
Zwelitsha 131 E5
Zwettl 81 D8
Zwickau 81 C7
Zwolle 80 B4
Żyrardów 82 B5

Projection: *Hammer Equal Area*

West from Greenwich